THE NEW ECONOMIC MODEL IN LATIN AMERICA AND ITS IMPACT ON INCOME DISTRIBUTION AND POVERTY

INSTITUTE OF LATIN AMERICAN STUDIES SERIES

General Editor: Victor Bulmer-Thomas, Professor of Economics and Director, Institute of Latin American Studies, University of London

The Institute of Latin American Studies, a member of the School of Advanced Study of the University of London, was founded in 1965. The Institute is dedicated to research on Latin America in the social sciences and humanities. The purpose of this series is to disseminate to a wide audience the new work based on the research programmes and projects organised by academic staff and Associate Fellows of the Institute of Latin American Studies.

Victor Bulmer-Thomas (*editor*)
THE NEW ECONOMIC MODEL IN LATIN AMERICA AND ITS
IMPACT ON INCOME DISTRIBUTION AND POVERTY

Victor Bulmer-Thomas, Nikki Craske and Mónica Serrano (*editors*)
MEXICO AND THE NORTH AMERICAN FREE TRADE
AGREEMENT: WHO WILL BENEFIT?

Walter Little and Eduardo Posada-Carbó (*editors*)
POLITICAL CORRUPTION IN EUROPE AND LATIN AMERICA

Eduardo Posada-Carbó (*editor*)
ELECTIONS BEFORE DEMOCRACY: THE HISTORY OF
ELECTIONS IN EUROPE AND LATIN AMERICA

Rachel Sieder (*editor*)
CENTRAL AMERICA: FRAGILE TRANSITION

John Weeks (*editor*)
STRUCTURAL ADJUSTMENT AND THE AGRICULTURAL
SECTOR IN LATIN AMERICA AND THE CARIBBEAN

The New Economic Model in Latin America and its Impact on Income Distribution and Poverty

Victor Bulmer-Thomas
Institute of Latin American Studies
University of London

St. Martin's Press
New York

in association with
INSTITUTE OF LATIN AMERICAN STUDIES
UNIVERSITY OF LONDON

St. Martin's Press, Scholarly and Reference Division,
175 Fifth Avenue, New York, N.Y. 10010

First published in the United States of America in 1996

Printed in Great Britain

ISBN 0–312–16038–0

Library of Congress Cataloging-in-Publication Data
The new economic model in Latin America and its impact on income
distribution and poverty / edited by Victor Bulmer-Thomas : with a
preface by Alejandro Foxley.
p.   cm. — (Institute of Latin American Studies series)
Includes bibliographical references and index.
ISBN 0–312–16038–0 (cloth)
1. Latin America—Economic policy.   2. Latin America—Economic
conditions—1982–   3. Income distribution—Latin America.
4. Poverty—Latin America.   I. Bulmer-Thomas, V.   II. Series.
HC125.N483   1996
338.98—dc20
96–490
CIP

CONTENTS

PART II. CASE STUDIES

* * * * * * *

ACKNOWLEDGEMENTS

This book arose out of a Study Group held at the Institute of Latin American Studies, University of London, in 1994/5. Meetings were held approximately every month over an 18 month period. On each occasion one of the authors presented a paper that had been circulated in advance. Revised versions were sent to all members of the Study Group and were subsequently presented to an international conference in May 1995 at which Dr. Alejandro Foxley was the keynote speaker. The editor wishes to express his thanks to all participants in the conference, in particular Suman Berry (World Bank) and Barbara Stallings (Economic Commission for Latin America and the Caribbean).

The Study Group included, in addition to the contributors to this book, a small number of specialists based in the United Kingdom. Among these were Sarah Bradshaw (London School of Economics), Jean de Bolle (Foreign and Colonial Emerging Markets), Sylvia Chant (London School of Economics), David Knox (former Vice-President for Latin America and the Caribbean at the World Bank), Peter Lloyd-Sherlock (London School of Economics), Sheila Page (Overseas Development Institute), and Rosemary Thorp (Oxford University). Their comments and criticisms were very helpful for the authors in this volume.

LIST OF CONTRIBUTORS

Victor Bulmer-Thomas is Director of the Institute of Latin American Studies and Professor of Economics, Queen Mary and Westfield College, London University.

Raúl Fernández is a Research Fellow at the Centro de Estudios de Estado y Sociedad (CEDES) in Buenos Aires.

Francisco Ferreira is at the SunTory International Centre for Research in Economics and Related Disciplines (STICERD) and a doctoral candidate at the London School of Economics.

E.V.K. FitzGerald is Director of the Centre for International Finance at Queen Elizabeth House, Oxford, and a Fellow of St Antony's College, Oxford.

Alejandro Foxley is President of the Christian Democrat Party in Chile. From 1990-94 he was Minister of Finance for Chile.

Stephany Griffith-Jones is a Senior Research Fellow at the Institute of Development Studies, University of Sussex.

Julie Litchfield is a Research Officer at the SunTory International Centre for Research in Economics and Related Disciplines (STICERD).

Humberto Pánuco-Laguette is a doctoral candidate at Queen Mary and Westfield College, London University.

Christopher Scott is Senior Lecturer in Economics at the London School of Economics and an Associate Fellow of the Institute of Latin American Studies.

Miguel Székely is at the Centre for International Finance, Queen Elizabeth House, and a doctoral condidate at St Antony's College, Oxford.

Jim Thomas is Senior Lecturer in Economics at the London School of Economics and an Associate Fellow of the Institute of Latin American Studies.

Andy Thorpe is Lecturer in Economics, Portsmouth University. From 1990-1993, he was at the Universidad Nacional Autónoma de Honduras.

John Weeks is Director of the Centre for Development Studies, Professor of Economics, School of Oriental and African Studies, London University and an Associate Fellow of the Institute of Latin American Studies.

Laurence Whitehead is Official Fellow in Politics, Nuffield College, Oxford. With Victor Bulmer-Thomas, he edits the *Journal of Latin American Studies*.

LIST OF TABLES

LIST OF FIGURES

PREFACE*

Alejandro Foxley

If we look backwards to Latin America fifteen years ago, i.e. before the 1982 debt crisis, what most countries in the region were seeking was a process of full integration into a world economy that was becoming increasingly globalised. This process requires deep structural changes to make possible the extension of the boundaries of the national economy into the world economy. The importance of this for Latin America should not be underestimated. I remember very well a piece that was written in the *Financial Times* many years ago that was headlined *'Latin America: A Continent Adrift'*. Of course, it was a time when everybody was praising the East Asian miracle and thinking that Latin America would not be able to take part in this very interesting process that was happening all over the world. The structural changes were eventually triggered by the debt crisis in the early 1980s, but it is also a fact that Latin America had been in search of a new development strategy after the import-substitution phase had lost steam.

The subject matter of this volume is the New Economic Model (NEM) in Latin America and its impact on income distribution and poverty. Let me, as a starting point, say I do not think one can talk about a 'model'. Instead, one can speak about a process – a gradual process in which countries go through different phases. The World Bank has done some very interesting studies in an attempt to characterise these different phases. The first, immediately after the debt crisis, was dominated by the need simply to stabilise the economy. During the second phase, structural transformation started taking place – the opening up of the economy to trade; the process of privatisation and, in some countries, a very rapid process of financial liberalisation. Finally there is a third phase, a stage in which, having gone successfully through the two previous ones, countries are able to increase investment significantly and develop a capacity to increase productivity in a more or less constant way. If we accept the notion of these different phases, one would say that an important goal of the process of transformation is, obviously, to reach Phase 3.

Phase 3 is the old notion of a self-sustained development process. Thus, the relevant question is how do you go through economic stabilisation, through the opening up of the economy and all the disruptions these phases assume, in order to arrive successfully at Phase 3? To reach Phase 3 will take a long period of time and there will be a lengthy questioning of political legitimacy. Sound economic policies will become more and more relevant. The question of political legitimacy is very directly related to the impact that the policies in Phase 1 and Phase 2 have on poverty and on income distribution. It is certainly one of the fundamental factors that might strengthen the progress towards Phase 3 or might debilitate it; a second factor is simply the quality of political leadership and the strength of democratic institutions – countries that go through this painful period of adjustment must agree on certain shared goals, postpone instant gratification, perhaps sacrificing short-run wage increases or higher profits, and extend the time horizon for investment decisions. So both income distribution and the quality of politics are crucial for reaching Phase 3. And for preventing backsliding say if you are in Phase 2 and do not want to go back to Phase 1, but move to Phase 3 countries have to produce the sensation in the population, particularly among the main economic actors, that stabilisation is here to stay, that in fact the key decisions being taken in the economy are so sound that you have a kind of guaranteed progress towards the next Phase.

What does one usually see as the outcome of Phase 1? The economic stabilisation programmes after the debt crisis were always supported by international economic organisations, which were essentially proposing a uniform set of policies whose end result, at least during this Phase, was very often a deceleration of economic growth, increasing unemployment, reductions in real wages and reduced government expenditure where it was easiest, i.e. expenditure on the social sectors. This type of policy outcome could not but result in a deterioration in income distribution and very probably in an increase in the levels of poverty in the countries going through this stage.[1]

In Phase 2, where the opening up of the economy and the privatisation process are initiated, there are many possible different outcomes. Let me just stress two that are very likely to reinforce the negative impact on income distribution observed in the first stage:

1) Privatisation usually involves the selling of companies which are basically in the utility sector, e.g. energy companies . These are, by definition, 'natural monopolies'. Once they are transferred to the private sector, the companies then tend to use their leverage in the market to generate a set of prices that increase very sharply and produce, generally speaking, a negative impact on the purchasing power of the lower income households.

2) Given that this process of privatisation goes together with the opening up of the economy to international competition, firms in the tradeable sector have to adjust to competition and one of the aspects of adjustment is the wage and salary structure. These firms producing tradeables must attract highly

skilled management, professional staff and a skilled labour force. In order to attract them, they have to offer higher wages and salaries at the top and the final result is a more skewed wage and salary scale within the modernised firm, as compared to the one that stays in the traditional sector or in the non-tradeable sector of the economy.

Just by giving these examples one could very well argue that unless governments involved in the process of modernising and opening up the economy are committed to a very active social policy, the likely outcome of the structural transformation in Phase 1 and Phase 2 will be a deterioration in income distribution and perhaps an increase in the levels of poverty. That is why I think it is so important that this type of economic strategy – that some people call the 'neo-liberal' strategy – be re-formulated to include a strong social component that will neutralise the negative equity effects observed in Phase 1 and Phase 2.

Let us assume that we have now developed a strategy of structural adjustment with very active social policies. How can the economies make the transtition from Phase 2 to Phase 3? Can these efforts be sustained with improvements, more or less permanent, in income distribution afterwards? I would argue that the transition from Phase 2 to Phase 3 will depend critically on certain economic policies about which there has not been a lot of agreement in Latin America. The policies which are critical here are exchange rate policy and fiscal policy.

If you have the exchange rate policies wrong, it is very likely that an economy in Phase 2 will backslide into Phase 1. Let us take the recent example of Mexico and some of the difficulties being faced by Argentina. There is always the temptation, when you are in the middle of a process of economic stabilisation and you are opening up the economy, to show quick results by fixing the exchange rate to the dollar. In doing so, you can rapidly achieve a reduction in the rate of inflation but at the cost of developing a large, and in the medium-term uncontrollable, trade deficit. A fixed exchange rate makes imports cheaper through time because of the real appreciation of the domestic currency implied by the fixed exchange rate policy. After a while, the trade deficit is of such magnitude that the markets do not believe any more in the permanence of the exchange rate policy. This is a lesson we learned in Chile in the early 1980s, because the exchange rate policy adopted in 1978-9 had disastrous effects on the economy and particularly on the financial and banking sector. Once the markets believe that you are going to devalue, almost immediately you are faced with a massive capital flight. You are then forced to increase interest rates and reduce government expenditure in a very drastic way. A long recession then begins, if the policy choice is to stick to the fixed exchange rate, or stagflation where the domestic currency is devalued.

Consider the situation of Argentina today *vis-à-vis* Mexico. Capital flight in the two countries, after rapid appreciation of the domestic currency, happened very quickly. Mexico had net capital inflows of $30 billion in 1993, but only $5 billion in 1994. Argentina received $10 billion in 1993 and will be lucky to have $2 billion in 1995. As a consequence, in spite of being very advanced in the process of economic transformation, Mexico and Argentina are faced with the need to start the process of economic stabilisation once again, with the consequence of a new recession or a new process of stagflation. After devaluing in December 1994, Mexico faced in 1995 rates of inflation of around 50% and a reduction of GDP of perhaps five per cent. Argentina does not expect to grow very much in either 1995 or 1996. Thus the exchange rate policy that is followed becomes a key to the successful transition from Phase 2 to Phase 3.

The other economic policy decision concerns fiscal adjustment. Let me just mention one aspect on which I think it is worthwhile reflecting. In Phase 2 the economies are opening up and privatising companies. The big temptation for a Minister of Finance[2] is that, because privatisation produces so much revenue in such a short period of time, the fiscal adjustment becomes cosmetic – that is, you can show a rapid decrease in the fiscal deficit by including as government revenues the proceeds of privatisation. If the programme of privatisation is taking several years to implement, then you have several years in which you can show very good, healthy fiscal accounts. Once this process is over, then reality sinks in and you are again faced with a deep imbalance in the fiscal accounts. To some extent, this is what is happening today in some countries in Latin America. As we have seen, Argentina is fighting a very hard battle to produce a fiscal adjustment which is done under very difficult conditions, because some of these problems were postponed – and they were postponed because the privatisation process allowed them to do so.

So key policy mistakes that I think should be avoided in the future are (i) overvaluation of the domestic currency, (ii) too much liberalisation of capital inflows – in Chile we have applied restrictions to the inflow of capital precisely to avoid a rapid overvaluation of the domestic currency – and (iii) the fiscal adjustment must be implemented upfront, at the very beginning when your political capital is intact.

Let me now suggest some of the new themes and new problems that are likely to emerge when the economy succeeds in passing from Phase 2 to Phase 3: that is to say, when economies are able to open up, to restructure, to privatise, to stabilise their prices and as a consequence experience a rapid increase in investment and domestic savings. The stylised facts of Phase 3 can be presented by the type of parameters the Chilean economy shows today. Rates of investment in the period 1990-1994 of around 27% of GDP, domestic savings around 25%, an average growth rate in the economy of around seven per cent a year and rapid increases in labour productivity of nearly four per cent. This was accompanied by a fiscal surplus of around 2.4% of GDP and a small current account deficit which is not too large – not larger than 2% of GDP.

What are the new problems emerging here? I will very quickly outline them because I think they are very important as a topic of reflection. It seems to me that a key aspect to consider is the imbalance between growth of the private sector in the economy – in Chile the private sector probably has grown at a steady rate of nine per cent a year – and the insufficient investment in infrastructure that is needed for a sustained increase in productivity after the process of structural adjustment has taken place. This question of the supply and quality of public goods and services becomes critical to avoid bottlenecks in roads, ports, airports, telecommunications and so on, but it also becomes critical for the impact on income distribution or, if you wish, on the impact on the quality of life for people in the lower income strata.

Just to give one example, one of the lagging sectors during the first part of the process is the rural sector, and if you are thinking seriously about reducing poverty in the medium- and long-term, large investments have to be undertaken in such things as rural electricity programmes, water and sewage programmes, and secondary roads. Now the issue I would like to pose here very briefly is the following: if you want to maintain fiscal balance in the long-run, that is to say fiscal equilibrium or fiscal surplus, and you do have all these needs and deficits in infrastructure, I think it is inevitable that you invite the private sector to participate in the investment process. In the Chilean case, we have requirements beyond what the government can do in terms of public investment of about $6 billion from now until the year 2000; either the private sector will finance these investments or they will never take place, with a negative impact on growth and also a negative impact on income distribution.

Let me finally mention other problems during Phase 3. After privatisation you have all these natural monopolies transferred to the private sector and there is no real capacity in the hands of the government to regulate this sector. If you do not regulate, as mentioned above, the rates people pay for running water each month, for the electricity bill and so on, go up very fast. As a consequence, one is bound to go backwards in terms of income distribution. So the need for regulation of the privatised natural monopolies becomes a key problem.

The reform of the health and education sectors are also problems that have been generally postponed and that have to be tackled at this stage. The educational reform becomes critical once unemployment has gone down. You do need a more skilled labour force. The educational system is basically obsolete at the secondary level, and technical education trains people in the wrong skills. Thus, total transformation of the educational system, in particular the public side of the system, has to be undertaken and the same can be said about the health service. The open economy requires mobility in factors of production. During the liberalisation, several sectors are declining very rapidly and other sectors of economic activity are expanding very rapidly – how do you facilitate the process of mobility of the labour force from the former to the latter? How do you protect mobility instead of protecting jobs? How can unemployment insurance schemes be designed so as to avoid huge fiscal deficits as seen in Europe today? I think that this is a very important new element that has to be considered for countries in Phase 3 to be successful.

The whole exercise at the end rests on two basic political notions. For people and countries to be able to sustain a long process of increasing domestic savings, gradually – but only gradually – increasing real wages, two elements must be present at all times. First, there must be a certain notion of a 'fair deal' on the part of the government. That is why social policies that are targeted on specific groups are so essential. Pensioners, women, heads of households or the poor in the rural areas are obvious targets of such policies. You have to have some component in your policies that tells these people that they will not be waiting forever – some notion of a 'fair deal'. These policies usually go together with tax reform programmes that imply an increase in taxes and not a reduction. Secondly there must be a certain level of cooperation in society and particularly in political life. What Robert Putnam has called 'the social capital' in society must be increased. His book *'Making Democracy Work'* reflects on the notion that countries performing very well are countries that have been able to develop networks of cooperation, civic networks based in cooperation, in trust and reciprocity – elements that should be present not only at the level of social organisation, but also hopefully in political life.

Notes

*   This is a revised version of the author's John Brooks Memorial Lecture, given at the Institute of Latin American Studies, University of London, in May 1995. The lecture was the keynote speech in the Institute's conference on the New Economic Model in Latin America and its Impact on Income Distribution and Poverty.

1.   This is supported by the evidence in this book and elsewhere. See for example Table 5 in Chapter 12.

2.   The author was Minister of Finance in Chile from 1990 to 1994.

CHAPTER 1

INTRODUCTION

Victor Bulmer-Thomas

The extent of poverty and the degree of inequality in Latin America are both problems with a long history. The first is a reflection above all of the low average level of income and the gap in living standards between Latin America on the one hand and developed countries on the other. The second is a consequence of both the region's colonial heritage and the style of development pursued since independence in the 19th century. Yet the differences between Latin American countries in both the extent of poverty and the degree of inequality suggest that there are some degrees of freedom open to policy-makers pursuing greater equity. As the countries of the region enter the 21st century, subject to political systems that now give more voice to the most disadvantaged groups, the need to understand the forces that shape poverty and income distribution has never been greater.

The improvements in data collection and statistical analysis in Latin America in the last fifty years have confirmed earlier suspicions: the degree of income inequality in Latin America, even before the 1980s debt crisis, was extremely severe and greater than in other parts of the world. The skewed nature of income distribution meant that in 1980 some 70 per cent of households had incomes below the national average,[1] while the income of the richest 20 per cent has recently been estimated as 10 times greater than the poorest 20 per cent.[2] By contrast, the ratio of richest to poorest quintile is five in Organisation of Economic Cooperation and Development (OECD) countries, and less than seven in less developed countries (LDCs) outside Latin America.[3] If poverty indicators were not the worst in the world, it was still the case that in 1980 an estimated 41 per cent of the population lived in poverty with nearly half (19 per cent of the total) living in extreme poverty.[4]

These figures are so shocking that it is tempting to assume that both poverty and income distribution had been deteriorating rapidly even before the debt crisis. This epoch, which was marked in general by inward-looking development strategies and state intervention, has never been noted for its commitment to egalitarianism and the proportion of the *urban* population living in poverty was indeed rising.[5] Yet it coincided with a rapid rate of growth of real GDP in many countries that lowered the proportion of the *total* population living in poverty and extreme poverty.[6] This was due to the reduction in poverty in rural areas.[7] If rapid population growth meant that the *absolute* numbers living in poverty continued to increase, it was still the case that the *proportion* classified as poor was falling and in *rural* Latin America even the absolute numbers of those in extreme poverty fell between 1970 and 1980.

A decline in poverty is no guarantee of an increase in income equality. Indeed, there are frequent examples in Latin America before 1980 of rapid GDP growth being associated with an increase in inequality despite a fall in poverty. The sharp rise in the Gini coefficient in Brazil in the 1960s[8] and Mexico in the 1950s has been widely reported.[9] There was also a fall in the share of income received by the bottom two quintiles in many countries, including Argentina in the 1960s and 1970s.[10] However, there were also cases where the growth of real GDP before 1980 was associated with an improvement in income distribution. Inequality was reduced in Colombia and Costa Rica in the first decade after reliable surveys in 1964 and 1961 respectively,[11] while an improvement was also observed in Venezuela between 1971 and 1981.[12] The distribution of urban income, a more widely available statistic, improved in Peru between 1968/9 and 1981.[13]

The inward-looking model of development did not, therefore, lead necessarily to a deterioration in equity. Rapid growth implied a fall in overall poverty as measured by the headcount index and occasionally yielded an improvement in income distribution. By contrast, outward-looking neo-liberal policies in the Southern Cone after 1973 were not noted for their favourable impact on equality, with Argentina, Chile and Uruguay all experiencing a sharp rise in the Gini coefficient.[14] Indeed, these three experiments are the only ones in Latin America before the debt crisis in which rising GDP per head may have been associated with an increase in the headcount index of poverty (see footnote 6).

The debt crisis in 1982 brought to an end the growth of the Latin American economies; in the 1980s, the evolution of poverty and income distribution took place against a background of stabilisation, adjustment and macroeconomic stagnation. Real GDP per head fell by an average of one per cent a year in the ten years after 1980,[15] giving rise to the legitimate phrase 'the lost decade'. Only Chile and Colombia recorded an increase in income per head during this period with the growth in both cases concentrated in the second half of the decade.

The impact of stabilisation and adjustment programmes on poverty in the lost decade was all too predictable at the regional level. Just as economic growth before 1980 had yielded a reduction in poverty, so GDP stagnation and falling income per head in the 1980s produced an increase (see Table A.1 in the Statistical Appendix). The proportion living in poverty and extreme poverty in both urban and rural areas rose between 1980 and 1990 with the increase concentrated in cities. Indeed, 87.8 per cent of the 52.6 million additional poor people in Latin America were classified as urban.[16] By 1990, the urban poor were estimated at 115.5 million out of the total poor of 195.9 million and a total population of some 420 million.[17]

The position of the bottom 40 per cent of households, in which poverty is concentrated, is broadly consistent with the evolution of poverty at the regional level. Table 1 reports the 36 'observations' collected by the Economic Commission for Latin America and the Caribbean (ECLAC)[18] for eleven republics. These observations cover different time-periods since 1980 and report rural and urban income separately where both are available. In the 15 cases where average household income was falling, the average income of the bottom 40 per cent of households also fell; however, in seven of these cases the average income of the top 10 per cent still rose despite the fall in average household income. In the four cases where household income was unchanged, the bottom 40 per cent improved their income while the top 10 per cent experienced a decline.[19] Finally, in the 17 cases where household income rose, there were five cases where the income of the bottom 40 per cent of households failed to improve and two cases[20] where the top 10 per cent of households failed to increase their income.

Table 1:
Average Household Income Change and the Distribution of Income (1980 - 90)

Income Change		(-)	(0)	(+)
Bottom 40%	(-)	15	0	5
	(+)	0	4	12
Top 10%	(-)	8	4	2
	(+)	7	0	15

Source: Derived from CEPAL (1993), Tables 18 and 19.

With rare exceptions income distribution also deteriorated during the 1980s (see Table A.2 in the Statistical Appendix). Only three cases can be found where the distribution of income actually improved between 1980 and 1990: urban incomes in Colombia and Uruguay and rural income in Costa Rica.[21] Not a single case can therefore be found of an unambiguous improvement in national income distribution and in most countries for which data are available there was a clear deterioration over the course of the decade.[22] The most obvious conclusion is that the lost decade made a bad situation worse both in terms of the extent of poverty and in terms of the degree of inequality.

The New Economic Model

The debt crisis effectively ended the long period of inward-looking development that had begun in Latin America in the 1930s. Signs of decay in the model had been apparent for many years and a number of countries, notably in the Southern Cone (Argentina, Chile and Uruguay), had already experimented with alternatives – albeit without much success.[23] However, the need to generate a trade surplus after 1982 to accommodate debt service payments required a new approach to the external sector.[24] Similarly, the inability of state-owned enterprises (SOEs) to continue to finance investments through external borrowing obliged each republic to reevaluate the boundaries between the public and the private sector.

These pressures led to a shift in the development paradigm after the mid-1980s towards a New Economic Model (NEM) in which inward-looking development was to be replaced by export-led growth and state intervention by market forces. At an ideological level, it was assumed that the emphasis on market forces would reinforce export-led growth and *vice versa* so that the possibility of inconsistencies between the two approaches was not at first taken seriously by policy-makers. To a large extent the NEM simply derived its contours from opposition to what had gone before; if inward-looking development and state intervention were responsible for the debt crisis, it was natural to assume that the NEM should emphasise outward-looking growth and market forces, providing a more dominant role for the private sector.[25]

The new development paradigm crystallised in what has become known as the Washington Consensus (WC). Although not practised in Washington and never representing a consensus, the WC has a logical structure that appears at first to be both coherent and consistent, i.e. given certain assumptions and shared goals, the WC claims to have both sufficient theoretical and empirical support to offer countries implementing the new paradigm good prospects for high and sustainable long-run rates of growth following the introduction of the necessary reforms.

The cornerstone of the new development paradigm is provided by trade liberalisation. Given the trade barriers erected by Latin American countries since 1930 and the associated anti-export bias, it would be difficult to imagine a NEM without some dismantling of tariff and non-tariff barriers.[26] With an unchanged real exchange rate, however, such changes would simply erode the trade surplus needed to service the debt. Thus, a depreciation of the real effective exchange rate (REER) must be seen as an intrinsic part of the NEM, leading to an increase in the relative price of tradeables. With importables squeezed by tariff and non-tariff barrier reductions, trade liberalisation is then assumed to give an unambiguous boost to exportables and therefore to export-led growth.[27]

Trade liberalisation provides opportunities for exportables that were previously absent. This change in relative prices is a necessary, but rarely sufficient, condition for rapid export growth. Technological modernisation is also crucial. However, even rapid expansion of exports will not lead to export-led growth if the import-competing sector is unable to respond to the lowering of trade barriers. Thus, *both* exportables and importables need to be able to compete more effectively through technological modernisation. Trade liberalisation, by providing access to imported capital goods on more favourable terms, is an important ingredient in successful modernisation, although liberalisation of the capital account in general and the promotion of direct foreign investment (DFI) in particular are usually assumed to be relevant as well.

The change in relative prices induced by trade liberalisation is unlikely to be permanent if inflation is not reduced to international levels. Accelerating inflation and hyperinflation are notorious for the distortions they introduce in relative prices; even chronic, but stable, inflation has a habit of undermining the tradeable goods sectors.[28] Thus, the NEM places a high premium on inflation stabilisation. The consensus after many years of orthodox and heterodox stabilisation programmes is that a reduction in the budget deficit is a *sine qua non* for a permanent reduction in the inflation rate. Fiscal reform therefore plays a crucial part in the NEM with an emphasis on both expenditure reductions and revenue increases.[29] Furthermore, as privatisation can be treated as both cutting expenditure (through eliminating subsidies) and raising revenue (through asset sales or increased tax receipts), the divestiture of SOEs tends to play a leading role in fiscal reform.

Since the inefficiency of SOEs is often attributed to labour hoarding, it is safe to assume that privatisation leads to massive lay-offs. At the same time, firms in the tradeable goods sector need to lower labour costs in order to compete internationally. This implies the reform of labour markets since the inward-looking model of development had left as its legacy inflexible requirements for formal sector firms with regard to the hiring and firing of workers. Furthermore, a large part of the labour costs paid by formal sector firms are received by governments in the form of social security payments, pension contributions etc. These additions to the wages received by workers amount in effect to a tax on labour in the formal sector, discouraging the employment of workers in large-scale enterprises and driving them into the informal sector.

Labour market reform is intended to lower the cost of labour in the formal sector, leading to greater employment and an increase in the competitiveness of firms producing tradeable goods. Thus, labour market reform in the NEM is linked to trade liberalisation through the promotion of labour-intensive tradeable goods. However, technological modernisation is designed to enable firms to move towards a new isoquant lying inside the old one for all different combinations of labour and capital. Whether this results in the employment of more or less labour depends both on how labour-saving are the new techniques of production in practice and how the firm responds to the new relative price of labour. The latter, however, depends not only on the price of labour, but also on the price of capital and this will be affected in turn by the reform of the capital market.

The capital account controls in force before the debt crisis, coupled with restrictions on foreign investment, left the domestic financial system isolated from international competition. Huge spreads between lending and borrowing rates often left depositors with negative real rates of interest, discouraging domestic savings.[30] The reform of domestic capital markets aims to eliminate restrictive practices through deregulation, permitting a rise in real interest rates and an increase in domestic savings. This rise in real interest rates increases the cost of capital and encourages a shift away from capital-intensive activities.

Capital market reform, however, under the NEM applies also to the capital account of the balance of payments. Access to capital at international rates of interest represents a *fall* in the cost of capital for most firms provided that the REER is not depreciating. Furthermore, access to the international capital market is almost invariably restricted to large firms whose capital intensity *ceteris paribus* is greater than small or medium-size firms. Liberalisation of the capital account may be needed to promote technological modernisation, but its impact on relative factor prices and labour use is at variance with the outcome expected from reform of domestic capital markets.

Even under the best of circumstances, therefore, trade-offs can be found within the NEM. Privatisation leads to rising unemployment, but labour market reform may not be sufficient to absorb the surplus labour. Export promotion requires a depreciation of the REER, but inflation stabilisation may require the opposite. Technological modernisation requires access to capital, but the reform of domestic capital markets may make the needed investments more expensive. Fiscal reform requires increases in revenue, but tariff reductions and the elimination of employment taxes lead to a fall.

Under the right circumstances, the NEM in Latin America can still be expected to lead to export-led growth. Whether it does so, however, will depend on how it is implemented. The thematic chapters in this book show how complex is each area of reform and the case studies demonstrate the gap between rhetoric and reality in the application of reforms in many countries. Yet there is a strong domino effect at work in Latin America. When pioneer countries implement reforms that appear to function efficiently, other republics are quick to follow. Despite the ideological discourse, there is a strong dose of pragmatism in the NEM in Latin America.

What, however, will be its impact on income distribution and poverty? The

NEM was not adopted primarily to improve equity and yet each of the areas of reform on which we focus – trade liberalisation, fiscal adjustment, the labour market, the domestic capital market and the capital account of the balance of payments – is non-neutral with regard to changes in poverty and income distribution. By altering the relative prices for tradeable and non-tradeable goods, for exportables and importables and for the main factors of production, while at the same time altering the balance between the public and private sector over the provision of goods and services, the NEM is bound to affect both the functional and size distribution of income as well as the extent and depth of poverty.

The Measurement of Poverty and Income Distribution

Both poverty and income distribution present formidable philosophical and measurement problems. The former have been the subject of sustained analysis through the work of Amartya Sen in particular, but will not be discussed further here.[31] The macroeconomic data collected each year as part of the national accounts exercise do not provide the raw material for any of the standard measures; although the functional distribution of income (wages, profits etc.) is available for the larger countries on an annual basis, this is generally considered to be of limited use in societies, such as those in Latin America, where the distribution of wage income itself is highly skewed and where non-wage income may account for most of what the bottom decile receives.[32]

Measurement of poverty and income distribution therefore depends on household surveys, which are always samples and which are inevitably subject to a series of distortions (in particular, under-reporting of income). Furthermore, while the raw data from household surveys can be used to derive measures of income distribution relatively easily, they can only be used to produce measures of poverty after a series of adjustments have been made. These adjustments involve assumptions on which not all researchers agree. This can lead to huge discrepancies in the measurement of poverty derived from the same data set.[33]

Neither income distribution nor poverty can ever be measured directly. All indicators are proxies. This is particularly true of poverty, where indicators seek to reflect the degree of deprivation of the population. Yet it is also true of income distribution, since the degree of inequality within society can only be roughly approximated by a small household survey which in turn can rarely do justice to the degree of intra-household inequality, inter-regional price differences and non-monetary income sources.[34]

There is a huge theoretical and methodological literature on income distribution and poverty. As so often in economics, this literature runs far ahead of the options available given the empirical data. It was not the purpose of the Study Group to contribute to this literature nor were we able to carry out our own surveys or questionnaires. Thus, the Study Group was obliged to use the existing primary sources. However, numerous measures of both poverty and income distribution can be derived from these and it was necessary to ensure that the measures used were as far as possible comparable across countries.

Measures of income distribution and poverty should ideally have the following properties:

(i) Available for each country at a series of different intervals. A measure, however ideal, which is only available for a single year is not of much use.

(ii) Readily comparable over time and across countries. This seemingly simple property is in fact quite demanding, since the use of different assumptions in deriving indicators from raw data can undermine comparisons even for a single country at different time periods.

(iii) Robust. Indicators that are relatively insensitive to the assumptions that have to be imposed by researchers are preferable to those that are very sensitive. The ideal measure would be one which was very similar when estimated by different researchers using the same data set.

(iv) Decomposable. There is a class of measures which can be decomposed to reveal characteristics about the sources of inequality and poverty (e.g. region, age, gender). These measures are very useful in the discussion of policy issues.

Income distribution indicators, being relative measures, are also expected to exhibit a number of desirable properties or axioms. These include (a) the axiom of scale irrelevance, (b) the axiom of symmetry and (c) the axiom of rank-preserving equalisation. Fortunately, the available measures for Latin America all satisfy these axioms.[35]

A number of different measures for income distribution and poverty are listed in Table 2 with an indication of the presence or absence of the desirable properties. None of the measures are entirely satisfactory so difficult choices must be made. We begin with measures of income distribution (see Part A of Table 2):

A.1. Bottom Quintile (Decile). This widely available measure, recording the share of income received by the poorest 20% (10%) of households or population, can be obtained easily from household survey data. In Latin America it nearly always refers to household *per capita* income with household income assumed to be divided equally among the members of the household (occasionally it refers to household consumption). It therefore seeks to measure the proportion of total national income received by the poorest 20% (10%) of individuals. It is sensitive to the inclusion or exclusion of non-monetary income/consumption (especially non-marketed farm output) and this can cause problems of comparability for both cross-section and time-series work.

A.2. Top Quintile (Decile). Like the bottom quintile (decile), this is widely available and always refers to the same concept of income/consumption as the bottom quintile (decile), although the concept itself will vary from survey to survey. It is widely quoted in the Latin American context because it is so high by international standards (the bottom quintile is not always such an outlier in international comparisons). If unadjusted, it may be seriously affected by under-reporting of income which varies significantly from country to country.

A.3. Gini. The Gini coefficient, derived from the Lorenz curve and the size distribution of income,[36] is usually available.[37] Although it can contradict the information provided by the top and bottom quintiles (deciles), in practice this is not common. Thus, a recent World Bank (1993) study found that in every case in the 1980s where the share of the bottom quintile fell, both the share of the top quintile and the Gini coefficient rose (implying greater inequality). It could be said, therefore, that it adds little to our knowledge of income distribution and it suffers from the fact that, when two Lorenz curves cross, it may not change. Nevertheless, it is widely available, it is spectacularly high in many countries of Latin America and can (with some difficulty) be decomposed.[38] It may also start to provide different information to that provided by the bottom and top quintiles (deciles) in the 1990s.[39]

A.4. Pen's Parade. This is a graph that records on the horizontal axis each income recipient in ascending order of income with their actual income given by the vertical axis. The 'parade' is usually quite spectacular, because most of the population appear as 'dwarfs' when set against a few 'giants' with high incomes. Pen's Parade is a visually very striking way of presenting much the same information as is contained in both the Lorenz curve and the Gini coefficient.

A.5. Theil. The Theil index is easy to calculate, but difficult to interpret intuitively as a measure of inequality. It can be decomposed and a decomposition formula was used by Fishlow (1972) in a famous study of the sources of Brazilian inequality. It is not easily comparable because its maximum value depends on the sample size, but it can be normalised to make comparisons possible.[40]

A.6. Atkinson. The great attraction of the Atkinson index[41] from a theoretical point of view is that it allows different assumptions to be made about the degree of poverty aversion, each of which gives a different value of the index. It is also decomposable in a straightforward fashion. It is, however, only rarely computed for Latin American countries.

A.7. The Coefficient of Variation. This is similar to the Theil and Atkinson indices (see footnote 41), but is more sensitive to differences at the top end of

Table 2:
Measures of Income Distribution and Poverty

	Widely Available	Easily Comparable	Robust	Decomposable
(A) Income Distribution				
1. Bottom Quintile (Decile)	Yes	Some problems	Yes	No
2. Top Quintile (Decile)	Yes	Some problems	Yes	No
3. Gini	Yes	Yes	Yes	With difficulty
4. Pen's Parade	No	Yes	Yes	No
5. Theil	No	With some adjustment	Yes	Yes
6. Atkinson	No	Depends on degree of aversion	Yes	Yes
7. Coefficient of Variation	No	Yes	Yes	Yes
(B) Poverty				
1. Headcount Index	Yes	No	No	No
2. Poverty Gap	No	No	No	No
3. F G T	No	No	No	Yes
4. DBN	No	Yes	Yes	No
5. Real Minimum Wage	Yes	No	Yes	No
6. Real Wages	Yes	Only by sector	Yes	No
7. Unemployment	Yes	No	Yes	No
8. Informal Sector	Yes	No	No	No

the income distribution (it is therefore known as a top sensitive inequality measure).

Before turning to poverty, it is necessary to discuss the relationship between the first three poverty measures in Table 1 (B.1-B.3). The most general formula for poverty measurement is:

(1)
$$P_\alpha = \frac{1}{n} \sum_{i=1}^{q} \left\{ \frac{[z - y_i]}{z} \right\}^\alpha$$

where z is the poverty line, n is the total number of people, q refers to all poor people (i.e. whose income falls below z), y(i) is the income of the ith poor person and alpha is a parameter whose value is yet to be determined. When alpha is set at zero, the formula becomes:

(2)
$$H = \frac{q}{n}$$

where H is the Headcount Index that measures the proportion of the population in poverty.

The Headcount Index (B.1.) is often criticised because it tells us nothing about the depth of poverty. The poor in eq(1) can either all be close to the poverty line or far away from it. However, if alpha is set to one, the formula becomes:

(3)
$$PG = \frac{1}{n} \sum_{i-1}^{q} \frac{[z - y_i]}{z}$$

This can be rewritten as PG = I.H where I is the income gap ratio and is defined as:

(4)
$$I = \frac{[z - y^p]}{z}$$

where y^p denotes the mean income of the poor.

This new measure can be interpreted as the poverty gap (PG) as it measures the gap between the average income of the poor and the poverty line. It has been criticised, in turn, because it does not tell us anything about the distribution of income among the poor themselves. If, however, alpha is set equal to two, the formula becomes:

(5) $$FGT = \frac{PG^2}{H} + \frac{\left[H - PG^2\right]}{H} CV_p^2$$

where CV_p^2 denotes the squared coefficient of variation of income (or consumption) amongst the poor. The first term on the right-hand side then measures the contribution of the poverty gap to the index and the second term refers to the contribution of inequality among the poor. The measure is known as FGT in honour of its authors (Foster-Greer-Thorbecke).[42]

It is now possible to turn to the different measures of poverty in Table 2 (Part B):

B.1. The Headcount Index. This is widely used and quoted. However, it is not particularly robust, because so many assumptions have to be made before it can be estimated. Indeed, it is worth indicating the steps that must be taken to estimate B.1 (and its derivatives B.2. and B.3.):

(a)   Adjustment of raw data for under-reporting of income.[43]
(b)   Calculation of minimum nutritional standard (this is usually taken from United Nations publications).
(c)   Calculation of food requirements to meet (b) (this varies from country to country, e.g. relatively more meat in Argentina, relatively more basic grains in Guatemala).
(d)   Calculation of cost of (c). This should use different prices for different regions (e.g. higher for urban than rural areas).
(e)   Derivation of non-food component of minimum consumption required to avoid poverty (CEPAL typically assumes a multiple of 2.0 of the cost of food in calculating its poverty line for urban areas and 1.75 for rural areas).

Since any combination of these assumptions can produce changes in the height of the poverty line, it is not surprising that estimates differ so greatly over the proportion of the population living in poverty. Nevertheless, if the assumptions are the same for each different observation for a given country, the Headcount Index has obvious merits.

B.2. and B.3. Despite their attractions, these measures are not widely available. This may change in the future as their calculation becomes a standard feature of household survey data. The World Bank (1993) has calculated both indices for a number of countries.[44]

B.4. Dissatisfaction of Basic Needs (DBN). The attraction of the DBN index is that it is based on a series of quantitative measures (e.g. access to running water) with households/individuals defined as 'poor' if they do not enjoy the facility in question. It does not therefore depend on the use of prices and is relatively robust. It is, however, rather arbitrary and in some respects paternalistic. It is also not widely used.

B.5. Real minimum wages. These are widely available and can be considered an important indicator of poverty in situations where the wages of the bottom quintile are largely determined by minimum wage decrees. In the 1980s, however, the minimum wage was not raised in line with inflation and no longer provides the reference point for as many wage bargains as used to be the case. Studies of Mexico, for example, show that the proportion of the labour force receiving one minimum wage or less declined sharply between 1984 and 1989. For some countries, it may be still be a useful proxy for the extent of poverty, but it should be used with considerable caution and is not strictly comparable between countries.

B.6. Real wages. These are difficult to compare across countries because of major intra-sectoral differences in average wage rates. If comparisons are made for the same sector, however, real wage indices can be helpful. The biggest problem in using real wage data to study poverty is that the bottom quintile (decile) is usually the least dependent on formal sector employment, while the distribution of wage income is itself highly skewed. Real wage data are therefore most useful when referring to unskilled workers.

B.7. Unemployment. It has been traditional to regard unemployment in Latin America as a luxury that the very poorest cannot afford. According to this received wisdom, unemployment rates would then be negatively correlated with quintile income. There are countries where this is still true,[45] but this negative correlation is increasingly breaking down and being replaced with a positive correlation. Thus, unemployment is a much more useful indicator of poverty than it has been in the past, although it is still far from perfect.

B.8. The Informal Sector. It is well-established that the extent of employment in the informal sector varies inversely with the level of income by group. Thus, the bottom quintile is the most heavily dependent on jobs in the informal sector and this makes it a useful indicator of poverty. It is usually measured as the proportion of the labour force in the informal sector.

The minimum requirements for a comparative study of income distribution in Latin America are the top and bottom quintile (decile) and the Gini coefficient. The minimum requirement for the study of poverty is the Headcount Index. These are the measures on which we concentrate in this book, while other measures (e.g. the Theil index and real wage rates) are used when available and as appropriate.

Thematic and Case Studies

The NEM consists of a series of reforms that are analysed in depth in Part I of this book. In Chapter 2, E.V.K. FitzGerald examines trade liberalisation both in terms of what has been achieved and also in terms of its expected impact on income distribution and poverty. The approach, as in the other thematic chapters in Part I, is to isolate as far as possible the causal links between the reform in question and income shares, while recognising that in any given country many other factors will have contributed to the final outcome.

The need for macroeconomic stability, associated with trade liberalisation and export-orientation, has produced a new emphasis in favour of fiscal reform in Latin America. This is the theme of Chapter 3 by Laurence Whitehead, where the difficulties of combining fiscal balance with social expenditures designed to combat poverty and improve income distribution are examined. Whitehead pays particular attention to the problem of social security reform and the privatisation of pensions, which – in the short-run at least – can often increase rather than decrease fiscal stress.

Labour market reform is the subject of Chapter 4 by Jim Thomas. While exchange rate policy is crucial at the beginning of the reform process to shift resources towards the tradeable goods sector, real depreciation cannot be used indefinitely to promote international competitiveness. Thomas examines the impact of the NEM on the labour market in the region and examines the steps taken to reform the labour market so as to reduce the unit cost of labour and enhance efficiency.

The theme of factor market reform is continued in Chapter 5, where Raúl Fernández reviews the changes in the domestic capital market associated with the NEM through financial liberalisation. Fernández demonstrates that a fall in inflation will have redistributive consequences through the capital market, although the major impact on the size distribution of income occurs as a result of the reduction in the inflation tax. Meanwhile, deregulation of financial markets leads to higher real interest rates from which the top decile benefits disproportionately.

Part 1 closes with a study by Stephany Griffith-Jones in Chapter 6 on the link between international capital flows, macroeconomic performance and income distribution. While she notes the positive impact on inequality associated with the return of foreign capital to Latin America, she also emphasises the negative distributional consequences of the periodic financial and liquidity crises to which Latin American countries are subject. She stresses the need for a stronger regulatory environment to smooth out the flows of capital to Latin America over the long-run.

The thematic chapters in Part 1 explore both the reform process within the NEM as well as the implications of each reform, *ceteris paribus,* on income distribution and poverty. What actually happens to income distribution and poverty is a consequence of the whole reform process together with other longer term changes (e.g. demographic and educational) inherited from the past. This is the subject of the country studies in Part II, which also contains a case study of the impact of the NEM on the manufacturing sector.

The first country study, Chapter 7, is devoted to Chile, where the NEM began more than twenty years ago and where the reform process is the most advanced. It is therefore the most important country to study in terms of the impact of the NEM on income distribution and poverty. The author, Christopher Scott, finds clear evidence of an improvement in equity in recent years. However, this has still not fully reversed the deterioration associated with the first phase of the model and Scott argues that at least some of the improvement can be attributed to reforms adopted in Chile even before the start of the NEM.

The theme of (severe) pain followed by (modest) gain continues in Chapter 8 with the case study of Mexico by Humberto Pánuco and Miguel Székely. The increase in both inequality and poverty in the first five years of the NEM was not reversed in the subsequent period. Furthermore, the authors argue that the most recent financial crisis in Mexico (1994/5) will have reversed even the modest gains recorded in the *sexenio* of President Salinas de Gortari (1988-94).

Chile and Mexico are the only two countries in Latin America that have been operating a version of the NEM for at least a decade. Other countries have still to complete the reform process or have only just begun it. In Chapter 9, Andy Thorpe looks at Honduras where the NEM only began to operate after 1990. The author stresses the difficulties encountered in implementing the NEM in a coherent fashion in a country where institutions are weak, democracy fragile and interest groups powerful. Nevertheless, despite data deficiencies, he finds that the Honduran version of the NEM has strong equity implications and that some of these are positive.

The study of Brazil in Chapter 10 by Francisco Ferreira and Julie Litchfield is rather different. Although Brazil began to implement its own version of the NEM in 1990, there are no data on income distribution and poverty that can be used to test the relationship between reform and equity. The authors therefore concentrate on the changes in income distribution and poverty in the decade leading upto 1990 – a decade when all scholars are agreed the NEM was *not* being implemented. The Brazil study can then be interpreted as a counterfactual – an example of what can happen to income distribution and poverty when countries postpone the reforms associated with the NEM.[46]

The final chapter in Part II is a case study of the manufacturing sector. The main beneficiary of inward-looking policies under import-substituting industrialisation (ISI), the manufacturing sector is still seen by many as a potential beneficiary of the NEM through the impact of reform on manufactured exports. In Chapter 11, however, John Weeks shows that the impact of the NEM on the manufacturing sector has in many cases been negative rather than positive. Weeks then raises the question of whether an industrial policy needs to be integrated into the NEM, a theme that is addressed by several other authors in this volume.

The conclusions are given in Chapter 12. It is now possible to identify a number of patterns both in the operation of the NEM in Latin America and in its impact on income distribution and poverty. The Study Group conclusions are that the NEM has done little to improve poverty and has a tendency to harm income distribution. While this may seem very negative, it should not be forgotten that the alternative to the NEM before 1990 was not much better and that non-NEM experiments since 1980 have been very unsuccessful. Thus, the main policy implication is not the rejection of the NEM, but its refinement to place equity considerations at the centre of the model's operation.

Notes

1. See CEPAL (1993), Table 17, pp. 95-7.
2. See Lustig (1995), p.2. For individual countries see UNDP (1995), pp. 178-9.
3. See Lustig (1995) p.2.
4. See CEPAL (1993), Table 20, p.100. There are, however, other estimates of poverty in 1980. The World Bank, for example, gives a figure of 26.5% for the headcount index of poverty as a result of different assumptions and the use of a different methodology. See World Bank (1993), p.66.
5. Between 1970 and 1980 the proportion of the *urban* population living in poverty rose from 27% to 30%, although the proportion living in extreme poverty fell from 12% to 11%. See CEPAL (1993), Table 20, p.100.
6. Fields (1992) could not find a single case in which expansion of real GDP per head before 1980 was not accompanied by a fall in *national* poverty as measured by the headcount index. Using a less restrictive definition of 'national', Altimir (1994) found three cases before 1980 where rising GDP per head was accompanied by rising poverty. However, in two cases – Argentina and Chile (1970-80) – the rate of growth of GDP per head was close to zero and both economies were subject to severe fluctuations during the decade. In the third case – Uruguay (1970-81) – the increase in poverty is clearly proven only for urban areas.
7. The decline in the headcount index of poverty in rural areas was due both to agricultural modernisation and rural-urban migration. Given the rise in urban poverty, it is not unreasonable therefore to argue that poverty was in large part exported from rural to urban areas. See Altimir (1994).
8. See Maddison (1992), Table 4-3, p.82.
9. See Altimir (1982).
10. See Altimir (1986). The fall took place over a period in which GDP per head

was rising, albeit at a modest 1.7% per year. See SALA (1993), Table 3466.

11. The Gini coefficient improved in both cases; see Londoño (1990) for Colombia and Fields (1980) for Costa Rica. However, the share of the bottom quintile in Costa Rica fell.

12. See Márquez and Mukherjee (1991).

13. See CEPAL (1989).

14. The Gini coefficient rose by 10% in urban Argentina between 1974 and 1980, by 21% in urban Chile over the same period and by 32% in urban Uruguay between 1973 and 1979. See Altimir (1994), Table B-1.

15. See IDB (1994), Table B-2, p.239.

16. See CEPAL (1993), Table 20.

17. See CEPAL (1993), Table 20. The World Bank estimates a lower level of poverty, but a similar increase in poverty (41.3 million) for the period 1980 to 1989 with 75% of the increase classified as urban. See World Bank (1993), p.66 and Morley (1995), p.44.

18. ECLAC and CEPAL, the Spanish acronym, are used interchangeably in this volume to describe the United Nations Economic Commission for Latin America and the Caribbean. In the case of references CEPAL is used for Spanish-language publications and ECLAC for English-language ones.

19. One should not read too much into this surprising result. Only one case refers to urban households – Costa Rica (1988-90) – and the time-period is very short. The other three cases all refer to rural households where the statistics are less reliable: Costa Rica (1988-90); Guatemala (1986-9); Venezuela (1986-90). See CEPAL (1993), Table 18 and Table 19, pp.98-9.

20. The two cases are urban incomes in Paraguay from 1986 to 1990 and in Colombia from 1980 to 1986. The former refers to Asunción only, while the latter is almost certainly subject to measurement error (see Berry, (1995).

21. In each case, caution must be exercised before assuming that the degree of inequality declined. In Costa Rica, for example, the rural Gini only fell from 0.355 in 1981 to 0.351 in 1990 – see CEPAL (1993), Table 17. In Uruguay, the urban Gini decline was also very small and one study – Bucheli and Rossi (1993) – suggests virtually no change. The strongest case for a decline is provided by Colombia, but this is the exception that perhaps proves the rule since GDP per head continued to grow during the 1980s.

22. In some cases the deterioration was very marked. The Gini coefficient, for example, rose sharply in Brazil, Panama and Venezuela during the 1980s in both rural and urban areas. See CEPAL (1993), Table 17.

23. For an excellent account of the Southern Cone experiment, see Ramos (1986).

24. Before the debt crisis the net capital inflow (K) exceeded the payment of interest and profits on foreign capital (F), allowing imports (M) to exceed exports (E). For most of the 1980s the opposite was true, i.e. (F) exceeded (K), leading to a negative transfer of resources and the need for a trade surplus (E > M). See Bulmer-Thomas (1994), pp.377-8.

25. A number of influential books capture the intellectual odyssey towards the new development paradigm. See, in particular, Balassa *et al.* (1986), De Soto (1987), Williamson (1990) and World Bank (1993a).

26. These barriers have become legendary, although the combination of tariff and non-tariff barriers makes it difficult to quantify them. See Jenkins (1995), Table I.1.

27. This point cannot be stressed too much. Some studies of trade liberalisation erroneously imply that REER devaluation is optional.

28. High inflation rates, even if stable, tend to promote financial over real investment, reducing the importance of productive activity in generating profits. See Welch (1992) for a case study of Brazil.

29. See Perry and Herrera (1994).

30. See Frenkel (1994), Chapter 1.

31. Sen's Kuznets lectures delivered in 1988 have been published and have much to say on income distribution and poverty. See Sen (1992). For a discussion of Sen's philosophical approach to inequality and his attack on revealed preference theory and welfarism, see Sugden (1993).

32. The share of income received from wages and salaries is highest in the middle deciles and lowest in the top and bottom. In the case of Mexico in 1989, for example, the bottom decile received only 38% of its total income in the form of earnings from labour compared to 73% for the eighth decile. The top decile received 48% of its total income from this source.

33. The proportion of the population estimated to be living in poverty in Costa Rica in 1986 varied from 17.8% to 52%. See Morley and Alvarez (1992), Table 2. For 1981 it varied from 9.9% to 62%. See World Bank (1993), Table 4.5. In both cases the same household survey was used.

34. The problem of comparing indicators of income inequality even for a single country are well illustrated by Moll (1992). His article seeks to demonstrate that the improvement in income distribution in Taiwan since 1950 is largely a statistical illusion.

35. See Fields (1980), pp.108-9. For a detailed axiomatic treatment of each of the main income distribution indicators, see Kakwani (1980).

36. The size distribution measures the share of income received by each decile (or some other equal division) of the population. When the information is presented cumulatively, it can be used to construct a Lorenz curve in which the horizontal axis records population and the vertical axis income. The

graph can then be used to measure the share of income received by any given proportion of the population starting from the poorest.

37. The Gini coefficient is written:

$$G = \frac{1}{2n^2 \bar{y}} \sum_{i=1}^{n} \sum_{j=1}^{n} |y_i - y_j|$$

where n = number of individuals

y_i = gross *per capita* household income for individual i:

(arithmetic mean income) $\qquad \bar{y} = \left(\frac{1}{n}\right) \sum y_i$

38. The overall Gini requires households to be ranked in increasing order of income. The different components of income (e.g. wages, transfers, interest) may not be monotonically related to one another, so the overall Gini is not simply a weighted average of the different factor Ginis. However, there are solutions to the problem (see Fields (1980), pp.102-3) and some studies for Latin America do use the Gini coefficient to decompose inequality.

39. In the 1960s and 1970s, for example, there were cases in Latin America where the share of the bottom decile fell while the Gini coefficient improved (i.e. declined).

40. The Theil index of inequality (T) can be written:

$$T = \sum_{i}^{N} y_i \ln \frac{y_i}{1 / N}$$

where y(i) is the share of the ith individual in total income and N is the sample size. This can be normalised to

$$T^* = \frac{T}{\ln N}$$

where T* is roughly comparable between countries.

41. The Atkinson index, like the Theil index, is in fact a special case of what are known as General Entropy (GE) measures. These can be written as:

$$GE = \frac{1}{\alpha^2 - \alpha} \left[\frac{1}{n} \sum_{i=1}^{n} \left[\frac{y_i}{\bar{y}} \right]^{\alpha} - 1 \right]$$

Using l'Hôpital's rule (Cowell, 1995) this becomes the mean logarithmic deviation when $\alpha = 0$; the entire subfamily of Atkinson indices when $\alpha < 1$; the Theil index when $\alpha = 1$; and the squared coefficient of variation divided by 2 when $\alpha = 2$.

42. See Ravallion (1992), pp.35-40. The FGT index is sometimes written as FGT(2) since $\alpha = 2$ in eq. (5)

43. The World Bank reports 'income expansion coefficients' for a variety of household surveys used to measure poverty. They vary from 1.0 (i.e. no underreporting assumed) in the case of urban Honduras to 4.14 in the case of rural Costa Rica. See World Bank (1993), Appendix 9.3.

44. The FGT index in the World Bank study is highest for Guatemala and lowest for Costa Rica. Brazil is in an intermediate position. Results from the measurement of the Poverty Gap (PG) index are similar.

45. In Guatemala, for example, the lowest unemployment rate in the 1989 household survey was found in the bottom quintile and the highest in the top quintile. See World Bank (1993).

46. The 1992 household survey data for Brazil became available as this book went to press.

PART I

THEMATIC STUDIES

CHAPTER 2

THE NEW TRADE REGIME, MACROECONOMIC BEHAVIOUR AND INCOME DISTRIBUTION IN LATIN AMERICA

E.V.K. FitzGerald*

The aim of this chapter is to explore the consequences for income distribution in Latin America of the new trade regime (NTR), which almost all governments in the region implemented during the 1980s in reaction to the perceived failure of the import substitution strategy of industrialisation and the need to recover investor credibility in the wake of the debt crisis.

The NTR in this context I understand to be a combination of trade liberalisation (removing quantitative controls on exports, imports and all other current account transactions), and the reduction of import tariffs (and exports taxes or subsidies) to a minimal level; in other words to come completely within the rules of the World Trade Organisation (WTO). This is accompanied at the macroeconomic level by a fiscal policy designed to avoid excess domestic demand and promote private investment. At the microeconomic level mechanisms for government intervention in product and factor markets are dismantled in order to permit the reallocation of capital and labour towards internationally competitive activities.

Broadly speaking, NTRs explicitly based on orthodox principles of comparative advantage and structural adjustment were first implemented in Chile during the 1970s, and subsequently in Mexico and Argentina in the 1980s; Brazil and Colombia have been much more cautious and retained heterodox features in their trade regimes into the 1990s, while Peru and Venezuela both have attempted to liberalise along orthodox lines with some difficulties throughout the decade. The re-emergence of regional trade blocs and Latin American participation in bilateral and global trade negotiations are important features of current trade regimes, but lie beyond the scope of this chapter; nonetheless, the two main arrangements – NAFTA and Mercosur – both involve lowering of trade barriers within the area and common external protection consistent with WTO rules.

As might be expected, opinion is mixed as to the success of the NTR in terms of both its contribution to export growth and balance of payments stability, and its implications for income distribution and longer term growth. The 'Washington view' (e.g. the World Bank) is that the NTR has been an almost unqualified success on both criteria, while the 'view from Santiago' (i.e. from CEPAL) is almost the diametrical opposite.[1] However, no systematic attempt seems to have been made to evaluate the impact of NTR on income distribution in Latin America as such, possibly because it is usually considered as part of the broader process of structural adjustment and market reform.

In this chapter I shall first outline the main methodological problems involved in the *ex-post* evaluation of the relationship between a new trade regime and income distribution. Second, the standard 'trade reform model' (TRM) based on trade liberalisation and real devaluation is set out and the expected behaviour of key economic variables and income distribution are derived; the alternative version of a trade regime based on an explicit industrialisation strategy is also examined in similar terms. Third, I shall examine aggregate economic data for the major economies of the region in order to suggest the extent to which the observed NTR in the major Latin American economies actually conforms to the standard model, and thus whether the distributional consequences are likely to be as expected. Fourth, some 'stylised facts' about the observed outcome of the NTR for the region as a whole are put forward and the possible distributional consequences examined in an attempt to approximate reality better. Finally, by way of a conclusion, I suggest how the effect of the new trade regime on income distribution in Latin America might best be understood.

The Problem of Method

The evaluation of the impact of the NTR on income distribution involves at least five serious conceptual problems:

First, the NTR is based on a standard economic model, but this conceptual definition does not usually correspond to reality as observed, whatever the intentions of the government may be; in other words, we are engaged in positive rather than normative analysis. This slippage may arise from partial implementation (e.g. the frequent attribution of continued unemployment to a failure to liberalise labour markets) or from unrealistic assumptions about market behaviour (e.g. on price formation or Organisation of Economic Cooperation and Development (OECD) protection) in the model itself.

Second, the transmission mechanisms between trade and income distribution are extremely complex and difficult to observe in practice, all the more so when economies are undergoing multiple exogenous shocks as well as other shifts in policy regime. For instance, export growth may raise employment directly in the exportables sector and indirectly (by permitting faster GDP growth under a foreign exchange constraint) allow non-traded employment to rise too. Again, the level of poverty after a trade reform may depend more on the nature of an accompanying fiscal structure (often simultaneously undergoing reform) than on changing production techniques.

Third, the lags between trade reform and distributional consequences vary considerably. The negative impact of real devaluation on real wages is almost immediate, but positive effects on employment rely on investment response (which may take five years or more), while skilling and technological shifts take even longer. This poses interesting dynamic problems in welfare theory, and the practical problem that trade reforms probably require at least a decade of *sustained* implementation before they can be evaluated properly.

Fourth, the expected impact of a trade regime is expressed in terms of the 'primary' (i.e. functional or institutional) income distribution through levels of output, relative prices, resource utilisation and so on. Even if this impact were known, the 'secondary' (i.e. personal or household) distribution that results from this primary distribution depends upon how incomes are distributed by market institutions (both public and private) on the basis of assets, entitlements and so on. For instance, even if it could be unambiguously shown that the NTR leads to lower real wages and higher employment, the net effect on poverty is still ambiguous.

Fifth, a rigorous evaluation of the impact of the NTR on income distribution would require comparison at best with the impact of alternative trade regimes, and at least with the continuation of the previous regime. In principle, this can be done by applying simulation models (usually of the Computable General Equilibrium (CGE) type,[2] but in practice the construction of such models requires behavioural assumptions and parameter imputations which are heavily biased by the theoretical approach taken by the model-builder.

In consequence, there seems to be little point in trying to match, say, indicators of trade openness with Gini coefficients. I shall thus proceed in this chapter by the application of intuitive analytics and inference from the available aggregate data. Formal theoretical proof or rigorous econometric testing will not be attempted, and my approach is largely macroeconomic, so no reference will be made to micro-level studies of individual sectors – which in any case are difficult to compare on a cross-country basis.

Models of Trade and Income Distribution

Broadly speaking, the emerging trade strategy in Latin America in the 1980s was based on a standardised 'trade reform model' (TRM) proposed by the Bretton Woods Institutions. The elements of this model are well known, and form an integral part of structural adjustment policies recommended by the multilateral agencies in order to overcome underdevelopment (Krueger, 1982). Removal of trade barriers, rapid reduction of tariffs and elimination of subsidies are seen as part of a wider process of domestic market deregulation, including the privatisation of state enterprise. There are two theoretical pillars to this policy edifice:

(i)   Familiar neo-classical trade theory (Corden, 1993) which argues that the welfare gains from free trade are unambiguous, because adjustment to world prices will allow resources to be allocated most efficiently and growth to be maximised; cheaper natural resources and labour (in the case of Latin America) will be used more intensively as exports and imports adjust to comparative advantage and costly scarce capital will be used less; exports and output will grow more rapidly, while trade will balance through a variable exchange rate.

(ii)   In view of the prior distortions in the economy, textbook open-economy macroeconomic theory (Dornbusch, 1980) suggests that to reap the advantages of trade liberalisation, specific policies need to be implemented in support of the removal of trade barriers: in particular real effective exchange rate (REER) devaluation in order to shift labour and capital away from non-traded towards traded sectors, and fiscal closure in order to reduce aggregate demand and thus control inflation in non-traded sectors and prevent import surges.

The implications of this model for income distribution in the short and long term are said to be unambiguous (Dornbusch & Helmers, 1988). In the short-run real wages will fall (which is the logical corollary of real devaluation) as will employment in non-traded sectors, so that although real costs of imported consumption will also decline, income dispersion may widen and absolute poverty increase in the short-run. However, the market should react rapidly to the new price set and traded output will rise generating greater employment and reducing dispersion and poverty, although (indeed because) the real wage remains low. Eventually, with increased private investment in the traded sectors, full employment returns and labour productivity begins to rise leading to higher wages. In the longer run, growth will provide fiscal resources for poverty alleviation, but meanwhile foreign assistance can be used to provide a 'targeted safety net' (World Bank, 1993).

The basis for tracing the income-distribution effects of trade in standard theory is, of course the Stolper-Samuelson Theorem (SST) (Stolper & Samuelson, 1941): within a two-factor (capital and labour), two-commodity neoclassical model, liberalisation of foreign trade – typically by tariff reduction – increases the income of the factor which is relatively most used in the export sector and which (on the principle of comparative advantage) is most abundant, this factor being conventionally assumed to be unskilled labour; so income distribution improves. However, as Bourguinon and Morrison (1989) point out, while the SST may provide a useful point of reference, it does not determine the relationship which may exist between trade and distribution for at least three reasons: (i) the ambiguous relationship between functional and personal income distribution, discussed above; (ii) the existence of factor immobility and product market imperfections, to be discussed below; and (iii) the possibility of more than two factors of production. In fact, when further production factors are introduced to the model – such as natural resources or skilled labour – the results become indeterminate and lack precision except in specific cases. Two such problems are of relevance to the subject in hand. First, if the exporting sector is the only user of a specific factor (land or minerals), the total increase in income arising from trade liberalisation will accrue in rent, its distribution depending on the pattern of ownership in the sector – so the effect might be positive in, for example, Costa Rican small-holdings and negative for Brazilian estates. Second, the removal of import protection from a sector will reduce employment (and factor rewards) there but raise them in exports, so that the net effect depends upon whether exports are more or less labour intensive than import-substituting activities – e.g. a case might be made for Colombian flowers production, but not for Chilean mining. These theoretical difficulties are compounded when more than two intersectorally mobile factors are considered.

In practice, trade liberalisation has been one of the more easily implemented aspects of Latin American structural adjustment programmes within the orthodox paradigm (FitzGerald, 1995). On the export side this has involved removing state marketing systems and export duties, but the main change is in the shift away from quantitative restrictions on imports, adoption of uniform tariffs, and their subsequent virtual elimination. The stimulus to exports is expected to arise initially from reduced marketing costs and the greater availability of imported raw materials, spares and plant; subsequently the competition faced by domestic producers of inputs to the export sectors will force greater efficiency. The resulting increase in export profitability will stimulate increasing supply from existing capacity (and switching away from domestic markets) in the short term and further investment in the sector in the longer term.

Trade reform is supposed to be accompanied by policies designed to achieve REER depreciation (Collier & Gunning, 1993). A real devaluation aims at raising the price of tradeables relative to non-tradeables, with three consequences: (i) exports (and import-competing domestic production) become more profitable and supply rises – initially through diversion of existing production and subsequently through greater investment; (ii) imports fall as their higher price forces down effective demand and domestic products are substituted; (iii) non-traded production becomes less profitable and supply declines from existing capacity, followed by a fall in investment; and (iv) real wages decline,[3] leading to a substitution of labour for capital.

The expected results of the TRM in terms of the major macroeconomic variables would logically be: a) an increasing share of exports in GDP as 'trade openness' increases and traded prices rise relative to non-traded ones; b) rapid growth of total exports, particularly those based on natural resources and labour-intensive manufacturing, derived from inter-sectoral trade; c) strong depreciation of the REER due to consistent macroeconomic policies; with real wages falling initially,[4] in order to make this possible, but subsequently rising as the employment generated tightens the labour market; d) import penetration rises as previously protected import-competing industries shrink, concentrated on capital-intensive goods as private investment rises.

What might be called the 'new-Keynesian' critique of this essentially 'new-classical' model suggests that it is not a plausible account of the relationship between trade, growth and industrialisation. This critique suggests the following: first, that the TRM does not (and cannot) form the basis for sustained export growth; second, that successful export growth depends upon specific government intervention, particularly in order to support corporate investment, technological innovation and labour skilling; and third, that such an alternative strategy would have better consequences for income distribution than the TRM.

On the one hand, the central *cepalino* tradition is based on a different vision of world trade, where Latin American exports are constrained by market access, and their growth is based on income growth and technological change in OECD countries (ECLAC, 1992a).[5] In consequence, attempts to exploit comparative advantage will not accelerate export growth. Real devaluation is seen as difficult to implement (due to price formation, wage setting and fiscal behaviour) and, if achieved, will lead to a production collapse without significant export gains (Taylor, 1991). Real wage cuts are seen as not only socially undesirable and macroeconomically unnecessary, but also as reducing labour effort (the 'efficiency wages' approach). Trade liberalisation would thus lead to considerable welfare costs without significant gain, while sustained industrialisation requires positive protection and infrastructure provision – particularly in order to establish a technologically dynamic capital goods industry which can raise productivity (and thus labour incomes) throughout the economy.

On the other hand, 'new trade theory' (NTT) has tended to modify but essentially strengthen this view; NTT stresses the importance of domestic markets as the prelude to export efforts, of public investment in human capital formation ('skilling'), specific incentives to large competitive firms ('economies of scale and scope') and above all of export growth based on intra-sectoral trade in increasingly sophisticated manufactured products (Grossman & Helpman, 1991; Helpman & Krugman, 1985).

In terms of the key variables mentioned above, the following trends would be expected from trade liberalisation within a new-Keynesian point of view that brings together these neo-structuralist and NTT elements: a) a stable share of exports in GDP due to the foreign exchange constraint limiting the growth of output, a constraint which is not lifted by trade liberalisation and relative price movements; b) slow growth of total export volume, but more rapid growth of 'high-tech' exports (as opposed to 'low-tech' or natural resource-based exports dependent on inter-sectoral trade) due to intra-sectoral trade by those countries which have moved beyond reliance on natural resource development to full industrialisation – involving higher rates of both public and private investment; c) a real depreciation of the exchange rate that is only temporary, as domestic price- formation rules dominate in the medium term; the real wage decline is not reversed in the long-run because new technologies save labour and increase wage dispersion; d) import penetration continues to be limited by real export income and autonomous capital inflows; it is concentrated on luxury consumer goods after trade liberalisation in the case of natural resource exporters, and on capital goods only in industrialising countries as private and public investment rise together.

The implications for income distribution, from this critical viewpoint, depend upon whether the orthodox trade reform model (TRM) is implemented or not. The TRM, according to the new-Keynesian view, would increase both income dispersion and absolute poverty in the short- and long-run, due to the slow rate of growth, lack of skilling, depressed real wage rate, recessive fiscal retrenchment and increased structural unemployment. In contrast, if an appropriate industrial strategy were implemented, then faster growth would increase employment, real wage cuts would be unnecessary and welfare expenditure would be maintained.

Figure 1:
Hypothetical Distributional Outcomes of Trade Reform

	Rapid Export Growth	Slow Export Growth
Rapid Trade Reform	**Trade Reform Model (TRM):** – less dispersion – less poverty	**New Trade Regime (NTR) in practice?:** – more dispersion – more poverty
Slow Trade Reform	**Industrial Strategy proposed by NTT:** – more dispersion – less poverty	**Old Trade Regime (ISI):** – less dispersion – more poverty

Figure 1 contains, in a summary form, a representation of the expected outcomes of the four models, characterised in two dimensions – whether export growth is rapid or not (with implications for labour demand and thus poverty) and how rapidly the trade reform itself is implemented (with implications for employment composition and thus dispersion). The northwest quadrant reflects the outcome of the TRM as expected by its orthodox proponents, with both inequality and poverty falling as the result of rapid export growth and a shift towards labour-intensive traded production after liberalisation. The southwest quadrant reflects the expected results of an industrial strategy with slow trade liberalisation, such as that of East Asia, where inequality rises but poverty declines as the result of skills dispersion and rapid export growth. In contrast, the southeast quadrant reflects the supposed experience of the 'old trade regime' in Latin America, where import-substituting industrialisation (ISI) leads to slow export growth (and thus poverty), but less wage dispersion as trade is only liberalised slowly. Finally, the northeast quadrant reflects the worst possible distributive outcome – increasing inequality and increasing poverty – arising from a combination of radical trade liberalisation combined with slow export growth: this possible outcome of the NTR will be a hypothesis to be tested in the empirical section of this chapter which follows.

An Overview of the Empirical Evidence

There is no consistent body of research on trade liberalisation in Latin America upon which a comparative analysis can be based. The large scale study by the World Bank on the subject (Papageorgiou *et al.*, 1991) includes six economies from the region[6] among the 19 developing countries covered, but suffers from two serious weaknesses. First, the period covered is 1960-82, so it does not coincide with the period of interest to us in this chapter, and what is more, does not include the major trade reform initiatives since the mid-1980s. Second, the study explicitly takes the benefits of trade liberalisation as given and focuses entirely on problems of policy execution.[7] Third, as mainstream reviewers have pointed out (e.g. Greenaway, 1993), there are serious methodological flaws in the World Bank study, including the lack of a common analytical or quantitative framework and the derivation of overall conclusions inconsistent with the case studies.

In any case, it is extremely difficult, for the reasons discussed above, to establish a methodologically satisfactory and empirically testable direct link between trade liberalisation and income distribution. In this part of the chapter I shall therefore briefly discuss aggregate data on the trade performance of the major seven economies in the region (Argentina, Brazil, Chile, Colombia,

Mexico, Peru and Venezuela) between 1980 and 1993, in order to ascertain which of the three models discussed seem to best explain observed behaviour, and thus derive – albeit by deduction – the probable consequences for factor earnings dispersion and employment. The reader can then compare them with the individual country studies and the comparative data on personal income distribution trends and labour market conditions in the other chapters of this volume.

Table 1:
Summary of Trade Regimes of Western Hemisphere Developing Countries

Regime	QRs		Tariffs		Combined	
	1990	1993	1990	1993	1990	1993
Total Number of Countries	15	15	15	15	15	15
Open	7	13	0	1	0	1
Moderate	2	1	6	12	4	12
Restrictive	6	1	9	2	11	2

Note: QRs = Quota Restrictions

Source: International Monetary Fund (1994).

Trade Regimes
It is notoriously difficult to measure the degree of protection offered by trade regimes in practice,[8] but it is clear that as a result of individual country action and the Uruguay Round negotiations during the 1980s, the degree of 'trade openness' (Table 1) in terms of both the reduction of quota restrictions (QRs) and tariffs has been considerable throughout the developing countries of the Western Hemisphere. The Uruguay Round itself resulted in an average tariff regime of around 13%, with Argentina, Chile and Colombia having the lowest average rate (11%) and Peru the highest (17%) – see Table 2. However, the degree of effective trade liberalisation is often exaggerated. On the one hand, external trade taxes collected as a proportion of imports have declined in all seven countries by about a half (with Chile, Mexico and Peru making the most drastic reductions). On the other hand, for industrial products (Table 3) the IMF estimates show that average import-weighted bound rates for our seven countries only fell from 41% to 30% during the Uruguay Round, indicating considerable residual industrial protection which is now built into the various regional agreements.

Table 2:
Comparative Tariff Regimes c. 1994 (Percent)

Country	Maximum (%)	Average (Excluding Other Charges) (%)	Other Charges (%)	Number of Tariff Bands
Argentina	20	11	10	8
Brazil	35/40	15	6	13
Chile	15	11	0	1
Colombia	20/35	11	0	4
Mexico	20	13	1	4
Peru	25	17	n/a	2
Venezuela	20/30	12	0	4

Source: International Monetary Fund (1994). Status based on information available in May, 1994.

Table 3:
Uruguay Round Tariff Reductions on Industrial Products (Percent)

Country	IMPORT-WEIGHTED AVERAGE Bound Rates Pre-Uruguay Round	IMPORT-WEIGHTED AVERAGE Applied Rates Pre-Uruguay Round	IMPORT-WEIGHTED AVERAGE Bound Rates Post-Uruguay Round
Argentina	38.2	20.0	30.9
Brazil	40.7	15.0	27.0
Chile	34.9	15.0	24.9
Colombia	44.3	11.0	35.3
Mexico	46.1	13.0	33.7
Peru	34.8	15.3	29.4
Venezuela	50.0	12.0	31.1
Average	41.3	14.5	30.3

Source: International Monetary Fund (1994).

In other words, the degree of trade liberalisation undertaken under the NTR may well be rather less than the TRM supposes because (i) the previous degree of protection was not as high as the stylised critique of the previous trade regime suggested, and (ii) the residual degree of protection is rather higher than the proponents of the NTR would claim.

Export Performance

The share of exports of goods and services in GDP for Latin America as a whole (see Table A.3 in Statistical Appendix) rose steadily through the 1980s from about 10% to 15%, despite the declining share of the region in world exports. However, among the major economies only Argentina strictly reflected the regional aggregate, which was made up of quite different trends. Brazil, Chile, Colombia and Mexico were stagnant in the first sub-period (1980-85) and expanded rapidly in the second (1985-90), while Peru and Venezuela had poor performance throughout. Export volume indicators (Table 4), which might suggest the success of trade regimes independently of world price movements, show large and fairly steady increases in the cases of Argentina, Brazil, Chile, Colombia and Mexico with Peru and Venezuela making little progress.

Table 4:
Export Volume (Quantum) Index 1980 = 100

Year	Argentina	Brazil	Chile	Colombia	Mexico	Peru	Venezuela
1981	117	132	102	90	123	90	94
1982	115	120	109	90	137	102	85
1983	127	130	110	96	159	99	82
1984	119	157	117	106	177	106	90
1985	135	158	122	107	160	103	83
1986	121	127	136	117	169	100	85
1987	108	162	135	166	190	87	85
1988	138	199	153	147	203	77	93
1989	137	205	166	185	199	92	105
1990	162	179	171	248	189	83	112
1991	159	182	196	270	209	93	111
1992	151	201	217	290	213	97	96

Source: UNCTAD (1992) and (1993)

This degree of volume expansion has probably only had a marginal effect on traded sector employment. The average compound growth rates in export volume between 1981-83 and 1990-92 were not sufficiently greater than labour force growth rates to allow for loss of import-competing jobs except in the case of Colombia. Moreover, generally deteriorating terms of trade (see Table A. 3) offset export volume growth so that the purchasing power of exports grew at less than the rate of population growth in the cases of Argentina and Mexico, with absolute declines in the cases of Peru and Venezuela, and net *per capita* gains only in the cases of Brazil, Chile and Colombia.

Trade Openness and Composition

In terms of the proportion of GDP exported (see Table A.5 in Statistical Appendix), a clear upward trend is observable only in the cases of Chile and Colombia, while in the other countries the trend is erratic and it is difficult to make a case for a major structural shift. Even in the two former cases, where the ratio of exports to Colombian GDP rose from 11% in 1981-83 to 19% in 1991-93 and that for Chile from 20% to 31%, at least half of this change is accounted for by the relative price shift arising from real devaluation and not from changes in the volume of output. The composition of exports (Table 5) – particularly the share of manufactures – has not changed significantly in Argentina, Chile, Peru or Venezuela (once oil prices are taken into account), all of which remained predominantly primary exporters during the period and thus potentially still

Table 5:
Export Structure by Main Categories and Selected Commodity Groups (%)

Year	All Food	Agricultural Raw Materials	Fuels	Ores and Metals	Manufactured Goods	Manufactured Exports/Manufactured Value Added
Argentina						
1980	65.0	6.2	3.5	2.2	23.1	7.6
1985	66.1	3.5	7.6	1.7	21.1	6.1
1990	56.3	4.3	7.8	2.4	29.1	11.5
1991	60.1	3.8	6.3	1.7	28.2	n/a
1992	61.0	2.8	8.7	1.2	26.3	n/a
Brazil						
1980	46.3	4.0	1.8	9.4	37.2	10.4
1985	36.8	2.6	6.3	9.4	43.9	14.6
1990	27.8	3.5	2.2	13.8	51.5	22.0
1991	24.9	3.4	1.4	14.3	54.9	n/a
1992	25.4	3.3	1.6	11.9	57.0	n/a

Table 5: continued

Year	All Food	Agricult-ural Raw Materials	Fuels	Ores and Metals	Manufact-ured Goods	Manufactured Exports/Manu-factured Value Added
			Chile			
1980	14.9	10.0	1.3	64.1	9.1	8.4
1985	25.1	8.3	0.5	58.3	6.9	5.4
1990	23.1	9.5	0.5	53.1	9.7	9.4
1991	27.1	8.0	0.5	49.2	13.4	n/a
1992	28.5	9.2	0.3	46.8	13.6	n/a
			Colombia			
1980	71.8	4.7	2.8	0.2	19.6	10.8
1985	59.3	5.5	16.3	0.4	16.9	8.9
1990	32.8	4.3	36.9	0.2	25.1	20.6
1991	32.4	5.2	28.8	0.3	33.3	n/a
1992	33.1	6.3	28.5	0.3	31.9	n/a
			Mexico			
1980	12.4	2.3	66.8	6.5	11.9	4.3
1987	12.0	1.1	31.4	5.1	50.3	n/a
1989	12.3	2.0	33.9	6.9	44.9	n/a
1990	11.7	1.6	37.0	5.7	44.1	20.5
1992	11.3	1.9	29.9	4.5	52.4	n/a
			Peru			
1980	15.6	3.6	20.3	42.3	16.7	11.1
1985	15.8	6.0	20.5	40.8	15.7	11.8
1989	21.8	4.7	12.6	40.2	17.0	n/a
1990	22.4	3.9	10.9	42.6	18.4	8.3
1991	22.0	3.6	11.6	42.1	18.8	n/a
			Venezuela			
1980	0.4	0.1	94.0	3.9	1.7	2.3
1985	3.2	0.1	80.0	7.5	9.2	10.5
1990	2.0	0.5	81.0	5.7	10.6	15.0
1992	2.6	0.1	81.3	5.0	11.0	n/a

Source: For the composition of exports, UNCTAD (1992) and (1993) was used. For value added UNCTAD (1993/94) was used.

Note: Rows may not sum to 100 due to unallocated entries in source.

subjects of the SST model. Only Brazil, Colombia and Mexico appear to have shifted structurally towards manufactures and are thus potential candidates for the NTT model. However, the proportion of technologically advanced branches in manufactured exports is relatively stable in the case of Brazil and Mexico and has actually fallen in that of Colombia.

Imports have grown much faster than exports for the region as a whole and in our seven countries (see Table A.4) due to net private capital inflows – either in the form of debt relief or in that of fresh portfolio inflows resulting not only from fiscal reform and privatisation, but also the strong signals sent by trade liberalisation itself. It is these inflows, rather than trade reform as such, which transformed the balance of payments position by the end of the 1980s. However, average import penetration in our seven cases has remained remarkably stable over the period, reflecting the fact that GDP rose with increased foreign exchange availability: there are notable increases in Colombia and Mexico, marked *declines* in the cases of Brazil and Peru, and no discernible long-term trend at all in the cases of Argentina, Chile and Venezuela.

As far as the composition of imports is concerned, if we compare 1980 with 1991-2, it is difficult to find major structural shifts. All countries continued to import producer goods (i.e. chemicals, fuels, machinery and equipment) in fairly stable proportions, although there does appear to be a steady rise in 'other manufactures', which presumably correspond to imported consumer goods as a result of lower tariffs and the lifting of QRs. Nonetheless, the changes in the import structure are much less than might have been expected from radical trade liberalisation.

Real Effective Exchange Rates and Investment

The REER is one of the linchpins of the TRM, reallocating resources towards the traded sector and reducing the real wage. The REER can be measured by using the consumer price index (CPI) or the wholesale price index (WPI) in the absence of direct estimates of traded and non-traded prices.[9] The TRM assumes that trade liberalisation will be accompanied by sharp real devaluation, expressed as a *rise* in the REER indices. The CPI index should reflect the prices faced by consumers, and thus a rise should depress import demand and real wages; the WPI index should reflect prices faced by producers, and thus a rise should shift output towards the traded sector and reduce labour costs. The Latin American experience after 1985 (see Table A.6 in the Statistical Appendix) has not conformed to the standard orthodox view of exchange rate policy discussed above. Chile, Colombia (before 1994) and Venezuela have all experienced sustained real devaluations, which should have depressed real wages and stimulated the primary export sector in the fashion expected by the TRM. In sharp contrast, Brazil, Mexico and Peru all show sustained revaluation after initial devaluation periods; this unexpected behaviour appears to be the result of private capital inflows resulting from the expectations raised in part by trade liberalisation itself, which had the perverse consequence of stimulating non-traded sectors, raising imports and sustaining real wages. In the most complex case, Argentina, the CPI index shows real revaluation after devaluation in the mid-1980s, when the nominal anchor was adopted, leading to increased import penetration and sustaining real wages; however, the WPI index (not shown in Table A.6) continues the devaluationary trend, maintaining low labour costs and stimulating the primary export sector.[10]

For the region as a whole, the investment rate has declined sharply, much of this due to fiscal constraints on public investment that undermined human capital and infrastructure provision for private investment (FitzGerald *et al.*, 1994). The average private investment rate for the region fell from 15% of GDP in 1980-82 to 12% in 1991-92; circumstantial evidence indicates, moreover, that there has been a shift towards non-traded sectors such as real estate and services modernisation. In Argentina and Peru there was a secular decline in the private investment rate, in Brazil and Mexico an apparent cycle of decline and recovery, and erratic stagnation in the other three cases. This poor record is puzzling in view of the undoubted conversion of policy-makers to 'the market' and the observed increase in profitability and investment incentives throughout the region. Econometric tests by the World Bank, however, show that private investment levels were positively associated with domestic demand growth, low real interest rates, real exchange rate stability and low debt burdens (Cardoso, 1993). In other words, the negative impact of macroeconomic policy on these variables in most cases depressed private investment and thus limited severely the response to the shock of trade liberalisation.

Real Wages and Earnings Dispersion

Average real wages (see Table A.8) fell considerably between the mid-1980s and the early 1990s in Argentina, Peru and Venezuela, while in Brazil (São Paulo), Chile, Colombia and Mexico (until 1995) they rose considerably as output recovered. In contrast, real minimum wages declined substantially almost everywhere.[11] Even after allowing for problems of representativity, two broad interpretations do seem to be justified. First, that although trade liberal-isation has been accompanied by substantial real wage declines (and corresponding increases in capital rents) in the case of primary exporters such as Argentina and Peru, the factor price change does not seem to have been enough to achieve the structural shift towards exports and/or labour-intensive technologies predicted by the SST (see also Chapter 11). Indeed, if anything, labour-intensive non-traded sectors may have been perversely stimulated by low real wages and REER overvaluation. Second, wage dispersion (as reflected by the ratio between average and minimum wage indices) has increased dramatically in Argentina, Brazil, Mexico and Peru, while declining slightly in Chile and rising slightly in Colombia. The explanation for this shift would logically differ as between primary and industrial exporters (Wood, 1994): it can be seen as responding to excess supply of unskilled labour in the case of primary exporters such as Argentina and Peru, but in that of Brazil and Mexico it may be evidence for segmented labour demand of the kind predicted by the NTT. In Mexico, however, detailed branch-level data indicate that the technologically-derived shift in skilled labour demand arises from foreign investment rather than trade as such (Hanson & Harrison, 1995).

Data on the share of earnings in manufacturing value added – and by extension, the gross profit share – appears[12] to have fluctuated around a falling trend in all our cases except that of Brazil, where it was relatively stable. A falling earnings share implies increasing industrial profitability so long as capital-intensity remains stable, but as we have seen investment did not respond. However, real interest rates also rose considerably during the 1980s throughout the region, so that part of the increased profitability would have been transferred to financial asset holders, thus further increasing the dispersion of factor incomes under the reasonable assumption that financial asset ownership is even more concentrated than that for industrial capital.

Productivity and Employment

Employment figures are not available disaggregated by traded and non-traded sectors in order to test the SST directly, and in any case it is not clear what they would mean in the face of large-scale informal activities. Industrial productivity does not seem to have risen in general as a result of trade liberalisation (see also Chapter 11). Since the mid-1980s, manufacturing output per worker actually declined in Brazil, Colombia, Peru and Venezuela and was roughly stable in the case of Chile. Productivity only rose in Mexico, where it was mainly due to labour-shedding as the manufacturing share of output rose by less than its share of employment fell. Only in one case (Chile) did the manufacturing sector increase its share of both GDP and employment.

When the real GDP growth rate is lower than that for the economically active population (EAP), then the labour market is presumably loosening, although how much higher the former must be than the latter to maintain equilibrium depends on the rate of average labour productivity growth. For the 1980-93 period as a whole,[13] GDP grew less rapidly than the EAP in the cases of Argentina, Brazil, Mexico, Peru and Venezuela so that labour markets must have become considerably less tight, although this does not necessarily show up in open unemployment rates (see Table A.9). For the reasons given above – principally import penetration and slow export growth – a considerable part of this underemployment can be attributed to the NTRs. Only in the case of Chile and Colombia did GDP grow more rapidly than EAP, but for Colombia the margin of 1-2% per annum is not sufficient evidence, once productivity growth is taken into account, to argue for a significant tightening of labour markets – let alone attribute this to successful trade reform. Indeed, to reverse the argument, it cannot be argued that the meagre results of the TRM in most of our country cases are due to 'distorted labour markets', because generally real wages have fallen and unemployment risen.

A Tentative Interpretation

Clearly reality (as always) is far from homogeneous. Moreover *ex post* it cannot be plausibly argued that the region as a whole has experienced a profound change in trade structures or even in basic macroeconomic ratios. Can it be said that some countries conform to the TRM (at least in its basic SST variant) and others to the NTT alternative? Not really:

Argentina has experienced radical trade opening, but exports have not expanded rapidly (until 1995) or assumed a dynamic role in growth; rather their composition reflects a process of 'de-industrialisation' without a new natural resource based comparative advantage. Real wages have fallen, despite real exchange rate appreciation, while real interest rates have risen and industrial employment has fallen due in part to import penetration. Thus, increased dispersion and increased poverty are the probable consequence of the NTR *ceteris paribus*.

Brazil only implemented the TRM in 1990, and the process is still incomplete. Slow export growth (due to problems of market access and monetary stabilisation) has been accompanied by a standstill in the previous technological upgrading of exports. Real wages have not fallen excessively. Thus, no increase in dispersion is the probable outcome of the NTR, combined with some increase in poverty *ceteris paribus*.

Chile is the only country to fit the TRM properly, and also the only case where even medium-term evaluation is possible because the NTR had been in place since the previous decade. Exports accelerated and real wages recovered after an initial decline, so that the virtuous long-term reduction in both income dispersion and poverty is the probable consequence of the NTR. However, the continued dominance of natural resource exports implies a lack of skilling and long-run income growth potential.

Colombia has combined the advantages of sustained export growth, steady industrialisation and real wage recovery as the TRM predicts, although trade has only been liberalised slowly until recently and the real exchange rate has

Figure 2:
Aspects of Trade Reform Affecting Income Distribution

	Argentina	Brazil	Chile	Colombia	Mexico	Peru	Venezuela
Export volume growth	+	+	+	+	+	-	-
Export purchasing power growth	=	+	+	+	=	-	-
Export structure shift	=	+	=	=	+	=	=
Import penetration	=	+	=	-	-	+	=
Real exchange rate	+	+	-	-	+	+	-
Private investment	-	+	=	=	+	-	=
Average real wages	-	+	+	=	+	-	-
Wage dispersion	-	-	=	=	-	=	=
Labour market tightening	-	-	+	=	-	-	-
Score	**-2**	**+5**	**+3**	**0**	**+2**	**-3**	**-5**

Note:
'+' indicates a change favourable to income distribution
'-' indicates a change unfavourable to income distribution
'=' indicates no change

remained high. Reduced dispersion and reduced poverty are the probable consequence of the NTR in this heterodox form.

Mexico entered the GATT quite suddenly in 1985, and subsequently experienced real wage recovery, but increased import penetration accompanied by high real interest rates and real exchange rate appreciation due to capital inflows caused unemployment and thus dispersion in non-wage incomes. The trend towards industrialisation of exports was maintained, although overall growth was modest due to the declining terms of trade and the aftermath of the debt crisis. An increase in both dispersion and poverty is thus the probable consequence of the NTR even before the December 1994 crisis.[14]

Both **Peru** and **Venezuela** have attempted trade reform without enjoying export growth or industrialisation of exports; real wages have fallen with GDP and there is little or no trade-induced employment growth. In consequence, a fairly stable dispersion and increasing poverty are the probable outcome of the NTR.

In sum, only Chile and Colombia can be said to have conformed to the TRM and its SST foundation, and even Chile has taken two decades to implement the model while Colombia still operates a somewhat unusual variant. The only candidates for the NTT model are Brazil and Mexico, where exports have become more industrialised and wages more dispersed due to skilling, but the reduction of poverty to be generated by export-led growth is still not apparent. Figure 2 gives a very crude set of summary indicators of the distributional effects of trade reform in our seven countries based on the above discussion. On this basis, Chile and Mexico come out reasonably well and Peru and Venezuela very badly, which seems reasonable. The surprise is that Brazil does rather better than expected and Colombia rather worse, but it should be remembered that the analysis in this chapter only refers to the net effect of the NTR, not the overall trend in income distribution.

To the extent that the evidence suggests that the new trade regime (NTR) has had macroeconomic effects rather different from those supposed in the standard trade reform model (TRM), it also implies that the distributional consequences are also quite different. The behaviour of the main trade variables themselves, let alone those for wages and employment, reflects different responses to broadly similar liberalisation policies (albeit at somewhat different dates) and a comparable international environment. What is clear is that after an extended period of trade reform the results are rather different from those expected by policy-makers (and certainly much less positive for the bulk of the citizenry) and thus the renewed interest in customs unions, industrial strategies and selective protection is hardly surprising.[15]

While the combination of these distributional forces is not entirely unambiguous, it does seem reasonable to expect that overall income dispersion would increase in practice unless export-driven growth is quite rapid or welfare structures are maintained. Within groups, we would also expect increased dispersion: rising property incomes in the upper terciles; separation between skilled and unskilled employees in the middle tercile; and increased absolute poverty in the lower tercile. The crucial factor, apart from more rapid export growth and the labour-intensity of primary exports, is the response of private investment upon which the creation of new capacity and jobs depends. Structural adjustment measures in general – and trade liberalisation in particular – can have perverse effects on private investment due to the initial shock effect on implementation lags, the impact of subsequent macroeconomic instability on expectations and the lack of public investment under the fiscal restraint required to control the balance of payments (FitzGerald, 1995).

It might be argued, as in World Bank (1993a), that the longer-term effect of the new trade regime (NTR) will be to improve income distribution and reduce absolute poverty in the way that the standard trade reform model

(TRM) would indicate. My own inclination would be to suggest that the NTR as it currently operates in Latin America has little potential for dynamic growth as it is still largely based on limited primary export markets and cheap labour, with insufficient attention to industrial export promotion on the one hand and the sequencing of trade reform in order to sustain macroeconomic stability and thus investment on the other. The particular distributional benefits predicted by the SST for primary exporters do not seem to apply to the relatively capital (and natural resource) intensive activities of mining and agribusiness in the countries discussed in this chapter. Moreover, the East Asian experience (as well as the earlier experience of the industrialised countries themselves) is that manufactured export growth and intra-industry specialisation is the best way to achieve sufficient macroeconomic dynamism in order to absorb labour and finance welfare provision, while the concerted industrial policy that this approach requires (focusing on human capital formation and technological development) also has positive distributional characteristics.

Finally, in view of the limited degree of success in trade reform to date, despite the bold efforts at tariff reduction, it is perhaps worth asking why this major shift in Latin American economic doctrine took place – particularly in view of the fact that 'political economy' theories of trade liberalisation (Rodrik, 1989) indicate that *ex ante* at least, reform will have more opponents than supporters. There are three possible reasons: (i) much of the policy argument for the benefits of the TRM was conducted in theoretical terms, which was compared with the perceived failure of the previous 'import substitution model', although without much attention being paid to Latin American historical experience (OECD protectionism, efforts at export promotion since the 1960s etc) or to the basis for the East Asian manufactured export boom; ii) the domestic pressure for trade reform (as opposed to, say, labour reform or reduced inflation) appears to have come from state managers themselves – allied with their Bretton Woods counterparts – rather than from local business groups as such; indeed, import liberalisation was often officially presented as a means of reforming the 'rent seeking' and 'inefficient' private sector to the benefit of consumers; (iii) the distribution between 'North' and South' of the mutual gains from trade liberalisation are ambiguous at best (and Latin American governments signally failed to obtain equivalent tariff concessions from the USA and the European Union (EU)), but trade liberalisation did act as a strong signal of irreversible policy commitment to foreign investors in the wake of the debt crisis.

Conclusions

In this chapter I have tried to deduce the *additional* (i.e. partial equilibrium) effect of the trade regime actually implemented during the 1980s on income dispersion and poverty levels by deduction from the observable macroeconomic and aggregate structural characteristics of the seven major Latin American economies. I have not attempted to guess what the distributional consequences of the new trade regimes will be in the longer term, and still less to suggest what would have happened had the standard trade reform model (TRM) been implemented 'properly' – whatever that might mean. It is of course possible to build a formal general equilibrium model of any one (or all) of these economies and subject it to exogenous shocks in the form of, say, tariff cuts. However, this exercise requires the incorporation of numerous assumptions about just those patterns of sectoral behaviour (particularly private sector response) that are in dispute and thus cannot 'prove' much about the effect of liberalisation on distribution.[16]

The conclusions of this chapter can be summarised as follows: i) despite a common policy of trade liberalisation, applied at different speeds, the resulting trade regimes have differed widely in practice due to differences in economic structure, export performance and macroeconomic management; ii) the effect of trade liberalisation depends to a considerable degree on the initial structure of the economy, the effect on natural resource exporters (such as Argentina and Chile) differing from that on manufacturing exporters (such as Brazil and Mexico); iii) the generally slow growth of export volume and the failure of private investment to recover has contributed to continued unemployment (exacerbated by job losses in previously protected industries) and thus to poverty; iv) the widespread phenomenon of increasing wage dispersion (and thus decreasing equity) derives from oversupply of unskilled labour in the case of natural resource exporters, and from technological job differentiation in the case of manufacturing exporters; v) the real devaluation and fiscal retrenchment that initially accompanied trade liberalisation in the standard structural adjustment programmes necessarily involved declining real wages and increased unemployment in the short term; vi) macroeconomic management has not delivered a stable and competitive real exchange rate, nor adequate public capital, nor sufficient long-term finance, to accelerate private investment in traded goods sectors in the medium term and thus reverse the negative short-term income distribution effects; vii) even if the relative price shifts had been sufficient to achieve the capital reallocation supposed by the standard TRM, non-traded and protected sectors are generally more labour-intensive than export sectors (the reverse of the SST assumption) and thus there would be a net employment loss.

The main thrust of my analysis has been that, whatever the ultimate distributional virtues of the standard TRM in theory, the new trade regime as experienced in Latin America in the past decade has in many (if not most) cases probably contributed to greater income dispersion and increased absolute poverty. This outcome is presumably due in part to poor policy management and exogenous trade shocks, but it also reflects the fact that markets are inherently imperfect. The more recent advances in the theory of trade (Bliss, 1989) and open economy macroeconomics (Dixon, 1994) suggest that these imperfections are inherent and are not just the result of government regulation or special interests, and thus cannot be removed by liberalisation alone – and, indeed, specific trade interventions may be needed in order to correct them.

The implication of this conclusion is presumably that the current trade regime should be modified by integrating it to an industrial development strategy, rather than relying on imperfect market forces alone (ECLAC, 1992). To the distributional benefits that would result directly from this strategy – increased skills and employment - would be added the economy-wide employment growth and fiscal resources for welfare provision arising from accelerating export income.

Notes

* I am very grateful to Miguel Székely for his assistance with data collection and to members of the Study Group for perceptive comments on two earlier drafts of this chapter.

1. For the former view, see for instance World Bank (1993a) and Edwards (1993); for the latter, ECLAC (1992) and Agosín & Ffrench-Davis (1993).
2. See Bourguinon & Morrison (1989) for a careful survey of exercises of this type, the value of which depends of course on the plausibility of the underlying behavioural assumptions. It should be noted that 'mainstream' CGE models of the distributional consequences of structural adjustment are based closely on the Stolper-Samuelson Theorem (SST), so the real exchange rate plays the central role in reallocating labour and capital between traded and non-traded sectors, thus 'showing' that the distributional result is positive.
3. This is quite simple to demonstrate, following Dornbusch (1980). The real effective exchange rate (E) is defined as the ratio of traded (P_t) to non-traded (P_n) prices, where traded prices are determined by the world price (P_s) and the nominal exchange rate (e), and non-traded prices the result of a mark-up (r) on unit labour cost – itself the product of the nominal wage (w) and

the unit labour input (j)

$$(1) \quad E = P_t/P_n = e.P_s/\{(1 + r)w.j\}$$

In other words, for a given set of world prices (P_s), labour productivity $(1/j)$ and profit margin (r), the REER depends on the nominal wage and the exchange rate (w, e).

The real wage (W) is defined as the nominal wage (w) deflated by the two domestic prices weighted by the proportion (a) of traded goods in the wage-goods basket

$$(2) \quad W = w/\{a.P_t + (1 - a)P_n\}$$

Since $P_t = E.P_n$ (see ([1])), we can show that the real wage rate (W) is inversely related to the real exchange rate (E) by two structural parameters (a, j) and the markup rate (r):

$$(3) \quad W = \{w/P_n\}/\{a.E + (1 - a)\}$$
$$= [j\{1 + r\}\{a.E + (1 - a)\}]^{-1}$$

4. Note that in the World Bank's view (Edwards and Cox-Edwards, 1994), the distributional benefits of trade reform may be thwarted by labour market distortions – that is, by minimum wages and job protection preventing factor substitution along the production function. There is little theoretical justification or empirical evidence for this view (FitzGerald & Perosino, forthcoming).

5. In view of the frequent attribution to *CEPAL* by the Bretton Woods institutions of 'intellectual responsibility for ISI' (e.g. World Bank, 1993a), it is worth noting that the original *cepalino* post-war proposals had been for export-led industrialisation, but barriers to Latin American access to US markets led to support for ISI as a second-best solution (FitzGerald, 1994).

6 Argentina, Brazil, Chile, Colombia, Peru and Uruguay.

7. 'The benefits of open trading have by now been sufficiently demonstrated and described by economic historians and analysts. In this study we take them for granted and turn our minds from the ''whether'' to the ''how'''. (*op cit*. Vol 1, p. vii). For further criticisms, see Jenkins (1995).

8. As Collier (1993, p. 504) points out 'the fundamental step in an empirical study of trade liberalisation is to measure that liberalisation. This is extremely difficult: trade restrictions are partly quantitative – and must be translated into their price equivalent, and the myriad of different implicit and explicit tariff and subsidy rates must be aggregated into a summary

scalar or vector. Possibly in no other field of economic policy is the mapping of policy instruments to macroeconomic and general equilibrium effects so obscure. ... (moreover) often governments are changing policies at the micro level which have offsetting aggregate implications; at times they think they are liberalising and they are not (and *vice versa*)'.

9. Dornbusch & Helmers (1988). Note that the REER indices calculated by ECLAC (see Table A.6 in the Statistical Appendix) are much more reliable than those usually employed (e.g. by the IMF) which are essentially the US dollar exchange rate deflated by the CPI for the USA and the country in question.

10. In terms of the Dornbusch model discussed in fn. 3, the difference between the directions of the two trends can be explained by a sustained increase in the markup (r) over the period. This appears plausible.

11. See Chapter 4, Table 3.

12. See World Bank, *World Tables* (various years).

13. Calculated from Inter-American Development Bank (1994) and International Labour Organisation (various years).

14. The distributional effects of NAFTA lie in the future, but are the subject of much debate (Bulmer-Thomas *et al.*, 1994). The main features are: collapse of employment in traditional farming and small industry due to cheap imports; growing demand and wages for skilled workers; overall wage and public welfare restraint due to macroeconomic convergence rules; continued high interest rates and asset dispersion; long-term recovery of employment in the non-traded sector as the overall economy grows. However, much depends upon the behaviour of private investment, which has undoubtedly been slowed down by the recent (1994/5) financial crisis.

15. In retrospect, it is also clear that Latin America sacrificed considerable potential benefits from both the Uruguay Round and bilateral negotiations by cutting tariffs and deregulating trade unilaterally during the 1980s; in particular, enhanced access to USA, European Union (EU) and Japanese markets could probably have been achieved if Latin America had negotiated collectively and demanded more in exchange for its own concessions.

16. Despite this admonition, I have attempted elsewhere to build a dynamic macroeconomic model in the new-Keynesian tradition where trade liberalisation impacts on private investment directly through changes in profit rates in the traded and non-traded sectors on the one hand, and indirectly through the macroeconomic effects on expectations and public investment on the other (FitzGerald & Perosino, forthcoming).

CHAPTER 3

CHRONIC FISCAL STRESS AND THE REPRODUCTION OF POVERTY AND INEQUALITY IN LATIN AMERICA

Laurence Whitehead*

About 15 years have elapsed since the Latin America-wide 'debt crisis' began, and about half as long since the post-debt crisis framework of a new economic model (sometimes loosely labelled 'the Washington consensus', or more polemically 'neo-liberalism') took shape. The sub-continent was notorious for the levels of poverty and economic inequality prevailing *before* the debt crisis, and in broad terms these have either been reproduced or even in some cases intensified during the 1980s. The new economic model (NEM) of the 1990s will have to gather further momentum before it can be expected to make a sustained impact on these long-established inequities. Even if this occurs, conclusive evidence will not be available for some years to come. The best provisional assessments so far available reveal clear conflicts of interpretation.[1] Legitimate disagreement in this field is easy to explain. Thus, the quality of the data varies greatly, both within and between countries; individual country studies can be quoted to support one thesis or another, but it is far from clear that, say, a Chilean success story foreshadows similar outcomes in other countries; the disproportionate size and deviant pattern of the Brazilian economy means that counting countries and counting poor people can produce very divergent interpretations of poverty trends; such trends are in any case affected by demographic and structural forces as well as by policy choices; moreover, any given economic model may produce a variety of effects depending on how well or badly it is implemented, and whether the broader context is supportive or destabilising; internationally comparable 'poverty lines' are conceptually questionable, since above the bare minimum required for physical survival, basic capabilities (job-seeking) depend on the living standards of others; finally, of course, the time lags separating policy change from poverty results are long and variable, and secular shifts or continuities may be masked by strong cyclical effects.[2]

This chapter focuses on one dimension of Latin American economic reality that has frequently been linked with the region's strong socio-economic inequalities. In many Latin American countries, both before import-substituting industrialisation (ISI) and since, an inefficient and unjust fiscal system has been identified as a significant source of economic inequity, and social instability. Some recent theorists have also postulated a reversal of this causal relationship: the strains of acute social inequality are said to have produced strong intermittent demands for a rapid alleviation of hardships and the redistribution of resources through the fiscal system, regardless of the long-term damage to economic equilibrium. This is 'macroeconomic populism' in the language of Dornbusch and Edwards.[3] Thus, a poorly functioning fiscal system may aggravate existing inequality and instability; but, also, inequality and instability may generate further fiscal mismanagement.

The puzzle here is to explain why these cycles seem to be repetitive, despite the fact that everyone (including the intended beneficiaries of populism) seems to lose. Why is there so little learning from past mistakes, or from the sorry experiences of neighbouring countries? Why have the simplest and most fundamental tenets of conventional economic analysis been so regularly ignored, even by those with substantial academic training and good external advice? The answer is that the pressing and immediate needs of the poor exert such an intense demand on policy-makers and on the political process, that governments are more or less forced to adopt 'populist' redistributive measures which may alleviate the situation tomorrow, albeit at the price of perpetuating stagnation and inequality in the long-run.

There is then a fair amount of ambiguity about the implications of fiscal reform. One possibility is that by 'insulating' the economic policy-makers from popular pressures, it may be possible to avoid the self-destructiveness of this cycle, gradually alleviating long-run inequalities through sound policies that appear insensitive to the poor in the short-run. A second possibility is that a more democratic system, backed by strong international support, could assist the processes of 'political learning' and assuage the most destabilising pressures for fiscal irresponsibility. A third is that perhaps there are some variants of 'controlled' populism that can be reconciled with strict overall fiscal control. Finally, if all these remedies fail and the cycle still persists, there is always a fall-back position. Perhaps the real explanation is that the populists have a covert agenda. Knowing full well what they are doing, they deliberately repeat these cycles in order to generate the instability and inequality which is essential if their style of politics is to survive.

According to this argument, whatever happens from now on can be accommodated within its ample framework. Is not the real focus on identifying wilful practitioners of macro-economic error, and seeking ways to reform, control, or in the last analysis condemn them? In any case, following the argument in these very general terms, a NEM, that comes into operation precisely at the point when Latin America's characteristically severe poverty and inequality have reached a cyclical peak, could be expected to succumb to the same cyclical patterns of destabilisation as its predecessor.

Beyond such relatively timeless 'tendency statements', the economic policy changes of the past decade call for a more precisely specified explanation. Although it is inevitably rather over-simplified to counterpose a unified old economic 'model' against a coherent new one, it is nevertheless striking that over such a short period so many governments have shifted their development strategies so much in parallel. There does seem to have emerged a remarkably wide consensus that old inward-looking and state-directed strategies and policy instruments are no longer viable, and that the main tenets of economic liberalisation must be actively embraced. A serious account of the political economy of this transformation lies beyond the scope of this chapter, and would need to incorporate various factors that are absent from the 'macro-economic populism' interpretation. Such factors would presumably include changed international opportunities and constraints (dramatised by the debt crisis, but also including broader changes in global economic ideology); the impact of technological developments; and the (largely unforeseen) shifts in popular expectations about what public policy can achieve that have accompanied democratisation. It may be that this relatively *ad hoc* list of considerations can be unified (for example, under some revised version of a 'peripheral capitalism' analysis – see below). But here we shall focus on just one (albeit strategically central) element in the change of model. By concentrating on 'fiscal crisis', fiscal stress, and the relationship of this area of public policy to patterns of economic inequality, the chapter inevitably directs attention mainly to *domestic* 'learning processes' and patterns of consensus formation, more than to external pressures for a change of economic model, although these are always present in the background. The second section deals with the impact both of acute and of prolonged experiences of fiscal difficulty.

The third section examines the distributive implications of protracted fiscal stress, and discusses respects in which a well-designed version of the new model might temper the resulting inequities and policy strains. But the possibilities are diverse; the consequences are imprecise, and the evidence so far available is mostly inconclusive. So the fourth section of the chapter focuses more narrowly on one major subset of fiscal issues, with clear distributive connotations, which can be analysed with more precision. Social security systems are relatively predictable structures with fiscal properties that can be analysed on a medium to long-term view. Under Latin America's NEM endemic fiscal stress can be materially alleviated (or intensified) depending on the approach to social security reform adopted in the early years. The conclusion emphasises the incomplete and provisional character of the analysis presented here, and the probability that the new model will produce a considerable range of equity outcomes. However, it also raises the possibility that the present broad consensus underlying the NEM could prove relatively shallow, insofar as it rests on an unsubstantiated assumption that a successful and sustained implementation of a liberalisation strategy can be counted on not only to reduce absolute poverty levels, but also to mitigate Latin America's deeply entrenched experiences of acute inequity.

Fiscal 'Crisis' and the Change of Economic Model

During the 1980s most Latin American countries experienced at least one serious fiscal 'crisis'. In addition, for about a decade after Mexico suspended interest payments on its foreign debt (August 1982), virtually all the governments of the region laboured under chronic fiscal stress. More intermittently Latin America was also afflicted by both acute fiscal crisis and chronic fiscal stress for many years *before* 1982, and it is to this milder condition that the region has returned since the early 1990s. But what do 'crisis' and 'stress' really mean in this context, and how can either identify or explain specific episodes?

Most indicators give only very crude approximations to reality, but here that is all we need. If the fiscal deficit increases by more than, say, five per cent of GDP in a single year, that is a fairly reliable sign of imminent economic crisis. The scale and speed of the corrective austerity measures likely to be required will almost invariably exceed the smooth adjustment capacity of the economy, producing marked 'adjustment costs' and dislocations. Even a smaller increase than this can precipitate a 'crisis' (i.e. a situation obliging the public authorities to correct the imbalance through the adoption of drastic emergency measures) if the pre-existing fiscal deficit was already close to some danger limit (e.g. ten per cent of GDP). Thus chronic 'fiscal stress' (running public finances close to the danger limit on a regular basis) is likely to be associated with relatively frequent and acute fiscal crises.

The public sector deficit is only a rough and ready indicator, of course, because in some cases it is much easier to finance a large or a recurrent deficit than in others. Thus, where for example the external public debt is very heavy, or domestic savings are particularly meagre, or the capital market is distorted or underdeveloped, a much lower deficit increase can precipitate a fiscal crisis, or a much lower level of deficit can signal endemic fiscal stress. In other words, the government can exhaust (or simply lose even through no fault of its own) its credit-worthiness. Multiple indicators could be assembled to test for this condition: rating agencies grade government bonds, the prices of some dollar public debt instruments are quoted in the secondary markets, etc. In general, these indicators would all reinforce the picture of recurrent fiscal crisis and persistent fiscal stress throughout Latin America in the 1980s, followed by a patchy and uneven remission in the first half of the 1990s.

Annual series for the 'inflation tax' as a percentage of GDP can be used as a second simple summary indicator to back up the fiscal deficit number.[4] For illustrative purposes, interest on Argentina's public debt peaked at 46 per cent of current public sector revenues in 1982 (a moratorium followed) and in Mexico by 1987 the total financial burden (domestic and foreign interest payments) peaked at 80 per cent of the public sector's revenues.[5] It is noteworthy that in 1995 both of these countries were again experiencing acute fiscal crisis as defined here, notwithstanding their status as leading practitioners of the NEM. In neither of these most recent episodes is it tenable to attribute fiscal crisis to policy errors caused by 'populism'.

With these considerations in mind we can attempt to identify the fiscal policy dimensions of the recent change in Latin America's prevailing economic model. Under the old inward-looking regime a notable component of fiscal policy (broadly conceived) was the possibility – frequently the actuality – of resolving fiscal conflicts between the state and the most dominant resource-based private enterprises by resort to discriminatory imports, price controls and, in the last resort, nationalisation. An equally notable and widespread characteristic of the NEM is not just that the state is precluded from resolving fiscal difficulties in this way, but that it is induced to tackle fiscal reform by the reverse procedure – i.e. by shifting from discriminatory to universalist principles of taxation, by reducing or eliminating market-distorting transfers and subsidies, and by privatising state-owned enterprises (SOEs). Such fiscal measures are so prominent and consistent a feature of the NEM that they cannot be assessed in a partial or *ad hoc* manner. It is necessary to think through the overall logic of the new model as a whole, in order to specify the framework within which the reformed fiscal and social security systems must necessarily nest.

In the case of this specific topic, there is a very powerful institutional component to the change in fiscal system from the old model to the new, and the poverty and inequality consequences of (and feedback from) these changes involves a large element of political bargaining. This makes it appropriate to use a political economy approach, rather than a purely technical economic analysis. That is to say, we need to consider not just what the fiscal component of the new model happens to be, in terms of the economic evidence and the coherence of the project, but also (and this may be something quite different) what policy-makers must claim to be, and what voters will believe to be, causes and consequences of these reforms. In analysing the trajectory and limitations of the fiscal reform process, it will normally be quite inadequate to rely on abstract reasoning about economic optimisation. The actual range of possibilities available will be heavily conditioned by constitutional, institutional and electoral restrictions, and by the lobbying and bargaining processes through which the public authorities will seek to obtain the acquiescence or co-operation of the powerful interests that are bound to be affected, either by expenditure rational-isation, tax reform or restructuring of the system of welfare provision. The NEM may assign a larger role to the market, but it does not abolish political processes of policy formation. On the contrary, it is generally associated with attempts to establish a more democratic institutional system. This is not to deny either the political importance or the inventive potential of well-grounded economic analysis, but only to insist that in fiscal matters policy alternatives must also be situated in a precise context of political opportunities and constraints.

In principle, it should be possible to identify a fairly clear connection between the overall shift from the old economic model to the new, and the specific fiscal and social security reform consequences of that shift. Under the old model the fiscal system was (at least on paper) centrally concerned with regulating the distribution of income, and mitigating various market-generated sources of inequality. In practice, of course, it is argued that over time (and for reasons that can only really be understood by using a political economy analysis) these redistributive policies not only lost their potential effectiveness, but indeed became major elements in the manufacture of additional poverty and inequality, beyond that which could be attributed to the market acting alone. It would seem to follow from this analysis that the dismantling of an interventionist state apparatus ought to mitigate those sources of poverty and inequality attributable to 'state failure', which would no longer be perpetuated under the new externally-oriented and market-sensitive model. In view of the centrality of this debate between the 'market failure' and 'state failure' explanations for social inequality and poverty in Latin America, we should in principle be well placed to trace relatively direct connections between each fiscal system and the distributional consequences thereof.

Despite an extensive 'political economy' literature on 'fiscal crisis', however, the general dynamics of such processes do not seem to have been well specified.[6] At the most general level, Hirschman (1991) traces the characteris-tically reactionary features of the contemporary critique of welfare states, highlighting its three dominant themes – perversity, futility, and jeopardy. But this does not explain the construction of a consensus in support of an alternative model.

In any case, this volume needs a more specifically regional theory, to account for the dynamics of fiscal crises in contemporary Latin America. Such a theory would need to give considerable weight to such factors as the build-up of sovereign debts, the extensive and prolonged resort to inflationary financing, and the policy leverage of capital flight. These are all central features of the regional experience of fiscal crisis, and are all critical factors affecting the change from one economic model to another, but none of them are essential features of any more global analysis. A Latin American theory which gave full weight to these three elements would almost certainly have to be couched in terms of 'peripheral capitalism', since that provides a framework for identifying what differentiates our region from the 'core' (roughly OECD) countries. Within this framework, the relative weakness of the internal market system and the 'inferiority' of the local currency limits domestic savings and renders the economy more than usually dependent upon access to external capital, which may be secured through sovereign lending, through the attraction of private international capital or through the repatriation of domestic flight capital. Each of these three alternatives tends to be associated with a distinctive fiscal strategy, and each tends to be unstable over time, with the result that periodic fiscal crises may be predicted each time one source of external funding becomes exhausted, and it becomes necessary drastically to reorient the internal fiscal system in order, first, to cope with the unavailability of external finance and, subsequently, in order to mobilise alternative sources when they become available. There are, of course, some stylised facts that would enable us to interpret Latin America's most recent, generalised, and prolonged fiscal crisis within this framework, which would also help to explain why regional currencies have remained consistently 'inferior'.

However, this is still a very loose theoretical apparatus, which fails to discriminate between what we know to be strikingly diverse cases, and which attributes so much causation to external structural forces that it could become an excuse for fatalism. In particular, it may distract attention from internal sources which are of particular relevance to the theme of this chapter – notably the inter-relationships between the weakness of the fiscal system, the inequalities of income and wealth, and the low and unstable rate of domestic savings. Even if international capital markets are as powerful and as fickle as the 'peripheral capitalism' analysis assumes, countries which achieve a competitive edge in the processes of state and fiscal reform may be able to achieve a durable re-ranking, especially if reinforced by the supporting conditionalities provided by the international financial institutions (IFIs). But at least the peripheral capitalist perspective does generate relatively specific (and even testable) explanations for the incidence and duration of recent fiscal crises, and for their evolutionary dynamics. It also contains an implicit prediction, namely that in due course Latin America's current efforts at fiscal discipline will again be severely destabilised by further shifts in the behaviour of international capital markets, which will force further abrupt and discontinuous shifts in fiscal policy.

In principle, the main linkages between fiscal discipline and each of the other main aspects of the outward-oriented and market-sensitive model are presumably:

(i)   *Trade liberalisation,* which directly involves a reduction in import tax revenue (and also perhaps a reduction in export subsidies), thus implying a shift in tax effort to other sources if fiscal discipline is even to be maintained. More indirectly, trade liberalisation increases the incentives for fiscal rectitude, and the penalties for fiscal slippage, since it empowers private trading partners who are sensitive to such indicators.

(ii)   *Financial liberalisation,* which involves the freeing up of interest rates, often with substantial costs to the public accounts when the government sector is a major borrower. This may reinforce the necessity for fiscal discipline as captive sources of domestic finance (such as social security funds) can no longer be tapped at negative real interest rates. In the longer run, however, it should also lower the rate of inflation, and thus the *nominal* cost of government borrowing.

(iii)   *Privatisation,* which may enable the public sector to dispose of a flow of commitments to pay subsidies and it may also bring in substantial one-off payments from the private sector for the asset transfers. The longer-term fiscal consequences are more ambiguous, however. Thus, a short-term source of fiscal relief may or may not generate healthier public finances in the long run. However, the breathing space created by the privatisation programme could be vital to the process of fiscal reform if this is tackled energetically before privatisation receipts are exhausted.

(iv)   *External debt reduction,* which, like privatisation, should involve substantial short-term fiscal relief, although again its longer term fiscal consequences could be quite mixed, depending on the cost and priority assigned to the rescheduled service payments.

(v)   *Less reliance on the inflation tax,* which *ceteris paribus* increases the pressure to tax in other ways. However, recent Latin American experience indicates that at least for a transitional period the control of inflation may strongly enhance government tax capacity, via a reverse 'Tanzi effect' (taxpayers comply better in a stable price setting).

The eventual success of the new model will strongly depend upon the regime's ability to transform fiscal austerity and stabilisation measures into a new structure of public revenue and expenditure commitments which are not so prone to run out of control, and which provide a stable structure of incentives for outward-directed investment and growth. Looking beyond the period of transition one must anticipate a recovery in the demand for certain types of public expenditure (e.g. when public sector wages have been depressed to unsustainably low levels, or when infrastructure spending has been postponed for too long). It is therefore essential to set in place a system for monitoring expenditure that guards against a recurrence of other types of (unjustifiable) outlay. It is equally necessary to provide a steady and secure flow of tax revenue to support essential public spending. All this must be done in a way that assists the other forms of structural adjustment inherent in the new model, which is administratively manageable, politically legitimate, and rational in micro-economic terms.

Having listed the requirements for a sound long-term fiscal policy under the new model, it should be apparent that: a) although there have generally been big improvements in the early 1990s (see Table A.7 in the Statistical Appendix), it is difficult to determine how much of this is cyclical; b) the new model will not deliver its expected benefits unless past improvements are maintained, and perhaps even reinforced; and c) the scope for including specifically redistributive measures, or large programmes devoted to poverty alleviation, will necessarily be heavily restricted, at least until the other requirements of sound fiscal reform have been convincingly met.

As should be apparent from the discussion of fiscal stress above, sound fiscal reform involves more than just a few years of low recorded public sector deficits. For example, public expenditure can be artificially suppressed (infra-structure maintenance can be postponed, the real salaries of public employees can be pegged far below inflation, acute regional imbalances can be temporarily disregarded), without reducing the 'equilibrium' level of outlay as much as the reported figures suggest. In some circumstances the federal budget may seem well under control, but the banking system may be accumulating heavy contingent liabilities that will eventually force the issue of a taxpayer bail-out (e.g. this was the case in Chile before 1982, and in Venezuela before 1994). More generally, the relevant target of fiscal control should be the consolidated public sector budget (including state enterprises, semi-autonomous public entities, provincial and municipal governments, and social security funds, which we discuss below). It is not uncommon for Latin American governments to over-correct the federal budget, while failing to extend adequate discipline to these other, institutionally more elusive, agencies of public spending. There can also be serious distortions arising from exchange rate misalignment (e.g. in 1994, when the Mexican peso became overvalued the authorities accumulated dollar liabilities – *tesobonos* – which proved far more burdensome to the treasury than anticipated, after the peso collapsed). Any of these 'off-budget' provisions and contingencies may reflect continuing fiscal stress despite a superficial appearance of good management. Each of these possible problem areas has its own strong and distinctive distributive implications (dividing young from old, in the case of social security; or public from private; or centre from regions; or savers from debtors; or those with access to foreign currency from domestic asset-holders). If sound fiscal control is to be established on a broad basis and over the long term, this will have major distributional 'side effects', but will leave limited scope to use the fiscal system for explicitly redistributive purposes.

This is not to say that there will be *no* scope, especially since so much of the ostensibly redistributive spending under the old model was poorly adminis- tered, unpredictable and unstable in its effects, so that even in the short-run there may be considerable scope for combining the goals of administrative efficiency and micro-economic rationality with the objective of poverty alleviation. In the medium term, a more stable fiscal system which is better defended against intermittent collapse can therefore deliver such 'public goods' as price stability and economic security that may be disproportionately advantageous to, and desired by, the poor. Obviously if the NEM can produce accelerated long-term growth (as appears to be the case at least in Chile), it will thereby eventually reduce the numbers in extreme poverty. More optimistically, a new model which in the long run delivers a more flexible, open, and dynamic economy governed by democratic processes could have a built-in tendency to channel incremental resources into reductions of social inequality.

Some Distributional Aspects of Protracted Fiscal Stress

It seems clear that at least under the *first* stages of the NEM, as in much of what preceded it, Latin American economic policy-making will continue to be characterised by a significant (albeit lesser) degree of latent fiscal stress. In this section we need to consider the consequences of this medium-term situation for income distribution and poverty trends in the region. But such consequences are complex, variable as between countries, and difficult to isolate. Moreover, from a 'political economy' perspective, if we are to take into account arguments about macroeconomic populism and the problems of legitimising the NEM, we need to consider not just the raw allocative effects of fiscal policy, but also the changed principles of distribution. The same crude distributive results may have quite different socio-political connotations depending upon whether it is viewed as the product of political bargaining on the one hand, or of impersonal market forces, on the other.

In principle, the focus should be on the distributive consequences of protracted fiscal stress (comparing the old economic model with the new), rather than on the shortlived cyclical effects of acute fiscal crisis. But in practice the two are difficult to disentangle, especially when fiscal crises recur periodically and when they acquire the virulence of many recent Latin American episodes. There is now considerable evidence that what has really changed the 'political economy' of macro-economic decision-making over the past decade has been the shattering impact on popular expectations of what government can achieve produced by brief episodes of extreme fiscal collapse (notably those associated with extreme bursts of inflation that characteristically cause greatest dismay among the unorganised poor).[7]

At the upper end of the income scale, chronic fiscal stress has not infrequently forced the public authorities to pay very high real interest rates over sustained periods in order to raise short-term finance from domestic sources (this has been a particularly pronounced feature of policy in the larger countries, which have relatively deep financial markets). Clearly, the largest beneficiaries from this policy have typically been a very small sector of the population with high net worth and liquid assets. In the same vein, the shift to the NEM has characteristically been associated with sweeping (and often poorly regulated) privatisation programmes, which may have transferred public assets to private wealth holders at fire sale prices.[8] Some of the private monopolies thereby created have frequently proceeded to eliminate social subsidies and to charge heavily for the utilities and basic services they provide.

All region-wide generalisations about fiscal trends must be carefully qualified, given the range of outcomes apparent from statistical series so far available. Nevertheless, the following summary statement represents a fair overview of the distributional impact of public expenditure changes in the 1980s: 'The drop in consumption expenditure had a negative effect on the coverage, regularity and quality of social services, especially in those countries where they were extensively provided by the State, and had a firm, decades-long tradition. The quality of those services was markedly affected by the lack of resources, both in administrative areas as well as in education, health and social welfare. This deterioration aggravated distributive effects of the adjustment process ...... since for a large section of the population the loss in real income was exacerbated by the reduced coverage and lower quality of essential public services. The higher-income segments of the population sought protection in private services that had previously been the State's exclusive domain; meanwhile, worsening quality notwithstanding, the hard-hit middle class defended its share of access to available public services. Under these circumstances, it became increasingly difficult for public policy to provide assistance to the most destitute and poverty-stricken sectors which, in turn, were expanding considerably as a result of the severe crisis'.[9]

Between 1989 and 1992 there was evidently some reversal of these trends in public expenditure, but the available evidence does not reveal whether these regressive distributional patterns are also being reversed, and it is in general too early to tell whether durable improvements are in prospect.[10] (Chile, since 1989, appears the main exception – see Chapter 7.) Taking into account this recent recovery, real *per capita* social expenditure had still not, in general, regained the levels recorded prior to 1982 – although the countries with traditionally relatively high levels of such expenditure performed considerably better than those with moderate levels, and far better than those with traditionally low levels.[11] Consequently, this increase in inter-country variation probably signified a regressive shift in the region-wide distribution of social expenditure, but on the other hand real expenditure in the health and basic education sectors seems to have held up better than social expenditure on housing or social security.[12] This would have a progressive distributive effect, since the first two categories of expenditure are more concentrated on the poor than the last two. However, according to a CEPAL study, 'although social expenditure continues to have a major positive effect on low-income groups, the composition of such spending as well as the variations recorded during the 1980s did not generally contribute to improving its redistributive potential or its progressivity.'[13]

The only empirical work directly linking trends in public expenditure to data on the distribution of household income derived from periodic household surveys comes from three rather atypical Latin American countries – Chile (1983-90); Costa Rica (1983-86); and Uruguay (1982-89). 'In the three countries analysed social expenditure represented a significant fraction of the effective incomes of poor sectors' (those in the bottom quintile), 'varying from 26% in Uruguay to around 50% in the cases of Costa Rica and Chile. ...... In Costa Rica it was found that the distribution of social expenditure was focused in a more equitable manner in 1986 than it was in 1983 ..... still the increment in social spending aimed at the lowest income groups (0.4% of GDP) hardly managed to compensate them for the fall registered in the component of their autonomous incomes (0.5% of GDP), ... in the case of Chile during the adjustment process (1983-85) overall social expenditure was curtailed, while ...... redistribution arose mainly owing to the decrease of resources transferred to higher income groups ..... which in turn could be attributed to the improved targeting of health and housing expenditure in favour of the poorest ..... with the advent of economic recovery (1985-90) the contraction in social spending became more acute ..... towards the end of the decade social expenditure in Chile not only had sunk to lower levels than before the crisis, but was moreover flawed by a worse distribution ...... In the case of Uruguay ...... the contraction of social expenditure .... between 1982 and 1989 was distributed among all income strata, with the exception of ...... the first quintile. In spite of this positive targeting, however, social spending did not succeed in compensating for the worsening in the distribution of autonomous incomes.'[14] The limitations of this data should be noted: it only refers to short-term changes in the 1980s, it only concerns three long-established welfare states, and it only concerns public *expenditure* patterns, omitting the sources of public *revenue* by income quintile. A further limitation of all data of this kind concerns the variable composition of income deciles over time. It is not always the 'poor' who are the most 'vulnerable', but this is a distinction that is easily overlooked in the design of 'targeted' programmes of assistance.[15]

Between 1988 and 1993 twelve Latin American governments created special 'social investment funds' aimed at providing new forms of public assistance targeted on the most needy.[16] (Prior to 1988 only one Latin American country had created such a fund – Costa Rica in 1974.) Seven of these programmes were described as temporary, but five (including the well-known PRONASOL of Mexico, and the widely commented social funds of Bolivia and Chile) were intended to provide permanent new mechanisms for the efficient delivery of public policy to those in greatest need.[17] The same concept was taken up by the Cardoso government in Brazil in 1995. Thus, although it is too early to be sure, these targeted social funds may turn out to be standard components of the NEM, differentiating its mode of social intervention from the ineffective universalism which typified its predecessor. In principle the new model could contain elements of targeting on the revenue side (selective user charges, vouchers, etc.) as well as through direct social expenditure, but so far this potential has been little developed.

Under conditions of protracted fiscal stress these social funds are designed to avoid imposing large and persistent burdens on the public exchequer. The temporary funds obviously reflect this reality, but even most permanent funds should be seen in this light. The Bolivian fund, for example, concentrates on recycling aid funds from abroad, and the Mexican fund has apparently been heavily reliant on privatisation receipts. So far, at least, the resources channeled in this way have been quite modest, certainly in relation to the stated objectives of the funds – usually of the order of one per cent of GDP. Given this, it would be unrealistic to anticipate any very major global redistributive impact. Nevertheless, from a political economy perspective these funds could be large enough to dissipate potentially destabilising sources of social tension, and if well targeted they could in principle significantly alleviate pockets of extreme poverty. In practice, however, the obstacles to precise targeting are quite formidable. Certainly, the evidence so far is mixed. PRONASOL, for example, spent heavily on the state of Chiapas, without averting the indigenous uprising which took place there in 1994. The only quantitative study of the distributional impact of one of these funds found that most (51.3%) of the income generated by the Bolivian fund accrued to those in the middle of the income distribution range (fourth to sixth deciles). By contrast the lowest three deciles obtained 27.2% of the income, and the top four deciles 21.5%.[18]

The Fiscal Challenge of Social Security Reform

This section focuses on one major sub-sector of fiscal policy, namely social security. The social security system takes several generations to mature. As it does so, social security can produce powerful long-term effects both on the stability of the fiscal system as a whole, and on the overall distribution of income. Indeed, recent changes in Latin America's economic model can in significant part be explained by the cumulative problems which arose as ISI-based social security schemes reached maturity, thereby depriving the fiscal authorities of this initially captive source of domestic savings. In the first phase of such schemes there are many more contributors than beneficiaries, and the government can more or less dictate the placement of the surplus funds, but in their later stages most Latin American schemes generated ever more unmanageable burdens of social spending commitments, causing substantial public dissaving. The structure and management of each scheme go far to determine whether and when it may mitigate, aggravate, or distort either the interpersonal and the intergenerational distribution of resources. The old economic model typically included financial repression, corporatist incorporation of wage-earners, and statist management of nationally self-contained welfare systems. The new model includes financial liberalisation, a market-oriented and internationalised provision of financial services, and the erosion of political entitlements to state benefits. Thus, a survey of emerging trends in the region's social security systems should shed light both on the long-term fiscal prospects of the NEM, and on its distributional characteristics.

A financially sound social security system must contain an effective mechanism for balancing the long-term flow of real payments obligations against the long-term stream of contributions that are to be expected. But if inflation is high and unstable, and if the structure of the relatively formal (and therefore potentially contributing) labour force undergoes rapid and unpredictable mutations, it becomes impossible to make realistic valuations of the system's assets and liabilities, and even if such valuations were available, it would be impossible to adjust the balance of the system sufficiently rapidly and extensively to ensure its solvency. In such circumstances, it is inevitable that the overall public accounts will acquire some imprecise, but potentially very large, contingent liability to bail out or restructure the social security system should its insolvency become apparent. Annual budget figures will only reveal the explicit transfer made between the government accounts and the social security accounts in any given period. To identify the additional contingent liabilities which may eventually turn into explicit transfer payments, it is necessary to look beyond the budget figures.

It is only possible to establish reasonably plausible estimates of these contingent liabilities after the acute phase of fiscal crisis and structural adjustment has passed, and a relatively stable and durable price system, and a more or less predictable labour market environment, have been restored. It is at this point that the true macroeconomic significance of social security insolvency may become apparent, and it is only in the light of such information that viable social security reform can be attempted. The durability of the current crop of social security reforms will therefore depend not only on the technical skill and actuarial precision with which they are designed, nor only on the 'political will' of policy-makers to adhere to the new rules, however much political heat that may generate. It will also depend on the durability and predictability of the price and employment parameters displayed by the NEM over the longer run. Given this, we must regard current reform efforts as highly provisional, and subject to possibly large further revisions in the future. All estimates of the macroeconomic significance either of the old system, or the transition to the new, could be subjected to large retrospective revisions at a later date, if changing parameters alter the scale of the revealed assets and liabilities.

A central argument for the privatisation of much social security provision is that this may sever the link between the government budget and the financial performance of the social security system. If that performance proves better (or worse) than expected, the manager will have to transmit the consequences to the participants in the system, supposedly without further consequences for the public finances. A parallel argument is used to justify the privatisation of state-owned directly productive enterprises (the equity of which may become available as assets of the social security system). Whether or not the associated contingent liabilities really have been separated from the fiscal accounts, only time will tell; neither laws, nor constitutional guarantees, nor international treaties can guarantee the durability of such a separation in all future circumstances, although such steps may raise the costs of future policy reversals.

In practice, the situation in contemporary Latin America is much messier than this. Had the old social security system been unified in its finances, uniform in its coverage, and clearly distinct from directly provided government service provision in such areas as health, sanitation, emergency relief, etc., then a clear separation between the fiscal accounts and the social security accounts would be quite straightforward. But in many Latin American countries what grew up was a patchwork of different coverages; each with a complex and distinct financing regime (in which participant contributions were almost never more than a variable proportion); in some cases substituting for the universal provision of basic social services which the government had failed to deliver.[19] Consequently, disentangling the two sets of accounts is, even in principle, a far more complex and uncertain process than it might initially appear. This is an additional reason why annual budget accounts may fail to reveal the true macroeconomic (and distributive) impact of social security under the old system, and also why the stability of the emerging, more privatised, systems characteristic of the NEM must remain in question.

As is well known, early Latin American social security systems were often constructed on a piecemeal and stratified basis with specific benefits confined to limited groups of participants (public employees, railway workers, etc.). As these systems were expanded under conditions of ISI and often in a context of state corporatism, they gradually lost their initial autonomy, and not infrequently became used as sources of 'forced savings'; these were then channelled into government paper which, if inflation accelerated, might turn out to produce negative real returns. In 1983, 90% of social insurance and family allowance spending was concentrated on pension and sickness-maternity programmes, with only 10% for employment injury, unemployment compensation and family allowances. In the early stages of such systems it was possible to generate useful net savings, since the participant base was expanding rapidly and there were as yet few beneficiaries. As these schemes matured they were inevitably prone to turn from net provider of savings to a net drain on public savings. The original schemes were often constructed on capitalisation principles that ought to require the accumulation of a large stock of financial assets earning real returns in order to meet future liabilities, but since these capital funds were frequently poorly managed or even virtually misappropriated, it became the norm to switch from full capitalisation basis to partial capitalisation (i.e. with smaller reserves to cover a shorter period) or even to a pay-as-you-go (PAYG) basis, in order to delay the moment of reckoning when the scheme's eventual insolvency would become apparent (for example, the Argentine National Pension Scheme was reconstituted on a PAYG basis in 1968/9). By the 1980s virtually all the contributory social security schemes in Latin America (outside Cuba) were operated on a partial capitalisation or PAYG basis, which implied that at some future date when the scheme's expansion of coverage was completed, and if the formal labour force ceased to expand, or even began to contract, a major actuarial imbalance was likely to emerge (particularly if legislators added to the range of benefits provided, as post-employment life expectancy rose).

Even on this basis, by the early 1980s almost half of these systems faced accounting imbalances before state transfer, some of them quite severe. The most recent year for which comparable data is available is 1983, at which point the social security deficit for Chile was equivalent to 5.7% of GDP, 4.3% for Uruguay, 2.3% for Argentina, and 0.4% for Brazil (by 1989 the Brazilian figure had risen to 1.8% of GDP).[20] In five Latin American countries in the early 1980s social security spending approached 10% of GDP. This was at a time when the system's overall coverage for the whole of Latin America was put at 61% of both total population and economically active population.[21] It has also been estimated that if the social security programmes existing in 1980 had been extended to provide universal coverage on the same basis as before, the expenditure required would have been the equivalent of 39% of GDP for Ecuador, 25% of GDP for

Nicaragua, 18% of GDP for Colombia, 16% for Peru, 12% for Panama, Honduras and the Dominican Republic, 11% for Bolivia and Guatemala, etc.[22] In other words the low coverage systems were not a source of fiscal strain only because they were so immature. Their design was such that, as they expanded, they would tend to replicate the same macroeconomic imbalances as had already been experienced by the 'pioneer' countries. If the demographic structure was not sufficient to ensure this result, these systems frequently displayed other characteristics that signified the same tendency. For example, between 1980 and 1987 the real rate of return on invested capital in the Mexican system was minus 20.8% per year, while administrative costs were 12.8% of total spending.[23] Similarly for Peru, the real rate of return was about -25%; and about -10% for Costa Rica and Ecuador.[24] Administrative costs exceeded 10% of total expenditure in fourteen countries, and 15% in seven.[25]

The case of Brazil deserves a separate comment, because it is the largest system in the region, because its actuarial problems will mount as it matures, and because current financing problems of the social security system constitute an important ingredient in the present debate over public sector reform. In 1986 the new civilian government found itself inheriting a potentially large financial deficit (two per cent of GDP) in the system, which was closed in part by cutting the share of system revenues allocated to health care from 30 % to 20%. However, the 1988 Constitution mandated benefit enhancements which, if implemented, would according to the World Bank's 1990 study increase system expenditure in 1995 by between 80% and 120% compared to the baseline, producing financial deficits forecast at four per cent of GDP in 1990, over six per cent in 2000, and eight per cent of GDP in 2010 (compared to baseline deficits of about one per cent of GDP in each case).[26] Although these projections are obviously quite shaky, and the outturn has not (as yet) proved so dramatic, they give some order of magnitude by which old model security systems can potentially destabilise overall fiscal discipline. They therefore highlight the extent to which the region-wide change from the old economic model to the new may have been propelled as much by a domestic economic logic as by the pressures arising from the external debt crisis.

Whatever the advantages of the various current initiatives to reform old model social security systems (which were certainly in need of reform), it should not be assumed that early fiscal relief is likely to be forthcoming. On the contrary, reforms which face up to the magnitude of the inherited problem almost certainly require large-scale public financing over a sustained period. The 1981 Chilean reforms are the most long-established, and the most far-reaching (see Chapter 7). Important parts of the old system (excluding the military) were privatised, with pensions administered by private corporations and health-care services operated partly by private health care organisations and partly by the government. The private system has been financed on a full capitalisation basis, with fairly clear separation of the public and private accounts, so that over time the fiscal burden inherited from the old system will fade away. During a half-century long interim period, however, the public treasury will continue to subsidise the deficits associated with the old pension system, and to support welfare pensions, unemployment benefit and family allowances.

In the early 1980s over 40 per cent of the benefits being paid out under Argentina's three pension systems were financed from general treasury revenues. Later in the decade a tax on fuels equal to 1.5% of GDP was earmarked for this purpose. Between 1986 and 1989 the Alfonsín administration drafted several reform plans, but they were never implemented, and in any case even after such reform, annual state funding would have been required at around seven per cent of GDP. At the time of the 1991stabilisation programme the National Pension System (NPS) was also receiving earmarked shares of taxes on gas, telephone and foreign exchange equivalent to $1 billion per year to cover its 'system deficit'. In August 1991 this was reformed, and instead the NPS was allocated 10% of Value Added Tax (VAT) revenues, and 100% of the proceeds of a new tax on so-called unproductive goods of personal wealth. Temporarily the NPS also received a 30% share of all privatisation proceeds. After much negotiation, in October 1993, Congress enacted a partial privatisation of the system somewhat along Chilean lines, although less radical. It came into effect in the second half of 1994.

As was initially the case in Chile, the Argentine public treasury is left with a major burden in order to meet old pension obligations while waiting for the partly privatised system to take its place. According to a 1993 World Bank report, the NPS will run a deficit of $2.4 billion in 1993, rising to $5.6 billion a year in 1994-7 on optimistic assumptions, or to over $7 billion annually on more pessimistic assumptions. It will therefore require earmarked tax revenues to rise from $6.1 billion in 1993 to $7.7 billion per year thereafter (15% of co-participation revenues, generating over $4 billion per year and 10% of VAT revenues, generating $2.2 billion per year).[27] This is an incomplete measure of the scale of the problems, even in the Argentine pension system, since it omits the provincial pension schemes that fall outside the scope of the new reformed system. These payments just about correspond to the forecast size of Argentina's annual gross public borrowing requirement 1993-2000 (an average of $5.9 billion per year, or 2.5% of GDP), forecasts which lead the World Bank to refer to a 'lack of cushion in the near-term' fiscal projections, with a risk that a larger than expected public sector financing gap could easily emerge, in part due to 'the uncertain costs of transition to the capitalised social security system'.[28] Employees can choose whether to keep their schemes within the state system, or switch to private pension provision, or select some combination of the two. Those remaining within the state system will have their funds administered (and guaranteed) by the Banco de la Nación Argentina, with the result that the Argentine state may end up with a much larger contingent liability than the Chilean.

Other social security reforms in Latin America are either recent (Mexico and Peru in 1993) or are still at the design stage (Brazil and Uruguay), so that judgement would be premature. Although the Peruvian law was heavily modelled on the Chilean precedent and adopted in a climate of enthusiasm for Pinochet-style restriction from above, it is not yet clear that similar results will emerge. Initial start-up costs have been high because the average affiliate receives only $250 dollars per month, and therefore contributes only about $25 per month. Moreover only about one-tenth of the workforce is on a formal company payroll. In more democratic Uruguay, by contrast, social security spending accounts for 15% of Uruguayan GDP and generates a $400 million annual deficit, so the fiscal consequences of inaction would be severe. Most of the labour force, however, has been entitled to earnings-related occupational pensions since the 1940s, and the electorate is wary of any change that might jeopardise this national tradition. The reform currently under consideration is therefore much more gradualist than the Chilean scheme. The 80% of the labour force earning less than $800 per month would remain in the state scheme, and only higher earners would have access to private pensions.

Endemic Fiscal Stress and the Reproduction of Inequality in Latin America

This chapter has directed attention to certain distinctive and recurrent features of Latin American political economy – exceptional, and exceptionally persistent, levels of economic inequality; prolonged and repetitive episodes of fiscal crisis and fiscal stress; deep and long-term structural weaknesses in the financing of social security provision, which have undermined domestic savings rates and reinforced patterns of politico-economic instability. It has also accepted, at least as a 'stylised fact', that these recurrent features go far to account for the region-wide shift to a NEM which took place in the late 1980s and early 1990s. Yet it must also be acknowledged that the various national experiences traced elsewhere in this volume are strikingly diverse, and that the comparative evidence should warn us against over-simplistic attributions of regularity and causation. In particular, even if the NEM can be understood as a necessary response to the failings of the old system, in general the evidence is not yet available to either vindicate or refute theoretical arguments linking a flexible outward-orientation to the narrowing of inequalities, the elimination of fiscal stress, or the raising of domestic rates of savings. There *is* some evidence of this kind from Chile, and East Asian examples can to some extent be quoted in the same sense, but the NEM now being implemented in other parts of Latin America is not a straightforward transfer of Chilean experience, nor would a uniform prescription necessarily produce the same results in all contexts.

In fact the recent change of economic model may not be that decisive a factor affecting inequality patterns in most of the region. Some of the major forces accounting for the reproduction of gross inequality are so deep-rooted that the mitigating effects of even the most successful economic reform would take a long time to work through. This would apply to racial and ethnic inequalities in agrarian societies forged through the subjugation of an indian peasantry, or the importation of slave labour.[29] It is also relevant where extreme poverty is increasingly concentrated among children under five, or where basic education and health provision have been disproportionately affected by government retrenchment. Chapter 7 on Chile highlights the long lead times involved, suggesting that good economic performance in the 1990s may represent in part a pay-off from education spending by the pre-Pinochet democratic regime (a similar case could be made concerning the land reforms of the late 1960s and early 1970s). In the same vein, Guatemala's capacity to achieve equitable growth under a NEM in the 1990s will not be unaffected by the post-1954 reversal of agrarian reform and the denial of educational opportunities. This is not to argue that the forces affecting the reproduction of inequality are immutable, only that they may be very slow acting, so that not too much should be expected of a mere decade or so of more market-oriented economic policy.

No doubt there are *some* changes of economic model that may make a relatively rapid and profound impact on inherited patterns of inequality, but the current NEM is not of this kind. The oil wealth of Venezuela permitted the construction of a rather universalist welfare economy after the 1950s, and the Peronist welfarism of the 1940s could constitute another example of this kind. The efficiency costs of pursuing such a model need not concern us here, but the fiscal burdens involved are of direct relevance to this chapter. For it has been shown that under the present NEM, at least over the short-to-medium term, nearly all Latin American economies seem likely to continue to labour under conditions of persisting fiscal stringency, perhaps bordering on what I have labelled 'fiscal stress'. For limited periods and in certain countries only, these conditions may be much less constraining than in the recent past (e.g. because of temporary privatisation revenues, or cyclical capital inflows or debt relief programmes). But only in Chile and perhaps Colombia is there a strong likelihood that the public authorities can durably attain the kind of comfortable margin of fiscal discretion that could permit policy-makers (if so instructed by the electorate) to use the budget to make a real impact on the underlying incidence of poverty and inequality. Elsewhere the discretionary fiscal route to poverty alleviation and income redistribution will continue to be heavily constrained for the foreseeable future. If the NEM is to curb the reproduction of gross inequalities of income in Latin America, it will not (in general) be through the use of fiscal (or monetary) instruments of redistribution, but by other means.

According to mainstream opinion the key is for the new model to produce a high and sustainable rate of economic growth. But three doubts arise here: i) it is not entirely clear why the new model should be expected to produce a higher average rate of growth (or lower variation in the rate) than under the normal (i.e. pre-crisis) functioning of the old model – which of course regularly reproduced large inequalities; ii) even if it did, some features of the new model (e.g. those rewarding those who can compete best in liberalised international markets) might be expected to produce new forms of economic inequality;[30] and iii) in any case 'some of the most important contributions to poverty reduction, reflected in what poor people actually want, do not show up in production and growth figures, and are not achieved by economic growth'.[31]

Even if the macroeconomic setting is as given, it does not follow that choices concerning public sector income and expenditures need be distributionally neutral. On the contrary, in principle there could still be considerable scope for variance at the 'meso' level of decision-making, i.e. the level affecting 'particular groups, such as rich and poor, men and women, urban and rural residents, people belonging in different regions or belonging to different ethnic or religious communities, groups paying direct and indirect taxes .... If we are concerned with poverty reduction and employment creation, the meso level is crucial. The same reduction in a budget deficit has a very different impact according to whether social services to the poor or subsidies to the middle class are cut, or if indirect taxes on necessities or progressive taxes on land-holdings are increased. The same amount of credit restriction has different consequences for employment according to whether it hits small-scale informal sector firms or large firms using capital-intensive methods'.[32] Under the NEM 'meso' structures favouring those with marketable skills may to some extent cut across the income inequality divide, but the new balance of power is unlikely to favour the very poor. In liberalised financial markets it is those with liquid assets who are most likely to be rewarded, particularly if the new model requires incentives to boost the level of domestic savings.

One of the most striking characteristics of Latin American fiscal structures, both during the crisis of the 1980s and in the course of the subsequent recovery, turns out to be their diversity, a range of variance that is, if anything, still increasing during the transition to the NEM. Every variety of 'meso' level formula can be found in some part or other of the region. Patterns of income and asset distribution and strategies of poverty alleviation are also highly diverse. Clearly, one implication of this diversity is that *in principle* (i.e. disregarding political constraints) there must be considerable scope for more redistributive 'meso' level policies in those countries with the worst current performance levels. But in practice, even if we assume that the NEM will eventually be successfully generalised throughout the region at the macroeconomic level, this inherited structural heterogeneity, combined with the range of 'meso' level policies likely to be generated by relatively open competition for political office, should mean that distributional outcomes will be far from uniform. The most effective lobbyists may press social funds for distribution towards the middle of the income scale, or privilege certain highly valued symbols of universalism, rather than concentrating scarce resources on the most vulnerable or the most in need. Neither Uruguay's relatively egalitarian patterns nor Brazil's gross inequalities will be easy to change, and there may be no very reliable tendency towards regionwide convergence (let alone towards greater regionwide income equality). Latin America's overall distributional patterns owe much to inertia and to a structure of political economy that replicates strong inequalities.

It therefore seems likely that at least over the medium term and in most countries fiscal policy will normally remain too constrained (or too much a reflection of existing socio-economic structures) under the NEM to exert much countervailing pressure against the reproduction of long-standing inequalities. In the longer run this picture may change, but even then the NEM is unlikely to produce uniformly more egalitarian outcomes. There probably will be some 'success stories' under which faster growth produces greater fiscal discretionality and the additional margin for manoeuvre is then channeled into effective redistributive ('social democratic') policies. In assessing such cases it will be important to consider how much is due to the new model, how much to the cumulative consequences of long-standing social interventions (i.e. dating back to the best days of the old model), and how much to the policy bias imparted by redemocratisation. There will also very probably be some clear failures, but again care will be needed in determining how far the new model is responsible. Insofar as the present consensus in favour of the NEM rests in part on the assumption that it will eventually generate more equitable growth, that consensus could become increasingly frayed. Those who believe that the model is essentially sound and that all alternatives are worse, need to argue for equality-promoting policies from the outset, otherwise support may evaporate before their ideas can be fully tested.

Notes

*I wish to thank Tony Atkinson, Victor Bulmer-Thomas, Valpy FitzGerald and Frances Stewart for helpful comments on the penultimate draft of this chapter. The remaining errors are, of course, my own work.

1. Compare 'reviving economic growth in a sustainable way is the only truly effective policy' (Morley, 1994, p. 1), and 'the prospects for poverty alleviation through growth alone, without improvement in the relative distribution of incomes and vigorous social policies, appear so limited as to be disheartening, and seem likely to be counterproductive for social integration and, ultimately, for sustained growth' (Altimir, 1994a, p. 29). Both these studies draw on a wide range of household survey enquiries, and both reveal a perplexingly diverse pattern of results which resist single paragraph synthesis.

2. CEPAL (1994) contains standardised data on inequalities in household income in eleven Latin American countries for 1980, 1989, and 1992. If comparisons are made only between 1989 and 1992, in five countries inequality diminished, in four it increased, and in two it was unchanged.

3. Dornbusch and Edwards (1991). They argue that populist policy cycles almost invariably end in fiscal crises that necessitate growth-reducing austerity that destroy the political capital of those responsible, and that far from improving the long-run distribution of income, worsen it, while also generating a wide variety of perverse micro-economic consequences.

4. See ECLAC (1992), Part 3, Tables 22 and 23, and for the 1990s recovery ECLAC (1994), Vol. I, Chapter VI.

5. ECLAC (1992), p. 186.

6. The early work by O'Connor (1973) is flawed in theoretical terms, and dated in its reliance on stylised facts about the USA in the late 1960s.

7. In 1984 the 'inflation tax' in Bolivia peaked at 20.8% of GDP. Since then the (mostly very poor) electorate has consistently endorsed the new economic model, a drastic break with previous political traditions. The same happened in Peru, after the inflation tax peaked at 11.1% of GDP in 1988, and in Argentina after the 9.6% level recorded in 1989. (ECLAC 1992, p. 248). In none of these countries was the fiscal system capable of intentionally redistributing resources on anything like the scale achieved unintentionally through these hyper-inflations.

8. In the six largest countries total privatisation receipts were recorded as $782 million in 1989; $5,391 million in 1990; $18,044 million in 1991;

and $15,807 million in 1992. (ECLAC 1994b, Vol. I, p. 285). In Brazil alone, privatisation receipts under the Cardoso administration (1995-8) are currently forecast at up to $50 billion.

9.	ECLAC (1992), p. 192.
10.	ECLAC (1994b), p. 114.
11.	CEPAL (1994), p. 162. See also Cominetti (1994).
12.	CEPAL (1994), p. 58.
13.	CEPAL (1994), p. 63. For a broader assessment see also Infante and Revoredo (1993), Chapter 1.
14.	See Infante and Revoredo (1993), pp. 153-4.
15.	See Graham (1994) and Grosh (1995).
16.	See Grosh (1993) and Grosh (1995). There are good case studies for Bolivia, Chile and Peru in Graham (1994).
17.	However, in the wake of the Mexican devaluation crisis, PRONASOL was effectively closed in June 1995.
18.	See Pollack (1992). For a useful comparative survey of the main funds, see Wurgaff (1993) and Graham (1994). For the distributional impact of PRONASOL, see Guevara (1995).
19.	For a 48 page outline of the institutional provisions distinctive to each country in our region in 1990, see Inter-American Development Bank (1991), pp. 221-269.
20.	Inter-American Development Bank (1991), p. 192.
21.	Inter-American Development Bank (1991), pp. 179, 185.
22.	See McGreevey (1990), p. 59.
23.	McGreevey (1990), p. 4.
24.	McGreevey (1990), p. 28.
25.	McGreevey(1990), p. 25.
26.	McGreevey (1990), p. 34.
27.	See World Bank (1993b), pp. 154-9
28.	World Bank (1993b), pp. 199-200.
29.	For the reproduction of racial inequalities in post-abolition Brazil, see Hasenbalg and do Valle Silva (1992).
30.	'There are grounds for believing that the new form of operation and the new rules followed by public policy in these economies may involve still greater inequalities as regards income distribution', Altimir (1994a), p. 7.
31.	See Streeten (1994), p. 35. He lists such features as safe water, adequate nutrition and shelter, more and better schooling, which 'do not register in higher income per head, at least not for some time'. In Latin America one might add a safe medium of exchange and store of value accessible to poor people, and some minimum of physical security. Alejandro

Foxley (see Preface) suggests that the *quality* and *reliability* of public goods and services are as important to the poor as their price and quantity.

32.   See Streeten (1994), p.29. See also Cornia and Stewart (1990) for a comparative analysis which stresses the scope for 'pro-poor' choices at both the macro and the meso levels.

CHAPTER 4

THE NEW ECONOMIC MODEL
AND LABOUR MARKETS
IN LATIN AMERICA

Jim Thomas*

As FitzGerald makes clear in Chapter 2, the implementation of the New Economic Model (NEM) involves replacing the earlier import-substituting industrialisation (ISI) strategy with a drive for export-led growth (ELG). This requires a shift in production from non-tradeable to tradeable goods and services, with a corresponding movement of factors of production from the first sector to the second. This process represents one of the major impacts of the NEM on the labour market, since changes in the relative price of labour are required to send the appropriate signals to employers and employees in order to bring about these changes.

A further impact of the NEM on the labour market is through the effect the reduction of tariffs has on firms that have been protected from competition during the ISI period. When faced with more competition, they are forced to lower their costs. In the long-run this has to be achieved through increasing efficiency, but in the short-run it may be easier to lower costs directly by seeking ways to cut wages.

Although most analysts treat labour market adjustment as a secondary stage in the implementation of the NEM, the World Bank (1993a) argues that the labour market plays a key role in the NEM:

> Most policy discussions on the mechanics of structural adjustment and market-oriented reforms ignore labor market deregulation. And yet, labor markets in many countries are highly distorted, introducing efficiency costs and making adjustment more difficult. A dynamic and flexible labor market is an important part of market-oriented policies. It helps reallocate resources and allows the economy to respond rapidly to new challenges from increased foreign competition. Moreover, freeing the labor market of distortions improves the distribution of income because it encourages employment expansion and wage increases in the poorest

segments of society. In most Latin American countries, labor market distortions have been segmented, with protected and unprotected sectors coexisting side by side. Removing the most serious distortions usually increases the unprotected sector wage rate, and increases overall employment. (p. 92)

Any study of labour markets in Latin America and the impact of the NEM needs to be set in the context of long-term demographic and locational trends. The level of urbanisation has grown in all countries in the region between 1965 and the mid-1990s, with some countries reaching levels comparable to those of the UK and the USA. While there is considerable variation between countries (from 40% in Guatemala to nearly 90% in Argentina in 1991), the average is much higher than that found (on average) in either Africa or Asia.

This trend towards increasing urbanisation is reflected in changes in the ratio of the urban to the total Economically Active Population (EAP) whereas in 1950 only four countries in Latin America had a ratio greater than 50%, by 1980 12 had passed the 50% mark and the trend has continued since that date. Labour markets in Latin America are now largely urban. They reflect the relocational effects of the region's earlier policies, which led to massive levels of migration from rural to urban areas, with growing employment opportunities in the modern (formal) sector. This expansion, coupled with policies to subsidise basic food products for urban workers, produced an 'urban bias' that operated against agricultural producers and, in many countries, led to a lack of long-term planning for rural development (see Bautista and Valdés (1993) and Twomey and Helwege (1991)).

Urban labour markets tend to be more homogeneous than those in rural areas. Throughout Latin America, the urban labour market is characterised by a division into a formal (modern) sector and an informal (traditional/survival) sector and, while these vary in size and detailed composition, they show marked similarities, as will be illustrated below. Rural labour markets are more heterogeneous, since they respond to a wider range of influences, such as the effects of climate, the crops being produced, the size of land-holdings and the ownership of the land. For example, wage labour (often seasonal in nature) is important in the production of plantation crops, such as bananas and sugar cane, while small-holders are important in other cases (such as coffee production in Colombia). In many countries, an important group of rural workers is the peasantry, who may operate outside the wage system producing at a subsistence level or offering, at most, small surpluses in local markets (see Pérez (1991) and De Janvry *et al.* (1991)).

The structure of this chapter is as follows. The next section presents a theoretical analysis of the linkages between urban and rural labour markets and presents the available data on labour markets in Latin America. I then outline the likely effects of the NEM on labour markets in Latin America and present data to explore recent trends in labour market variables. Women and young people represent particularly vulnerable groups and evidence on their experience during the period of structural adjustment is presented in the next two sections. Finally, I present some conclusions on possible changes in income distribution and poverty.

One feature of the analysis is the emphasis on short- to medium-term effects, rather than long-run equilibrium results. The reason for this is that structural adjustment is a difficult process and likely to be particularly painful for the poor, for whom the disequilibrium costs may be very high. Hence disequilibrium effects, which might be ignored in macroeconomic analysis of long-run equilibrium, need to be considered in any study of poverty.

The Labour Market in Latin America

Theoretical considerations
The starting point for the economic analysis of the labour market in developing countries (including those of Latin America) has been the work of Harris and Todaro (Todaro 1969, Harris and Todaro 1970). It was observed empirically that the real urban wage, W_U, was greater than the real rural wage, W_R, and that urban unemployment existed, but that there seemed to be no movement of wages to bring about labour market adjustment of the kind neo-classical theory would suggest. One solution proposed was that the equilibrating adjustment failed to occur because of market imperfections and, in particular, the problem was the *segmentation* of the labour market.

Harris-Todaro (HT) models assume a duality between rural and urban sectors. Both W_U and W_R are set exogenously (the former through government policy, trade union pressure or efficiency-wage considerations and the latter possibly at the minimum-subsistence level, but available to all who wanted to work for it). W_U determines the level of urban employment in the *protected* urban sector (given the marginal product of labour) and the model sets out to explain the flow of migration and the level of unemployment. This is done by assuming that equilibrium is obtained when the *expected* urban wage equals the rural wage. The expected urban wage reflects the probability of finding a job in the urban sector (p) and, in the simple versions of the model, this is given by the ratio of the total number of urban sector jobs to the total urban labour force, i.e. the sum of the urban sector jobs plus the urban unemployed. The flow of migrants adjusts *via* the total urban labour force and equilibrium comes about when

$$(1) \qquad p.W_U = W_R$$

Further theoretical developments occurred when economists became concerned about a major weakness of the basic HT model – the urban dichotomy between having a job in the protected sector or being unemployed ignored the obvious empirical evidence that many urban dwellers were working informally outside the protected sector. Models by Mazumdar (1975, 1976, 1976a) and, especially, Fields (1975) maintained the original rural/urban dichotomy of the HT model, but introduced further options for urban dwellers within the concept of a job-search model. All members of the urban labour force wanted a job in the protected sector, now usually referred to as the Urban Formal Sector (UFS), since the real wage in this sector, W_F, was greater than the rural wage, W_R. However, those without UFS jobs now had the choice between remaining unemployed and searching full-time for such a job, or taking a job in the Urban Informal Sector (UIS) and searching part-time for a UFS job.[1] Searching part-time gave a lower probability of finding a UFS job than being unemployed and searching full-time, but the worker in the UIS received a wage, W_I, in compensation for this reduced probability. Equilibrium within the new model is obtained when the three expected wages are equal, i.e.

$$(2) \quad E(W_F) = E(W_I) = W_R.$$

As far as the direct modelling of segmented labour markets is concerned, there has not been much theoretical development since the mid-1970s (see the survey in Fields, 1990). The assumption that all urban dwellers wanted a UFS job was questioned in Cole and Sanders (1985), but their alternative model assumed that only the unemployed were searching for UFS jobs, since only they possessed sufficient human capital. They also assumed that all those working in the UIS were going to stay there, since they did not possess sufficient skills and education for UFS jobs – an assumption criticised by Todaro (1986) and Fields (1990).

An interesting variation on the *protected sector* version of the segmented labour market was proposed in a model by Mezzera (1981). In this model, segmentation results not from trade union pressure or the other direct labour market effects, but through imperfect capital markets in which small enterprises are unable to obtain large loans. Given capital-intensive technological change, large firms are able to obtain credit for investment, while small firms are forced to continue with the old technology. In order to compete, they are forced to adjust the relative price of labour to capital downwards and this leads to a lower wage in small firms.[2]

Issues of Measurement
Ever since the UIS was proposed by the ILO in the 1972 Kenya Report (ILO,

1972), the concept has been the subject of considerable debate. First, there are problems of how to define the UIS and the question of whether it is possible to arrive at a definition sufficiently general to apply to all developing countries. Second, the assumption in early ILO writings that the UIS and UFS were independent caused confusion and brought criticism from Marxists, who argued that the UIS represented Petty Commodity Production (PCP) as an integral part of an international capitalist system.[3]

The definition of the UIS that was proposed in the ILO Kenya Report was obtained by inverting the characteristics of the UFS. Thus, in contrast to the capital-intensive, large-scale enterprises of the UFS, with imported technology and highly protected final markets, the UIS involved (i) ease of entry, (ii) a reliance on indigenous resources, (iii) family ownership of enterprises, (iv) small scale of production, (v) labour-intensive and adapted technology, (vi) skills acquired outside the formal schooling system, and (vii) unregulated and competitive markets.

During the debates that followed, various attempts were made to clarify whether an activity must exhibit *all* or only some of the characteristics listed above to be classified as UIS or UFS, or *one or more* of some alternative set of conditions (see Sethuraman, 1976, 1981).[4]

In Latin America, PREALC, the former regional office in Santiago for the ILO's World Employment Programme,[5] adopted a different approach and Souza and Tokman (1976) considered two alternative definitions of the UIS. The first, which provided the basis for much of their early work, defines the UIS as including (i) domestic servants; (ii) casual workers; (iii) own-account (i.e. self-employed) workers; (iv)all persons (employers, employees, hired workers and family workers) working in enterprises employing four persons or fewer.[6] The second definition identified informality with low productivity and low incomes and included in the UIS individuals with incomes below some minimum level, usually based on the legal minimum wage.[7]

More recently, PREALC and the ILO changed their views on who should be included in the UIS and both have concluded that domestic servants should be excluded. For example, Mezzera (1989, p. 52) argues that:

> For two reasons PREALC analysts have concluded that domestic servants should not be included in the informal sector. The first is theoretical: the informal sector is a set of productive units, not of people, and an individual who works in domestic service is not a productive unit, but a wage-earner who generally depends on income from the modern sector. The second reason is empirical: including domestic service in the informal sector introduces an enormous conceptional bias of the informal sector in favor of the

personal characteristics of this particular group, which is quite large and homogeneous. The vast majority are women, particularly unskilled young women who are migrants and wage-earners with low incomes and long working hours. The result is that the informal sector becomes identified with unskilled women who are migrants and wage-earners who have no relationship to microenterprises.

Haan (1989, p. 8), in explaining the ILO's approach as it moves towards an international agreement on how the UIS will be measured for inclusion in the national accounts, argues that:

> At the same time, there are good reasons to exclude domestic servants from the informal sector in spite of their 'ease of entry': domestic servants generally have fixed salaries (with sometimes even a formal contract and coverage of social security) and do not own any capital equipment but make use of the (usually modern) household appliances of their employer.

These arguments have their merits, since for policy purposes it is important to treat domestic servants as a separate group. Policies that are directed towards the UIS need to focus on the economic operations of producing and selling goods and services and the needs of those involved, such as access to training and credit. The needs of domestic servants may not be the same. For example, if in general they are not as well cared for as Haan believes, the answer may be special legislation to deal with this particular case.

Currently, there is general agreement that own-account workers (excluding professionals) form the core of the UIS and that some small enterprises should also be included. Ideally, sufficient information would be available from household surveys to filter out UFS small enterprises from the count. Where this is not possible, it is best to report own-account workers and small enterprises separately, as the aggregation will overstate the size of the UIS.[8]

Table 1 presents data on the structure of the urban labour force from 1950 to 1970. What is striking (in percentage terms) is how little change in structure took place for Latin America as a whole over the period. There are differences across countries, though no very clear patterns. On the whole, there was some growth in the size of the UFS in most countries between 1950 and 1960, but between 1960 and 1970 the picture is more mixed, with some increases and decreases in the size of the UFS during that period.

Table 1:
Structure of Urban Labour Force (% of Total), 1950, 1960 and 1970

YEAR	1950			1960			1970		
COUNTRY	UIS	DS	FS	UIS	DI	FS	UIS	DS	FS
Argentina	13.2	7.9	78.9	11.3	7.0	81.7	11.6	7.5	80.9
Bolivia	43.6	18.7	37.7	42.4	16.7	40.9	41.4	14.6	44.0
Brazil	17.6	9.7	72.7	22.9	9.7	67.4	17.4	10.5	72.1
Chile	21.7	13.2	64.9	18.9	12.6	68.5	16.5	7.4	76.1
Colombia	21.7	17.3	61.0	23.1	14.9	62.0	20.4	11.0	68.6
Costa Rica	15.0	14.3	70.7	14.4	12.1	73.5	12.8	9.8	77.4
Dominican Republic	17.4	12.8	69.8	30.4	12.0	57.6	25.2	8.8	66.0
Ecuador	23.2	12.0	64.8	37.3	11.8	50.9	33.5	24.4	42.1
El Salvador	23.3	19.3	57.4	20.4	17.7	61.9	21.9	17.6	60.5
Guatemala	35.0	16.6	48.4	35.8	13.0	57.4	32.4	11.1	56.5
Honduras	23.8	15.9	60.3	23.6	17.6	58.8	27.5	11.2	61.3
Mexico	28 .1	9.3	62.6	21.9	7.7	70.4	27.8	7.1	65.1
Nicaragua	21.5	17.2	61.3	24.5	16.1	59.4	26.5	17.1	56.4
Panama	13.5	11.8	74.7	13.7	12.7	73.6	17.4	9.1	73.5
Peru	27.2	19.7	53.1	30.8	12.3	56.9	33.7	7.3	59.0
Uruguay	11.6	7.1	81.3	12.6	7.0	80.4	13.7	7.0	79.3
Venezuela	22.3	9.8	67.9	22.3	9.4	68.3	22.4	9.0	68.6
Latin America	20.0	10.8	69.2	21.0	9.9	69.1	20.2	9.5	70.2

Source: PREALC (1982), various tables

UIS: Urban Informal Sector, defined as Own Account Workers plus Unpaid Family

DS: Domestic Service

FS: Formal Sector, defined as (100 - UIS - DS).

The New Economic Model and the Labour Market in Latin America

Theoretical Issues

Labour market 'distortions' have been one of the targets for neo-liberal policies. These include legislation to reduce the power of trade unions; reduction in the number of public servants (who are often highly unionised) and hence a reduction in trade union power; reduction in the level of legislated minimum wages through the effects of inflation not being offset *via* indexation.

The neo-classical analysis of the effects of cutting the formal sector wage is that, *ceteris paribus*, this will lead to a higher demand for labour in the formal sector and, by reducing the supply of labour to the UIS, will cause a rise in the real informal sector wage (see, for example, Edwards and Cox-Edwards, 1990). However, this analysis may be questioned on several grounds.

First, it assumes a fixed supply of labour being allocated between the two sectors and, as Fiszbein (1992) shows, whether the UIS benefits from cutting the minimum wage in the formal sector depends on the relative elasticities of the demand for the output of the two sectors. Secondly, it ignores the rural sector and the fact that the urban labour supply is not fixed. Hence, the adjustment following a cut in the formal sector real wage also depends on the response of rural sector workers.

Working with the theory outlined in the previous section, the predictions for labour markets would be as follows: the fall in W_F and increase in formal sector employment outlined above would have opposite effects on the *expected* real formal sector wage, since the probability of finding a job and hence earning the lower W_F has now increased. If the net effect is a rise in the *expected* real formal wage, then the urban labour supply would expand as a result of migration from the rural sector. Hence, the overall effect on urban employment is more complicated than the simple neo-classical analysis would suggest.[9]

In reality, the adjustment process in the urban labour market is more complex, as a high proportion of formal sector employment in many Latin American countries is in the public sector, which is characterised by over-manning and where it is unlikely that workers are either paid or deliver the marginal product of labour. In this situation, a more plausible short-run scenario might be: (i) The removal of restrictions on UFS labour markets would make W_F endogenous and restructuring, together with moves to reduce the size of the public sector ('cut bureaucracy'), would lead to falls in both W_F and UFS employment. (ii) Policies designed to move the terms-of-trade in favour of tradeables and against non-tradeables would produce falls in employment and real wages in labour markets associated with non-tradeable activities. There should be some gains for those associated with tradeable activities, but these are unlikely to offset the losses, at least in the short-run. Within this period, the net effect is likely to be a loss in UFS employment and lowering of W_F. (iii) Those displaced from the UFS (plus rural migrants) have the choice of being unemployed and searching full-time for UFS jobs, or (given its perfectly competitive nature) entering the UIS. Many will choose the latter option. (iv) This influx of new workers into the UIS will lead to a fall in W_I. This prediction might not arise if there were to be a simultaneous increase in the demand for UIS output that was sufficient to absorb the increased UIS labour supply without W_I falling. This possibility will depend on, among other things, whether UIS workers are in tradeable or non-tradeable activities and whether they are supplying goods and services directly to the public or are sub-contracted to firms in the UFS. (v) Other features of labour market adjustment are the privatisation of state enterprises (often with subsequent labour shedding), changes in legislation to make the labour market more 'flexible' (by reducing the permanence of employment and making it easier to dismiss workers) and reducing employers' contributions to various fringe benefits for workers (such as pensions, accident insurance, etc.). In the short-term these policies are likely to involve a net transfer from labour to capital and make the distribution of income more unequal.

The demand for output in the rural sector is likely to benefit from the shift towards tradeables, as part of agricultural production is potentially exportable. This growth should raise employment and increase wages in the rural sector, so that the pressures to migrate may be reduced. Given the adverse short-run urban labour market effects of the NEM, there may even be some reverse migration from urban to rural areas.

Measuring the effects of the NEM on urban labour markets.
Table 2 covers the period 1980 to 1992 for seven countries as well as Latin America in the aggregate, but the results are not directly comparable with Table 1, as the informal categories here are own-account workers and *all* small enterprises.[10] However, the patterns are very clear with large increases in the percentages of those working on own-account and in small enterprises and a fall of about 13% in those working in large private firms. Looking at individual countries, there are increases in the percentage of own-account workers in Argentina, Brazil, Costa Rica and Mexico, hardly any change in Colombia and Venezuela, while the percentage falls in Chile. All countries, except Mexico, show increases in the percentage of those employed in small firms and all countries, except Chile, show decreases in the percentages employed in large private firms.

Aggregating in absolute terms across these seven countries, in 1980 out of a working population of 68 million persons, 13 million were own-account workers, 10 million were employed in small firms, 30 million in large firms, 11

Table 2: Structure of Non-Agricultural Employment in Some Latin American Countries, 1980-1992

COUNTRY	YEAR	INFORMAL SECTOR				FORMAL SECTOR		
		Own Account Workers	Domestic Service	Small Firms	Total	Public Sector	Large Private Firms	Total
ARGENTINA	1980	20.4	6.0	13.0	39.4	18.9	41.8	60.7
	1985	22.9	6.5	13.3	42.7	19.1	38.2	57.3
	1990	24.7	7.9	14.9	47.5	19.3	33.2	52.5
	1992	25.9	7.8	15.9	49.6	17.7	32.7	50.4
BRAZIL	1980	17.3	6.7	9.7	33.7	11.1	55.2	66.3
	1985	21.1	9.1	14.5	44.7	12.0	43.4	55.4
	1990	21.0	7.7	23.3	52.0	11.0	36.9	47.9
	1992	22.5	7.8	22.5	54.1	10.4	35.4	45.8
CHILE	1980	27.8	8.3	14.3	50.4	11.9	37.7	49.6
	1985	24.4	9.8	19.1	53.3	9.9	36.8	46.7
	1990	23.6	8.1	18.3	50.0	7.0	43.0	50.0
	1992	23.0	7.5	19.0	49.5	8.1	42.3	50.4
COLOMBIA	1980	25.3	6.7	20.5	52.5	13.8	33.7	47.5
	1985	28.0	7.0	20.7	55.7	12.4	31.8	44.2
	1990	25.1	6.2	27.8	59.1	10.6	30.2	40.8
	1992	25.4	5.9	29.0	60.3	9.9	29.6	39.5
COSTA RICA	1980	16.3	6.1	14.0	36.4	26.7	36.9	63.6
	1985	17.2	6.2	17.1	40.5	26.3	33.1	59.4
	1990	17.6	5.6	22.0	45.2	23.0	31.7	54.7
	1992	20.9	5.8	23.0	49.7	20.9	29.4	50.3
MEXICO	1980	18.0	6.2	24.9	49.1	21.8	29.1	50.9
	1985	23.5	6.4	21.4	51.3	25.5	23.2	48.7
	1990	30.4	5.6	19.5	55.5	25.0	19.6	44.6
	1992	30.5	5.5	20.0	56.0	24.5	19.5	44.0
VENEZUELA	1980	21.2	4.5	8.8	34.5	25.6	39.8	65.4
	1985	21.3	4.9	13.7	39.9	24.5	35.6	60.1
	1990	21.4	5.0	22.1	48.5	22.6	28.9	51.5
	1992	22.3	5.0	23.6	50.9	20.0	29.1	49.1
LATIN AMERICA	1980	19.2	6.4	14.6	40.2	15.7	44.1	59.8
	1985	22.6	7.8	16.6	47.0	16.6	36.5	53.1
	1990	24.0	6.9	21.8	52.7	15.6	31.7	47.3
	1992	25.0	6.9	22.5	54.4	14.9	30.8	45.7

Source: PREALC (1993), p. 4, Table 2

million in the public sector and 4 million were domestic servants. In 1992, out of a working population of 105 millions, the number of own-account workers had risen to 26 million, 24 million were employed in small firms, 32 million in large firms, 16 million in the public sector and 7 million worked as domestic servants. While all categories grew in absolute terms, the increases of 13 million in own-account workers and 14 million in those employed in small firms together represented nearly four times the combined growth of two million in those employed in large firms and five million in public service. Hence, Latin America has seen a major re-alignment in the distribution of labour across categories since the start of the debt crisis. While one cannot attribute all the changes to the NEM, the movement is consistent with the predictions of a movement out of the UFS.

Open unemployment
Annual household surveys are used to collect information on rates of open unemployment (see Table A.9 in the Statistical Appendix). Given the debt crisis and a good deal of structural adjustment, the rates appear quite low.[11] Some countries, such as Argentina after 1992, Chile before 1988 and Panama after 1987, do show some high annual unemployment rates, but the rate stays well below ten percent for a number of important countries (eg. Brazil). Kritz and Ramos (1976) pointed out that one might expect the open rate of unemployment to be low in economies in which a high proportion of the workforce are own-account workers, since a reduction in the demand for the services of such workers is likely to be reflected in declining incomes and *under*employment, rather than in open unemployment.[12]

It is unfortunate that there are no regional data available on open unemployment disaggregated by the former employment (where appropriate) of the individual, as well as by sex, age and education, so that one could see whether the official statistics bear out the findings of smaller surveys. For example, Hirata and Humphrey (1991), in a survey of industrial workers in Brazil who lost their jobs in the early 1980s, found that women and unskilled men were more likely to enter the UIS than remain unemployed. Unemployment and a return to UFS employment was more likely for skilled male heads of households.

Since there are very few unemployment or social security benefits to be obtained by being unemployed, it is not surprising that rates of open unemployment are often low. For this reason, this statistic may not be very helpful in analysing labour market adjustment to NEM policies in the absence of similar data on rates of underemployment. It is worth noting, however, that economic crisis in Argentina and Mexico in 1995 *was* reflected in the rate of unemployment (see Table A.9).

Table 3:
Evolution of Urban Real Minimum Wage, 1985-92 (1980 = 100)

	1985	1986	1987	1988	1989	1990	1991	1992
Argentina (1)	113.1	110.0	120.8	93.5	42.1	40.2	56.0	48.0
Brazil (2)	88.9	89.0	72.6	68.7	72.1	53.4	59.9	57.3
Chile (15)	76.4	73.6	69.1	73.9	79.8	87.5	95.6	99.8
Colombia (3)	109.4	114.2	113.0	109.9	110.8	107.9	104.3	101.6
Costa Rica (1)	112.2	118.7	117.9	114.6	119.4	120.5	111.8	111.5
Dominican Rep (1)	80.2	86.0	84.1	87.4	77.7	65.2	66.2	80.2
Ecuador (4)	60.4	65.0	61.4	53.4	47.3	39.6	33.5	32.5
El Salvador (5)	66.2	57.5	46.0	43.6	37.0	34.8	34.1	35.2
Guatemala (1)	94.0	68.6	61.1	75.9	68.1	48.2	38.9	35.0
Haiti (6)	91.3	84.8	94.7	94.8	95.7	99.7	n/a	n/a
Honduras (7)	89.1	85.3	83.3	79.7	72.6	87.1	84.4	97.0
Mexico (8)	71.1	64.9	61.5	54.2	50.8	45.5	43.6	42.1
Nicaragua (9)	45.1	n/a	n/a	n/a	n/a	n/a	n/a	n/a
Panama (10)	101.0	101.1	100.1	99.7	99.9	99.3	97.7	96.0
Paraguay (11)	99.6	108.3	122.6	135.2	137.5	131.6	125.8	115.5
Peru (12)	54.4	56.4	59.7	52.0	25.1	23.4	15.9	15.9
Uruguay (13)	93.2	88.5	90.3	84.5	78.0	69.1	62.0	60.0
Venezuela (14)	96.8	90.4	108.7	89.5	72.9	59.3	55.1	60.7

Source: SALA (1995), Part 1, Table 1408

(1) National minimum wage.
(2) Rio de Janeiro, deflated by the corresponding consumer price index.
(3) For upper-level urban sectors.
(4) Includes legal supplementary benefits.
(5) Nonagricultural activities in San Salvador.
(6) Minimum daily wage paid in manufacturing.
(7) Central District and San Pedro Sula for manufacturing.
(8) Mexico City, deflated by the corresponding consumer price index.
(9) Department of Managua industrial workers.
(10) Excludes construction and domestic service.

(11) Asunción and Puerto Stroessner.
(12) Metropolitan Lima for nonagricultural activities.
(13) National minimum wage for workers over 18 years of age.
(14) National minimum wage for nonagricultural activities, deflated by the consumer price index corresponding to the lowest income quartile.
(15) Minimum income.

Minimum wages

Data on urban real minimum wages (as indices based on 1980 = 100) are presented in Table 3. In only three countries (Colombia, Costa Rica and Paraguay) did the index stay close to 100 throughout the period and finish with a value above 100. The index in Panama also stays close to 100 throughout the period, while in Chile it had recovered to its earlier level by 1992. Some of the other countries (e.g. Argentina) did show some gains during part of the period, but the general picture is one of declining real minimum wages, spectacularly so in the case of Peru, where in 1991 the index had fallen to 16% of its 1980 value.[13]

For proponents of the NEM, the data on real minimum wages represent good news, as the lower the minimum wage (in real terms) the less its distortionary effect on the performance of the labour market. Its effect on poverty is more difficult to gauge without data on the structure of wages in relation to minimum wages.

Labour market flexibility

The World Bank (1993a) cites a number of sources of market inflexibility, such as high costs of dismissal, restrictions on hiring temporary workers and high levels of fringe benefits for labour.[14] Efforts to make labour markets more flexible have varied within Latin America (see García, 1993). For example, in Brazil the powerful links between organised labour and important political factions have protected the position of the unions. In Chile, the powers of the unions were greatly reduced in the early years of the Pinochet regime, when many trade union officials were arrested or 'disappeared' and most union activities were forbidden (see Leiva and Agacino, 1994). Some relaxation of the controls was permitted towards the end of the regime and the unions were able to play an important role in the economic dialogue that took place under President Aylwin (see Calderón, 1993).[15]

Regardless of the changing position of trade unions, there has been encouragement for employers to make more use of casual labour, often through legislation designed to reduce the length and permanence of labour contracts. For example, in Peru, legislation was introduced in 1991 permitting workers to be hired on a range of 'probationary' contracts at the end of which time they may be dismissed without compensation and during which time they enjoy few (if any) fringe benefits. The number of workers on one-month contracts rose from 35,000 in 1990 to 176,000 in 1993 (see Ahmad, Amieva and Thomas, 1994, Table 4.2).[16]

Subcontracting

One strategy for employers in the UFS to avoid paying high wages and fringe benefits to their workers is to subcontract out some of their work to small enterprises or individual workers in the UIS. This provides increased demand for the output of UIS firms involved in the process and creates some UIS employment, but since these jobs are lower paid and carry few (if any) benefits compared with the corresponding jobs in the UFS, the net effect *ceteris paribus* is to reduce the income going to labour.[17]

Privatisation
In addition to the attraction of providing governments with considerable amounts of revenue rapidly and without their having to face the more fundamental political problem of reforming the tax system, privatisation has also been seen as a way of reducing restrictive practices and over-manning in state enterprises. Case studies of privatisations in Latin America suggest that many resulted in a considerable reduction in the size of the post-privatisation labour force, but inexperience on the part of both governments and bidders and the failure to prevent some former public monopolies becoming private monopolies has meant that it is too early to see what the net gains from privatisation will be (see Galal and Shirley (1994) and Sánchez and Corona (1993)).

Measuring the effects of the NEM on rural labour markets
Rural labour markets are more heterogeneous than urban labour markets and it is therefore more difficult to summarise the possible effects of the NEM in this area. Given the underlying assumptions of the model, one would predict (i) an important role for agriculture in the ELG process and (ii) a switch in technology towards more labour-intensive methods of production.

At the aggregate level, it is not easy to find evidence of the first effect occurring. First, the data on agricultural trade in food and raw materials from 1980 to 1992 show no discernable trends towards increasing exports (see Chapter 2, Table 5) and there is also no evidence of a decrease in imports. Secondly, FAO (1988) forecasts of the growth in world trade in crop and livestock products to the year 2000 are somewhat pessimistic, being 1.6% and 0.5% per annum respectively. If these predictions are correct, it is unlikely that rural employment will expand fast enough (at least in legal activities) to absorb the growing rural population without a very rapid switch to more labour-intensive methods of production.

Systematic data on agricultural technology for the region is scarce, but studies on individual countries suggest that the expansion of output in some branches of agriculture is through the use of more capital-intensive methods of production. For example, successful agricultural export activities, such as fruit processing and wine production in Chile, have been very capital-intensive (see IICA (1990) and Estrella Díaz (1991)). While conventional theory would predict that the export sector in Latin American agriculture should exploit its comparative advantage in being labour-intensive, this does not seem to be happening in the short-run. Here the pattern is one of capital-intensive methods of production with relatively small numbers of jobs for skilled labour combined with a high demand for unskilled labour at seasonal peaks, with this demand being provided for by former agricultural workers who have migrated to the towns (often making jobs in the UIS), returning to the rural areas to work during the period of peak demand at harvest time. In Mexico, the pattern is different, as Barrón (1994) shows in her study of female agricultural workers; these women are able to obtain longer periods of agricultural employment by migrating to different regions in Mexico to match the varying peak harvest time of vegetables rather than migrating to the cities.

Land reform
Further implications of the NEM for rural labour markets are policies to 'improve the efficiency of land markets'. In Mexico, with the *ejido* system, and in parts of Central America, there has traditionally been communal land tenure without individual titles, so that land sales normally did not occur. The system was criticised on the grounds that without a land market, land would not be directed to its most productive use. The Mexican Constitution was changed in February 1992 to enable *ejido* lands to be sold into private ownership. The lands were offered to *ejido* owners, but many were too poor to pay the market price for the land. Corporations (both domestic and foreign) are allowed to own this former *ejido* land and, with the arrangement within NAFTA that the Mexican grain market will be opened to competition in return for liberalisation of North American fruit and vegetable markets, Plant (1994, p.120) suggests 'that as many as 700,000 Mexican farmers could lose their livelihood through Mexican maize market liberalisation, adding to the flow of up to 400,000 persons migrating annually to urban areas.'[19]

Migration and labour market adjustment.
The importance of migration in the process of labour market adjustment was stressed in the theoretical discussion above. One of the linkages between urban and rural labour markets that is not stressed in the theory is the importance of remittances. If the decision to migrate is made by a household as a group rather than by an individual potential migrant, then the marginal contribution to the household of a migrant sending back remittances may represent an optimal strategy.[20]

Clearly, migration and return remittances are not new features in Latin America and Martínez Pizarro (1993) discusses the flows of skilled workers involved in intraregional migration in the 1970s and 1980s. What has increased is the scale of the movement and the range of workers involved (see Stalker, 1994).

There are considerable problems in gauging the importance of remittances in Latin America and their effects on income distribution and poverty. First, no regional data are available that measure the inflow of remittances. Second, even if such aggregate data did exist, analysis of the effect of remittances on income distribution would require further disaggregation in terms of the destination of the inflow.

Stalker (1994, pp. 275-80) contains data for a few Latin American countries for 1990 on the number of migrants, showing that there are both sending and receiving countries in Latin America. For the number of economically active abroad (as a percentage of the total population), Colombia (3.9%) and Uruguay (6.5%) were sending countries, while for the foreign-born population (as a percentage of total population) Argentina (over 5%) and Venezuela (over 5%) were receiving countries.[21]

Some information on the importance of remittances in the Dominican Republic is available. Vargas-Lundius (1991, p. 336) reports estimates that in the mid-1980s, annual remittances from the United States averaged US $229 million, which may be compared with foreign exchange earnings from sugar exports of US $288 million in 1984. Ferguson (1992, pp. 77-8) suggests that '[r]egular monthly sums of US$50 or US$100 keep many rural families in the Dominican Republic above the poverty line.' He concludes that such remittances 'merely cover everyday consumption' and that 'the remittance economy is largely non-productive in development terms'. The same is true of El Salvador where remittances are now the single largest source of export earnings.

Gender Issues in Labour Market Adjustment[22]

So far, the data presented have mainly been at an aggregate level and it would be desirable to obtain data that have been disaggregated to investigate to what extent gender plays a role in the degree and distribution of poverty. Table 4 presents data and projections on the percentage of women in the labour force (including agriculture) for Latin America from 1950 to 2000. The data show considerable differences across countries in 1950, a steady increase in the percentage over the five decades and a tendency for the percentages to converge in the projection for the year 2000. With regard to the sectoral composition of the female labour force, there are clear patterns over the period, with the percentage of women in agriculture and industry falling for Latin America overall and for most individual countries. The percentage of women in services rose for Latin America from 49.2% in 1950 to 65.2% in 1980 and it rose in all countries during the period. In twelve of the countries the percentage was over 65% by 1980 and there is no reason to believe that the trend has been reversed since then.

This high concentration of women in service activities has implications for the switch from non-tradeable to tradeable production imposed by the NEM. To the extent that some of these jobs will be indirect service jobs in the production of tradeble goods, they may benefit from the switch. However, most of those providing services as a final good will be involved in non-tradeable activities and are likely to be negatively affected by the NEM.

Table 4: Percentage of Women in the Labour Force (including agriculture) for Latin America, 1950 - 2000

COUNTRY	YEAR					
	1950	1960	1970	1980	1990	2000
Argentina	19.7	21.0	24.9	26.9	28.1	29.1
Bolivia	19.5	20.4	21.4	22.5	25.8	25.6
Brazil	15.3	17.5	21.7	26.9	27.4	28.8
Chile	20.0	21.7	22.4	27.3	28.5	28.9
Colombia	18.5	19.4	21.3	22.4	21.9	22.3
Costa Rica	15.0	15.8	18.1	21.2	21.8	22.6
Dominican Republic	12.9	15.3	17.8	27.0	27.1	27.7
Ecuador	16.8	16.3	16.3	19.3	19.3	19.7
El Salvador	16.4	16.8	20.4	24.9	25.1	25.3
Guatemala	12.9	12.3	13.1	13.8	16.4	19.5
Honduras	11.6	12.3	14.2	15.7	18.8	22.7
Mexico	9.0	10.0	10.9	12.3	15.0	17.9
Nicaragua	13.6	17.9	19.7	21.6	25.2	29.1
Panama	19.1	20.9	25.2	26.2	27.1	28.7
Paraguay	21.3	21.4	21.3	20.8	20.7	20.8
Peru	20.9	20.9	20.3	24.2	24.1	24.4
Uruguay	22.6	24.1	26.3	29.6	31.2	32.5
Venezuela	17.9	18.3	20.7	25.8	27.6	28.8
Latin America	17.9	19.2	21.7	26.1	26.6	27.5

Source: IDB (1990), pp. 222-3, Table 3.

Table 5 presents some data on male/female income differentials across a range of UFS occupations, based on 1985 household surveys in five cities. The statistics are constructed by relating incomes to the average for the entire population (male and female) across all occupations (= 100). Thus in Bogotá, overall in comparison to this average of 100, men earn 116 and women 74, while male professionals earn 313 and female professionals 193. With the exception of a few cases, such as secretaries and cashiers in Panama, women earn less than their male counterparts. This should be borne in mind when considering the real wage cuts predicted for the NEM; on average, the real wage for women that is being cut will be lower than that for men.

Table 5: Index of Average Incomes of Labour Force by Sex and Occupation, 1985

	Bogotá		Caracas		Panamá		San José		São Paulo	
OCCUPATION	M	F	M	F	M	F	M	F	M	F
Professionals	313	193	240	154	317	180	200	175	340	142
Technicians, etc.	197	154	138	71	164	118	167	125	168	72
Managers, Executives, Public Administrators	540	373	205	175	195	158	234	124	347	191
Secretaries and Cashiers	105	85	77	70	91	101	98	50	95	102
Commercial Employees	89	43	102	76	110	76	93	69	114	52
Independent Business-Persons	163	78	118	49	67	51	116	79	149	69
Skilled and Semi-Skilled Workers	75	49	89	60	88	67	81	73	86	93
Unskilled Workers	61	51	75	46	69	65	75	63	40	33
Domestic Employees	58	54	48	40	60	33	80	46	28	20
TOTAL	**116**	**74**	**116**	**70**	**106**	**88**	**107**	**85**	**117**	**62**

Source: IDB (1990), pp. 219, Table 2b.

M = Male

F = Female

Note: Average income of the entire population = 100.

Women and the UIS

On the basis of studies of the UIS in a number of countries, some general patterns emerge concerning the position of women in this sector: (a) a higher proportion of women in the UIS are heads of households as well as the main breadwinner than is true of women in the UFS. (b) Women in the UIS tend to have less education than men in the UIS. (c) Within the UIS, women are found predominantly in Commerce and Personal Services, two activities which are basically non-tradeable . (d) On average, women earn less than men in the UIS. This is partly because Commerce and Personal Services are low-earning activities, but also because male/female differentials similar to those illustrated in Table 5 have also been found in the UIS.[23] (e) Generally, *household* incomes for female-headed households are lower than for male-headed households, largely because the former lack the earnings brought in by a male partner.[24]

Poor women face particular hardships in Latin America because of the *machismo* culture and the opposition of the Catholic Church to most forms of family planning. This means that many women must devote a considerable amount of time to domestic duties in addition to earning a living. The constraints of having to look after small children coupled with a lack of formal education can severely limit the range of options open to many women (see López, Pollack and Villarreal (1992)).

The Labour Market and Youth

Turning to the experience of youth in relation to the labour market, one has access to only limited information (see PREALC, 1992). Table 6 presents data for twelve Latin American countries and some general patterns emerge. First, youth unemployment is higher than total unemployment in all countries. Second, while only available for six countries, the data show unemployment to be much higher for urban than for rural youth. Third, except in Chile and Paraguay, the unemployment rate is higher for female than for male youths.[25]

Youth unemployment would seem to be a problem, but the PREALC study suggests that it is not a problem confined to Latin America. To put the figures in perspective, the range for the ratios of youth unemployment to total unemployment presented in Table 6 is from 1.4 in Costa Rica to 2.9 in Uruguay. PREALC present the corresponding ratios for twelve OECD countries, giving a range in 1989 from 1.4 in Germany and Great Britain to 2.8 in Italy.[26] The major differences are that (i) youths in OECD countries are more likely to be involved in training schemes than is the case in most Latin American countries and (ii) potentially poor families in OECD countries may be less reliant on the earnings of youths to supplement family incomes.[27]

Table 6: Structure of Youth Unemployment for Twelve Latin American
Countries (percentage of total)

Country	Year	Total Unempl- oyed	Youth Unempl- oyed	Area		Gender		Age		
				Urban	Rural	Male	Female	10-14	15-19	20-24
Brazil	1987	3.5	6.6	8.4	2.1	6.2	7.4	-	6.8	6.5
Chile	1990	5.7	13.1	15.1	4.1	13.4	12.4	-	15.9	12.0
Colombia	1990	8.2	22.5	-	-	21.5	23.0	25.7	20.4	-
Costa Rica	1990	6.0	8.3	10.5	6.9	7.6	10.0	-	11.5	6.2
Ecuador	1990	6.1	12.7	-	-	10.2	16.8	6.6	14.6	12.7
El Salvador	1990	10.0	18.6	-	-	17.0	20.5	-	19.2	18.0
Guatemala	1989	2.3	4.0	-	-	3.1	6.3	2.0	5.0	4.2
Honduras	1990	4.2	6.3	10.7	3.4	5.1	9.9	-	5.4	7.6
Panama	1989	16.3	31.5	41.6	21.1	25.9	42.7	-	33.5	30.3
Paraguay	1990	6.6	15.8	-	-	15.8	15.7	-	18.2	14.1
Uruguay	1990	9.3	26.6	-	-	23.7	30.2	-	30.5	18.1
Venezuela	1990	9.9	17.8	19.3	10.8	17.6	17.8	-	20.0	16.6

Source: PREALC (1992), p. 3.

- signifies data not presented in original PREALC table.

Conclusions

This chapter presents a theoretical analysis of the potential effects of the NEM
on the labour market and the information contained in the tables provides
evidence (at the aggregate level) relating to these effects. Unfortunately, data
are collected neither at a sufficiently disaggregated level nor frequently enough
for strong quantitative results to emerge that link the NEM *via* the labour market
to changes in income distribution and poverty. At best one can obtain a series
of snapshots for various countries at different points of time. However, these
data do provide support for the proposition that, in the short-run, it is likely that
NEM policies have reduced labour's share of income, reduced employment in
the UFS and shifted some workers into lower paying employment. The details
are summarised below.

The rural labour market is heterogeneous and there are many differences between countries, but two important features have emerged. First, in countries where peasants hold land in common, moves to improve the market in land have tended to move some of this land away from ownership by peasants, leading to an increase in landless rural labour and more migration to the cities. Second, at least in the short-run, increased agricultural output as part of an ELG strategy has tended to be capital-intensive with a tendency to displace labour from agriculture, except at the seasonal harvesting peaks.

The urban labour market has been subjected to two kinds of 'informalisation'. First, there is 'top-down' informalisation, a strategy on the part of governments and of employers in the UFS to cut labour costs by making labour markets more flexible through reducing the powers of trade unions, employing more workers on short-term contracts and sub-contracting work to enterprises in the UIS. In the short-term, this process of informalisation is likely to lower wages and employment in the UFS.

Second, there is 'bottom-up' informalisation, a process whereby many of those ejected from the UFS or newcomers who are excluded from it are forced to enter the UIS and create their own employment. While there may be a switch in demand from the UFS to the UIS for some goods and services during a recession, it is likely that the demand for UIS output is relatively inelastic. If this is the case, the increase in the UIS labour force will lead to a fall in average earnings in the sector.

Taken together, the two processes are likely to lead to a fall in average wages in both sectors, combined with a transfer of labour from the UFS to lower paid jobs in the UIS. This will result in a fall in the net share of national income going to labour. Given the short-run move towards capital-intensive methods of production in agriculture, the overall picture is one of lower wages and substantial underemployment in the labour markets of Latin America.

In an analysis that concentrates on the long-run, these short-run costs are unimportant and what is more important is whether adjustments are being made in the right direction. The conclusion of a recent World Bank study was that they were, but that some labour markets may have over-adjusted during structural adjustment programmes:

'The evidence on real wages casts considerable doubt on theoretical concerns about aggregate real wage rigidity and labor market inflexibilty as a hindrance to adjustment. Real wage declines have been dramatic, and often far greater than the fall in GDP. For some countries the real wage declines may have been excessively large and led to a fall in domestic demand, which inhibited recovery'. (Horton, Kanbur and Mazumdar (1994), pp. 54-5).

Those at the bottom of the income distribution will be particularly vulnerable in such situations and the conclusion must be that NEM labour market policies have imposed considerable welfare costs on the poor in Latin America.

Notes:

*   The help of Victoria Contreras in the preparation of tables for this chapter is gratefully acknowledged.
1.   The UIS is characterised by ease of entry, which was one of the empirical characteristics ascribed to that sector by the International Labour Organization (ILO) in early attempts to define it. This was picked up by economists associated with the World Bank, such as Mazumdar and Fields, and incorporated in their models as an assumption that the UIS operated perfectly competitively, in contrast to the protected UFS. I shall discuss the work of the ILO in defining and measuring the UIS below.
2.   Mezzera's capital market imperfections could be combined with the protected-sector type of labour market discussed above. The interesting implication of this model is that simply getting rid of whatever protects the UFS (e.g. trade union pressure, minimum wages) would not remove labour market segmentation unless the capital market imperfections are also addressed.
3.   For a fuller discussion of this debate, see Lubell (1991), Moser (1978, 1984) and Thomas (1992 and 1995).
4.   John Weeks (a contributor to this book) also shared in the early development of the concept of the UIS, but put the emphasis on the relationship of enterprises to the state. 'Basically, the *formal sector* includes government activity itself and those enterprises in the private sector which are officially recognised, nurtured and regulated by the State. ... Operations in the *informal sector* are characterised by an absence of such benefits.' (Weeks, 1975, p. 3).
5.   Officially PREALC ceased to exist as such at the end of December 1993 and it is unclear exactly what its new role as the Multidisciplinary Technical Team for Argentina, Brazil, Chile, Paraguay and Uruguay will imply for continuing research on the labour market in Latin America.
6.   One missing component of the UIS in the statistical data is any measure of moonlighting. De Soto (1987) does have some discussion of this phenomenon, but his estimates of the magnitude of moonlighting in Lima seem very odd – see Rossini and Thomas (1990) for a critique. See also Van den Gaag, Stelcner and Vijverberg (1989).
7.   This definition has not been widely used, as empirical studies demonstrated that (i) not all workers/employers in the UIS were poor and (ii) not all poor workers were employed in the UIS (for example, see Carbonetto, Hoyle and Tueros, 1987).

8.   However, in Table 1 the UIS is defined as own-account workers plus unpaid family workers. This measure is likely to *under*state the size of the UIS.

9.   For a critique of the neo-classical theory of the labour market, see Weeks (1991).

10.   PREALC data are the best available on the urban labour market in Latin America, but they have to be checked carefully to see what countries are covered when data for 'Latin America' are presented. In general, 'Latin America' will *not* mean all the seventeen countries listed in Table 1, but may represent the aggregation over, or an average (usually weighted), of a sub-group of Latin American countries. This is the case for the data presented in Table 2.

11.   The ILO has obtained international standardisation over its definition of *open unemployment*; a person who is (i) without work, (ii) available for work and (iii) seeking work is openly unemployed (see ILO (1990), p. 97). This was the basis for questions in household surveys used to construct Table A.9. However, Kritz and Ramos (1976) found that the response was sensitive to the wording of the question and so the data should be interpreted with caution. Wainerman (1992) presents Latin American case studies to demonstrate that the choice of questions in household surveys has underestimated the participation rates of women in the Economically Active Population.

12.   Underemployment may be divided into *visible* and *invisible* components. The former applies to those who would like and are available to work more in a given activity, but are unable to do so. The latter relates to individuals in 'jobs which generate insufficient productivity and insufficient income and/or fail to take full advantage of the capacity of the workers'. (PREALC, 1984, p. 6). Underemployment is an important form of labour market adjustment in Latin America. For example, household surveys in Lima suggest that while open unemployment increased from 4.8% in 1987 to 9.9% in 1993, the rate of underemployment rose from 34.9% to 77.4% (see Ahmad, Amieva and Thomas, 1994, Table 4.1).

13.   These falling values of real minimum wages have serious implications for the derivation of a poverty line that is a function of the minimum wage. Unless adjustments are made for the falling real value, such a measure would underestimate changes in poverty over time.

14.   In the case of dismissals, there is an important distinction between 'just' and 'unjust' dismissal, with the latter involving the employer in stiff penalties. The World Bank is critical of the fact that in most countries 'just' dismissal 'excludes economic reasons, such as financial distress

and increased international competition'. (1993a, p.93). In many countries, payment for 'unjust' dismissal varies positively with a worker's seniority, so that firms tend not to dismiss older workers, a further distortion of the labour market in Edwards's view.

15. For a detailed discussion of institutional changes in labour market regulations, see IILS (1993).

16. For arguments against treating minimum wages and legislation to protect workers as 'market distortions', see ILO (1995) and Plant (1994).

17. It is difficult to find quantitative data on the scale of these subcontracting links between the UFS and UIS in Latin America, but Díaz (1993) discusses the case of Chile.

19. Binswanger, Deininger and Feder (1993) report that small landholders lost out during land reforms in Bolivia, El Salvador and Guatemala. Gómez and Klein (1993) present case studies of the increasing numbers of casual rural workers in Brazil, Chile, Ecuador, Guatemala and Mexico, while Dirven (1993) discussed some of the social and political costs of land reform in Latin America.

20. Stark (1991) contains a number of theoretical models of migration and remittances. During recent years wars and terrorist activity have meant that in some countries, migrants are motivated by political objectives or the need for physical survival rather than economic incentives.

21. Verdera (1994, p. 31) reports that since 1990, between 8,000 and 12,000 Peruvians of Japanese descent (between 20% and 25% of the total number in Peru) have gone to work in Japan. He also reports that about 80,000 Brazilians of Japanese descent are working in Japan.

22. See Collier *et al* (1994).

23. See MacEwan Scott (1979, 1991) and Thomas (1995).

24. Whether expenditure on the family is lower or not depends on what proportion of the missing male earner's income would have been allocated to family expenditure. See Chant (1985, 1991).

25. The data on youth unemployment by age is more difficult to evaluate. No data exist for the age category 10 - 14 years in a number of countries, as at least the lower bound for this group lies below the *legal* minimum age for employment.

26. The (unweighted) averages of the ratios across the groups are 1.99 for the Latin American countries and 1.89 for the OECD countries.

27. Bequele and Boyden (1988), a study on the theme of combating child labour, contains a number of Latin American case studies that suggest that the effect on regular school attendance of having to work may be a major problem for poor children.

CHAPTER 5

THE NEW FINANCIAL REGIME IN LATIN AMERICA

Raúl Fernández*

The aim of this chapter is to evaluate the effect of the new financial regime (NFR) in Latin America on wealth and income distribution. The NFR has emerged from the process of removing capital market distortions in connection with: (1) the policies of setting interest rates and credit allocation, and (2) the practices of financing large public deficits in the domestic capital markets.[1]

Traditionally, Latin American countries have exerted control over capital markets in order to promote their development strategies of industrialisation through import substitution. State interventions were aimed at solving the lack of long-term financing and at fostering pre-selected activities through interest rate subsidies and direct credit allocation. It was believed that these policies would speed up the process of capital accumulation, as well as generating a positive efficiency effect on the global rate of investment.[2] Nevertheless, in practice, these economic goals were distorted by actions stemming from both the government and the private sector. In general, the use of domestic capital markets to finance a growing expansion of national fiscal deficits caused an acceleration of inflation and a crowding-out of private lending. In the private sector, low and negative real interest rates gave rise to a great disincentive to save in domestic financial assets, as well as misallocating resources in the economy.

The policy of government intervention in capital markets was reinforced with the appearance of the external debt crisis in the early 1980s. In most cases, financial regulations were intensified in order to ameliorate the domestic consequences of the external transfer of national savings. Macroeconomic instability and the financial policies of 'market manipulation' have accentuated the distortions and inefficiencies of capital markets in the region. During the 1970s and 1980s, this process was consolidating a 'typical' financial structure which comprises the following general features: (1) financial instruments of short-term maturity; (2) low degree of financial depth; (3) insufficient market competition; (4) abundant government regulations; and (5) high levels of financial fragility.

Within an unstable macroeconomic scenario, the above-stated distortions in the financial structure are the elements which explain the weakness and inefficiencies of the Latin American capital markets. These facts are manifested in terms of: (1) high costs of financial intermediation or *financial spread*; (2) significant differences between domestic and foreign interest rates; (3) high volatility in nominal and real return of assets; (4) important levels of credit rationing and market segmentation; and (5) large concentration in the distribution of credits. In other words, the 'typical' Latin American capital market is characterised by its weakness in providing a wide range of financial instruments to satisfy the portfolio choices of investors and savers in connection with risk, liquidity and returns.

The features and operation of a country's capital markets are a mixture of the microfinancial policies designed for this particular sector (i.e. interest rate, credit policies, etc), and the macroeconomic scenario in which it operates. In order to take this into account, the next section is devoted to revealing the macrofinancial conditions which affected the performance of capital markets in Argentina, Brazil, Chile, Colombia and Mexico during the 1982-93 period. Section three contains a cross country evaluation of the financial policies adopted by these countries in three main areas: capital account, stock exchange and financial or banking system. Section four deals with the impact of the NFR on income distribution. The final section presents the conclusions.

Macrofinancial Relationships Since the Debt Crisis

From the debt crisis onwards, Latin American economic performance as a whole can be explained by the evolution of two macro-disadjustments: the fiscal and the external gaps. Indeed, a huge negative external shock impacted the region in the early 1980s. The main reasons which help to explain the worsening of the external conditions are found in: (1) a deterioration in the terms of trade of the Latin American countries; (2) a significant increase in the industrial world's interest rates; and (3) a tight credit rationing in the international capital markets after 1982.

The foreign sector crisis did also impact heavily on the countries' fiscal accounts. Given that in most cases the external debt was mainly owned by the public sector, the increase in the international interest rates reinforced the original fiscal imbalance. In addition, some countries proceeded to nationalise a large part of the private foreign debt, including Argentina and Chile. The deepening of these macro-imbalances and the policies designed for adjusting the economies to the new international scenario have had strong macroeconomic consequences in the region (Damill *et al*, 1994).

By considering the evolution of the sectoral net financial positions, this chapter aims to identify those economic units that were demanding financing from those supplying assets. The interaction between the external and fiscal gaps has induced important changes in the financial relationships amongst the economic sectors in Latin America.[3] Table 1 presents the surpluses/deficits, on average, of the Foreign, Private and Government Sectors for the years 1982-93. Notice that the whole period under analysis was divided into sub-periods by taking into account the type of financial regime which was operating in each country (see next section).[4]

Table 1:   Sectoral Surplus/Deficit as a Proportion of GDP and the Annual Inflation Rate (%)

COUNTRY	FOREIGN SECTOR	PRIVATE SECTOR	GOVERNMENT SECTOR	INFLATION RATE (%)
ARGENTINA				
1982-93	1.7	3.4	-5.1	728.4
1982-90	1.4	5.1	-6.5	958.7
1991-93	2.8	-2.1	-0.7	37.41
BRAZIL*				
1982-91	1.2	10.4	-11.6	595.7
1982-86	2.4	5.0	-7.4	192.5
1987-91	0.1	15.7	-15.8	864.5
CHILE				
1982-93	4.3	-4.9	0.6	19.8
1982-85	8.5	-5.7	-2.8	23.3
1986-93	2.1	-4.4	2.3	18.1
COLOMBIA				
1982-93	2.2	-0.7	-1.5	24.0
1982-89	3.7	-1.8	-1.9	22.6
1990-93	-0.8	1.7	-0.9	26.9
MEXICO				
1982-93	2.3	3.5	-5.8	57.0
1982-89	-0.1	9.5	-9.4	76.7
1990-93	7.1	-8.4	1.3	17.8

(*)   the data for the government sector was available only until 1991

Source: Inter-American Development Bank (1991 and 1994)

The figures above show that Argentina, Brazil and Mexico present the largest government disequilibria during the 1982-93 period. Moreover, given that these countries received the lowest levels of external savings in relation to their fiscal disequilibria, the private sector had to bear most of the fiscal burden. With the smaller fiscal imbalances and the higher external surpluses, Chile and Colombia have exerted the lowest pressure on the private sector.

Thus, in the first sub-period, although Chile and Colombia had fiscal deficits, they did not create great pressure on their capital markets. In these two countries the proportion of external sources financing the public deficit was important, and the fiscal policies were very effective for closing each governments' imbalance in the second half of the 1980s (Damill *et al*, 1994). The opposite occurred in Argentina and Brazil, where the magnitude of fiscal imbalance implied rates of growth of domestic assets which were incompatible with the monetisation parameters of these economies. Naturally, this inconsistency resulted in a growing contribution of the inflation tax to the financing of the public deficit. Finally, Mexico represents an intermediate situation in terms of the degree of macroeconomic instability of our country studies. In this case, although the public sector exerted a significant pressure over the capital markets during 1982-89, the private sector voluntarily financed a high proportion of the government's imbalance.

In the second sub-period, the elimination of fiscal pressures on the domestic capital markets was the most important change observed in Argentina, Chile, Colombia and Mexico. Moreover, the external constraint was relaxed by the return of Latin America to the international capital markets at the beginning of the 1990s. Following an opposite trend, Brazil accentuated its fiscal disequilibrium and its external transfer during the 1987-91 period. In the Brazilian case, greater pressure on the private sector increased macroeconomic instability which, in turn, was reflected in a higher rate of inflation in the second sub-period (Table 1).

The examples above suggest that, given severe restriction in the access to foreign resources, both the magnitude of sectoral imbalances and the way they are financed will have a strong impact on the performance of national capital markets and this, in turn, will affect income distribution.

Capital Market Reform in Latin America

As a part of the New Economic Model (NEM) in Latin America, institutional and regulatory changes in capital markets are considered as a basic policy reform. The general thrust of these policies was a movement towards market mechanisms that included greater integration into the international capital market. This section is two-fold: (1) it outlines the main stylised facts of the capital markets in Latin America; and (2) the major institutional and regulatory reforms that were implemented recently in the areas of financial (or banking) systems, stock exchanges and capital accounts.

Financial systems

Argentina. The experience of financial liberalisation during the late 1970s resulted in a severe financial crash in 1981. In a turbulent macroeconomic scenario and financial distress, the Central Bank became the main 'actor' in the domestic financial system. The monetary authority started rescuing, refinancing and liquidating financial intermediaries and, at the same time, the monetary authority was backing – to a large extent – the huge public deficit.

In the period 1982-83, financial policy had another important objective: the redistribution of financial wealth between private and public sectors, and within the private sector itself. The policy of debt redistribution was promoted under the belief that the productive sector was collapsing. To begin with, the private external debt was redistributed through a mechanism of foreign exchange insurance and subsidies. In addition, interest rate ceilings were imposed in order to create significant negative returns on deposits which were expected to 'liquidate' the private domestic debt (Damill and Fanelli, 1994).

The macroinconsistency of this financial policy was soon evident. In effect, the demand for domestic assets quickly shrunk as a consequence of the incredibly low negative real returns on financial instruments. Meanwhile, the public sector was raising its supply of assets used for financing a growing fiscal imbalance. The evolution of this process ended up as the hyperinflationary episodes of 1989 and 1990. In order to stop this inflationary explosion, the Bonex Plan forced a rescheduling of the domestic debt and most of the private banking deposits for public bonds in dollars with ten-years maturity. This operation affected private assets valued at $8 billion (Frenkel, 1994).

The economy initiated a process of remonetisation after the implementation of the Bonex Plan. This process was consolidated with the economic stabilisation of 1991 – the Convertibility Plan (Rozenwurcel and Fernández, 1994). During this period, the monetary authority implemented a broad programme of financial reform which included: (1) freeing of the interest rates; (2) substantial reduction in the mandatory reserve requirements; (3) changes in the legal and regulatory framework, including the independence of the Central Bank; (4) privatisation of banking institutions; and (5) a radical opening up of the financial system to deposits denominated in dollars.

Although the 'liberalisation' was more a process imposed by the internal and external conditions of Argentina rather than an active financial policy, these measures did change completely the features of the financial sector. In effect, the financial activities experienced a rapid expansion and this, in turn, improved markedly the efficiency of the banking institutions. In addition, the process of remonetisation driven by capital inflows gave rise to a financial structure in which more than 50% of the assets are denominated in dollars (Rozenwurcel and Fernández, 1994). Furthermore, real lending rates stayed at very low – even negative – levels (see Table A.10 in the Statistical Appendix).

Brazil. For more than thirty years (1961-94), the financial system evolved with an inflationary rhythm. Two distinguishing features have characterised this process: (1) institutional changes have allowed the indexation of financial contracts since the 1960s; and (2) the Central Bank has developed an important role in the intermediation of public debt with the private financial sector. The conjunction of these elements gave rise to the most important characteristic of the Brazilian capital markets: its strong association with the government for developing 'money substitutes' in order to circumvent a demonetisation of the economy (Dias Carneiro *et. al.*, 1994).

Through indexation mechanisms, Brazil succeeded in avoiding the massive 'dollarisation' of financial assets that have characterised the process of high inflation in other countries, for example, Argentina, Bolivia and Uruguay. However, these institutional arrangements could not bypass some distortions and inefficiencies in the capital markets generated by the enormous fiscal deficit. In particular, the remarkable contraction of the private sector's borrowing from around 35% of GDP at the end of the 1970s to less than 12% of GDP at the beginning of the 1990s (Dias Carneiro *et al,* 1994). This led to a situation where the capital markets did not accomplish efficiently their function of providing resources to the private sector. Brazil instituted a sort of 'financial repression' with no interest rate ceilings, but an implicit 'forced' credit allocation into short-term 'overnight' deposits (Frenkel, 1994).[5] Real lending rates, however, remained very high (see Table A.10).

It should be stressed that any financial reform in Brazil needs to deal mainly with the government's deficit, as well as with the public internal debt. From 1986 to 1993, all five stabilisation attempts included significant changes in the capital markets. They tried to prevent the general use of financial indexation in order to soften the impact of the domestic debt on the fiscal burden. The deepest intervention in private contracts was accomplished by the Collor Plan I in May 1990. It blocked investors' access to their financial assets, which amounted approximately to 10% of GDP. As a result M4 fell from 15.7% to 5.2% of GDP. However, liquidity soon recovered. The rate of inflation increased sharply in the following months, and the financial system continued to operate without significant changes (Dias Carneiro *et. al.*, 1994).

Chile. In the early 1980s, following the 'fate' of other Southern Cone liberalisation attempts, Chile faced a financial crisis. The political response was a massive intervention into the capital markets, which included re-nationalisation of the financial institutions, re-scheduling of the domestic debt and subsidising foreign exchange for external debtors (Eyzaguirre, 1993).

In the Chilean case, the cost of the financial restoration was high. Debt liquidation implied a huge redistribution of wealth in favour of the domestic banking system and private debtors. These operations were estimated at around US$ 7 billion and US$ 9 billion respectively.[6] This 'price' is even higher if one includes the quasi-fiscal deficit of the Central Bank which appeared with the financial crisis. It reached two per cent of GDP in 1990-91 (Eyzaguirre, 1993).

In order to avoid the clear failures on bank monitoring that characterised the pre-crisis period, a new legislation for financial control and supervision was initiated with a financial reform in 1986. With better regulation, Chile followed an effective policy for recapitalisation and rehabilitation of financial institutions. Moreover, attempting to regain confidence, an explicit deposit guarantee scheme helped the financial system to recover from the crisis in the second half of the 1980s. This process was, in turn, strongly supported by the steady macroeconomic improvement of the country from 1985-86 onwards. Real lending rates, however, remained quite high (see Table A.10).

Colombia. At the beginning of the 1980s, several financial intermediaries underwent a crisis of solvency. Economic recession and weaknesses in the mechanisms of control and supervision gave rise to a noticeable deterioration in the quality of the banks' portfolios (Lora *et al.,*1994). These troubles continued until 1985, when several institutions went bankrupt, and the monetary authority had to intervene in the capital markets in order to avoid further problems. At that time, several institutions were nationalised, a bank was liquidated and a set of market restrictions were implemented.

Between 1986 and 1990, sectoral policy aimed at solving the financial difficulties caused by the crisis.[7] In a scenario of growing macroeconomic stability, there was a gradual change in the country's financial arrangements towards market mechanisms. It was not until 1990, however, that capital market reform acquired a special importance. It developed as a larger economic programme including reforms in the trade, financial, exchange rate and labour markets.

Regarding financial reform, the major policy change included the deregulation of the activity of financial intermediaries. This appears as the first step for moving from a structure of 'specialised banking' towards a system of 'universal banking'. Moreover, interest rates were liberalised, and new financial intermediaries were authorised to operate. Legislation for mergers, acquisitions and transformations of financial institutions were updated, and the restrictions for foreign investments in the financial sector were lifted (Lora *et al*, 1994).

All of the above measures were aimed at achieving greater competition within the capital markets, as well as ensuring that resource allocation was made by market forces. However, it should be stressed that the policy of financial deregulation in Colombia has been implemented since the 1970s. The conjunction of this sectoral strategy and the early control of the public imbalance during the 1980s are the elements that help to explain the relatively low fragility of the country's capital markets (Martínez, 1993), although real lending rates are still high (see Table A.10).

Mexico. A deep financial crash followed the Mexican economic crisis of 1982. Attempting to restore depositors' confidence, the government decided to nationalise the financial system and to implement a policy of 'debt relief' for reducing the real burden on borrowers. The process of debt liquidation was carried out through the following measures: (1) negative real rates on peso-denominated deposits; and (2) a forced conversion of deposits denominated in foreign currency at an unfavourable exchange rate. In addition, as happened in Argentina and Chile, private debtors were 'rewarded' by receiving a favourable exchange rate for their foreign liabilities.

From the beginning of the crisis, the public sector exerted a growing pressure on the domestic capital markets. In effect, banking credit to the government increased from 35% in 1982 to over 60% in 1986, and interest rates were fixed at negative (or low) real levels. This financial strategy continued until 1988, when the reduction of the rate of inflation made possible a positive real interest rate on both deposits and lending (for real lending rates see Table A.10). This was complemented with a programme of financial deregulation which began in 1989. The reform combined a liberalisation of interest rates with a gradual elimination of mandatory reserve requirements forcing banks to keep a rigid asset structure. In addition, changes in the legal and regulatory framework were established in order to: (1) encourage the creation of a system of universal banking; (2) avoid the emergence of large financial conglomerate groups (banks-industry); (3) allow the participation of foreign investors in domestic financial institutions – upto 30% of total capital; and (4) implement a vast privatisation programme of financial institutions. In the period 1990-93, fifteen of the eighteen commercial banks held by the government were sold for more than $11billion (Ortiz, 1993).

Stock Exchange Markets

Traditionally, stock exchange markets have had marginal importance in Latin America. Recently, however, several countries have experienced a rapid expansion of their bond and equity markets. Numerous factors account for this, such as inflation reduction, domestic financial deregulation, technological and financial innovations, privatisation, social security reforms and, above all, large foreign capital inflows into Latin America.

Following the regional trend, the five economies under analysis show a remarkable enlargement of the index of stock market capitalisation in terms of GDP from the late 1980s onwards (see Table 2). The initial jump of the indices was due to price increases of existing stocks rather than increases in the quantity of bonds and equities. Subsequently, the issue of new stocks expanded the size of the market. New and already existing enterprises were expected to benefit from these untraditional sources of financing. Nevertheless, there was not a significant change in the number of listed companies and, therefore, the degree of market concentration remained very high (Table 2). The concentration index, measured by the market capitalisation held by the ten largest companies, was above 50% in all cases, whereas it was approximately 30% in many Asian countries including China, Indonesia, Korea, Malaysia and Thailand (IFC, 1994).

To a large extent, the capital flows into Latin America at the beginning of the 1990s conferred on these markets the characteristic of 'emerging'. Although Chile shares the same label, it appears to be a distinctive case in terms of the evolution and degree of the market's deepness in the 1980s (Table 2). After a poor performance in the first half of the last decade, the Chilean stock market *has* recovered rapidly from the mid-1980s (Rojas-Suárez and Weisbrod, 1994). The latest inflows of foreign capital were just another step in the development process of the country's stock market. However, in the other cases, such as Argentina, Brazil, Colombia and Mexico, these inflows of foreign capital have provided the basis for the transformation of the market during the past years (see Table 2).

Capital Account Reform

The opening up of the capital account has been an important policy in recent Latin American economic reforms. Following the trend towards globalisation, several countries have embarked on a process of integrating the domestic capital markets into the world's financial flows. A favourable international scenario, combined with policies of freeing capital movements, has had a strong impact on regional capital markets during the early 1990s (see Chapter 6.). But different economic objectives, and distinctive national circumstances, have determined – in every case – the policy instruments used by each country and the extent of financial liberalisation.

Chile and Colombia followed a gradual and selective strategy for the opening up of their domestic financial markets to foreign capital movements. In Chile, several restrictions have been retained for capital flows, including reserve requirements imposed on external borrowing, regulations on the overseas issues of stocks and bonds made by Chilean companies, as well as restricted access to the foreign exchange market related to: (1) obtaining and refunding foreign debt; (2) making investments abroad; and (3) purchasing hard

Table 2: Stock Exchange Indicators

ARGENTINA	1984	1987	1989	1990	1991	1992	1993
Local Index (1990 = 100)	0.00128	0.03	32.6	100	810.6	609.5	935.5
Market Capitalisation (in Million US$)	1171	1519	4225	3268	18509	18633	43967
Market Capitalisation/ GDP (%)	1.29	1.34	2.64	1.95	9.76	8.14	16.98
No. of Listed Companies	236	206	178	179	174	175	180
BRAZIL							
Local Index (1990 = 100)	0.00397	0.039	24.5	100	2415.6	26949.5	149225
Market Capitalisation (in Million US$)	28995	16900	44368	16354	42759	45261	99430
Market Capitalisation/ GDP (%)	13.9	5.78	9.89	3.41	10.54	11.71	25.1
No. of Listed Companies	522	590	592	581	570	565	550
CHILE							
Local Index (1990 = 100)	5.4	29.5	64.9	100	212.9	234.3	335.6
Market Capitalisation (in Million US$)	51	503	866	783	1.9	2029	2797
Market Capitalisation/ GDP (%)	10.96	28.17	37.76	49.07	89.33	78.23	110.82
No. of Listed Companies	208	209	213	215	221	245	263
COLOMBIA							
Local Index (1990 = 100)	15.5	61.1	70.1	100	25.7	35.9	53.8
Market Capitalisation (in Million US$)	762	1255	1136	1416	4036	5681	9237
Market Capitalisation/ GDP (%)	2.77	3.45	2.87	3.52	9.44	11.58	16.39
No. of Listed Companies	180	96	82	80	83	80	89
MEXICO							
Local Index (1990 = 100)	0.6	16.8	66.6	100	227.7	279.8	413.9
Market Capitalisation (in Million US$)	2.16	15554	6232	12212	31723	44582	62454
Market Capitalisation/ GDP (%)	1.26	5.98	11.02	13.56	34.75	42.98	57.67
No. of Listed Companies	160	190	203	199	209	195	190

Source: International Finance Corporation (1994)

currency for portfolio management (Eyzaguirre, 1993).

Meanwhile, in Colombia, restrictions on foreign investments and profit remittance were eliminated. The private sector was allowed to borrow from abroad term contracts of more than one year. However, despite this outward orientation, the reforms did not allow the internal 'dollarisation' of financial activities. In effect, deposits in foreign currency remained forbidden, and the banks could only lend foreign currency from either their own capital or from external sources (Martínez, 1993).

At the other end of the spectrum, Argentina and – to a lesser extent – Mexico have adopted a much laxer approach regarding foreign financial flows. In the Argentine case, the opening of the domestic economy was somewhat radical from its inception. Argentina's policy started by giving an egalitarian treatment to both national and foreign productive investments regarding: (1) a uniform tax rate on profits for capital of any nationality; (2) the elimination of the requirement for the approval of direct external investments; and (3) an allowance for the free repatriation of foreign capital. Moreover, the exchange market was liberalised, and a segment of dollar-denominated deposits was established in the financial system. In April 1991, the Convertibility Law ensured a complete liberalisation of the capital account by fixing the nominal exchange rate, by conferring full legality to the contracts agreed in any national currency, and by eliminating all restrictions on the buying and selling of foreign currencies (Fanelli and Machinea, 1994). It should be noticed that in Argentina these measures have institutionalised the long process of financial dollarisation which was initiated at the end of the 1970s.

Although Mexico was not as permissive as Argentina, the Mexican policy for attracting foreign capital was also quite liberal. In 1989, within a broader programme of financial innovations that attempted to promote an integration into the international capital markets, foreigners were allowed to undertake portfolio investments in equities by acquiring special thirty-years funds. During this period, even though foreign direct investment was not completely liberalised, there were important institutional changes facilitating and encouraging the establishment of external productive investments. But Mexico, unlike Argentina, did not pursue a policy of dollarising domestic financial contracts, including dollar-denominated deposits within the financial system.

Despite the turbulent macroeconomic conditions until the adoption of the *Plano Real* in 1994, and the absence of significant changes in the long tradition of controlling foreign capital movements, Brazil experienced a noticeable inflow of funds in the 1990s. It is argued that this process has been largely explained by the direct and indirect capital repatriation of Brazilian financial assets (Dias Carneiro *et al.* 1994). Without neglecting recent changes in the foreign sector, Brazil has not yet moved towards a comprehensive reform for deregulating its capital account as was so in the other cases considered above.

The main features of the NFR in Latin America are the deregulation of capital markets and the elimination of the excessive pressure exerted by the public imbalance over the domestic capital market. By considering these macro- and micro- conditions, the beginning of the NFR in the country studies is identified by the following dates: Argentina started in 1991, Chile in 1986, and Colombia and Mexico began in 1990. Finally, Brazil is the counter-example in this study, where the features of the NFR were not found during the period 1982-93. Instead, what characterises Brazil in these years is the distinctive degree of pressure exerted by the public deficit on the domestic capital market. In this case, the worsening of the macroeconomic conditions is the criterion which was used to divide the analysis into two sub-periods, before and after 1986.

Capital Markets and Income Distribution

In addition to the problem of information, the diversity and complexity of the financial effects on wealth and income distribution explain the noticeable scarcity of analysis (Reyes Heroles, 1988). Yet, in general, what contributes to the difficulty of working on this topic appears to be the lack of an adequate framework for making a consistent evaluation of the redistributive effects within capital markets. Problems may arise with partial studies, which do not differentiate real from financial variables that impact on the distribution of income.

Bearing in mind that this is a cross-country evaluation, a standard analytical structure needs to be applied for making useful comparisons. This process starts with a clear delimitation of the factors 'above' and 'below' the line which separate real from financial variables (see the definition of surplus in equation 3 below). In other words, it is a 'below the line' analysis. In addition, in this study capital markets include the money market; the financial or banking system; and the stock exchange.

The *redistributive effects* within capital markets are due to capital gains/ losses on financial and physical assets. It appears as a consequence of the structure of nominal returns on assets (or assets' prices) and inflation, which affect individual portfolios.[8] With large changes in asset prices – in mean and variance – this 'windfall effect' is likely to acquire a noticeable importance in Latin America.

This section presents a general framework for analysing the redistributive effects within capital markets. At the end, there is an evaluation of the reforms of financial markets in Latin America and their likely impact on the wealth-effect of different income groups.

A Macrofinancial Framework

The analysis starts by defining the concept of *net financial wealth (nfw)* in real terms for an individual (i) at time (t)[9]. It is made up of the difference between the agent's stocks of total financial assets (a) and liabilities (l). Note that the *nfw* can also be expressed as the difference between the net worth *(nw)* minus the stock of physical assets (k). The wealth constraint of an individual can be written as follows:

(1) $$nfw^i_t = a^i_t - l^i_t = nw^i_t - k^i_t$$

Financial assets held by an individual are the liabilities of other agent(s). This implies that when aggregating over all of the individuals in one economy, the financial relationships would cancel out and, therefore, the total wealth of that society would become just its stock of physical capital. Formally, it can be stated as:

(2) $$\Sigma nfw^i_t = \Sigma nw^i_t - \Sigma k^i_t = 0 \qquad \text{with } i = 1...n$$

The stock of capital assets increases with the flows of net physical investment, and the stock of financial wealth rises with positive net financial savings. The *surplus (sup)* is defined as that part of the total disposable income which is allocated to increase the stock of net financial wealth. Nevertheless, it should be noticed that the redistributive effects on financial assets/liabilities can cause differences between the real change in an individual's financial wealth and his/her net surplus during the same period.

(3) $$\Delta fw^i_t = sup^i_t - \Gamma^{fwi}_t$$

where:
sup = s - i   s = real savings   i = real physical investment
Γ^{fwi} = wealth-effect on financial assets

From the macroeconomic condition of consistency for the stocks [identity (2)], it can be shown that changes in financial wealth must always be zero:

(4) $$\Sigma \Delta fw^i_t = \Sigma sup^i_t = 0 \qquad \text{with } i = 1...n$$

The wealth-effect (Γ^x) is defined as the capital gain/loss in real terms for keeping an asset (X) during the period between (t-1) and (t). Formally, it can be written as:

(5) $\Gamma^x_t = (X_{t-1}/P_{t-1}) - (X_{t-1}/P_t)$

Equation (5) can be rearranged as follows[10]:

(6) $\Gamma^x_t = x_{t-1}(\pi^x_t - \pi_t)/(1+\pi_t)$

where:
x_{t-1} = value of real asset at time (t-1)
π = rate of inflation
π^x = nominal interest rate or changes in nominal prices of the asset (X)

Assuming that r^n is the 'natural rate' of interest, the wealth-effect for an individual holding the asset (X) can be positive, neutral or negative depending on whether the expression $\{(\pi^x_t-\pi_t)-[r^n*(1+\pi_t)]\}$ is greater, equal or less than zero. Notice that the inflation tax is a particular case of wealth-effect in which the financial instrument being considered contains a fixed price and zero nominal return (for instance, domestic currency).[11]

Finally, the difference between distribution of capital gains/losses – *redistribution* within the capital markets – and the concept of the *distribution* of incomes from financial assets among individuals should be stressed. It is acknowledged that both real and financial variables can affect the evolution of the stock of financial wealth and, therefore, the distribution of financial income amongst individuals. This point can be understood with the following example: a reduction in real wages can affect the magnitude of the workers' surplus, and therefore, the evolution of the stock of financial wealth. When this happens, there may be a deterioration of financial incomes for the working class, without there being redistributive effects – capital gains/losses – within capital markets.[12]

Capital Markets and Redistribution Effects in Latin America

The analysis now turns to show the relative magnitude and the evolution of the capital gains/losses on a 'common set' of financial assets for the country cases since 1982.[13] In this 'standard' financial structure, the domestic instruments are divided into assets with zero (Mz), low (Ml) and high (Mh) nominal returns. In addition, the analysis includes an asset denominated in foreign currency (Me).

Empirical estimations of capital gains/losses on the above assets' structure were obtained by applying equation (6) to the following variables: inflation, deposit, lending and official exchange rates. These estimations must be taken only as an indication of *changes and dispersions* in connection with the return of assets since the beginning of the 1980s.[14]

As was done in Table 1, the period 1982-93 was divided into sub-periods in order to explore the impact of different financial regimes on the real yield of financial assets. Table 3 presents with positive/negative sign the percentage of capital gain/loss on average suffered by the asset holder. Moreover, the standard deviation (S-D) was calculated for the wealth-effect on each financial asset, as well as on the rate of inflation for the years 1982-93.

Table 3
Wealth-Effect on Financial Assets and Inflation Rate (%)

Country	Γ^{Mz}	Γ^{Ml}	Γ^{Mh}	Γ^{Me}	Inflation Rate
Argentina					
1982-90	-77.21	-13.67	43.72	14.34	958.74
1991-93	-24.41	-6.27	16.42	-9.57	37.41
S-D	29.22	27.20	50.83	56.69	1372.79
Brazil					
1982-93	-76.93	16.30	86.62	1.11	769.77
1982-86	-59.10	14.45	24.74	-2.18	192.50
1987-93	-89.66	20.79	130.81	-0.35	1200.69
S-D	18.57	22.70	86.60	13.05	726.60
Chile					
1982-85	-18.88	8.84	18.81	21.34	23.30
1986-93	-15.21	4.28	10.15	-5.68	18.13
S-D	3.54	5.91	7.67	18.92	5.03
Colombia					
1982-89	-18.36	6.64	13.76*	7.18	22.59
1990-93	-21.13	3.65	11.41	-3.60	26.89
S-D	2.79	2.81	2.76	13.94	4.28
Mexico					
1982-89	-40.84	-6.40	-2.78	4.02	76.70
1990-93	-14.79	1.82	4.18	-10.23	17.83
S-D	16.88	12.53	13.61	24.5	44.03

Note: (*) *the data start in 1986*
Source: IMF, International Financial Statistics, various years

The first general comment on the above figures refers to the inflation tax (Γ^{Mz}) and the perceived changes in the financial regimes in the country studies. In all cases, the NFR was implemented in a scenario of relatively low and stable inflation. This implies that in the post-liberalisation period, the inflation tax was reduced substantially (Argentina and Mexico) or it remained around its previous low level (Chile and Colombia).

The second observation is that the difference between real returns on domestic assets with low (Ml) and high (Mh) nominal returns – *financial spreads* – increases when inflation accelerates. This effect is clearly observed in the highest inflationary countries during the 1980s, such as Argentina and

Brazil. In the third place, the country cases present a negative wealth-effect on assets denominated in foreign currency (Γ^{Me}) at the beginning of the 1990s. This is due to an overvaluation of the nominal exchange rate which could be explained – to some extent – by the foreign capital inflows to Latin America during the recent years.

Finally, during the period 1982-93, the wealth-effect on assets denominated in domestic currency shows a much greater dispersion (S-D) in those countries that have experienced a higher macroeconomic instability. In connection with the capital gains/losses on foreign currency, the lowest deviation from its mean value suggests that Brazil, Chile and Colombia are the countries that have applied a more consistent exchange rate policy during the whole period 1982-93.

By contrasting the wealth-effect on domestic assets in the country cases, we observe that the policy of financial liberalisation had its strongest impact in Argentina and Mexico. In effect, a sharp reduction in the differential rates between assets in Argentina and a turning around from negative to positive real rates on domestic assets of Mexico were two unambiguous effects of these national financial reforms (see Table 3). At the other end of the spectrum, with much lower degrees of government intervention in the capital markets, are Chile and Colombia. By comparing these two economies, the relatively higher impact of the financial reform in Chile is due to: (1) its larger financial regulation until 1985; (2) its greater competition in the banking system since 1986; and (3) a better performance of Chile in terms of the rate of inflation in the first years of the 1990s (Table 3).

The last case study, Brazil, represents the country where institutional arrangements in the capital markets did not change – on a permanent base – during the period under analysis. However, the Brazilian 'type' of financial repression is a peculiar one. In this case, through indexation mechanisms on financial contracts, the dispersion of assets' returns observed in Argentina was avoided. Moreover, the monetary authority did not generate a disincentive for savings in domestic assets as did the Mexican policy (Table 3). The transfer of most of the banking 'overnight' credits to finance the public sector is what characterises the Brazilian 'manipulation' of its domestic capital markets.

It should be stressed that the financial strategy of Brazil was not one without costs in terms of the wealth-effects within the financial markets. In addition to the redistributive impact of this policy in connection with the crowding-out effect on private lending, the fast expansion of the government's domestic debt was to be highly monetised in the second half of the 1980s.[15] This has had two clear effects: (1) the inflation tax increased sharply in the second sub-period, and (2) the dispersion between low and high assets' returns was augmented after 1986 (Table 3). In Brazil, although there were indexation mechanisms in capital markets, a higher rate of inflation in the second sub-period caused an increase of the dispersion on real returns of different domestic assets.

In short, with the highest degree of government intervention in financial markets, Argentina, Brazil and Mexico are the countries with the largest 'mean' and 'variance' in capital gains/losses on domestic financial instruments. At the other end, in Chile and Colombia, the countries with relatively more stable economies and less government intervention in the capital markets, the policies of financial reforms are expected to have had a smaller impact on income distribution than in the first group of countries.

The Wealth-Effect by Income Groups

The likely distribution of the wealth-effect by income groups can now be evaluated using the above approach. The identification of creditors and debtors, and the structure of asset holders by income groups, is an essential input for a quantitative analysis of the capital gains/losses in financial portfolios (see eq. 3). The present study will, therefore, attempt to focus on the expected 'direction' of changes in financial earnings by income groups in: (1) the money market; (2) the financial or banking system; and (3) the stock exchange.

First, the financial asset held by the vast majority of individuals is the domestic currency (Mz). Assumptions about the inflation tax (Γ^{Mz}) and its distributional consequences are based on the belief that opportunities for substituting currency for other assets is not uniform by income group. In effect, individuals with high income levels are expected to have access to better 'technologies' of currency substitution than agents with lower incomes. Evidence of the regressivity of the inflation tax is given by the following argument: when the income of an individual increases, he/she keeps a lower real monetary balance in relation to his/her income. Formally, this fact is represented by an income elasticity which is lower than one in the demand for money (Ahumada *et al*, 1992).

Economies of scale, information costs and different institutional access to physical and financial assets are among the reasons that help to explain the regressive effect of inflation on income groups. This thesis has been tested in a recent study on Argentina during the period 1980-90 (Ahumada *et al*, 1992.). Table 4 presents the impact of the inflation tax on the personal and functional distribution of income.

The figures below fully confirm the hypothesis that the inflation tax is regressive.[16] In connection with the personal distribution of income, the poorest quintile suffered an inflation tax which was three times higher than its equivalent for individuals of the richest quintile. In effect, during 1980-90 the poorest quintile suffered on average an erosion of 8.6% of its income, whereas the richest group suffered losses of only 3% .

Similar results are obtained by analysing the impact of the inflation tax on the functional distribution of income. Table 4 shows that wage earners represent the group that suffered the most. While wage earners paid 5.2% of their income during 1980-90, the contribution of others was only 3.8%.

The likely distribution amongst income groups within the financial or banking system can now be evaluated. This includes an estimate of the capital gains/losses on domestic assets with low (Ml) and high nominal returns (Mh). The analysis follows the same logic applied to the distribution of wealth-effects by income groups in connection with the domestic currency (inflation tax). That is, if low income individuals pay a higher proportion of their revenue in inflation tax, it is because they cannot have access to the 'better choices' which are available to agents with higher levels of income. In addition, because these 'better choices' appear directly associated with the level of income, the inflation tax declines for wealthier individuals (see Table 4).

Table 4:
Estimations of the Inflation Tax by Income Groups (%) -
Argentina, 1980-90

PERIOD		QUINTILE					WAGE EARNERS	OTHERS
		1	2	3	4	5		
1980	I	1.6	1.2	1.1	0.9	0.6	1.0	0.8
	II	1.6	1.2	1.0	0.9	0.6	1.0	0.8
	III	1.3	1.0	0.9	0.7	0.5	0.8	0.6
	IV	1.4	1.1	1.0	0.8	0.6	0.9	0.7
1981	I	1.5	1.1	0.9	0.8	0.5	0.9	0.7
	II	2.0	1.5	1.2	1.0	0.7	1.1	0.9
	III	2.3	1.7	1.4	1.2	0.8	1.3	1.0
	IV	1.9	1.5	1.2	1.0	0.7	1.1	0.9
1982	I	2.2	1.7	1.4	1.1	0.8	1.6	1.0
	II	1.4	1.1	0.9	0.7	0.5	1.0	0.6
	III	2.8	2.1	1.7	1.4	0.9	2.0	1.2
	IV	2.7	2.1	1.7	1.4	1.0	1.9	1.2
1883	I	2.7	2.0	1.7	1.4	1.0	1.7	1.2
	II	2.5	1.9	1.6	1.3	0.9	1.5	1.1
	III	2.9	2.2	1.8	1.5	1.0	1.8	1.3
	IV	2.9	2.2	1.8	1.5	1.0	1.8	1.3
1984	I	2.8	2.1	1.8	1.5	1.0	1.6	1.3
	II	2.9	2.2	1.8	1.5	1.0	1.6	1.3
	III	3.0	2.3	1.9	1.6	1.1	1.7	1.4
	IV	3.0	2.2	1.9	1.6	1.1	1.7	1.4

Table 4: continued

PERIOD		QUINTILE 1	2	3	4	5	WAGE EARNERS	OTHERS
1985	I	3.1	2.3	2	1.6	1.1	1.8	1.4
	II	3.0	2.3	1.9	1.6	1.1	1 .8	1.4
	III	2.4	1.8	1.5	1.3	0.9	1.4	1.1
	IV	0.7	0.5	0.4	0.4	0.2	0.4	0.3
1986	I	1.0	0.7	0.6	0.5	0.3	0.5	0.4
	II	1.2	0.9	0.7	0.6	0.4	0.6	0.5
	III	1.7	1.2	1.0	0.8	0.6	0.9	0.8
	IV	1.6	1.2	1.0	0.8	0.5	0.8	0.7
1987	I	2.0	1.5	1.2	1.0	0.6	1.1	0.8
	II	1.5	1.1	0.9	0.7	0.5	0.8	0.6
	III	2.4	1.7	1.4	1.1	0.7	1.3	1.0
	IV	2.6	1.9	1.6	1.3	0.8	1.4	1.1
1988	I	2.2	1.6	1.3	1.1	0.7	1.3	0.9
	II	2.3	1.6	1.4	1.1	0.7	1.3	0.9
	III	2.6	1.8	1.5	1.2	0.8	1.5	1.0
	IV	1.9	1.4	1.1	0.9	0.6	1.1	0.8
1989	I	1.2	0.9	0.8	0.6	0.4	1.4	0.9
	II	3.1	1.3	2.0	1.6	1.1	1.7	1.1
	III	3.4	2.6	2.2	1.8	1.2	1.1	0.7
	IV	1.5	1.2	1.0	0.8	0.5	1.6	1.0
1990	I	3.3	2.5	2.1	1.8	1.1	N/A	N/A
	II	2.4	1.8	1.5	1.3	0.8	N/A	N/A
	III	1.5	1.1	1.0	0.8	0.5	N/A	N/A
	IV	1.1	0.9	0.8	0.6	0.4	N/A	N/A

Source: Ahumada et al (1992)

The above analysis suggests the following general hypothesis: the lower the level of income of an individual, then the greater the probability of having a relatively lower real return on assets. In turn, this implies that the greater the differential of wealth-effects between financial assets – with low and high returns – the higher the probability of having a greater *inequality* in the redistribution of financial incomes amongst asset holders.[17] Once again, economies of scale, information costs and institutional restrictions are the factors which explain the different assets structure of individuals' portfolios and, therefore, the distribution of the capital gains/losses – across assets– by income groups.

According to our analysis, there is a positive association between inflation and the mean-differentials between capital gains/losses on (Ml) and (Mh). This is observed by considering the financial spreads of the banking institutions in Table 3. Thus, it can be argued that the distribution of windfall-effects across assets in our countries' financial systems would be more unequal when inflation accelerates. Nevertheless, by using the same line of reasoning, if it is suggested that the acceleration of inflation increases the inequality in the redistribution of financial earnings, the relationship also has to hold when considering the distributive effects of a higher inflation on the domestic currency. This thesis is also validated by the above-mentioned empirical study. In effect, during the hyperinflationary period in Argentina (1989-90), the inflation tax differential between the poorest and the highest quintile increased from its average value of 8.6% and 3% respectively to 13.6% and 4.8% respectively (see Table 4).

By taking the above analysis into account, the impact of the NFR in a particular case will depend on the following elements: (1) the degree of previous country financial repression; and (2) changes in the levels of inflation between the periods of the pre- and post-liberalisation of the capital markets. These factors are essential in reaching conclusions about the redistributive effects within the money market and the financial system. In the country studies these two conditions suggest that the NFR would have caused a more *even* redistribution of incomes in Argentina, Chile and Mexico. In the post-liberalisation period of these three countries, a lower inflation tax and a reduction in the dispersion of the wealth-effect on assets with 'low' and 'high' nominal returns are the reasons which support this hypothesis.

Conclusions

This chapter has touched upon several issues regarding the impact of capital market reforms on income distribution in Latin America. The general finding of this study is that the well known Fisher's equation of arbitrage is not observed in an economic scenario of high and unstable inflation. In effect, the real return on assets does not evolve at the 'natural rate' when inflation accelerates. When this phenomenon happens, there is a transfer of financial incomes (wealth-effect) amongst individuals. Furthermore, this study has proved the following two hypothesis: (1) the dispersion of capital gains/losses among different financial assets increases with the magnitude of the rate of inflation; and (2) there is a positive association between negative redistributions of financial incomes and the dispersion of wealth-effects among different assets.

With macroeconomic stability, the reforms in the financial systems have reduced the 'opportunities' for obtaining large capital gains/losses within the banking sector of Latin America. In this sense, the NFR has a positive impact on the *redistribution* of financial incomes in Argentina, Chile and Mexico, albeit among a relatively wealthy group of individuals. In Colombia, however, the ambiguous result of the financial reform on income distribution is explained by: (1) the financial liberalisation of 1990 that did not represent a major break with the previous financial regime and (2) a macroeconomic scenario which remained relatively unchanged during the 1982-93 period. Finally, Brazil is the case where the NFR was not implemented during the 1982-93 period. With a deeper financial repression and a higher macroeconomic instability after 1986, this country increased the inequality in the distribution of financial incomes.

In connection with the stock exchange, the large concentration of shares and bonds in the upper income class indicates that inequality in the personal distribution of income would have increased in these markets in the early 1990s as a consequence of windfall gains. Although, in general, this happened in Latin America, Chile appears to be somewhat different. In effect, the privatisation of public enterprises with the aim of '*capitalismo popular*', and the reform of the social security system, have considerably reduced the degree of concentration in the stock market. With a policy of increasing the number of individuals and enterprises participating in the stock market, Chile has avoided a larger concentration in the distribution of income.

In short, the Latin American experiences since the debt crisis suggest that negative redistributions of income within capital markets are likely to appear in an unstable and inflationary economic scenario. If these macroeconomic conditions prevail, then it is hard to believe that there will be a type of financial regime able to avoid a higher concentration of earnings from financial assets at the top of the income distribution. This suggests that the NFR in Latin America can reduce the scale of capital gains/losses and this, in turn, implies a more even redistribution of incomes amongst individuals within capital markets.

This, however, does not imply that the NFR will necessarily cause a more even distribution of personal income in the whole economy. The reason is that the capital gains/losses referred to above occur almost exclusively in the upper decile of the economy. The lowering of the inflation tax *does* contribute positively to reducing the inequality of income distribution, but this chapter has argued that this cannot be attributed to the NFR – on the contrary, the NFR works best where macroeconomic stability has already been established. Furthermore, the increase in real interest rates often associated with the NFR (see Table A.10) can itself be very regressive. Thus, while the NFR is needed to promote greater efficiency in capital markets, it is unlikely to make much of a contribution to improving the size distribution of income.

Appendix to Chapter 5

Definition: the capital gain/loss on asset (X) is given by:

(1a) $\Gamma^x_t = (X_{t-1}/P_{t-1}) - (X_{t-1}/P_t)$

Eq. (1) can be rearranged as follows:

$\Gamma^x_t = (X_{t-1}/P_{t-1})(P_t/P_t) - (X_{t-1}/P_t)(1+\pi^x_t)$

$\Gamma^x_t = (X_{t-1}/P_t)[1+\pi_t-(1+\pi^x_t)] = (X_{t-1}/P_t)(P_{t-1}/P_{t-1})(\pi_t-\pi^x_t)$

Therefore,

(2a) $\Gamma^x_t = x_{t-1}(\pi_t - \pi^x_t)/(1+\pi_t)$

A real change in the stock of one financial asset (Δx) in period (t) can be expressed by its nominal increment in real terms ($\Delta X/P$) minus (plus) the capital loss (gain) of this asset in that period. It is given by

(3a) $\Delta x_t = (\Delta X_t/P_t) - \Gamma^x_t = (\Delta X_t/P_t) - x_{t-1}(\pi_t - \pi^x_t)/(1+\pi_t)$

where: $(\Delta X_t/P_t) = SUP_t/P_t =$ real surplus allocated in (X)

Notes

*   I am grateful to Ernesto Piedras for his comments and suggestions.
1.   This includes the elimination of the inflation tax as a way of financing the public imbalance.
2.   Although these were common measures in most countries, the degree and the intensity of financial regulations were not identical in all cases.
3.   For an analysis of the causes that explain the evolution of the foreign and fiscal gaps, see Fanelli *et al.* (1990) and Damill *et. al.* (1994).
4.   The exception to this rule is Brazil where the financial regime has not experienced a clear-cut change (see below). In this case, the distinction between before and after 1986 was made in terms of the dimension of the imbalance of the public sector.
5.   The 'overnight' deposits, in turn, were shifted into public bonds of long-term maturity.
6.   Equivalent to 30% of Chilean GDP at the time.

7. It included measures for the recapitalisation of the institutions which were intervened, increase of banks' capital requirements, improvement of instruments of financial control and banking supervision.

8. Direct actions which affect the stock of assets (i.e. assets confiscation, etc.) will not be considered in this analysis.

9. This analysis is based on Tobin (1969), Tobin (1982) and Buiter (1983).

10. For a formal derivation, see the appendix to this chapter.

11. Notice that this 'normal return' (r^n) cannot be accounted for in the case of assets with fixed prices and zero nominal returns (i.e. domestic currency).

12. In order to isolate the impact of the financial variables on the distribution of income, the analysis has to concentrate only on the redistributive effects or on the distribution of capital gains and losses.

13. An evaluation of the wealth-effect on physical assets due to price changes in the stock exchange will be considered below.

14. To simplify, and taking into account the qualitative approach of this analysis, the estimations do not exclude the 'natural' rate of return $[r^n*(1+\pi_t)]$.

15. In this sense, Brazil matches the assumptions and the result of the 'monetary arithmetic' suggested by a number of authors. When the monetary authority cannot reduce a continuous government deficit and the real return of the public debt surpasses the rate of economic growth, a higher rate of monetisation or debt repudiation can be expected. See Cardoso and Dantas (1990).

16. The monetary aggregate – M_1 – was used to approximate the demand for money by each income group.

17. Notice that the distribution of capital gains/losses and the redistribution of financial incomes are synonyms.

CHAPTER 6

INTERNATIONAL CAPITAL FLOWS TO LATIN AMERICA

Stephany Griffith-Jones*

The main feature of the new economic model (NEM) in Latin America is its outward orientation through both trade and capital account liberalisation. The opening of the capital account, accompanied – or often preceded – by domestic capital market liberalisation (see Chapter 5), creates the pre-conditions for large capital flows from abroad. These flows will then take place if and when the international economic circumstances are favourable and if the particular countries are broadly seen to have achieved macroeconomic stability.

In the context of the NEM such foreign flows on a large scale are welcomed. They are seen as mobilising external saving, which it is expected will mainly supplement domestic savings, and therefore raise investment and boost growth; they are also seen as contributing to smooth out expenditure over time (for example, if a country faces a sharp deterioration of its' 'terms of trade'); also, these flows are expected to increase the micro- efficiency of production, by causing lower intermediation spreads between lenders and borrowers. In the case of foreign direct investment flows, micro or sectoral efficiency is expected to be boosted by the transfer of technology and management know-how, which it is expected accompanies such direct foreign investment (DFI).

Most analysts have therefore welcomed the surge of private capital flows to Latin America in the 1990s and have used it as a key indicator or even proof of the success of the NEM. Williamson (1993) has cautioned that, particularly in the Latin American context, we should not equate access to external financing with success as on several occasions in the past the region had access to abundant financing for a time, only to end up in crisis. Unfortunately, warnings of the risk of volatility of capital flows to Latin America were dramatically confirmed by the Mexican crisis that started in December 1994.[1]

The introduction of the NEM (and particularly the liberalisation of domestic capital markets, of the capital account and the process of privatisation) created important pre-conditions for attracting foreign private capital, and is therefore an important determinant of the large surge of capital flows to the region in the first half of the 1990s. However, it must be stressed that international factors (and particularly relaxed US monetary policy and low US interest rates) played a very important role in these flows,[2] as have new global trends, such as the 'securitisation' of flows.[3] This raises the issue, as well as the danger, of potential volatility of such flows, and – more crucially – of the impact which such volatility will have on key macroeconomic variables in the medium-term. The Mexican crisis in 1994-5 illustrated the scale and the speed with which capital in the 1990s can move out of countries.

It is in this context that we shall examine the impact of external capital flows on income distribution and poverty. We shall distinguish in this analysis between a first phase, with massive capital inflows into the region, and a later stage, where there is uncertainty both about the sustainability of those flows and of their developmental impact. In the next section, I will outline the main features of the surge in capital flows to the Latin American region that have occurred in the early 1990s. I will also discuss in more detail some of the benefits, as well as the risks, of future instability in such flows. I shall then examine the mechanism by which these surges in capital flows influence income distribution and poverty. The last section provides conclusions and some policy recommendations.

The Surge in External Capital Flows to Latin America

The first feature of the capital flows to Latin America in the early 1990s was their massive scale. As can be seen in Table 1, for the 1992-93 period, they reached an annual average of around US$ 62 billion (if the 1990-93 period is considered, the annual average was $45 billion). This is in sharp contrast to what occurred during the 1983-90 period, when on average only US$ 10 billion of net capital entered the region as it faced its external debt crisis. The large scale of the net capital inflows is also reflected in its high proportion of GDP. For the 1992-93 period, net capital inflows reached 4.7% of GDP, which is slightly above the previous historical peak, at 4.5% in 1977-81, and well above the 1983-89 average of 1.3% of GDP (see again Table 1).

Particularly dramatic has been the sharp increase in flows to Mexico. Thus, net capital inflows into Mexico were slightly above zero in the 1983-90 period, but reached eight per cent of GDP for the 1991-93 period, a ratio well above the previous peak during 1977-81 (at 5% of GDP). Capital flows into Mexico also represented a very large part of total inflows into the region, absorbing over 50% of the capital inflows to the region in the 1990-93 period. Argentina has also been a very important recipient of capital in the early 1990s with levels of over 4% of GDP. Similarly, Chile, Peru and even some the of the smaller countries like Guatemala and Costa Rica have received very large capital inflows in the early 1990s.[4]

Table 1:
Net Capital Flows to Latin America (Annual Averages)

	Total net flows (US$ billion)						Percentage of GDP					
	1977 -81	1983 -89	1990	1991	1992	1993	1977 -81	1983 -89	1990	1991	1992	1993
Latin America	29.4	10.1	21.6	37.0	59.4	64.2	4.5	1.3	2.0	3.2	4.7	4.7
of which Mexico	8.2	0.8	11.6	21.9	24.7	28.5	5.1	0.3	4.8	7.6	7.5	8.3

Source: Ffrench-Davis and Griffith-Jones (1995)

A second significant trend in these capital flows into the region has been the change in their composition, as compared with the previous major inflow in the 1970s. As can be seen in Table 2, the share of DFI more than doubled between 1977-81 and 1989-92, portfolio equity emerged as a new source of finance, bonds also saw their share increase significantly (a trend which accelerated very much further in 1993, the year in which the region raised US $24 billion in bond finance – see Table 3), while the share of commercial bank lending fell sharply.

It is interesting to note that similar changes occurred in the structure of flows to the Asian countries. Their share of commercial bank lending fell, but far less dramatically than for Latin America; the share of portfolio equity increased, but only to 3.6% of total capital flows. On the other hand, the share of DFI flows to the Asian region rose faster, as did that of bonds (see again Table 2). The argument has been made that the different composition of capital inflows into Latin America and Asia have important effects on both the impact and reactions to such flows.[5] Thus, for example the different composition of capital flows, as well as the different historical stability in the evolution of such flows, helps to explain why concerns over 'hot money' and the risk of a sudden reversal are more prevalent among Latin American policy-makers than among their Asian counterparts.

Finally, an important point to make – and one which is often forgotten in discussions in Latin America itself – is that trends in capital flows to the Latin America region follow very closely global trends. In particular, the main dynamism for borrowing both by Latin American countries and globally comes from securities (both bonds and equities). On the other hand, syndicated loans (which were the main source of borrowing both globally and for Latin America in the 1970s) played a far smaller role in the early 1990s (compare Tables 3 and 4).

Table 2:
Latin America and Asia: Capital Flows(a)
(as a percentage of total, unless otherwise stated)

	1977-1981	1989-1992
Latin America		
Direct Foreign Investment	10.6	24.0
Portfolio Equity	-	6.3
Bonds	4.5	6.3
Commercial Bank Loans	66.9	14.7
Suppliers', and Export Credits	6.2	7.7
Official Loans	11.2	35.9
Grants	0.6	5.1
Total (in Billions of US Dollars)	49.5	42.8
Total (in Billions of Constant US Dollars)(b)	57.8	34.8
Asia		
Direct Foreign Investment	6.1	18.4
Portfolio Equity	-	3.6
Bonds	1.4	4.4
Commercial Bank Loans	32.1	23.5
Suppliers', and Export Credits	14.8	13.3
Official Loans	35.5	30.9
Grants	10.1	5.9
Total (in Billions of US Dollars)	23.2	66.5
Total (in Billions of Constant US Dollars)(b)	24.3	53.4

Notes:
(a) Gross long-term flows
(b) 1985 prices
Source: International Monetary Fund (1993)

A comparison of Tables 3 and 4 also shows that the increase in global international borrowing between 1989 and 1993 has been very large (it has almost doubled during those four years); clearly the growth of borrowing by Latin America has been far greater, and is therefore to an important extent explained by factors relating to the region; however, the fact that borrowing is also growing so rapidly globally would seem to indicate that at least in part the overall increase in Latin American international borrowing is responding to these global trends.

Table 3:
Borrowing by Latin American Countries (US$ billion)

Instruments	1989	1990	1991	1992	1993
Bonds	-	1.0	4.6	8.2	23.7
Equities(a)	-	-	4.4	4.5	5.5
Syndicated Loans	1.9	3.3	0.9	1.0	2.2
Committed Borrowing Facilities	0.1	-	2.8	0.3	-
Non-Underwritten Facilities(b)	-	-	1.2	6.1	6.8
Total	**2.0**	**4.3**	**13.9**	**20.1**	**38.2**
Latin American Countries as a percentage of total borrowing of LDCs	9.2	15.0	30.1	42.5	45.3

(a) New issues and initial public offerings of common and preferred shares
(b) Including Euro-commercial paper and medium-term note programmes

Source: OECD (1993/4); Vols. 54, 55 and 57; elaborated on the basis of the statistical annex.

The sudden surge in capital inflows, without initially having very positive effects, has brought to light an important policy dilemma as regards efforts to restore economies to growth. They have provided the financing needed to continue, in a more socially efficient way, the structural adjustment programmes initiated by several countries in the 1980s. However, they have posed a challenge as regards introducing safeguards designed to prevent them from triggering financial crises, guarantee the stability and sustainability of macroeconomic equilibria and promote investment.

Table 4:
Borrowings on the International Capital Markets (US$ billion)

	1989	1990	1991	1992	1993
Securities(a)	263.8	237.2	321.0	356.2	521.7
Loans	121.1	124.5	116.0	117.9	130.1
Committed Back-up Facilities	8.4	7.0	7.7	6.7	8.2
Non-Underwritten Facilities(b)	73.2	66.2	80.2	127.9	150.5
Total	466.5	434.9	524.9	609.7	810.5
Year-on-year change (%)	+2.8	-6.8	+20.7	+16.2	+32.9

(a) Includes both bonds and equities
(b) Including Euro-commercial paper and medium-term note programmes

Source: OECD (1993/4); Vols. 54 and 55

For the region as a whole, the entry of capital had positive Keynesian-type effects, in that it has reduced the foreign exchange constraint, enabling existing productive capacity to be used more fully and production, incomes and employment to pick up as a result. The lifting of the external constraint, which was the dominant restriction to growth during the 1980s, from the beginning of the 1990s contributed to the recovery of economic growth, whose annual rate for the region increased from 1.6% in 1983-90 to 3.4% in 1991-93 (see Table 5).[6]

The recovery of output was based largely on the fact that the greater availability of foreign savings has made it possible to finance the higher imports associated with an increased use of existing productive capacity; this, through its effect on output and income, reactivated aggregate demand. The expansionary effect was general throughout the region, and particularly strong for some countries (for example, Argentina and Chile); nevertheless, there were exceptions. Thus Mexico, while experiencing a particularly large influx of private capital, did not see such a recovery of growth during the period. The extent to which private capital inflows lead to growth is greatly influenced by the existing gap between actual GDP and productive capacity, the nature of domestic economic policies, particularly macroeconomic ones, expectations of economic agents, political developments, and external factors such as the terms of trade and levels of debt service.

Table 5:
Latin America: Macroeconomic Indicators (in percentages)

	1976-81	1983-90	1991-93	1991	1992	1993
Rate of Growth of GDP (1980 US$)	4.6	1.6	3.4	3.8	3.0	3.4
Investment as percentage of GDP	24.2	16.9	17.5	16.6	18.1	17.9
External savings (net capital inflows minus change in reserves) as % of GDP	3.9	0.9	3.1	1.8	3.2	4.0

Source: ECLAC (1994)

Net capital inflows surged after 1990, reaching an annual average of around US $53.5 billion in 1991-93 (see again Table 1). About half of these net inflows in 1991 went to build up depleted international reserves; this share steadily decreased to 30% in 1993, *pari passu* with the increased absorptive capacity of the region.

It was not until 1992, however, that the investment rate for the whole region achieved a level above the 1983-90 average (see Table 5). In all, if we compare 1983-90 with 1991-93, net external savings (capital flows minus the increase in reserves) rose by slightly above two per cent of GDP, while the investment ratio increased only by 0.6 percent of GDP. The remainder has gone to consumption or to compensate worsening terms of trade.

The speed with which capital inflows closed the external gap and generated a surplus of foreign funds was reflected in a tendency towards exchange rate appreciation, a rapid reduction in trade surpluses and an increase in the current account deficit (see ECLAC, 1994c). These trends reflected, initially, the recovery of 'normal' levels of aggregate demand, imports and the real exchange rate, all of which were conditioned by external constraints during the period 1983-89. However, the continuing abundance of capital tended to maintain these trends over time, and confronted the economic authorities with a dilemma crucial to future stability in that, if capital inflows fall, the levels of aggregate demand and imports and the exchange rate clearly would not be sustainable in the medium-term.

During 1991-93 a larger proportion of capital inflows was devoted to the accumulation of reserves than in the 1970s, thereby moderating the impact of these resources on the region's economies; national savings were crowded out by external savings, as reflected in the fact that the increase in total investment was lower than that in external savings (see Table 5). Thus, the short-term or

Keynesian effect of this surge in capital flows was reflected in a short-term rise in the growth rate, caused by a reduction of the foreign exchange constraint and higher demand for locally produced goods. Furthermore, the surge in foreign finance allowed domestic spending to increase faster than output. However, it needs to be stressed that, to the extent that the foreign capital inflow is temporary, this Keynesian boom is also temporary. Once – and if – an external financial crisis starts, investment and growth of output falls, debt servicing grows, and the rate of growth – or the level – of national income could fall even more than output (see Corden, 1990).

This short-term Keynesian effect of surges in capital inflows needs to be carefully distinguished from the second, more long-term effect, which is on the growth of capacity. The proportion of the external flows going to investment is crucial in this second type of effect (how productive such investment is, and what proportion of it is – directly and/or indirectly – converted into tradeables). If enough efficient investment takes place and output rises sufficiently (and is converted into tradeables), it is more likely that future debt service or other flows generated by the original inflows can be financed without a problem. Indeed, it will have increased the rate of growth and made the country better off. If foreign capital not only increases investment, but also raises its productivity, the long-term positive effects on growth could be even larger.

However, there is also a less rosy scenario. If increased investment proves insufficient or inefficient, and if not enough production of tradeables is generated, then the initial output growth may be followed by a debt problem, leading possibly to reductions in total absorption, below levels that could have been sustained in the absence of the earlier surge. Thus, in this negative scenario, the total effect (through time) of the surge in capital flows on countries' retained income could be negative, even if the Keynesian effect on output was initially positive.

Though it is still rather early to evaluate the impact of such flows on productive capacity, the preliminary macroeconomic evidence presented above does give cause for concern, as the increase in the investment rate has been smaller than the growth of external savings (see Table 5). The results, however, vary from country to country, and some countries (notably Chile) have seen their rate of investment increase significantly in the early 1990s.

Furthermore, for some countries (especially those which have very over-valued exchanged rates, resulting to an important extent from the capital surge itself and the form in which the government's economic policy has reacted to such a surge), there are some indications that only a relatively low share of the investment linked to foreign capital inflows is going into tradeables. This is a second cause of concern, and it is also an area where far better monitoring and data collection is urgently required.

The benefits of interaction with private capital flows for the development of recipient economies is partly dependent on stable and predictable access to financial markets. The risk of abrupt restrictions in supply and/or inordinately sharp increases in cost and shortening of the maturity terms of external liabilities are partly determined by perceptions of risk and hence host country policies. But from the standpoint of Latin America economies access can also be heavily conditioned by exogenously determined supply-side dynamics, related to industrialised country policies in the areas of macroeconomics and prudential regulation.

As the Mexican 1994/5 crisis illustrated, there are considerable risks of volatility regarding the new financial flows of the 1990s. First, there is a degree of consensus that one driving force behind the new inflow of capital in the early 1990s was exogenously based in the relaxation of monetary policy in the OECD area, and a consequent dramatic decline in international interest rates, especially US ones. The increased differential yields on investments in the region attracted investors who had become accustomed to a decade of relatively high real interest rates in the low-risk OECD area. Moreover, given the special conjunctural setting in Latin America – recovery from a deep and protracted recession and especially profitable opportunities, linked to privatisations – investors were able to capture high returns, with low information costs, as the need to discriminate among countries and firms was not at first important. Significant rises in international interest rates, as occurred in 1994, induced a reversal in the flow of some of the less committed investors.

A major source of the new flows to Latin America are bonds (see Table 3). These have the advantage of being mainly at fixed interest rates. However, the average maturity for those bonds in the 1990s is very short (around four years). This implies that a high share of the stock could be rapidly withdrawn, should bonds not be renewed. The problem was far more serious in Mexico, where a high proportion of Treasury Bills was both very short-term and in the hands of non-residents; this made the problem of non-renewal of these Bills a major one during the financial crisis. Less dramatic, but also a cause of concern, is the risk that, if renewal of bonds is possible but with higher interest rates, the average cost of borrowing would increase significantly as maturities are so short.

A new form of external private funding for Latin America is equity investment. This has the advantage that dividends are cyclically sensitive. However, equity flows also carry important risks for recipient countries. Foreign financiers could, for different reasons, stop investing in equities, and even try to sell their stocks very quickly, if they feared a worsening prospect in the country. This could either lead to pressure on the exchange rate and/or lead to price falls in the domestic stock exchange. Though the latter effect would diminish the risk of a large foreign exchange outflow, it could have a negative impact on aggregate demand – via a wealth effect – and on the domestic financial system, especially if banks and firms dealing in securities are closely integrated through cross-holdings or investor leveraging. To the extent that a growing part of foreign investment in Latin American shares originate in institutional investors, who seem to allocate their assets using more long-term criteria, the risk of large reversals of flows is smaller. But as long as markets are moved to an important extent by players who specialise in short-term yields, and equity markets remain relatively thin, the risks of great volatility are inherent in this new form of external financing.

The Likely Impact of Capital Surges on Income Distribution and Poverty

Methodological Issues

The evaluation of the impact of capital surges (CS) on income distribution and poverty involves several conceptual problems, most of which are similar to those encountered in other chapters in this volume. As in the analysis of the 'new trade regime' in Chapter 2, the analysis of the impact of capital surges (CS) is complex and hard to observe (as several changes are occurring simultaneously); furthermore, the analysis is made more complex because the impact is both on the 'primary' income distribution and on the redistributive mechanisms, which affect 'secondary' income distribution; also, it would be too complex and possibly too biased by the theoretical approach used by the author, to model the impact of CS *via* simulation models that compare the economies with and without CS and their impact on income distribution. Finally, the lags between CS and their distributional consequences vary considerably. In fact, this is particularly true for the case of capital surges, where we will distinguish two phases for our analysis: a) the current phase of the initial capital surge and its impact and b) the following future phase which, as we shall analyse below, can imply either 'rosy' or 'grey/black' scenarios. The fact that part of our analysis will be based on likely future developments increases the complexity and uncertainty of their impact on income distribution and poverty. To reduce this uncertainty, we first rely on alternative scenarios; secondly, our analysis of the 'grey/black' scenario is made somewhat 'easier' by our knowledge of the impact of the debt crisis of the 1980s on income distribution and poverty.[7]

First phase

The capital inflows in the first phase have two types of major effects on the primary distribution of income. First, as already outlined, a reduction in the foreign exchange constraint has allowed an increase in the demand for locally produced goods; this has led to an increase in output (the expenditure increasing effect). In fact, Latin America's GDP grew 3.1% in the 1991-93 period, which is higher than the 0.9% growth rate of GDP during the debt crisis years of 1983-90. The share of imports in GDP rose from 9.0% in the 1983-89 period to around 12.0% in the 1990-92 period (ECLAC 1994). As a result of more rapid output growth, existing productive capacity has been used more fully, and both employment and real wages grew; therefore, the income of the poor would be expected to rise quite significantly due to this factor. Indeed, there is evidence that the increase in employment will particularly benefit the poorest. In most Latin American countries, the people in the bottom quintile are far more likely to be unemployed than the average, and therefore will benefit more from employment growth.[8] Secondly, the capital inflows have an expenditure switching effect – due to a revaluation of the exchange rate. Indeed, according to ECLAC (1994a), of *eighteen* countries in the Latin American and Caribbean region, *sixteen* experienced exchange rate appreciation between 1990 and mid-1994.

The extent of the appreciation varies significantly from country to country, depending on the magnitude and composition of the capital inflows, on other trends in the balance of payments, and on the policy response of governments to their inflows. To a certain extent, this shows that there are quite significant variations within the NEM. Thus, some countries (exemplified by the case of Argentina) have chosen a more pure market approach to capital inflows following the path of what is called non-sterilised intervention. This involves a more passive monetary policy, and a tendency towards greater revaluation of the exchange rate. Other countries (for example, Chile) have followed a more active stance, including sterilised intervention, which allows the country to have a more active monetary policy, thus avoiding excessive expansion of aggregate demand and excessive appreciation of the real exchange rate. A more active policy stance can also include measures to restrict or discourage certain capital inflows, for example *via* reserve requirements on some credits from abroad and various quantitative controls (e.g. minimum maturity periods, minimum volume for bond issues).

It is interesting to note in this context that, although large capital inflows are seen as – and to an extent are – a key favourable outcome of the NEM, they also (especially if not properly managed) pose an essential contradiction by putting pressure on revaluation of the exchange rate which, if excessive, may discourage exports – a key aspect of the model. Thus, an exchange rate revaluation, caused in this case by financial 'Dutch disease', that is a surge of capital inflows, will make exports less profitable. This may have negative long-term effects on output (and on the income of the poor), as it may discourage investment in exports, and thus undermine the logic of the model which is based on export-led growth, and needs to generate exports to help service the capital that is flowing in. Furthermore, if an overvalued exchange rate leads to a rapidly growing current account deficit, and if external capital becomes – as is likely – unwilling to fund this deficit, the resulting crisis, if it occurs, is very damaging for the poor (see below).

As regards the distribution of income in the short-term, the bias against exports will bring about changes in the demand for factors of production. If the exportable sector is relatively labour-intensive, as in Costa Rica,[9] then a revaluation of the exchange rate will have a negative effect on income distribution and poverty. However, if the exportable sector is relatively less labour-intensive than the rest of the economy, as in the case of Brazil, there can be a positive effect on income distribution from the switch in demand for factors of production.

A real revaluation of the exchange rate also reduces the cost of imports. Because this implies a reduction in the price of some wage goods, and because more generally this will lead to lower inflation, real wages can be expected to increase as a result of these inflows. As wages are a significantly higher proportion of the income of the lower decile strata, this will imply an improvement in income distribution and a reduction in poverty.[10]

Capital inflows can also be expected to have an effect on the income derived from capital. For example, the liberalisation of domestic capital markets and privatisation (which are an important part of the NEM) has already led to an important expansion of the stock market, as well as to increases in the prices of these stocks; however, the massive entry of foreign equity flows in the early 1990s (both by foreigners purchasing shares locally and by the placement of Latin American shares in New York and globally) has greatly accelerated this trend. As a result, capital inflows caused share prices to rise significantly. As the ownership of shares is very concentrated amongst the top deciles, and as such an important share of the income of the top deciles is derived from income from capital in Latin America, this could have an important effect on increasing the income of the rich and the concentration of income.

To the extent that large capital inflows lead to a significant reduction in real interest rates (which seems to be the case in some Latin American countries, such as Mexico, though falls in real interest rates are smaller than conventional theory would lead us to expect – see Rodríguez, 1994), this will imply a smaller return on financial savings. As this income will tend to be concentrated amongst the upper deciles (though perhaps somewhat less than in the case of stocks and shares), the decline in interest rates should reduce income disparities. It is noteworthy in this context that, as Rodríguez (1994) shows, though deposit interest rates (expressed in dollar equivalent) have declined in the late eighties and early nineties in Latin American countries, their level remains fairly high (with the exception of Chile). Indeed, for 1992, the average for Argentina,

Bolivia, Chile, Colombia, Mexico, Peru and Uruguay was 8.1%, with several countries having interest rates above 10% (see also Table A.10).

Finally, it should be mentioned that, especially initially, an important part of the private capital flowing in was return of domestic capital that had previously fled. To the extent that average returns on capital are currently higher in Latin America than in other parts of the world (e.g. the USA), this would imply increased concentration of income, as the income of the rich capital returners would rise. However, the fact that the income would now be taxed domestically, rather than abroad (this capital whilst abroad may not have been taxed at all or may have been taxed at a lower rate), may reduce *post*-tax income on this capital. Furthermore, if the increased tax is spent by governments in a progressive manner (that favours the relatively poor), then the return of capital would reduce income inequality somewhat.

In introducing the impact of taxes and government expenditure, we are examining secondary income distribution. Perhaps the most important effect in this category relates to the impact of the surge in capital flows on government spending. As mentioned above, one of the effects of foreign capital inflows is the lowering of domestic real interest rates. In particular, domestic government debt can on the whole be placed at lower real interest rates, as the supply of savings is increased *via* foreign capital. Furthermore, this coincides with the lowering of the level of the external debt that occurred in Latin America as a result of the Brady deals in the late eighties and early nineties, and the decline in US interest rates; as a result, government servicing of external debt also declined significantly. Furthermore, to the extent that debt equity swaps were used to sell shares in state enterprises abroad (which was quite common in countries like Argentina and Mexico), again government debt service requirements were lowered as a direct result of foreign capital inflows.

There is clear evidence (see Cornia and Stewart, 1990) that in the 1980s the increase in debt service payments (both domestic and external) within government budgets displaced resources from spending on the social sectors, that is on spending that benefits mainly the poor. This was general throughout Latin America, but particularly dramatic in Mexico. The trends described above for the early 1990s – to an important extent caused by large foreign capital inflows – led to a significant reduction in the proportion of government spending going to external and domestic debt servicing. As a result, potentially there was room for fairly large increases in spending on the social sectors (e.g. education, health, low income housing) that benefit relatively more the poorer sections of society. There is indeed evidence that the share of government spending on the social sectors began to increase in the early 1990s; It is too early to say, however, if this trend has been reversed as a result of the fall in capital inflow after the Mexican crisis of 1994/5.

On balance, it would seem that the impact of capital surges reduces income inequality and poverty *ceteris paribus* with the most important effect probably being created by the Keynesian recovery of output, employment and real wages, but with significant positive effects also derived from the indirect positive impact on greater government spending in the social sectors. One effect of capital inflows that does lead to greater income concentration, however, is the impact of such inflows on capital gains in financial asset markets.

Second phase

As mentioned above, it is also important to analyse the impact of the second phase of CS, especially because both history and economic analysis show us that there is no guarantee that such large inflows can be sustained. We will therefore distinguish two scenarios. In the first, 'rosy' scenario, a number of conditions have to be met: the foreign flows are mainly channelled to increase investment (and therefore domestic savings does not fall too much), a high proportion of investment goes into tradeables, this investment is efficient and no major external shocks occur or, if they do occur, the economy is assumed to be able to adjust to them; finally, external capital flows need to be sustained at current levels or taper off relatively slowly.

In this 'rosy scenario', output continues to rise, and the exchange rate ceases to appreciate (if flows taper off slowly, there would be a gradual devaluation). Income distribution would consequently continue to improve and poverty to decline, as the *status quo ante* continues.

However, as discussed above, there is unfortunately the risk of a less favourable outcome, the 'grey/black' scenario, exemplified by events in Mexico in late 1994 and early 1995. This would occur if too small a part of the foreign flows leads to an increase in investment and too low a proportion of that investment goes into production of tradeables; this could lead to an insufficient increase in the production of tradeables to allow foreign exchange to be available for debt servicing and/or profit remittances to take place. The situation could be made more serious if this trend interacted with an abrupt reduction or even a large reversal of capital inflows. The outcome of this latter scenario (including its impact on income distribution) would naturally depend on how the situation unravelled, which in turn would be related to the speed and the timing of events, and the mechanisms used by governments to handle any balance of payments problems/crises that occurred. We can, however, reach some tentative conclusions, and attempt to analyse their likely impact on income distribution and poverty.

In this 'grey' or 'black' scenario, there would first be an expenditure reduction effect that would imply a reduction in output, employment and in real wages. Declines in output, wages and employment will tend to be highest in companies that are heavily indebted (as interest rates rise sharply) and in those that sell mainly or exclusively in the domestic market; on the other hand, wages and employment in firms producing tradeables may rise especially in firms that were not heavily indebted. The history of the 1980s seems to show how in such critical situations, the poorer groups of the society are less able to protect themselves from the direct and indirect effects of adjustment.

Secondly, there would be an expenditure switching effect, as the response to a sharp reduction or reversal of capital inflows would be a devaluation of the exchange rate. This would lead to higher inflation. Both trends would tend to make income distribution more unequal. In particular, higher and more variable inflation is widely deemed to have a regressive effect on income distribution (see Chapter 5, Table 4). The impact of the devaluation on income distribution and poverty will also naturally depend on whether the export sector is more or less labour-intensive than the average. Here the inverse of the analysis made above for revaluation applies.

Thirdly, there could again be an important negative impact due to : a) a reduction in the level of government spending (related to the adjustment), and b) a reduction of the proportion of it spent on the social sectors. As regards the latter, the reduction in capital inflows or their reversal will tend to increase domestic interest rates and, thus, the servicing of public domestic debt. Devaluation will further increase the local currency cost of government servicing of external debt. This can also be increased if the government has *ex-post* to guarantee (or take over) part of the private external debt. Furthermore, if there is some kind of domestic financial crisis (or risk of it) linked to the abrupt change in foreign flows – particularly if these affect the domestic banking system, either directly or indirectly – then it is likely that the government may be involved in some bail-out of the domestic financial sector. As a result, governments would be forced to reduce spending on the social sectors, as both the level of government spending and the share of it 'available' for social spending would fall, increasing inequality and poverty in the process. Income from capital would also suffer to the extent that smaller inflows and/or outflows would very probably cause a fall (and possibly a sharp one) in the prices of shares. This could diminish income inequality. However, the likely increases in domestic real interest rates would augment the income of owners of capital.

On balance, a rapid outflow or even a reversal of external capital flows would tend to increase income inequality and, above all, poverty. These effects would be particularly strong if the previous inflow had not led to a significant increase in investment in tradeables, as higher levels of tradeables (and as a consequence a favourable trade account) could shelter the economy (and the poor) somewhat from shocks on the capital account.

Conclusions

Our analysis shows that the initial impact of the surge in capital flows to Latin America on income distribution and poverty is likely to have been positive. This is mainly because of the short-term Keynesian effect, that allows – as the foreign constraint is lifted – for higher output, employment and real wages. The revaluation of the exchange rate further allows for an increase in real wages; its medium-term impact on income distribution is less clear, as it depends on the relative labour-intensity of tradeables. The greater room for manoeuvre of governments to increase spending on the social sectors, partly made possible by changes brought about by the capital inflows, should also make income distribution more equal and lessen poverty; a similar effect should arise from lower real interest rates. One contrary effect – leading to greater concentration of income – is the significant increase in the price of stocks and shares associated with capital inflows as shares are owned mainly by the rich in Latin America.

Although the short-term impact on income distribution and poverty of the capital surges to the region seems positive, there are serious concerns about the medium-term. Unless these flows lead to increased investment in tradeables, and unless they are sustained or taper off only slowly, they seem to pose serious risks for the sustainability of the short-run growth that they have helped to generate. Should growth falter, or even worse, output fall as result of a serious balance of payments crisis, then the effects on the poor and on income distribution can be very negative.

A great deal seems to depend on how Latin American governments manage these capital surges. In the short-term, these flows seem to provide a valuable increase in the range of manoeuvre for governments to increase spending on social sectors, particularly that targeted on the poorest groups in the society. It is important that governments take this opportunity and that international institutions encourage them to do so.

Governments also face the challenge to follow policies that maximise the favourable impact of capital surges, as well as minimise the risk that future volatility of capital flows could lead to damaging foreign exchange crises. This requires in several cases striking a complex, sophisticated and pragmatic balance in economic policy. The challenges include: a) the appropriate management of macro-economic policy to sustain growth and avoid both excessive over-valuation of the exchange rate and excessive growth of aggregate demand; b) the management of capital account liberalisation, allowing economies the benefits particularly of long-term capital inflows, but protecting them from the volatility of short-term inflows (the latter can, where appropriate, include the need to regulate or discourage such short-term flows); c) deepening of capital markets in ways that encourage higher productive investment, particularly by smaller and medium-size enterprises, and d) greater prudential regulation of the financial system to protect it from external – or internal – shocks. This implies in particular broadening regulations to cover new developments linked to rapid capital surges. Finally, as an appropriate basis for action, governments need to monitor capital inflows and their impact on the domestic economy (both macro and micro-economic) carefully, so they have precise information on which to base their policy decisions.

There is growing evidence and acceptance that the impact of capital flows is most beneficial in the medium and long-term in those countries where governments use a wide range of policy instruments to manage such flows, and thus avoid serious distortions of key macroeconomic variables such as the exchange rate. This wide range of instruments includes both conventional measures (such as improving the fiscal position and liberalising imports as well as capital outflows) and less conventional measures (such as measures to discourage short-term capital inflows like the reserve requirements and taxes which were, for example, applied by the Chilean economic authorities). Though clearly not a panacea, measures to discourage short-term capital flows can be a valuable ingredient in a policy package to manage capital flows in a way that: a) maximises long-term benefits for growth; b) maintains competitiveness, essential for the success of the NEM and c) avoids financial crisis, which are so costly to the economy as a whole, but particularly so for the poorest sectors in the population.

Notes

* I wish to thank Professor Sir Hans Singer for his comments on an earlier draft of this chapter.

1. See Ffrench-Davis and Griffith-Jones (1995).
2. See Calvo, Leiderman and Reinhart (1993).
3. See Griffith-Jones (1995).
4. See ECLAC (1994c).
5. See Calvo, Leiderman and Reinhart (1993); Griffith-Jones and Stallings (1995).
6. The contribution to growth of capital flows would have been higher, if a deterioration in the terms of trade had not occurred during that period.
7. See, for example, Cornia and Stewart (1990).
8. On the profile of the poor in Latin America, see Fiszbein and Psacharopoulos (1995).
9. For a case study of Costa Rica, in which the exchange rate plays a key role, see Morley (1995), Chapter 5.
10. This may not be true of the bottom decile. See Chapter 1.

PART II

CASE STUDIES

CHAPTER 7

THE DISTRIBUTIVE IMPACT OF THE NEW ECONOMIC MODEL IN CHILE

Christopher Scott*

As compared to the other case studies, the Chilean experience is characterised by two distinctive features. First, the transition to the New Economic Model (NEM) began at a much earlier date. This can be fixed precisely to the immediate aftermath of the military coup which overthrew the Popular Unity government in September 1973. Secondly, and largely as a result of the country being ruled by a military dictatorship, the reforms which put in place the NEM in Chile were implemented at a speed and with a scope and ideological coherence which is unparalleled in Latin America. The new model constituted a major rupture with the former politico-economic regime of democratic government characterised by extensive state intervention in the economy, and its successful introduction represents a major discontinuity in Chilean history.

Because the country has such a long experience with the NEM, it is essential to begin by reviewing the evolution of macroeconomic policy in Chile during the last twenty years. This is the purpose of the next section which distinguishes two periods of economic development since 1974, encompassing the double transition made by the Chilean economy.[1] The first transition from a socialist to a neoliberal political economy was complete in Chile by the mid-1980s. The second transition, whereby a neoliberal economy passes from the control of a military to a democratic government, ended in 1990.

The third section of the chapter examines how well Chile has matched up to three characteristics of the NEM since 1974: (i) a commitment to macroeconomic stability; (ii) greater openness on both current and capital accounts of the balance of payments, and (iii) a more limited role for the state in the national economy. The priority assigned by the Pinochet regime (1974-90) and the Aylwin administration (1990-94) to the alleviation of poverty is also compared and evaluated.

The fourth section of the chapter identifies four sets of transmission mechanisms between the NEM and the distribution of income. These include (i) the redistribution of assets and liabilities between and within the public and private sectors; (ii) the process of macroeconomic adjustment; (iii) the social expenditure reforms, and (iv) the transmission mechanisms associated with the NEM in steady-state growth.

The fifth section examines changes in poverty and income inequality since 1974. The analysis is conducted at four levels of aggregation: national, regional, sectoral and for Greater Santiago. Finally, some conclusions are drawn regarding the extent to which changes in the Chilean income distribution since 1974 may be attributed to the effects of the NEM.

An Overview of Economic Policy in Chile, 1974-1994

The establishment of the NEM in Chile has resulted from a long process of learning-by-doing which began in 1974. The top priority of the military government after seizing power was to reduce the rate of inflation, which exceeded 600% in 1973. To this end the budget deficit was cut savagely from 25% of GDP in 1973 to only 1% by 1975. Between 1976 and 1981, the regime achieved a budget surplus. This rapid improvement in public sector finances was attained by a drastic reduction in government expenditure, while the elimination of most subsidies increased net tax revenue. An accelerated programme of privatisation contributed to reducing the budget deficit by eliminating the fiscal cost of covering the large operating losses of many state-owned firms, of which there were more than 500 in September 1973. By 1980, only 43 firms remained in the public sector.

At the same time as the stabilisation programme was being implemented, a drastic liberalisation of markets was undertaken. This made it more difficult to lower inflation in the short-run. The reduction of tariffs to a uniform rate of 10% decreased government revenue, while the elimination of subsidies and lifting of price controls put upward pressure on the general price level. This problem was made more acute when the exchange rate system was unified and a large real devaluation was implemented.

Despite the adoption of both a tight fiscal and monetary policy, which led domestic real interest rates to rise above 50% *per annum*, the rate of disinflation was deemed too slow. Consequently, it was decided in mid-1979 to fix the nominal exchange rate against the US dollar as an anti-inflationary measure. This proved to be a fateful decision.

Between 1982 and 1983, Chile experienced the most severe economic crisis since the 1930s. Domestic demand fell by 24%, domestic output was reduced by 14% and open unemployment rose to 20% of the labour force with another 10% enrolled on public employment programmes (Bosworth *et al*, 1994a, p. 8). GDP continued to fall in 1983 before recovering in 1984.

The severity of this recession is crucial for understanding the growth performance of the Chilean economy in the last decade. In 1984, the margin of underutilised capacity represented approximately 22% of actual GDP (Dornbusch and Edwards, 1994, p.82). This allowed rapid growth to occur during the period while the investment ratio remained relatively low. Only by 1989 had the economy returned close to full capacity utilisation.

The causes of the crisis were both external and internal. The country's foreign debt had accumulated to an unsustainable level as a result of a deterioration in the terms of trade, the rise in foreign interest rates and a drying up of external commercial loans in early 1982. However, Chile's vulnerability to external shocks had been increased by the adoption of a fixed nominal exchange rate (in mid-1979) while wages continued to be compulsorily indexed at 100% of past inflation. This led to a sharp appreciation of the real exchange rate with a consequent loss of competitiveness by Chilean exports.

The foreign debt had been accumulated largely by the private sector in response to the radical liberalisation of domestic capital markets without proper supervision and regulation. Financial intermediaries in Chile were able to borrow abroad at negative real interest rates (after adjusting for inflation) for much of the period between 1979 and 1982, while lending domestically at real interest rates which averaged 15% in 1979-80 and 39% in 1981 (Bosworth *et al*, 1994a, p. 7). Despite this incentive to cut real consumption, domestic savings had fallen to a low of 1.6% of GDP by 1982.

Owing to the severity of the crisis, the government was forced to reverse its previous policy stance in several key areas. The nominal exchange rate was devalued in 1982 and 1983, which resulted in a 49% real devaluation between 1981 and 1983 (Palma, 1995, p. 13). The average nominal tariff rate rose from 10% in mid-1979 to 20% in early 1983 and to 35% by late 1984 (Palma, 1995, p. 9). Selective protection of domestic foodstuffs was established as price supports were introduced for certain agricultural importables such as wheat and sugar. A large number of firms on the verge of bankruptcy were taken into the public sector, and the state took over the private external debt.

The economic crisis of 1982-83 might have induced a less confident and determined government to reconsider its long-term development strategy. However, this refusal to be knocked off course because of policy errors led to the consolidation of a revised NEM during the last six years of the military government (1984-1990).

After some vacillation, a pragmatic and consistent macroeconomic policy emerged in 1985. This had two main features: a sustained depreciation of the real exchange rate and a tight fiscal policy. The use of a fixed exchange rate as a nominal anchor to reduce inflation was abandoned in favour of a crawling peg to keep Chilean exports competitive. Unlike the *tablita* system adopted between 1978 and mid-1979, whereby fixed depreciations of the nominal exchange rate were preannounced, the new policy was passive and retroactive. The nominal exchange rate was adjusted *ex post* by (slightly more than) the difference between inflation rates in Chile and in its major trading partners. The cumulative effect of this policy was to achieve a real depreciation of 52% between 1984 and 1990 (Corbo and Fischer,1994, pp. 32-3). This was crucial to explaining the rapid growth of exports during the period.[2]

The Pinochet administration was able to sustain real devaluations over so long a period without increasing inflation for two reasons. First, the tightening of fiscal policy transformed a public sector deficit of 9.1% of GDP in 1984 into a public sector surplus of 1.2% of GDP in 1989.[3] Secondly, the elimination of wage indexation in 1982 and the persistence of high unemployment until 1987 reduced both the inertial element in inflation and any upward pressure on nominal wage rates which would have caused a real appreciation *via* an increase in the price of non-traded goods.

In 1985, a second round of privatisation was begun as firms that had been nationalised during the 1982-83 crisis were sold off by the state. A process of tariff reduction was initiated with average nominal tariff levels falling from 35% in late 1984 to 30% in 1985 and 15% in 1988. The financial system was reconstructed with the Central Bank having a stronger regulatory role. The government also introduced several debt conversion schemes such as debt-equity swaps which reduced the foreign debt by around 50% (Bosworth *et al*,1994a, pp. 9,14). These capital market reforms, together with the introduction of private pension schemes and a general recovery in business confidence, prompted a strong recovery in the domestic savings rate which rose from 2.9% of GDP in 1984 to a record 25.8% in 1994 (PET,1992, p. 18; EIU,1995a, p. 5).

In December 1989, President Aylwin of the Christian Democratic party was elected President of Chile and in March 1990 a broad coalition of centre-left parties (*Concertación*) came to power. The civilian government introduced two reform measures in its first year, but otherwise retained the policy stance of the military regime.[4] First, additional tax revenue was raised to fund new social programmes. Value Added Tax (VAT) was raised by two percentage points to 18%, and corporate income tax was increased from 10% of distributed profits to 15% of total profits. Revenue from personal income tax was increased by lowering the income threshold above which higher marginal tax rates applied (EIU,1994, p. 15).

Secondly, certain aspects of labour legislation decreed by former President Pinochet were reformed (García,1993, p. 139). The procedure for firing workers was modified to require employers to give a 'sound reason' (*causa fundada*), such as technological innovations or a change in market conditions, before sacking employees. Severance payments were increased and the formation of unions was made easier,while the range of issues subject to union-employer bargaining was extended (García,1993, p. 139).

The combination of a return to democratic rule and the tightening of the labour-market already noticeable in the late 1980s, led to an increase in real wages of 1.8% in 1990, 4.9% in 1991, 4.5 % in 1992, 4.2% in 1993 and 5% in 1994 (Velasco, 1994, p. 399; EIU, 1994, p. 19; EIU, 1995, p. 15). This, together with a rapid growth in capital inflows, precipitated a real exchange rate *appreciation* between 1990 and 1994 (see Table A.6).

The New Economic Model: A Characterisation and Some Simple Tests

The NEM has three defining characteristics: (i) a commitment to macroeconomic stability; (ii) greater openness on both current and capital accounts of the balance of payments, and (iii) a more limited role for the state in the national economy. In some quarters, the NEM is defined by a fourth element, namely a commitment to combat poverty more effectively (World Bank,1993a, p. 24). However, such a commitment is best viewed as a contingent feature of the NEM rather than as one of its constituent elements. Consequently, the priority assigned by the Pinochet regime (1974-90) and the Aylwin administration (1990-94) to the alleviation of poverty is compared and evaluated below.

This section of the chapter tests for the presence of these characteristics in Chile's economic development during the last twenty years. Various methods are employed for this purpose. Where secondary data exist in an appropriate form, they are used to evaluate the null hypothesis that a particular characteristic of the NEM is absent after 1974. Where such data are unavailable, certain primary indicators for each characteristic are chosen in order to establish by regression analysis whether the level and/or the annual rate of change in these indicators varied significantly between 1960-1973 and 1974-1992.

Chile's experience of inflation between 1940 and 1994 is shown in Table 1, which has three features worthy of comment. First, inflation remained persistently high during the first decade after the military coup, despite elimination of the public sector deficit. It took eight years to bring inflation down to the levels observed in the 1960s. While the commitment of the Pinochet administration to reducing inflation during the 1970s was never in doubt, the strength of inertial factors in the labour market (due to backward-looking indexation) together with the cumulative effects of supply shocks arising from the radical liberalisation programme (particularly in the capital market) delayed the achievement of price stability.

Secondly, between 1984 and 1992 when the NEM was consolidated and the country undertook the transition to democratic government, the annual inflation rate averaged 20% – the lowest figure in Chile since the 1940s. This achieve-

Table 1:
Inflation and Economic Growth in Chile, 1940-1994

	Average Annual Inflation Rate (%) (a)	Average Annual Inflation Rate among the Poor (%) (a)	Average Annual Growth Rate (%) (a)	Average Annual Fiscal Deficit (-) or Surplus (+) (% GDP) (b)
1940-53	18.1	-	3.84	-0.70
1953-58	48.3	-	2.23	-2.65
1959-64	27.1	-	4.33	-4.57
1965-70	27.3	-	5.07	-2.53
1971-73	295.9	-	1.20	-11.50
1974-83	115.5		1.65	+0.77
	87.3 (c)	115.3 (c)	1.65	+0.77
1984-92	20.0 (d)		6.21	+1.54
	20.4 (e)	21.7		
1993	12.2 (e)	10.2	6.00	+2.10
1994	8.9 (d)	-	4.20	+1.80

Notes:
(a) Arithmetic mean for the period
(b) Refers to central government only, so excludes state enterprises and local/regional governments
(c)1975-83. Both the official (INE) and the CIEPLAN (Cortazar/Marshall) inflation rates are measured annually from December to December. The inflation rate of the poor is calculated from September to September.
(d) December to December
(e) September to September
- = not available

Sources:
All data for period 1940-92, except inflation rate of poor, from Velasco (1994, p. 381), Table 8-1. Inflation rate of poor from PET (1994, p. 210). Both inflation rates and growth for 1993 from PET (1994, p.204,210). Fiscal surplus in 1993 from IDB (1994, p. 253). Inflation and growth rates for 1994 from Monthly Bulletin of Central Bank, March 1995. Fiscal surplus for 1994 from The Economist, 3 June 1995, p.20.

ment was at least partly the result of running a fiscal surplus over the same period which averaged 1.5 % of GDP. This was unparalleled in modern Chilean history since all other governments since 1940 have generated fiscal deficits.

At the same time, economic growth exceeded six per cent *per annum* which is the highest figure attained in forty years. This achievement of macroeconomic stability and high growth fulfilled a major objective of the NEM, and is an important indicator of the model's success in Chile since 1984. However, the high level of underutilised capacity existing in the economy in 1983-84 made this objective easier to attain than if full employment had existed at the beginning of the period.

Thirdly, the inflation rate among the poor was significantly higher than the average inflation rate during the first decade after the military coup.[5] This implies that the decline in the real consumption wage of the lowest paid workers has been underestimated. However, after 1984 the inflation differential borne by the poorest households declined, while in 1993 the poor experienced a lower rate of price increases than the population as a whole. This process suggests that the variation in income inequality in Chile over the last twenty years may have been greater than indicated by existing data sources (see below). Inequality probably rose faster in the mid to late 1970s than is usually assumed, while it also fell faster during the early 1990s.

Any assessment of Chilean economic performance since 1974 according to the first feature of the NEM must therefore be mixed. It took the military government approximately eight years to bring inflation down to the level of the 1960s, while the regime needed another decade after that to bring inflation below 20% *per annum* in two consecutive years. Nevertheless, during the last ten years Chile has experienced the lowest average annual inflation rate since the 1940s.

Figure 1: Export Ratio (X/GDP), 1960-1992

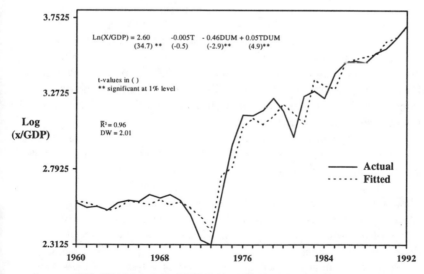

Sources: 1960-1974, Mamalakis (1978) Vol 1; 1975-1992, ECLAC (1994 and earlier years)

Economic openness, which is the second feature of the NEM, can be measured directly or indirectly. Direct measurement uses indicators such as the share of foreign trade in national income, while indirect measurement focuses on the difference between domestic and world prices of tradeable goods and on the interest rate differential between local and international capital markets.

Figure 1 plots the logarithm of the annual export ratio (X/GDP) over the period 1960 -1992. If the Chilean economy became more export-oriented after 1974, the annual rate of change in the export ratio should increase. This may be tested by regressing log (X/GDP) on a time trend (T), an intercept dummy (DUM) scored unity for the period 1974-1992 and zero for other years, and a trend dummy (TDUM). If the coefficient of the trend dummy is positive and significant, the evidence is consistent with the hypothesis of greater export openness after 1974. The results, shown in Figure 1, indicate that between 1960 and 1973 exports grew at approximately the same rate as GDP, so the export ratio remained constant. However, between 1974 and 1992 the export ratio grew at 5% *per annum* which indicates that recent economic growth in Chile has been export-led.[6]

Reducing the economic role of government has three aspects: (i) decreasing ownership and control by the state of productive facilities; (ii) reducing intervention in and regulation of product and factor markets; and (iii) decreasing the government's claims on current output. The privatisation of state enterprises since 1974 has been extensive (Muñoz,1993). By 1992, the state controlled production facilities only in the following industries: copper, water and sewage, oil and petrochemicals, and coal. The government also owned a bank (Banco del Estado) and a diversified holding company (CORFO). Public utilities such as electricity and gas were in private hands, as were telecommunications, airlines and part of the rail network. The state retains a responsibility for the provision of public goods (defence, law and order) and economic infrastructure, but where feasible user charges are being introduced and private sector financing of infrastructure development through Build-Operate-Transfer (BOT) projects began in 1993 (EIU,1994, p. 8).[7]

Deregulation of product markets has also been extensive as foreign trade was liberalised, price controls were lifted and subsidies removed. However, price support for selected agricultural commodities was re-introduced after the crash of the early 1980s. The capital market, which was almost wholly liberalised in the mid-1970s, has been subject to closer regulation since 1983. The labour market reforms introduced much greater flexibility of real wages and employment, which has not been significantly affected by the return of a democratic government.

The decline in government claims on current output since 1974 is shown in Figure 2 which plots government consumption as a share of GDP from 1960 to 1991.[8] A similar test to that applied in the case of the export ratio was conducted. The results suggest that over the period 1960 to 1973, the share of government current expenditure in GDP rose by 1.0% *per annum*. However, between 1974 and 1991 this share declined by 3.0% annually.[9]

Therefore, whether the economic role of the state is measured by the ownership and control of productive assets, the extent of intervention in markets or the share of government claims on output, there has been a significant reduction in its role since 1974. According to this criterion, contemporary Chile fits the NEM well.

Figure 2: Government Consumption Ratio (G/GDP), 1960-1991

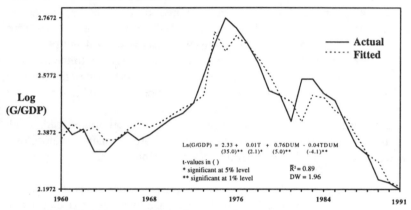

Sources: 1960-1974, Mamalakis (1978) Vol 1; 1975-1991, ECLAC (1994 and earlier years)

The New Economic Model: Transmission Mechanisms and the Distribution of Income

Four sets of transmission mechanisms can be identified which link character-istics of the NEM to the distribution of income. First, the introduction of the NEM in Chile involved property rights reforms which led to a significant redistribution of assets and liabilities in civil society. Secondly, after both the military coup in 1973 and the financial crisis ten years later, Chile underwent a stringent process of macroeconomic adjustment. The twin mechanisms of expenditure reduction and expenditure switching had important distributive consequences in the short- and medium-run. Thirdly, the military government undertook a radical restructuring of social expenditure in Chile, which has had profound effects on income distribution. These effects may be evaluated by the extent to which the fiscal system generates a distribution of total income which is more equal than the distribution of primary income.[10] Fourthly, in the period since 1990, it has become possible to identify certain transmission mechanisms associated with the NEM in steady-state growth.

Three processes of asset redistribution occurred under the Pinochet admin-istration: (i) state-sponsored transfers of assets between private agents; (ii) the redistribution of assets from the public to the private sector; and (iii) the transfer of liabilities from the private to the public sector in response to the economic crisis of 1982-83.

The most striking example of the state redistributing property rights among private agents under the NEM was the agrarian counter-reform. Between 1965 and mid-1973, approximately 43% of Chile's agricultural land (measured in basic irrigated hectares [BIH]) had been expropriated under a far-reaching land reform programme and had been assigned to producer cooperatives (*asentamientos*). This reduced the share of land held by the largest private farms from over 55% in 1965 to less than 3% in 1973.[11] Between 1974 and 1979, 28% of the expropriated land was returned by the military regime to the previous owners and a further five per cent reverted to the large farm sector through sale to the highest bidder at auction. The government retained another ten per cent for public use, most of which was transferred to the parastatal Forestry Corporation (CONAF).[12] Therefore, only 57% of the expropriated land, which amounted to 25% of the country's total agricultural area, remained in the reform sector after the military government's redistribution of property rights (Jarvis,1985, p. 11).

However, the reform sector itself underwent major restructuring. The producer cooperatives were forcibly dissolved and their land was allocated in individual holdings to a minority of the membership. This process of decollectivisation led to the expulsion of around 40,000 people from the reform sector between 1974 and 1978. This figure represented 55% of the coopera-tives' membership and seven percent of the entire agricultural labour force (Jarvis,1985, pp. 98-9). In the short- and medium-run, the dissolution of the *asentamientos* increased rural unemployment, prompted the establishment of new forms of settlement inhabited by landless labourers (*poblados rurales*) and led to a rise in rural poverty (Rivera and Cruz,1984).

In addition, many of the individual land reform beneficiaries (*parceleros*) sold their plots soon after receiving them. Although it was illegal to sell these *parcelas* before April 1980, it has been estimated that thirty per cent of *parceleros* sold their land between 1974 and 1979 and a further ten percent sold out between 1979 and 1982 (Crispi,1984; Jarvis,1985, p. 168). Therefore, it appears that within ten years of Pinochet's military coup, three-quarters of the *asentamiento* membership no longer enjoyed ownership rights over land assigned under the reform programmes of Presidents Frei (1964-70) and Allende (1970-73). Some of these ex-*parceleros* may have bought land elsewhere, while others used the proceeds of land sales to move out of agriculture into other activities such as transport and commerce. However, many of them spent their windfall gains on consumption (Gómez, 1994).

Although the counter-reform and the emergence of an active land market have led to some reconcentration of agricultural property, the inequality of land ownership in Chile by the late 1980s remained significantly below the level obtaining on the eve of the land reform in the mid-1960s (Rivera,1988, pp. 86-7; Gómez and Echenique, 1988, p. 101). The main beneficiaries of agrarian policies in the NEM have been a technically sophisticated and export-oriented medium-size farm sector together with a small number of transnational corporations which have purchased large tracts of land for afforestation. The main losers have been the ex-*asentados* who were not assigned plots, and the traditional *minifundistas* whose access to subsidised credit and agricultural extension was severely curtailed, while remaining excluded from the direct benefits of land redistribution (Scott,1990;1993).

The second process of asset redistribution was the sale of state-owned enterprises (SOEs). There have been several episodes of privatisation in Chile since 1974, but this chapter concentrates on the reprivatisation of firms nationalised during the crisis of 1982-83 and the sale of large long-established public enterprises after 1985 (Muñoz,1993; Bitran and Saez,1994). As yet, there has been no comprehensive study of the distributive impact of privatisation in Chile. Consequently, it is only possible to undertake a partial analysis which focuses on a few relevant variables in order to make use of the sparse information available.

Three factors are of particular significance in determining the distributive effects of privatisation: (i) the level of the share price; (ii) other conditions of the share sale, such as a ceiling on the number of shares which may be bought by a single investor and the existence of any preferential arrangements for allocating shares and (iii) the income levels of those buying shares.

The pricing of public sector assets determines the extent to which privatisation generates a resource transfer from society as a whole to those holding equity in the privatised firms. This remains a controversial issue in Chile, but most commentators agree that shares in the privatised enterprises were sold at a discount to the economic value of their assets.[13] The disagreement concerns the size of this discount which ranges from 15% to 41% (Cabrera, Hachette and Luders,1989; Hachette and Luders,1992; Marcel, 1989;1989a). Such calculations are fraught with methodological problems, but the evidence suggests that shareholders in SOEs (re-)privatised in the mid-1980s received a possibly substantial implicit capital gain as a result of this property rights reform.[14]

In contrast to the privatisations carried out in the mid-1970s, those undertaken in the 1980s sought to diffuse share ownership widely. In several instances, shares were sold in small blocks and an upper limit was placed on the number of shares which could be purchased by a single investor. Shares could be bought for a small down-payment with the balance met from an interest-free loan from CORFO repayable over 15 years. Prompt loan repayments reduced the value of the principal owed, and tax rebates could be claimed for 20% of the value of shares purchased. Indeed, for those facing marginal income tax rates of 30%, the value of the tax rebate exceeded the cash down payment for the shares (Saez, 1993, p. 90).

Although this attempt to promote 'popular capitalism' created 120,000 petty share owners, this group represented barely 2.1% of the adult population (Devlin, 1993, p. 201; Maloney, 1994, p. 374). Furthermore, such fragmentary evidence as exists on these popular capitalists suggests they are concentrated in the upper range of the income distribution. An analysis of share ownership in ENDESA, a large privatised electricity company, showed that 46% of shares sold to popular capitalists, i.e. those buying at a discounted price with subsidised credit, were held by residents of Santiago. More than half the shares held by these Santiago residents were acquired by households in only four districts (*comunas*), where 70% of the population was located in the top two deciles of the national income distribution (Devlin, 1993, p. 201). In short, it appears that the direct effects of privatisation were regressive, and that the attempt to reduce wealth inequality by promoting popular capitalism was no more successful in General Pinochet's Chile than it was in Mrs Thatcher's Britain in the 1980s.[15]

The last, and least publicised, element of the property rights reforms introduced under the NEM in Chile was the 'socialisation' of private sector debt by the Central Bank during the economic crisis of 1982-83. This transfer of liabilities from the private to the public sector was a precondition for the privatisation programme undertaken in the 1980s, and it had important distributive consequences in both the short- and long- run. The response of the military government to both the problems of the external and the internal debt was clearly regressive in its impact.

Unlike other Latin American countries, most of Chile's external debt had been contracted by the private sector and was not guaranteed by the state. Therefore, when the debt crisis broke in 1982, the military government attempted to leave private agents in Chile to negotiate a solution with their foreign creditors. In response, the international banks cut off all credit to Chile which was only resumed once the Chilean government had agreed to guarantee the external debt of the private financial (but not the non-financial) sector. This effectively transferred to present and future generations of Chileans losses of US$3.5 billion, which had been incurred by a small number of wealthy private agents (Meller, 1992, p. 58). The striking feature of this outcome to the external debt renegotiation was the asymmetry in the distribution of gains and losses from foreign borrowing. During the late 1970s, when the *grupos económicos* were expanding rapidly and large private fortunes were being made by a small group, neither the Chilean government nor Chilean society received any substantive benefits. However, once the speculative bubble burst, the costs of maintaining Chile's membership of the international financial community were immediately distributed over the whole of society.

The resolution of the internal debt problem also favoured the better off. The Central Bank provided large subsidies to three groups, which were not mutually exclusive: foreign currency debtors, Chilean local currency debtors and domestic private commercial banks.[16] The mechanisms for providing these subsidies were complex and involved preferential exchange rates, conversions of dollar debt to peso debt, the opening of special credit lines and the purchase of government bonds by the commercial banks with the proceeds of selling their bad debts to the Central Bank. It is difficult to put an aggregate value on these subsidies, but one estimate for part of the total suggests it amounted to 4% of GDP over a four year period (Meller, 1992, p. 77).[17] Since most domestic credit (whether in foreign or domestic currency) was held by high income groups, this rescue plan of the Central Bank had a clearly regressive impact on income distribution.[18]

During the mid-1970s, and again in the mid-1980s, Chile underwent a stringent programme of macroeconomic adjustment. The adjustment process lasted several years and had major effects on income distribution, largely through the labour market. The main transmission mechanisms were expenditure reduction and expenditure switching which increased unemployment and reduced real wages.

Figure 3: Unemployment Rate (UN), 1960-1992

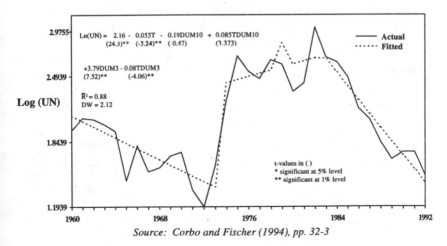

Source: Corbo and Fischer (1994), pp. 32-3

Figure 3 shows the evolution of unemployment for the period 1960-1992. From 1960 to 1973, the unemployment rate fell at 5.5% per year, but this declining trend was sharply reversed with the onset of the military government's adjustment programme in 1974. Between 1974 and 1982, the unemployment rate rose at 3% per annum. Employment recovered in 1984 and the unemployment rate fell by 13% *per annum* between 1983 and 1992 as a result of export-led growth.

Real wage movements show a different pattern. Between 1960 and 1973, real wages grew at over five per cent *per annum* which together with a falling unemployment rate should have reduced absolute poverty and possibly income inequality also. The hyperinflation of 1973 decreased real wages, which were further depressed by the fall in aggregate demand for labour in 1974 and the real devaluations in 1974-75 (Figure 4). Real wages began to recover in 1976 and continued to grow until the crisis of 1982-83. This recovery was associated with a sustained appreciation of the real exchange rate, as might be expected. In 1982, wage indexation was abandoned and a more flexible exchange rate regime was adopted which allowed a persistent real depreciation of the currency for the rest of the decade. In consequence, real wages fell again until 1987 when the economy was close to full capacity utilisation and aggregate labour supply had emerged as a constraint on growth. Since 1987 real wages (see Table A.8) have increased steadily.

Figure 4: Real Exchange Rate (RER), 1960-1992

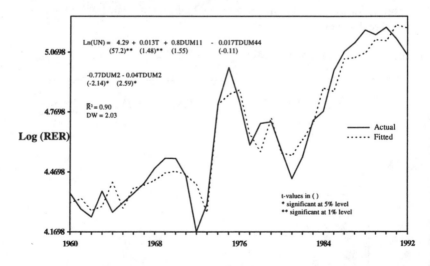

Source: Corbo and Fischer (1994), pp. 32-3

In an attempt to mitigate the regressive impact of adjustment measures on income distribution, the military government introduced several public employment schemes to provide low paid work for the unemployed.[19] At their peak in 1983, these schemes absorbed 13% of the country's labour force and had a total budget equivalent to 1.4% of GNP. They were successfully targeted on the poor and managed to recruit large numbers of women as well as men.[20] Although such schemes no doubt alleviated the most extreme forms of poverty, they could not compensate for the overall deterioration of labour market conditions in the mid-1970s and early 1980s.

The third set of transmission mechanisms between the NEM and the distribution of income in Chile is located in the major social expenditure reforms implemented by the military government. These involved not just the partial privatisation of supply of certain goods traditionally provided directly by the state, such as health care and education, but also the establishment of quasi-markets within the public sector itself, the use of increasingly sophisticated methods of targeting beneficiaries and extensive decentralisation of government services. The reforms in health and housing began in the mid-1970s, while those in education and social security were introduced in 1980-81. Each of these reform programmes was complex, lengthy and subject to revision over time. The *Concertación* government has modified some of these reforms, but has not attempted to change the basic institutional and organisational landscape which was redrawn by and inherited from the military regime.[21]

Any assessment of the distributive effects of these social reforms must distinguish between the period of military government (1974-90) and the period of democratic rule since 1990. The political priority assigned to alleviating poverty and reducing income inequality was much higher in the latter period. Detailed information for making a quantitative assessment is scarce before 1985, when the first CASEN survey was undertaken. This national household survey collected detailed information on income sources and was repeated in 1987, 1990 and 1992.[22] However, even with the CASEN data it is not possible to trace the evolution of the net redistributive effect of the reforms because of incomplete information on tax incidence.[23] Therefore, this section cannot claim to offer a comprehensive review of the distributional impact of the reforms.

Whether the poor receive more or less resources *via* the state under the NEM cannot be established *a priori*, because the outcome is the result of two opposed sets of forces. On the one hand, the new model seeks to decrease the share of government expenditure in GDP and reduce the state's claims on social resources, while on the other it acknowledges that a larger share of public expenditure and transfers should be allocated to providing a minimum safety net. Thus, the central distributional issue is whether the poorest deciles gain more from increased targeting than they lose through a reduction in aggregate social expenditure *per capita*. The evidence suggests that while the NEM was under military rule, the lowest deciles lost more than they gained, although particular groups among the very poor may have been net beneficiaries.

Castañeda has calculated the distribution of educational spending and housing benefits across different income groups between 1974 and 1986 using a variety of sources. In both cases, the distribution of these state expenditures was changed in favour of the poorest groups, although *per capita* spending on education and housing over the relevant period fell by nine per cent and 63% respectively (PET, 1992, p. 96). In 1974, the richest 40% of the population received 47% of all educational expenditure, but this had fallen to 34% by 1986. Conversely, the poorest 30% of households increased their share of educational spending from 29% to 37% over the same period.

In the case of housing subsidies, a sharply reduced total amount was allocated increasingly towards low income groups. In 1981, the richest 40% of the population received 42% of housing subsidies, but this proportion had fallen to 21% by 1986. Conversely, the poorest 30% of households increased their share of these benefits from 27% to 47% over the same period. However, the real value of total housing benefits accruing to the poorest 30% only regained its 1969 level in 1984.

Information from the CASEN surveys of 1985 and 1987 permits a more general assessment of the distributional consequences of social spending during the last five years of military rule. Both surveys show that the distributive impact of different types of social expenditure varied greatly (Haindl and Weber, 1986, p. 49; Haindl, 1989, p. 44). Monetary transfers which were (and remain) targeted had a progressive effect, as did the provision of basic health services – probably because of the concentration of children in the first quintile.[24] By contrast, fiscal transfers under the new pension arrangements are highly regressive. This is because the size of the transfer is positively related to the value of present and past pension contributions, which are in turn positively associated with income.

Because pension contributions by the state make up such a large proportion of social expenditure (around 40% by the early 1990s), any assessment of the distributive impact of the social reforms under the NEM will depend crucially on how these contributions are treated. If they are included in social expenditure, then the overall effect of social spending on income distribution under the military government (and under the Aylwin administration) is probably regressive. However, if pension contributions are excluded, then the impact of social expenditure was clearly progressive both before and after 1990. The progressive impact of social spending (net of pension contributions) is demonstrated in Table 2 which shows average total income in each income class as a proportion of average primary income in that class. In both 1987 and in 1990, this proportion declined monotonically from the first decile (or quintile) to the last decile (or quintile).

Table 2:
Total Income as a Proportion of Primary Income by Primary Income Decile, 1987 and 1990 (in %)

Decile	1987	1990
1	294.1	172.8
2	172.0	
3	145.6	124.1
4	131.5	
5	123.6	111.2
6	117.0	
7	113.4	104.6
8	110.9	
9	108.0	100.4
10	102.1	
Total	**114.2**	**107.4**

Source: Haindl (1989. p. 59); Schkolnik and Agüero (1993, p. 263)

Racyznski (1994) provides a concise summary of the changes in social policy under the NEM as Chile moved from military to civilian rule. Distributive objectives received a higher priority in an economic strategy characterised as 'growth with equity'. There was less emphasis on individual transfers which were viewed as encouraging passivity, dependency and social isolation among beneficiaries, and more stress was laid on enhancing the poor's capacity to help themselves, particularly through group formation.

A more discriminating approach was taken towards targeting benefits. Some programmes with evident positive externalities, such as primary education and health care, aimed at universality, while others such as nutrition programmes and training schemes, remained tightly focused on particular groups. New broader-based target populations were identified and new public agencies established to reach them, such as SERNAM (for women), INJ (for youth) and CONADI (for indigenous groups).

The process of decentralising government was extended by creating 13 regional authorities with greater resources. Local government was democratised and closer collaboration between the public, private and NGO sectors was promoted. The boldest organisational initiative was the creation of FOSIS, a nationwide public agency charged with financing (but not implementing) a diversified and decentralised portfolio of anti-poverty projects which would complement other public sector initiatives in education and health. The whole strategy was underpinned by a substantial increase in social spending *per capita*.

Despite these changes, the social reforms introduced by the military government had little effect on income distribution. Table 3 shows that pension contributions by the state made up nearly 40% of social expenditure in 1993 and were highly regressive. Monetary transfers and social investments such as nutrition and youth training programmes, which are both targeted, had a progressive effect as did the provision of basic health services. If pension

Table 3:
Distribution of Planned Social Expenditure by Primary Income Quintiles (in %), 1993 (a)

Quintiles	Subsidies	Monetary Transfers	Pension Contrib-utions	Basic Services (b)	Education	Health	Housing	Social Invest-ments	Admin-istrative Costs	Total	Total (excluding Pension Contrib-utions)
1	32.5	32.1	4.0	26.2	27.2	29.0	20.2	40.2	16.6	18.5	28.3
2	24.1	22.6	8.8	23.1	23.7	25.7	18.2	25.2	17.8	17.2	22.9
3	18.4	18.4	15.2	20.0	18.7	21.9	19.3	16.9	22.0	17.8	19.5
4	12.8	13.3	24.9	17.8	16.0	16.3	23.0	11.3	22.9	19.9	16.6
5	12.1	13.7	47.1	12.9	14.3	7.2	19.2	6.5	20.7	26.6	12.7
Total	100.0	100.0	100.0	100.0	100.0	100.0	100.0	100.0	100.0	100.0	100.0
% of Total	7.6	6.3	39.2	33.4	13.8	12.3	7.3	11.1	8.7	100.0	

(a) Calculated using distributive weights from 1990 CASEN survey
(b) Includes education, health and housing

Source: Larrañaga (1994: Table 2, p.11)

contributions are included in social expenditure, then in the last year of the Aylwin administration (1993), the lowest quintile of primary income recipients received 18% of social expenditure, while the top quintile received 27%. If these contributions are excluded, then this conclusion is reversed. The first quintile received 28% of social expenditure, while the fifth quintile received only 13%.

The increased commitment to poverty alleviation by the *Concertación* government is shown in Table 4 where the decline in the real value of monetary transfers between 1987 and 1990 was reversed between 1990 and 1992. This contributed to the decline in poverty incidence in the early 1990s, although as Table 4 also makes clear, it was the rise in primary incomes of the lowest deciles resulting from a tighter labour market and a higher minimum wage which was the main source of welfare improvement among the poor over this period.[25]

Table 4:
Variation in Primary Incomes and Monetary Transfers by Primary Income Quintiles (%), 1987-90 and 1990-92

Quintiles	1987-90			1990-92		
	Primary Income	Monetary Transfers	Total	Primary Income	Monetary Transfers	Total
1	12.6	-34.7	4.6	28.3	7.7	26.1
2	19.6	-26.1	16.7	18.8	10.3	18.4
3	19.5	-32.1	17.6	16.8	8.4	16.6
4	15.3	-36.9	14.3	16.9	2.7	16.7
5	11.0	-42.4	10.7	17.9	-20.3	17.8
Total	**13.6**	**-33.6**	**12.5**	**18.0**	**4.7**	**17.8**

Source: Raczynski (1994, Table 8, p. 66) quoting MIDEPLAN (1993)

There are both economic and political reasons for giving separate consideration to transmission mechanisms under the NEM in steady state. First, the long-run distributive effects of the new model may only become apparent once the state-induced redistribution of assets and liabilities in the short- and medium-run has been completed, once macroeconomic adjustment has been successfully achieved and once the structural reforms to social expenditure have been put into place. While the processes of asset transfer, structural adjustment and fiscal reform have had a profound impact on shaping Chile's economic future, other factors such as the growth rate of the country's labour force and the achievements in health and education of the public sector in the pre-NEM period must be taken into account in any assessment of the distributive effects of the new model in the long-run.

Secondly, the economy's return to full capacity growth coincided with the polity's return to democratic government. In the face of strong popular pressure, both the administrations of Presidents Aylwin (1990-94) and Frei (1994-) have assigned a high priority to the reduction of poverty and income inequality. This has had implications for fiscal policy, which in turn has affected the impact of the NEM on the secondary income distribution.

For present purposes, three transmission mechanisms may be identified in the steady-state NEM: (i) the existence of low and stable inflation; (ii) the achievement of sustained export-led growth; and (iii) the long-run distributive effects of the funded pension system. These are discussed in turn.

There are several reasons to believe that low and stable inflation should have a progressive impact on income distribution. Even where the minimum wage is indexed, many low-paid wage workers in the urban informal sector are likely to be outside the effective coverage of such labour legislation, and in consequence are not fully protected against rises in the general price level. The self-employed among the urban poor who are able to adjust quickly the nominal prices of their output in an inflationary environment may appear to be better protected than their wage earning counterparts. However, such households may need to hold a higher proportion of their meagre net wealth in cash (for working capital) than wage workers, so any advantage associated with their occupational status may be illusory.

The secular decline of payments-in-kind to agricultural workers has reduced the ability of the rural poor to protect themselves against inflation. This transformation of the nature of contracts in the agricultural labour market in Chile includes not just the disappearance of *inquilinaje*, but also a tendency for share renting to be replaced by wage labour (Ramirez, 1968, BID, 1986, p. 124). The reduction in average farm size among small holders due to the subdivision of properties at inheritance has reduced the capacity of *minifundistas* to produce directly their subsistence requirements (Scott, 1990).

Finally, low income households that are dependent on transfers, such as pensions or child allowances, will be protected against inflation only if indexation is forward-looking and fully anticipates future price rises. Therefore, if the NEM can sustain low and stable inflation in steady state growth, poverty and income inequality should be reduced *ceteris paribus*.

The distributive impact of sustained export-led growth depends on the size distribution of assets in the export sector, the characteristics of the production function in exportable industries and the tax regime. Chile's main exports vary significantly according to each of these three elements. Copper continues to provide more than one quarter of the country's export earnings, although this share has declined over the last twenty years.[26] CODELCO, the state-owned copper corporation, which accounts for approximately 65% of copper exports, has so far proved immune to privatisation, largely because such a move would involve at least partial foreign ownership. When the industry was nationalised in 1971, the relevant legislation was supported by all political parties. Any sale of CODELCO would require a constitutional amendment and is thus a very delicate political issue . This mining enterprise contributes a sizeable share of total fiscal revenues while ten per cent of copper sales accrues by law to the Armed Forces. CODELCO workers are among the highest paid in the country, although their productivity as compared to their counterparts employed in US-run mines in Chile is low (Hojman, 1993, p. 143).

The situation in the fruit and timber industries, which by 1992 accounted for over 11% of export revenues, is very different. The fruit industry has been one of the fastest growing new exports under the NEM. The area planted with fruit trees nearly trebled between 1974 and 1991, while the volume of fruit exports increased by 162% between 1984-85 and 1991-92 (Montero, Jarvis and Gomez, 1992, pp. 61-5). By the 1990-91 season, Chile accounted for 84% of total Southern Hemisphere grape exports and 93% of total Southern Hemisphere exports of nectarines and peaches (Barrientos, 1995).

The first difference with the copper industry is that the level of industrial concentration is much lower and there is little evidence of foreign management in fruit growing (Jarvis, Montero and Hidalgo, 1993). Much of the fruit area is in medium-sized farms owned by *parceleros* or recent (often urban resident) entrants to the industry. In 1986, two-thirds of the fruit area was in farms of less than 100 hectares (Venegas, 1992, p. 19), but concentration has been increasing. One survey conducted in 1992-93 found that the six largest farms controlled 30% of the fruit area (Jarvis, Montero and Hidalgo, 1993, p. 12). As in other food chains, concentration is higher in marketing. In 1991-92, the five largest export firms marketed 42% of total fruit exports (Montero, Jarvis and Gomez, 1992, p. 68).[27]

The second difference with the copper industry is that unskilled labour is complementary to natural resources in fruit production, although most employment is seasonal and much of it is female. A survey conducted in 1988 found that 79% of fruit workers were temporary and 21% permanent (Venegas, 1992, p. 91). For 60% of temporary workers their only employment was seasonal work in the fruit industry. Male workers made up 58% of the total labour force in the sample and 35% of them were permanent employees. By contrast, female workers accounted for 42% of the total, but less than two per cent of them were permanent labourers. Thus, almost all permanent workers (97%) were male while more than half of temporary workers (52%) were female.

In the early 1990s, there were approximately 200,000 women who participated in seasonal agricultural employment, of whom 90% lived (often in towns) and worked in the Central Valley (PET, 1992a, p. 2). This is a new phenomenon in the development of rural labour markets in Chile. In the past, large-scale temporary employment in agriculture such as cereal production was predominantly male, involved almost continuous migration throughout the year and mobilised the most marginal elements in rural society (Valenzuela, 1991; Bengoa,1988; Zemelman,1967).

The implications of this feminisation of rural labour markets for income distribution and for the evolution of gender relations in Chile are substantial. Anthropological evidence together with revealed preference indicates that, despite the burden of the *doble jornada*, many of these female workers welcome the opportunity to take paid employment outside the household (Bee,1995; Matear,1995; Vogel,1995).[28] The increased economic independence provided by such employment has not only changed the intra-household distribution of income, but has induced some women to leave their husbands and establish separate households of their own. A recent study of female-headed rural households in two districts of the III and VI Regions,where fruit growing is extensive, has shown that the largest single group of such households was headed by women who had separated from their husbands for precisely this reason (Aranda, 1994). This too is a new phenomenon because in the past many female-headed rural households were the result of wives being abandoned by migrant husbands (Scott,1986).

The forestry industry is characterised by extensive vertical integration, a high concentration ratio, significant direct foreign investment, and heavy reliance on male temporary workers recruited through labour contractors. Two conglomerates, Matte and Angelini, own nearly 50% of the country's pine plantations in addition to sawmills, paper and pulp plants (Gómez and Echenique, 1988, p. 106). Foreign capital from New Zealand, the United States and Japan has entered the industry – usually in the form of joint ventures with Chilean partners. This concentrated pattern of resource ownership implies a relatively unequal distribution of value added in the forestry sector.

Unlike the copper industry, which is a large net contributor of revenue to the state, the forestry industry has been a net recipient of government funds. Since the mid-1970s, the timber companies have received generous subsidies for afforestation, tax rebates and special credits. In 1980, it was estimated that nearly 90% of the investment costs in privately-owned plantations were being met by Chilean taxpayers (Rivera and Cruz, 1983, p. 20).

The rapid expansion of the forestry sector created significant employment opportunities while the new plantations were being established.[29] However, the recurrent labour requirements per hectare of conifers are low, so that permanent employment has fallen in areas where afforestation has occurred. Detailed studies of the distributive impact of forestry growth are rare. Gómez (1994) analysed the consequences of the industry's expansion in the X Region (Valdivia, Osorno and Llanquihue) between 1990 and 1993. He found that many peasant proprietors who sold land to timber companies improved their situation by buying smaller farms with better quality land and easier access to transport and communication. Nevertheless, wage labourers who were previously employed on these small farms often lost both their jobs and their homes when the land was sold. Gómez warns against drawing general conclusions from these results which may be specific to a particular time and place.

In summary, copper will remain the most significant exportable in the Chilean economy in the foreseeable future. The distributive impact of the copper industry's growth will depend on whether CODELCO remains in the public sector, and how tax revenues raised from the industry are used by the state. Growth in the fruit industry will lead to a wider diffusion of direct benefits given the unimodal agrarian structure in Chile and the labour intensity of fruit production.[30] Further development of forestry is likely to be disequalising, given the concentration of land ownership in the industry, the high degree of vertical integration and the low labour-intensity of production.

The last transmission mechanism under the NEM to be examined under steady-state conditions concerns the change from a 'pay-as-you-go' to a funded pension scheme. Given the significance of pension contributions by the state in determining the distributive impact of social expenditure during the transition from the old to the new pension system, it is important to compare the distributive consequences of the two types of system in the long-run.

Two impacts may be distinguished: that relating to the distribution of income between young and old, and that between rich and poor. Under 'pay-as-you-go' (PAYG) schemes like the traditional pension system in Chile, retirees may receive more in benefits than they paid in contributions. This constitutes an income transfer from young to old, which in the case of developed countries over the last few decades has been substantial (Barr, 1993, p. 225). Therefore, if a PAYG is replaced by a funded scheme, this redistributive effect in favour of the old will come to an end. This may well explain why it was younger workers who moved first and in the largest numbers to the new system. Contribution rates to the private pension funds (AFPs) were on average lower and take-home pay higher for such workers compared to the traditional system.

In the case of a funded scheme like the new system where pensions are not indexed, intergenerational redistribution can occur only as a result of unanticipated inflation. If the price level rises faster than predicted, real purchasing power is transferred from old to young (and *vice versa*). However, in the Chilean case, more than 70% of the accumulated funds held by persons retiring up to the year 2000 are held in the form of recognition bonds which *are* inflation-indexed, so this redistributive mechanism is likely to be of minor importance in the short- and medium-term (Castañeda, 1992, p. 185).

A prime objective of the new system is to make benefits proportional to contributions, which rules out any systematic redistribution from rich to poor or *vice versa*. The same income inequalities which exist during the working life of a given generation persist into the period of retirement. However, the new system in Chile is not a pure funded scheme, because the state guarantees a minimum pension to participants and an assistance pension to non-members and affiliates with incomplete contributions. This should induce a modest redistribution of income from rich to poor.

The Evolution of Social Equity: Evidence and Explanation

This section examines the evolution of absolute poverty and relative income inequality since 1974. An attempt is made to relate changes in these social equity indices to the transmission mechanisms discussed in the previous section.

The pioneering work of Altimir in ECLAC in the 1970s has made it possible in principle to track the incidence of poverty in Chile since 1970 using an invariant absolute poverty line. He defined two levels of deprivation: the *poverty* line represented the money income required to purchase a minimum basket of food and other necessities, while the *indigence* line represented the cost of the minimal diet (Altimir, 1979). Table 5 shows the headcount ratios for each of these two levels of deprivation in Chile over the period 1970 to 1992.

The most remarkable feature of Table 5 is the large rise in the headcount ratio between 1970 and 1987. This ratio more than doubled whichever poverty line is used. However, some doubts have been expressed about the values of the headcount ratio in the 1980s because of their apparent inconsistency with other data such as that collected by the INE's Household Budget Survey for Santiago. A reliable source, by no means sympathetic to the military regime, has suggested that the headcount ratio was exaggerated and that '..the percentage of Chilean families below indigence and poverty lines in the 1980s would seem closer to that of 1970 figures: that is, fewer than 10% of Chilean families would be below the indigence line and fewer than 20% below the poverty line' (Meller, 1992, p. 23).

With this important qualification, two conclusions may be drawn from Table 5. First, there has been a continuous decline in the incidence of poverty

Table 5:
Headcount Ratio of Poverty (% of households) in Chile, 1970-1992

		1970	**1987**	**1990**	**1992**
Poverty	Urban	12.0	36.6	34.2	27.4
	Rural	25.0	44.9	36.3	28.9
	Total	17.0	38.1	34.6	27.7
Indigence	Urban	3.0	13.0	10.8	7.1
	Rural	11.0	15.7	14.9	8.5
	Total	6.5	13.5	11.6	7.3

Sources: 1970-90, Schkolnik (1992, p. 112); 1992, MIDEPLAN (1994a, pp. 35-7)

since 1987 whichever poverty line is used, and this decline was faster after the return of a democratic government in 1990. However, both poverty and indigence were still higher in 1992 than in 1970.

Secondly, the increase in poverty between 1970 and 1992 was largely the result of immiserisation in the *urban* sector where the headcount ratio more than doubled. Rural poverty apparently changed little over the period. This process has led to a narrowing in the poverty differential between the urban and rural sectors. In 1970, there was proportionately twice as much poverty in the countryside as in the towns. By 1992, the incidence of poverty as measured by the headcount ratio was virtually the same in both sectors.

These results are consistent with an export-led growth strategy driven by a sustained real depreciation and supported by the increased targeting of state expenditures and transfers in favour of the poorest. If a larger proportion of agricultural output is tradeable than of non-agricultural output, then a real depreciation will tend to benefit rural producers. At the same time, a reallocation of the state's resources from higher quintiles, which are largely urban, to the lowest quintile, which is largely rural, will tend to benefit the countryside.[31]

Further evidence of a link between trade policy and poverty incidence may be examined at the regional level. Table 6 gives headcount ratios for the 13 regions of Chile in 1987, 1990 and 1992. In 1992, regional poverty was lowest in the Metropolitan Region (Santiago) and the VI region (O'Higgins).[32] Poverty appeared highest in regions IV (Coquimbo), VII (Maule), VIII (Biobio) and IX (Los Lagos). Table 6 also includes a regional tradeability index, which is defined as the share of regional tradeable output in regional GDP in 1990 (CIEPLAN-

Min. del Interior, 1994). If export-led growth (or more precisely, tradeable-led growth) reduces poverty, a negative association between the regional headcount ratio and the regional tradeability index may be expected.

A simple model of regional poverty determination is introduced to test this hypothesis using data for 1990. The regional headcount ratio $(=H_R)$ is considered to depend on (i) the level of regional income per head$(=Y)$; (ii) the degree of income inequality within the region, as measured by the Gini coefficient $(=G)$; (iii) the regional dependency ratio, measured by the average number of people supported by each employed person in the region $(=D)$, and (iv) the value of the regional tradeability index $(=T)$. In the absence of any clear guidance from economic theory as to the appropriate choice of functional form, a double logarithmic (ln) specification was chosen so that the regression coefficients may be interpreted as partial elasticities.

Table 6:
Regional Headcount Ratios (% of persons), 1987-1992 and Regional Tradeability Index (%), 1990

Region	Headcount Ratios (%)			Tradeability Index (%)
	1987	1990	1992	1990
I	44.2	31.1	29.3	34.9
II	38.6	34.8	29.7	67.1
III	44.1	37.4	28.8	66.8
IV	51.1	47.4	40.0	58.3
V	40.0	43.6	34.5	45.4
VI	45.2	42.6	27.1	64.4
VII	47.2	48.9	40.2	52.8
VIII	56.2	46.3	46.6	52.2
IX	61.3	47.5	43.4	36.5
X	50.6	43.8	34.9	42.6
XI	26.6	32.8	28.5	28.3
XII	19.3	32.1	26.2	66.1
Santiago	38.7	34.6	25.5	26.3

Note: The poverty line was invariant across regions, but was lower in the countryside than in the towns. In November 1992, the poverty line was Ch $25,750 per capita per month in urban areas and Ch $17,362 in rural areas.

Sources: MIDEPLAN (1994a, p. 13) for headcount ratios; CIEPLAN - Min. del Interior (1994) for tradeability index.

The results are shown in equation (1) in Table 7. The coefficient of Ln T is positive and significant at the 10% level, which suggests that increased tradeability of regional output *increases* regional poverty after controlling for other relevant factors. The only other significant determinant of regional poverty in eq.(1) is the level of regional income inequality (G), which as expected is positively associated with poverty incidence.

However, improved econometric results were obtained when the tradeability index was replaced by a regional real exchange rate index for exportables (REER).[33] In eq.(2), which uses a definition of the REER that includes the output of the state-owned copper corporation (CODELCO), the coefficient of the dependency ratio is positive (as expected) and significant, while the coefficient on the real exchange rate is negative and significant.

Table 7:
The Determinants of Regional Poverty, 1990

Dependent Variable: Ln Regional Headcount Ratio				
Independent Variables	Eq. (1)	Eq. (2)	Eq. (3)	Eq. (4)
Constant	2.498	3.936	3.668	6.928
Ln Y	-0.0008	0.036	0.025	
	(-0.02)	(1.37)	(0.99)	
Ln G a/	1.254	0.494	0.702	0.906
	(2.99)*	(1.79)	(2.64)*	(3.81)**
Ln D	1.074	2.217	1.980	1.165
	(1.66)	(4.52)**	(4.28)**	(1.93)#
Ln T	0.265			
	(2.16)#			
Ln REER1 b/		-0.489		
		(-2.67)*		
Ln REER2 c/			-0.346	-0.270
			(-2.85)*	(-2.17)#
Ln (Income Per Head) a/				-0.272
				(-1.49)
R^2	0.788	0.823	0.834	0.854
No. of Observations	13	13	13	13

Note:
a/ Refers to 1985   *b/ Including CODELCO*
c/ Excluding CODELCO   *# Significant at 10% level*
* Significant at 5% level   *** Significant at 1% level*
Source; Teitelboim (1992, p. 418); MIDEPLAN (1994, p. 13); CIEPLAN-Min. del Interior (1994); Escobar and Repetto (1993); Haindl and Weber (1986, p. 44)

Even better results were achieved with eq.(3), where the coefficients on the regional Gini and the dependency ratio have the expected signs (positive) and are both significant, while the coefficient of REER2, which excludes the output of CODELCO, is negative and significant. The goodness of fit of eq.(3) is also better than eqs.(1) and (2). However, a surprising feature of eqs.(1)-(3) is that the coefficient of regional income per head is not significant.

The best specification is shown in eq.(4) which is identical to eq.(3), except that regional income per head is replaced by regional (secondary) income per head from the CASEN survey. Unfortunately, the published results of the 1990 survey give neither regional Gini coefficients nor regional income per head, so these two variables are measured with data from the 1985 survey. In eq.(4), all the coefficients of the explanatory variables have the expected signs, while three out of four are significant at the 10% level or below. Only regional income per head remains insignificant, but given the small size of the sample its t-value is relatively high. The goodness of fit of eq.(4) is the best in Table 7.

These results suggest that the larger the devaluation of a region's real exchange rate for exportables between 1985-86 and 1990, the lower the incidence of regional poverty in 1990. Specifically, a ten per cent real devaluation between the mid-1980s and 1990 reduced the incidence of regional poverty by approximately 2.7%. However, the transmission mechanism whereby a real regional devaluation diminishes poverty is not clear, since it does not appear to operate via an increase in the tradeable share of regional output.[34] If the price elasticity of tradeable supply is low, which may be plausible in the short-run but not in the long-run, a real devaluation could still reduce poverty simply by increasing the real incomes of those factors used in tradable production. This result is more likely, the larger the proportion of the poor who are located in the tradable sector.

Before leaving the regional level, it may be noted that the VIII region, where the forestry industry has grown extremely rapidly, had the highest regional headcount ratio in the country in 1992, while the VI region where the fruit industry is significant had the lowest headcount ratio after the metropolitan region of Santiago. This finding is consistent with the predicted distributional impact of different exportable industries discussed above.[35]

An even more disaggregated analysis of the transmission mechanisms between trade policy and poverty incidence is offered by Larrañaga and Sanhueza (1994). They define 15 sectoral subgroups and using data from the CASEN surveys are able to decompose the change in the headcount ratio in each subgroup between 1987 and 1992 into a growth and a distributive component. The subgroups were classified by the level of educational attainment (high[H] and low[L]), and by the economic activity of the household member with the largest income, who was not necessarily the household head.

In 1992, the two largest subgroups were low educated commerce (18% of population), which includes part of the urban informal sector, and low educated agriculture (10% of population) which includes both landless labourers and peasant farmers. Poverty was highest among the unemployed (80%) and lowest among highly educated government employees (7%).

The decomposition procedure involves partitioning the change in the headcount ratio into three elements. The first element, termed the growth effect, holds constant the distribution of income (Lorenz Curve) within the subgroup but allows mean income to vary. The second element, termed the distributive effect, holds mean income constant but allows the distribution of income (Lorenz Curve) to vary. Since poverty measures are not usually additively separable between mean income and the parameters of the Lorenz Curve, there is a third element which represents the interaction between changes in mean income and the distribution of income (Larrañaga, 1993, pp. 9-12).

The results of the decomposition analysis are striking and also hold if other poverty measures such as the poverty gap or members of the Foster-Greer-Thorbecke class of poverty indices are used instead of the headcount ratio (Larrañaga and Sanhueza, 1994, p. 14). Table 8 shows that approximately 80% of the reduction in poverty occurring between 1987 and 1992 is accounted for by the growth effect. This suggests that 'trickle-down' was the major source of poverty alleviation over the period with a tightened labour market acting as the most likely transmission mechanism.

Furthermore, as theory predicts, the decline in poverty and the relative contribution of the growth effect to this decline were greatest in those subgroups associated with tradeable goods production. Households associated with importable and agricultural production, whatever their level of human capital, exhibited the largest reductions in poverty. Low educated households producing exportables also improved their position strongly. By contrast, in several non-traded subgroups, poverty either increased (high educated government) or where it fell, the distributive effect dominated the growth effect (low educated commerce, low educated services). The exception was construction where poverty fell sharply, largely due to the growth effect. This suggests that construction may be complementary to tradeable goods production (*via* an investment accelerator).

It is difficult to trace accurately changes in income inequality in Chile since 1974 owing to a lack of comparable nationwide data for the whole period. This section draws on information from the CASEN national surveys between 1985 and 1992, and the Survey of Household Income (SHI) in Greater Santiago conducted quarterly by the University of Chile since 1956.

Table 9 shows Gini coefficients for three concepts of income between 1985 and 1992. Two features of this table may be noted. First, inequality declined

Table 8:
Decomposition of Change in Headcount Ratio by Subgroup (%),
1987-1992

Subgroup	Growth Effect	Distributive Effect	Residual Effect	Total Change (No. of % points)
Unemployed	-4.0	-0.8	0.2	-4.6
Exportables L	-15.4	-2.1	2.1	-15.4
Agriculture L	-17.9	-5.0	1.5	-21.4
Construction	-16.6	5.0	-2.7	-14.3
Import-Competing L	-17.5	-0.7	-0.4	-18.6
Commerce L	-1.4	-7.9	-0.2	-9.5
Inactive L	-5.5	-0.6	-0.4	-6.5
Agriculture H	-13.7	1.1	1.6	-11.0
Services L	-5.8	-6.2	-1.6	-13.6
Government L	-6.3	-3.1	-2.3	-11.7
Import-Competing H	-12.5	-4.2	0.7	-16.0
Exportables H	-7.6	4.2	-0.7	-4.1
Inactive H	-2.2	4.5	-0.2	2.1
Services and Commerce H	-0.5	-1.8	0.0	-2.3
Government H	-2.9	5.9	0.4	3.4
National	-8.0	-2.7	0.5	-10.2

Note:
L= Low Education; H = High Education
Source: Larrañaga and Sanhueza (1994: Table 5, p. 15)

monotonically in each year as the definition of income is widened to embrace the value of monetary transfers and then the imputed value of goods/services provided by the state. Thus, the distributive impact of both monetary transfers and government-supplied goods/services was progressive, which is consistent with the objectives of the NEM.

Secondly, inequality fell steadily between 1985 and 1992 for each definition of income. However, as the last column in Table 9 indicates, this decline was proportionately greater for primary income (11.8%) than for total income (6.5%). In 1985, inequality of the primary income distribution was 20% higher than inequality of the total income distribution. By 1992, this differential had fallen to 13.5%.

Table 9:
Gini Coefficients of Primary, Secondary and Total Income at National Level, 1985-1992

Year	Type of Income a/	Gini Coefficient (G)	G as % of G for Total Income
	Primary	0.515	1.203
1985	Secondary	0.481	1.124
	Total	0.428	1.000
	Primary	0.496	1.195
1987	Secondary	0.479	1.154
	Total	0.415	1.000
	Primary	0.488	1.199
1990	Secondary	0.481	1.182
	Total	0.407	1.000
	Primary	0.454	1.135
1992	Secondary	0.443	1.108
	Total	0.400	1.000

a/ Definitions of each type of income are given in footnote 10

Sources: Haindl and Weber (1986, p. 48); Haindl (1989, p. 58);
Own calculations from MIDEPLAN (1994), pp. 121-3)

Since economic growth was high in the period 1985-1992 (Table 1), this result suggests that it was an improvement of conditions in the labour market which was the main factor in reducing inequality since the mid-1980s. This conclusion is corroborated by econometric evidence from the Santiago labour market (see Marcel and Solimano, 1994).

Conclusions

In this concluding section, the answers to the two central questions of the chapter are summarised: (i) how closely does the Chilean experience fit the NEM in the period since 1974? and (ii) to what extent can the changes in income distribution in Chile over the last two decades be attributed to the effects of the NEM?

As to the first question, Chile fits the NEM closely but not perfectly since

1974. Although certain long-run economic policy objectives have persisted virtually unchanged over the last twenty years, several periods can be distinguished according to the choice of policy instruments and to the priority assigned to short-run goals.

The NEM was only consolidated in Chile by the mid-1980s and it is only in the last five years that it has exhibited growth under steady state conditions. Macroeconomic stability (at least relative to other Latin American countries) was finally achieved by the mid-1980s, while the growth rate has exceeded 6.0% per annum since 1984. Growth has been export-led while the economy has opened up on both current and capital accounts of the balance of payments. However, price supports for certain agricultural importables, which were re-introduced after the 1982-83 crisis, are still in place and continue to provide nominal (and effective) protection. The state also continues to offer very generous subsidies for afforestation.

The role of the state has been redefined to offer an efficient enabling framework for private economic activity, while also providing a minimum safety net for the sick and the poor. The coverage of this safety net was substantially extended after 1990, when the country returned to democratic government. Widespread privatisation has led to a significant transfer of assets from the public sector, while the 'socialisation' of private sector debt by the Central Bank in 1982-83 led to a large transfer of liabilities in the opposite direction. The direct effect of both these processes on income distribution was regressive.

The agrarian counter-reform gave rise to a significant medium-sized farm sector in agriculture, and has created a much more active market in agricultural land. Sectoral efficiency has increased as a result, but so has the inequality of farm size and land ownership. The direct effects of industrial privatisation were probably regressive, and there is little evidence of a widespread diffusion of private share ownership.

The reform of public administration has led to improved efficiency through the introduction of better management, tighter budgetary controls and more decentralised decision-making. The increasingly sophisticated use of an extensive and regularly updated data base by well-trained civil servants to target government subsidies and transfers on the poorest has generated a secondary income distribution that is more egalitarian than the primary distribution.

As to the second question, it is important again to distinguish between the two periods of transition the country has undergone since 1974. During the first decade of the military government, it is clear that the combination of rapid and radical structural reforms, and stringent macroeconomic adjustment increased both absolute poverty and income inequality. However, infant mortality continued to decline and life expectancy to improve.

Since 1984, the decline in poverty (as measured by the headcount ratio) and the reduction in income inequality (as measured by the Gini coefficient) have been largely due to the fall in the unemployment rate (see Table A.9) and the increase in real wages (see Table A.8). This tightening of the labour market was largely the result of accelerated economic growth. The persistently high inequality at the top end of the distribution, where the richest quintile received more than 60% of income in the early 1990s, has been accentuated by such policies as the decollectivisation of agriculture, the privatisation of state assets and the decontrol of property rents.

State transfers and subsidies have been redistributed in favour of the poorest groups, but the overall effect of this redistribution was modest under the military government owing to the sharp reduction in real fiscal social expenditure *per capita*. The redistributive effect of social spending became more significant with the return to civilian rule in 1990. 40% of the increased social expenditure which occurred in 1990-91 benefited the poorest quintile, while 63% of such additional expenditure went to the poorest 40% of the population (Schkolnik, 1992, p. 90). More than half (51%) of the increase in real consumption by the poorest two quintiles in 1990 and 1991 was due to this increase in social spending. The corresponding proportion for the middle 40% of income earners was 28%.

However, the main factor reducing poverty and income inequality in the early 1990s was sustained export-led growth. In 1991, 70% of the increase in real consumption by poor households can be traced to the growth of their primary incomes such as labour earnings, while 30% was due to additional social expenditure (MIDEPLAN,1992 quoted in García,1993, p. 140). The predominant contribution of increased primary incomes to improved welfare continued in 1992 (see Table 4).

Finally, it is clear that certain longer run processes have been, and continue to be, at work in determining both economic performance and distributive outcomes in Chile. First, the country has now completed the demographic transition, as well as the other two transitions mentioned earlier in the chapter. The growth rate of the economically active population fell from 2.6% *per annum* in the quinquennium 1975-80 to 1.5% *per annum* in the period 1990-95. This represents a decline of 58% in the annual growth rate of the labour-force which partly explains the tightening of the labour market in the late 1980s.

Secondly, the achievements of both the pre-NEM welfare state and the public educational system in Chile have had important inertial effects on the evolution of social indicators such as infant mortality rates and life expectancy at birth. Recent research on Latin America suggests that, *ceteris paribus*, higher values for health outcomes and educational attainment in 1965 are associated with lower infant mortality and longer life expectancy twenty five years later

(Behrman, 1993, p. 199).

Thirdly, some investments in the export sector have long gestation periods which can be traced to the pre-NEM period. Some timber species which were harvested in the mid-1980s were planted in the late 1960s under the Frei government in response to tax incentives and exemptions from the land reform programme. The Chile-California scheme, which promoted the transfer of agricultural 'know-how' to Chile from the West Coast of the USA in the 1960s, may have also contributed to the successful expansion of the fruit industry twenty years later.

Overall, the distributive impact of the NEM in Chile has followed an inverted-U curve over time. In the short- and medium-run, poverty rose and inequality increased during a lengthy and painful period of stabilisation, macroeconomic adjustment and structural reform. Once this process of transition was complete, and after certain policy errors had been corrected (particularly with respect to the exchange rate), economic growth recovered, poverty declined and income inequality fell. In long-run steady state conditions under a democratic government, the NEM in Chile has been remarkably successful in providing both rapid economic growth and improved equity since 1990.

Whether this successful performance can be maintained in future depends on many factors, only some of which are subject to the control of Chilean policy-makers. Continued access to existing export markets and gaining entry to new markets will be vital, so a speedy completion of the NAFTA negotiations is very important. On the domestic front, a key factor will be developments in the labour market. Upward pressure on wages may jeopardise export growth unless labour productivity continues to rise. A resurgence of organised labour will also test how robust is the existing consensus in Chile as to the goals of the NEM and how they should be achieved.[36]

Notes

*The research for this chapter was supported by the Suntory-Toyota International Centre for Research in Economics and Related Disciplines (STICERD)

1. Having completed this chapter, I found that Petras and Leiva (1994) use the notion of a 'double transition' in Chile with essentially the same meaning as that given here.

2. An important policy initiative taken as part of the World Bank's Structural Adjustment Loan (SAL) to Chile between 1985 and 1988 was the creation of a Copper Stabilisation Fund. This sought to prevent outbreaks of Dutch disease by sterilising additional export revenues resulting from unexpected

increases in the world copper price. Thus, the growth of non-copper exportables would not be jeopardised by sudden real appreciations of the Chilean peso due to volatility in the world copper market.

3. The estimate of the public sector deficit in 1984 includes quasi-fiscal subsidies channeled through the Central Bank (Larrañaga,1989). These were discontinued after 1989. The distributive impact of these subsidies is examined below.

4. Tariffs continued to decline, and by the early 1990s the average nominal tariff rate had fallen to 11% (Bosworth *et al*, 1994a, p. 14)

5. Between 1974 and 1989, the inflation rate of the poor reflects annual changes in the prices of 38 products consumed by the poorest quintile of the population. In 1990, this index was revised to include changes in the prices of 64 products consumed by the poorest. For further details, see Teitelboim (1991). It also appears that low income households spend a higher proportion of their consumption budgets on tradeable goods than high income households. Therefore, real devaluation-induced increases in the general price level are regressive (Meller, 1992).

6. The regression equation in Figure 1 was estimated using the Newton-Raphson iterative method in MICROFIT-3 to correct for two period autoregression (AR2) in the error term.

7. The introduction of tolls on major roads into Central Santiago was announced in July 1991 (Hojman, 1993, p. 141).

8. Annual data on public sector investment are not readily available over this period.

9. The regression equation in Figure 2 was estimated using the maximum likelihood inverse interpolation method to correct for one period autoregression (AR1) in the error term.

10. Three concepts of income may be distinguished for the purposes of this chapter: (i) *primary income* which results from the independent activities of private agents before direct taxation and includes wage income, earnings of the self-employed, rental income and pensions; (ii) *secondary income* which is the sum of primary income and the value of money transfers from the government (excluding direct taxation); and (iii) *total income* which is the sum of secondary income and the imputed consumption value of goods and services provided free by the state. All three income concepts refer to pre-tax incomes and correspond to *ingresos autónomos, ingresos monetarios* and *ingresos corregidos* respectively in MIDEPLAN terminology (Haindl, 1989, p. 51).

11. The largest farms were those with more than 80 BIH.

12. Much of this land was subsequently sold off to the private sector (Rivera and Cruz, 1983, p. 15).

13. The economic value of a firm's assets is taken to be the expected net present value of the future stream of dividends.

14. A good discussion of the methodological problems involved in calculating whether a state enterprise was privatised at a discount to its new shareholders may be found in Saez (1993).

15. The process of privatisation was facilitated by the growth of private pension funds (AFPs). Initially, fund managers invested largely in government bonds and fixed-term deposits, but in 1985 they were permitted to hold debentures and equity of private firms. This boosted the domestic capital market as the AFPs increased their holdings of private stock (Diamond and Valdes-Prieto, 1994, pp. 302-4). Between 1988 and 1994 (June), the share of private pension fund assets held in equity and debentures rose from 8% to 40% (Banco Central, 1994, p. 202).

16. In 1982, foreign currency denominated loans made up nearly 50% of domestic credit.

17. This proportion of GDP in the UK would have been sufficient in 1995 for the Bank of England to have rescued 20 Baring Banks!

18. In 1995, the Senate Finance Commission approved legislation setting out a new regime for the payment of the 'subordinated debt' owed to the Central Bank by eight private commercial banks. They will have 40 years to settle their obligations and must allocate at least 70% of their monthly earnings to service the debt (EIU, 1995, p. 12).

19. The most important of these programmes were the PEM, which was introduced in 1975, and the POJH which was established in 1982 (Córtez Baldassano,1988). Both programmes were terminated in 1989 when the labour market had recovered. For a critical discussion of the PEM and POJH, see Graham (1991;1994).

20. In 1986-87, two-thirds of workers in public employment schemes were drawn from the lowest quintile of the income distribution, and half of the beneficiaries were women (World Bank, 1990, p. 119).

21. Space constraints preclude any discussion of the reforms in health, housing, education and social security under the military regime. Cástañeda (1992) provides a lucid, succinct and generally sympathetic account.

22. Schkolnik (1992) discusses the methodological differences between the CASEN surveys in 1985, 1987 and 1990. The income data in CASEN 1990 are not directly comparable with the data in CASEN 1985 and CASEN 1987.

23. Using the CASEN data for 1987, Haindl has estimated the net redistributive effect of the fiscal system. He found that the main loser was the top decile from which income amounting to 7.6% of GDP was transferred. The main beneficiaries were the third, fourth and fifth deciles which together received

an amount equivalent to more than 8% of GDP (Haindl, 1989, p. 49).

24. 32% of persons under 14 years old are located in the first quintile of households (Teitelboim and Chacon, 1993, p. 26).

25. The role of the minimum wage in reducing inequality and poverty is discussed below.

26. In 1975, copper accounted for 37.8% of export revenues while the corresponding figure in 1992 was 27.3% (ECLAC, 1993, p. 126).

27. Higher levels of industrial concentration among exporters than producers may partly explain why the share of the wholesale price paid in the importing country which accrues to fruit exporters is twice as large as that received by fruit producers (Codron, 1990, p. 12).

28. It has been claimed that 74% of a sample of female temporary workers in agriculture wish to secure full-time employment (PET, 1992a, p. 17). However, the source of this information is unclear.

29. In 1982, the area planted with timber amounted to 68,600 hectares (Gómez and Echenique,1988, p. 144). In 1992, this figure had risen to 130,000 hectares, an increase of 89% in a decade (Gómez, 1994, p. 32).

30. However, wage levels have now risen to the point where selective mechanisation of fruit harvesting has become attractive (*Panorama Económico de la Agricultura,*1994).

31. A complicating factor in this explanation is that since the mid-1970s an increased proportion of the agricultural labour force has become urban resident. The creation of *poblados rurales* in the wake of the agrarian counter-reform of 1974-75 and the greater use of temporary agricultural labour often drawn from nearby towns has contributed to this equalising trend in living standards between urban and rural areas.

32. Excluding the XII Region (Magallanes and the Antarctic) which has rather special features.

33. The methodology used to construct the real regional exchange rate indices for exportables used in the econometric analysis together with the actual data are given in Escobar and Repetto (1993). Two REERs are used: one which includes the output of the state-owned copper corporation (REER1), and the other which excludes this output (REER2). The information on regional GDP *per capita* is given in CIEPLAN-Min. del Interior (1994),while regional dependency ratios may be found in Teitelboim (1992, p. 418).

34. Equation (3) is in reduced form as the effect of changes in the real regional exchange rate for exportables (REER) on poverty would presumably operate *via* changes in the composition of regional output as between tradable and non-tradable goods. However, the simple correlation coefficient between the regional tradability index and the REER was only +0.01 when the output of CODELCO is included in the construction of the

exchange rate, and only rises to +0.30 when CODELCO is excluded. One reason for this low correlation may be that while the REER constructed by Escobar and Repetto refers only to exportables, the tradeability index includes both exportables and importables. Another reason could be that industrial exports not derived from natural resources (amounting to 10% of total Chilean exports in 1991) were excluded from the REER, because it was not possible to assign them to particular regions.

35. In 1990, agriculture and forestry contributed 27.1% of GDP in the VI Region and 10.5% of GDP in the VIII Region. The coal industry of Arauco, which is located in the VIII Region and is uncompetitive with imports, is an important source of regional poverty.

36. If draft legislation currently before Congress is passed, this will strengthen the position of workers in the labour market. The proposals would extend collective bargaining rights to seasonal workers in construction, agriculture and forestry. Employees in small firms would be able to join cross-company unions which would negotiate over wages and conditions of employment (*The Economist*, 13 May/3 June 1995). However, international experience suggests that it is extremely difficult to achieve effective unionisation of such groups of workers.

CHAPTER 8

INCOME DISTRIBUTION AND POVERTY IN MEXICO

Humberto Pánuco-Laguette
and
Miguel Székely*

Following the debt crisis of the first years of the 1980s decade, there has been a worldwide trend towards economic liberalisation that has resulted in a shift in development strategy away from import-substitution and government expenditure to export-led growth. In Latin America, the change to a new economic model (NEM) has implied a drastic redefinition of the role of the state, a commitment to macroeconomic stability and the adoption of trade liberalisation as the way to achieve sustained economic growth. In some countries, these measures have also resulted in a redefinition of the strategy to combat poverty.

Several studies[1] have analysed and mapped out in a theoretical way the transmission mechanisms by which economic liberalisation affects the welfare level of individuals, and there seems to be agreement that conclusions can only be reached by analysing the specific case of each country, as the conditions under which the NEM has been implemented vary widely. However, in general terms, economic liberalisation is expected to have generalised positive effects over the standard of living of the population in the long-run, as it will presumably result in high growth rates and a more efficient allocation of resources in the economy.

The purpose of this study is to analyse the impact of such policies for the case of Mexico and, in particular, to determine if the expected positive outcomes have in fact materialised. The most common approach to evaluate the effects of economic liberalisation on absolute and relative welfare is simply to assume that growth is itself poverty reducing, and that controlling inflation is highly progressive. Here we intend to take a closer look at the transmission mechanisms involved in the process.

Due to the availability of data at the household level, we will analyse the effects on poverty and inequality between 1984, 1989 and 1992. These observations constitute an adequate starting point, although they do not strictly coincide with the three different stages through which the Mexican economy has gone since the introduction of the first measures associated with the NEM.

The first stage, which encompasses the 1983-1989 period, was characterised by the efforts to control inflation and by a strong economic contraction, while the second one, starting in 1989 and continuing up to 1994, saw a partial recovery of growth. In December 1994 the country entered a severe financial crisis, marking the beginning of a third stage which seems to be particularly important in terms of the analysis of the NEM as it has led to doubts about the viability of the new economic strategy not only in Mexico, but also in other parts of the developing world.

This chapter consists of five sections. The first discusses the timing of the implementation of the policies identified with the NEM. The second examines the changes in poverty and inequality that have occurred in Mexico between 1984 and 1992 and explores the causes of such changes. The third deals with the distributive effects of fiscal contraction. The fourth analyses the implications of wage controls, privatisation, and trade and financial liberalisation for income distribution and poverty. The final section draws the conclusions.

A Macroeconomic Overview of the NEM in Mexico

From the early 1950s Mexico followed an inward-looking economic model, which involved the creation of an industrial sector through protectionism in a context of low inflation and high growth rates. Through the 1970s, this strategy was supported by high oil revenues, resulting in a very active role for the state as well as significant increases in GDP *per capita*. However, by 1982 the strategy was no longer sustainable and the country entered a deep economic crisis.

According to Aspe (1993), the Mexican response to the crisis involved a strong fiscal contraction, the privatisation and liquidation of state-owned firms, trade and financial liberalisation, tax reform, the introduction of measures favouring economic deregulation, the renegotiation of public debt, and the redefinition of the strategy to combat poverty, which are all in line with the NEM. The timing of these policies is described below.

The first phase of the NEM in Mexico can be traced to 1983, when the government reacted to a sharp rise in inflation by reducing government expenditures, by a monetary contraction, by increasing the prices paid for publicly provided goods and services, by devaluing the currency and by the liquidation and disincorporation of 200 out of 1155 state-owned firms. This marked the initial stages of the redefinition of the role of the state in the economy simultaneously with the first stabilisation attempts, and they indicate a clear shift away from the public expenditure-led growth model. The second major shift towards the NEM was observed in 1985, when Mexico launched a unilateral trade liberalisation movement by joining the GATT the following year. This unilateral measure marks the first step towards a clear export-oriented strategy.

At the same time international oil prices fell and this initiated a period of economic stagnation that lasted up to 1989. Inflation rates rose sharply (reaching a maximum of 159% in 1987) and the Mexican peso depreciated by almost 50% in real terms. This time, the government's strategy to combat inflation was the creation of the 'Pact for Economic Solidarity' at the end of 1987, a negotiation process between labour, peasants, business and the government through which the freezing of prices and wages were agreed, and the exchange rate was set as the nominal anchor of the system (exchange rate policy changed into one of a preannounced schedule of devaluations against the US dollar). Similar agreements followed the initial Pact, and they continued to be the instrument through which wage, exchange rate, tariff, and public sector pricing policies were defined.

President Carlos Salinas de Gortari came to power in 1988 after a hotly disputed election. The first full year of the Salinas administration, 1989, marked three major changes in the Mexican economy. The first was the liberalisation of the financial system. According to Coorey (1992), the main reforms were the freeing of interest rates, the elimination of direct controls on credit and the reduction in the high reserve requirements for commercial banks. Quantitative restrictions on credit allocation were also lifted and several different financial instruments were allowed to operate.

A consequence of financial liberalisation was a rise in interest rates. This hindered investment through increases in the costs of production and put pressure on the fiscal deficit due to the increase in domestic debt service costs. On the other hand, the amount of credit available to the private sector rose and this contributed to the recovery of growth. Financial liberalisation was reinforced by the introduction of a capital repatriation scheme, which provided incentives for the deposit of foreign resources by Mexicans in domestic banks by charging only a 1% tax rate. The measure seems to have been successful, as it resulted in the repatriation of around $10 billion.

An important step towards the completion of the financial liberalisation process was achieved during the 1991-1993 period, when 18 commercial banks were privatised, the role of development banks was redefined and a new pension-fund system for social security was introduced. However, the fact that the financial sector has continued to have a monopolised structure and has not yet been fully opened to international competition has hindered the possibilities of achieving high growth rates and constituted a bottle-neck for the whole economy.

The second change was the creation of the National Solidarity Programme

(PRONASOL) in 1989. This constituted a redefinition of the poverty alleviation strategy as a single mechanism that incorporated the main social policy tools; it replaced several government agencies, which were difficult to monitor and which sometimes had diffusive objectives (we consider PRONASOL to be of such importance to the theme of this chapter that we have devoted a large section to it (see below)).

The third change was the deregulation of foreign investment. As explained by Kalter (1992), although the efforts at attracting foreign investment (both direct and portfolio) began in 1983, regulations started to be lifted in 1989 when the authorisation procedures were simplified and the limits on foreign ownership of firms were redefined (from a maximum of 49% up to 100% in some cases) and portfolio investment in the stock market became possible. The deregulation of direct foreign investment (DFI) usually has positive short-run effects on growth and inflation, as it enhances government credibility, reduces borrowing requirements, raises taxable income and helps to close the foreign exchange and investment gaps by enlarging the stock of capital available in the economy (see Chapter 6).

One of the most important measures to be reinforced under Salinas was trade liberalisation. Import barriers continued to drop, the proportion of non-controlled items grew to almost 90% and the average tariff decreased. This contributed to a rise in the trade balance deficit from $883 million in 1990 to $15,934 million in 1992, which reversed the positive balance observed between 1983 and 1989. Indeed, imports kept on rising by around 20% each year (reaching 19% of GDP in 1992). Furthermore, while in 1986, imports of capital goods represented 24% of the total, their importance declined steadily up to 1992, while imports of intermediate goods maintained their share. In contrast, there was a significant rise in the proportion of consumption goods from 7% in 1986 to 13% in 1992.

Compared to imports, total exports have increased only modestly since 1986, but the main characteristic of exports has been a drastic change in their composition. Figure 1 shows that in 1985 oil exports accounted for around 55% of the total, but their importance declined consistently up to 1992 when they accounted for only 13%. The dynamic sectors have been the *maquiladora* assembling industry and the machinery and equipment manufacturing subsector (including the automobile and electronics industries). By 1992 these two groups accounted for two-thirds of total exports.

The export pattern indicates that the country has been following an intra-industry and intra-firm export pattern, which according to trade theory[2] requires relatively intensive use of medium-skilled labour and capital. This trade pattern is consistent with the large investments in some specific sub-sectors (such as automobile parts) that have flourished in recent years, as a result of the

Figure 1: Structure of Exports by Sector of Origin, 1980-1992

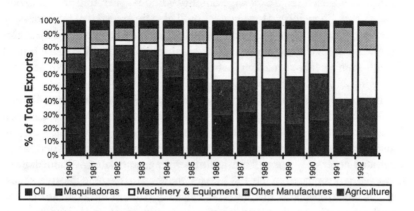

deregulation of DFI. The trade liberalisation measures were further consolidated by the initiation of the North American Free Trade Agreement (NAFTA) in 1994, which constitutes the starting point of a process of multilateral reductions of barriers to trade between Canada, Mexico and the USA.

One of the key features of the Mexican economy, all too apparent by the end of 1994, was its slow rate of growth. One explanation was that the flows of foreign investment had not yet resulted in production and employment increases due to the long maturation period required and also due to the fact that a large proportion of such resources had constituted short-term financial investments. Nevertheless, the transformation process through which the country had been going led to relatively optimistic expectations.

In December 1994, the combination of an overvalued exchange rate[3] (hindering growth and export performance while generating massive flows of imported consumption goods), the uncertainty surrounding exchange rate policy, a high trade deficit of around $18.5 billion for the whole year, the rise in interest rates in the United States and the political instability caused by various events, resulted in massive capital flight and thus a sharp devaluation of the currency. As the exchange rate had been held as the nominal anchor of the system, the result was a severe financial crisis due to the apparent insufficiency of international reserves to fulfill short-term obligations, especially from the issue of *tesobonos*, which amounted to more that $40 billion.

This event is highly significant in the context of the NEM, as Mexico had seemed to constitute a model country in terms of economic recovery and inflation control in the context of economic liberalisation. In fact, some critics have argued that one of the consequences of the NEM has been the flow of excessively 'volatile' foreign capital which proved to be harmful in the long-run, as it created a foreign exchange liability without generating greater export capacity (see Chapter 6). However, it could also be argued that the crisis was generated precisely by the fact that Mexico had not fully implemented the NEM, namely due to its incomplete financial liberalisation process and to the lack of liberalisation in labour markets, which have been a strong impediment for improving export performance.

In some senses, the December 1994 Mexican crisis can be compared to that of 1982, but in many respects it is significantly different. Perhaps the main advantage is that in 1994 the economy had already gone through an intensive transformation process that has helped to ease pressures on the public deficit and facilitated access to capital from multilateral agencies almost immediately. However, as compared to the 1982 crisis, there are also some disadvantages. Perhaps the main one is that an economic recession in the context of trade liberalisation may result in much higher unemployment levels leading to an intensification of social pressures. To this we should add that the possibilities of increasing the value of international reserves through 'speculative' invest-ment or privatisation revenues are highly limited, and that the chances of enhancing export performance are hindered by the incompleteness of the restructuring process in the private sector.

Inequality and Poverty in Mexico, 1984-92

Most of the authors who have analysed economic transformation in Mexico concluded that the fact that inflation had been controlled and that the economy had shown positive growth rates after 1988 were indicators of success.[4] The purpose of this section is to determine how poverty and inequality changed during the 1984-1992 period of economic liberalisation by using the informa-tion in the household income and expenditure surveys for 1984, 1989 and 1992 in order to explain the welfare implications of the macroeconomic programme.[5]

Income distribution in Mexico historically has been very unequal com-pared to other countries in the world, although inequality declined during the 1969-1984 period.[6] In what follows we will analyse how income distribution has changed in Mexico during the period 1984 and 1992 using three different methods. The first will be by comparing the shares of total income of each decile and the top and bottom percentiles; the second will be by the use of diagrams and the third will be by using different inequality measures.

Table 1 illustrates the share of each decile and the top and bottom percentiles in total national income using *per capita* incomes. From this table one can see

Table 1:
Size Distribution of Income in Mexico: 1984, 1989 and 1992

	Income Shares %		
Deciles & Percentiles	**1984**	**1989**	**1992**
Bottom 1%	0.04	0.04	0.06
Bottom 5%	0.60	0.46	0.50
1st Decile	1.60	1.29	1.30
2nd Decile	2.89	2.41	2.35
3rd Decile	3.78	3.30	3.20
4th Decile	4.72	4.22	4.16
5th Decile	5.91	5.26	5.14
6th Decile	7.32	6.56	6.42
7th Decile	9.18	8.26	8.33
8th Decile	11.94	10.67	10.94
9th Decile	16.52	15.51	16.10
10th Decile	36.13	42.50	42.06
Top 5%	24.15	30.76	29.36
Top 1%	9.07	14.02	11.81
Gini Coefficient	0.4740	0.5312	0.5313

Source: Own calculations from the Household Income and Expenditure Surveys. INEGI, 1984, 1989 and 1992 using per capita incomes.

the difference in the national income shares between the bottom and top percentiles and the top and bottom deciles. If we take the shares of the top (richest) and bottom (poorest) decile we can see that the top decile had 22.6 times the share of income of the bottom decile in 1984 and that this difference increased between 1984 and 1989, when the top decile received 32.9 times the share of the bottom decile. This difference between the share of the top and bottom decile, however, did not increase in 1992.

A striking feature of the table is that the top percentile (1%) increased its share of total national income considerably as it went from 9.1% of total national income in 1984 to 14.0% in 1989. This means that in five years (1984 to 1989) the richest one per cent of the population increased its already high share by almost 5% of total national income. The losers were the bottom nine deciles (90 per cent of the population) as each one of these deciles reduced its share of national income between 1984 and 1989 (see Table 2). Between 1989 and 1992 the top percentile lost some of its earlier gains, but was still considerably better off than in 1984.

Our calculations (see Table 2) show that between 1984 and 1989 average income rose by 16.9% in real terms, and between 1989 and 1992 by 15.6%, resulting in an aggregate rise of 35.0% for the whole period. These results do not coincide with the sharp decline in *per capita* GDP between 1984 and 1989 nor with the modest recovery from 1989 to 1992 shown in the national accounts. There are some explanations for this discrepancy. One of them is that GDP does not include all informal activities or non-monetary incomes, which are both more fully captured by the household surveys. Another explanation is that the degree of under-reporting may differ from one survey to another, but this argument is difficult to verify. By taking a closer look at the changes in the real value of each income source, our calculations show that the main discrepancies are registered in entrepreneurial incomes and imputed rents, which appear to have increased disproportionately as compared to those registered in the national accounts. However, it is not possible to determine if the discrepancy is due to inaccuracies in the national accounts or in the income and expenditure surveys.

Table 2:
Income Distribution by Deciles using Per Capita Incomes

Decile	Change in Decile Income Shares (%)			Change in Decile Real Average Income (%)		
	Between '84 &'89	Between '89 & '92	Between '84 &'92	Between '84 & '89	Between '89 &'92	Between '84 & '92
1	-19.1	1.0	-18.3	-5.6	16.34	9.86
2	-16.7	-2.6	-18.8	-2.4	12.81	10.12
3	-12.7	-3.1	-15.4	1.6	12.78	14.63
4	-10.6	-1.4	-11.9	4.2	13.14	17.95
5	-11.1	-2.3	-13.1	3.7	12.96	17.19
6	-10.3	-2.2	-12.2	5.3	13.80	19.82
7	-10.0	0.8	-9.3	5.5	15.74	22.08
8	-10.7	2.5	-8.4	4.3	18.90	24.03
9	-6.1	3.8	-2.6	9.8	19.63	31.35
10	+17.7	-1.1	+16.4	37.5	14.14	56.96
Total				16.9	15.55	35.04

Source: Own calculations from the Household Income and Expenditure Surveys. INEGI, 1984, 1989 and 1992 using per capita incomes.

Apart from increasing its income share by 16.4% in eight years, the 10th decile registers an increase in real average income of 57% during the 1984-1992 period, most of which was achieved between 1984 and 1989 (see Table 2). In contrast, the incomes of the individuals in the first and second decile only rose by 9.9% and 10.1% respectively, as they experienced a decline of 5.6% and

2.4% in real terms between 1984 and 1989. It is interesting to see that the first decile registers a higher rise in real income between 1989 and 1992 than most of the other deciles, but this was not enough to reverse the strong regressive redistributions that occurred in the previous years.

Another approach to show the changes in inequality is by using Pen's parade (see Chapter 1). This graph is built by plotting on the horizontal axis the number of income recipients as a proportion of the total, ranked from the poorest upwards. The vertical axis shows the income that each of the individuals receive. The result is the so-called parade of dwarfs and a few giants (see Figure 2). The name comes from the fact that each individual in the graph appears with a height according to their respective income. As a result, most of the people appear as dwarves as their income is relatively low, while there will only be few giants with very high incomes. This illustration shows clearly one of the main features of income distribution in Mexico - the huge inequality illustrated by the right-hand part of the curve.

One can see from Figure 2 that the parade for 1992 lies above the parade for 1989 except for the top percentile, as people in general had more real income in 1992 than in 1989 (see Table 2). Conversely, the parade for 1984 lies entirely below the parade for 1989 and 1992. This is a result of the fact that average income for each decile and for the population as a whole increased during the 1984-1992 period.[7] Another important feature that Figure 2 shows is that the main beneficiaries of the increase in real income are those people in the top decile as their real income during the period 1984-1989 increased disproportionately in comparison to the other deciles. We can see that there is a considerable difference between the right-hand tail of the parade for 1984 and the parades for 1989 and 1992.

Figure 2: Pen's Parade, Per Capita Monthly Income (In thousands of 1990 US dollars)

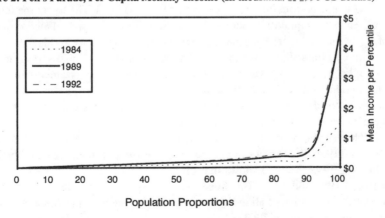

Population Proportions

Source: Own Calculations from INEGI, 1984, 1989 and 1992

The results obtained from Table 2 and Figure 2 are twofold. First, there is an unambiguous increase in inequality between 1984 and 1989, mainly due to the relatively high increase in the share of total income accruing to the top decile.[8] Secondly, economic welfare increased during the period as there was an increase in the real income of the population between 1984 and 1989 (except for the first and second deciles) and between 1989 and 1992. To make these results compatible, we can conclude that, although there was an increase in the real income of the population during the period, this did not increase the level of social welfare in Mexico due to the sharp increase in inequality between 1984 and 1989.

The next part of the chapter calculates different inequality measures using *per capita* income. For this purpose we use different indices, all of which form part of the family of General Entropy measures (Cowell, 1995). The general form of these types of indices is the following:

$$G.E. = \frac{1}{\alpha^2 - \alpha} \left[\frac{1}{n} \sum_{i=1}^{n} \left[\frac{y_i}{\mu} \right]^{\alpha} - 1 \right]$$

where μ is average income and α is an arbitrary parameter which may be given any value from $-\alpha$ to $+\alpha$. The values of α that we will adopt for the present study will be the same as the ones used by Cowell (1984) i.e. from -1 to +2. In general, a large positive value for the parameter α indicates that the measure is sensitive to income differences at the top end of the income distribution (this is known as a *top sensitive* inequality measure). Similarly, measures with negative values of α indicate that the measure is sensitive to income differences at the bottom end of the distribution (known as *bottom sensitive* measures).

The results from the exercise can be seen in Table 3. The lower the index, the greater the equality in income distribution and *vice versa*. Of all the values of α, the one of +2 is the one that shows the greatest inequality as this is the most sensitive to high incomes. Likewise, the value of α of -1 also shows higher inequality as at the bottom end of the distribution we find more inequality than in the middle range. As we find more people in the lower-middle and middle ranges of the distribution, the values of α that give more weight to the centre of the distribution give relatively more equality.

The results, without exception, reveal an increase in inequality between 1984 and 1989. We can say unambiguously that 1984 shows more equality than 1989 and 1992. Table 3 shows that on average inequality increased by 63% between 1984 and 1989. This huge rise in inequality was due to a very high increase in the value of all indices, especially the one with the value of $\alpha = 2$, as this index increased by 214.2%.

Table 3:
General Entropy Index (Per Capita Incomes)

Alpha	Value			Change (%)		
	1984	1989	1992	1984-89	1989-92	1984-92
2	0.7729	2.4283	1.2081	214.2	-50.2	56.3
1	0.4224	0.6238	0.5631	47.7	-9.7	33.3
0.5	0.3878	0.5144	0.4971	32.6	-3.4	28.2
0	0.3937	0.5056	0.5020	28.4	-0.7	27.5
-0.5	0.4541	0.5818	0.5754	28.1	-1.1	26.7
-1	0.6398	0.8140	0.7546	27.2	-7.3	17.9
Average				**63.0**	**-12.1**	**31.7**

Source: Own calculations from the Household Income and Expenditure
Surveys. INEGI, 1984, 1989 and 1992 using per capita incomes.

The results between 1989 and 1992 display some reduction in inequality. As illustrated in Table 3, inequality reduced on average by 12.1% between 1989 and 1992. The year 1989 shows considerable more inequality at the lower and at the top end of the distribution than 1992. Actually, the difference is substantially higher at the top end of the distribution where the value of the index reaches 2.4283 in 1989 in comparison to 1992 where the value reduces by half to 1.2081 (see Table 3). However, the distribution of income still remained more unequal in 1992 than in 1984 as Mexico did not recover from the crisis years with respect to the distribution of income of its population.

Table 4:
General Entropy Index (Household Incomes), Urban Areas

Alpha	Value			Change (%)		
	1984	1989	1992	1984-89	1989-92	1984-92
2	0.334	0.489	0.471	46.4	-3.7	41.0
1	0.278	0.367	0.359	32.0	-2.2	29.1
0.5	0.274	0.349	0.343	27.4	-1.7	25.2
0	0.284	0.354	0.349	24.6	-1.4	22.9
-0.5	0.312	0.386	0.380	23.7	-1.6	21.8
-1	0.365	0.452	0.443	23.8	-2.0	21.4
Average				**29.7**	**-2.1**	**26.9**

Source: Own calculations from the Household Income and Expenditure Surveys .
INEGI, 1984, 1989 and 1992 using household incomes aggregated by deciles.

For the analysis of inequality in urban (high density) and rural (low density) areas in Mexico, we use the same General Entropy measure as before. If we analyse the case of urban areas first (see Table 4), we can see that inequality increased on average by 29.7% between 1984 and 1989 although there was a reduction on average of inequality between 1989 and 1992 of 2.1% (Table 4).

The results for rural areas show that inequality between 1984 and 1989 increased, but not as much as in urban areas (see Table 5). Inequality appears to have fallen after 1989 at the middle and lower end of the distribution – even showing more equality than in 1984 at the bottom end. Inequality increased at the top end of the distribution, however, in 1992 compared with both 1989 and 1984. What happened during the period of recovery in rural areas (1989-92) is that people at the middle and bottom end of the distribution moved closer with respect to each others' incomes while the richest population moved outwards. As a result, inequality only increased on average by 0.3% between 1984 and 1992 (see Table 5).

Table 5:
General Entropy Index (Household Incomes), Rural Areas

Alpha	Value			Change (%)		
	1984	1989	1992	1984-89	1989-92	1984-92
2	0.321	0.337	0.341	5.0	1.2	6.2
1	0.272	0.282	0.279	3.7	-1.1	2.6
0.5	0.269	0.278	0.272	3.3	-2.2	1.1
0	0.282	0.290	0.280	2.8	-3.4	-0.7
-0.5	0.313	0.322	0.305	2.9	-5.3	-2.6
-1	0.369	0.380	0.352	3.0	-7.4	-4.6
Average				3.4	-3.0	0.3

Source: Own calculations from the Household Income and Expenditure Surveys. INEGI, 1984, 1989 and 1992 using household incomes aggregated by deciles.

For the analysis of inequality in urban and rural areas we have decomposed the General Entropy measure outlined above as this will enable us to compare inequality *between* and *within* rural and urban areas.[9] The results are shown in Table 6, where we can see that inequality *within* urban and rural areas explains most of the inequality in Mexico, while inequality *between* these areas is less significant. From these figures, we can also see that inequality *within* decreases its relative significance (from 89.6 to 84.3%), while inequality *between* increased its relative importance (from 10.4 to 15.7%) during the period.

Table 6:
Decomposition of Rural-Urban Inequality

	1984	1989	1992
Within	89.6	87.0	84.3
Between	10.4	13.0	15.7
Total	100.0	100.0	100.0

Source: Own calculations from the Household Income and Expenditure Surveys.

All these results suggest that the period of recession and stabilisation (1984-9) has adversely affected the high density areas, as the increase in inequality was more an urban phenomenon than a rural one. Furthermore, inequality *between* urban and rural areas has risen as inequality within urban areas has become considerably higher in comparison to inequality in rural areas.

By dividing the population into four socioeconomic groups (extremely poor, moderately poor, middle class and rich), we can form a clearer picture of the welfare changes registered in Mexico.[11] Table 7 shows the results. The increase in the proportion of extremely poor individuals between 1984 and 1989 is in line with the expected outcome of the contractionary policies implemented in the first sub-period under study. It is interesting to see that the short-run effects of trade liberalisation, devaluation and fiscal contraction seem to have been a large negative impact on the incomes of the moderately and extremely poor, little effect on the incomes of the middle class and a substantial improvement for the rich.

Table 7: Income Distribution by Class

	Population Share (%)			(%) Change in Real Income		
	1984	1989	1992	84-89	89-92	84-92
Extremely Poor	10.3	10.7	10.8	-4.0	15.9	11.4
Moderately Poor	19.5	17.6	17.1	-2.0	12.3	9.9
Middle Class	62.1	61.9	60.7	0.7	12.0	12.7
Rich	8.1	9.9	11.5	26.71	5.5	33.7
Total	100	100	100	16.9	15.6	35.0

Source: Own calculations from the Household Income and Expenditure Surveys. INEGI, 1984, 1989, and 1992.

In order to throw further light on the changes in poverty, we can compute the value of the three most common poverty indices (see Chaper 1). The results are presented in Table 8.[12] First of all, regardless of the index used, extreme poverty increased between 1984 and 1989, as the proportion of the extremely poor rose, the poverty gap (the average distance to the poverty line) widened, and inequality within the poor (FGT index) increased. However, in the case of moderate poverty the conclusion depends on the poverty index used, as the headcount ratio declined, but the poverty gap and the FGT index increased. This means that, although the proportion of moderately poor diminished, those who continued to be moderately poor were poorer in 1989 than in 1984.

Table 8: Poverty Measures: 1984, 1989 and 1992

Poverty Line	Poverty Index	Year		
		1984	1989	1992
	H	10.33	10.7	10.8
Extreme Poverty	PG	3.04	3.5	3.19
	FGT	1.38	1.73	1.37
	H	29.85	28.3	27.8
Moderate Poverty	PG	10.3	10.6	10.2
	FGT	5.10	5.53	5.16

Note:
H = Headcount, PG = Poverty Gap Index; FGT = Foster-Greer-Thorbecke Index

Source: Own calculations from the Household Income and Expenditure Surveys. INEGI, 1984, 1989, and 1992

Table 9 shows the results of decomposing poverty by occupation of the household head for 1984, 1989 and 1992. It is interesting to note that between 1984 and 1989, the share of agricultural workers in total poverty decreased, although the share increased sharply again by 1992. Indeed, between 1989 and 1992 poverty decreased for all the occupational groups except rural workers. The share of industrial workers in poverty has increased since 1984. During the first sub-period under study, the population share of this occupation declined slightly, perhaps due to the minimum wage deterioration experienced in that period which led to migration towards other occupations and to job losses occasioned by economic stagnation. During the 1989-1992 period, industrial activities attracted a larger share of the population perhaps as a response to the positive effects of trade liberalisation on some manufactures and the *maquiladora* industry. However, industrial workers continued to account for almost 16% of the overall FGT index in 1992 (see Table 9).

According to our results, the 1989-1992 period constitutes one of recovery in macroeconomic terms, as well as one of improvement in the relative position of the extremely poor with respect to the rest of the population, which constitutes a considerable reversal as compared to the stagnation period. Table 8 shows that the proportion of extremely poor remained practically constant, but the poverty gap and the FGT index declined, meaning that on average the extremely poor were better off in 1992 than in 1989. Regarding moderate poverty, there is an unambiguous decline in the proportion (H), in the average distance of their incomes to the poverty line (PG) and in the inequality level within the group (FGT). Despite the improvement during the second sub-period, the losses

Table 9:
Poverty by Occupation: 1984, 1989 and 1992

	Share (%) of Total Poverty (FGT Index)		
Occupation	**1984**	**1989**	**1992**
Workers in Agriculture	64.77	62.37	66.72
Industrial Workers	12.98	15.88	15.86
Other Occupations	11.19	9.75	8.62
Professionals and Technicians	0.25	1.00	0.67
High Level Officials and Directors	0.18	1.84	0.21
Middle Level Officials and Salesmen	5.45	3.54	3.00
Street Vendors and Domestic Servants	3.57	3.05	2.76
Drivers and Armed Forces Workers	1.62	2.58	2.16

Source: Own calculations from the Household Income and Expenditure Surveys. INEGI, 1984, 1989, and 1992.

suffered by the poor between 1984 and 1989 were strong enough to result in a deterioration in their relative position throughout the overall period under study. It is interesting to note that between 1984 and 1992, the proportion of individuals in extreme poverty increased by five per cent in a context of a rise in the real average income reported in the surveys of more than 35%. Since the total population expanded by around 15%, this resulted in a change in the number of individuals without sufficient income to acquire the minimal food bundle from 7,839,444 to 9,033,473 – an absolute increase of 1,194,029 individuals in extreme poverty.

Recalling the results concerning the changes in inequality during the period, it is obvious that economic growth does not guarantee poverty reduction as its benefits do not necessarily reach everyone. In the case of Mexico, simultaneously with the increases in extreme poverty registered during the 1984-1992 period, the standard of living of the richest 70% of the population increased and, as we argued before, the main gains were registered at the highest income levels.

During the 1989-1992 period inequality did not change significantly and this had some poverty reducing effects in a context of economic growth. INEGI-CEPAL (1993) argues that during the 1990s this inequality and poverty increasing trend has been reversed and that sustainable growth in the next few years will continue to have poverty reducing effects. In order to verify this argument, we would need to determine if the structure of the Mexican economy has remained unchanged in such a way so as to make this result likely. To analyse this, we can use some formulae suggested by Kakwani (1993), which allow us to analyse the fall in the poverty index when income distribution or average income improves.

The idea behind the definition of the formulae is that rises in average income will tend to have positive 'trickle-down' effects over the whole population when income distribution does not deteriorate simultaneously, while a redistribution of income from the poor to the rich would increase poverty when average income remains unchanged. Table 10 shows the results of computing the elasticities of the FGT index with respect to changes in mean income and changes in inequality for a range of poverty lines, and throws some light on structural change in the Mexican economy. If we take the extreme poverty line in 1984 (92, 986 monthly 1992 pesos), a one per cent positive growth rate would have reduced extreme poverty by 2.4% (given by the negative sign), while a one per cent improvement in income distribution (a one per cent decline in the Gini index given by income transfers from the rich to the poor) would have reduced extreme poverty by 16.3% (given by the positive sign).

Two main conclusions can be derived from Table 10. The first is that the lower the poverty line, the higher the difference between the two elasticities for each year. This means that for the extremely poor, improvements in the distribution of income have a much larger effect than the 'spill-over' effects from growth for reducing poverty. For all the poverty lines considered, the difference in elasticities declines as incomes rise, but the potential of income redistribution for poverty alleviation remains greater than that of economic growth.   The second important conclusion is that between the three years 1984, 1989 and 1992, the elasticities have changed considerably. Between 1984 and 1989, the elasticity with respect to economic growth declined (as the rise in the poverty gap made it more difficult to 'pull' individuals over the poverty line), while that with respect to inequality became higher. By 1992 both elasticities, but especially that with respect to inequality, increased again. These results indicate that the changes experienced between 1984 and 1992 make it less likely that the spill-over effects from economic growth will have any significant effect on poverty alleviation compared to the potential of inequality reductions.

Table 10: Poverty Elasticities: 1984, 1989 and 1992

Poverty Line (Monthly 1992 Pesos)	Elasticity With Respect to Mean Income Changes			Elasticity With Respect to Changes in Inequality		
	1984	1989	1992	1984	1989	1992
87,778	-2.42	-2.15	-2.75	17.49	19.76	23.58
92,986*	-2.41	-2.06	-2.66	16.32	18.18	21.70
117,037	-2.24	-2.04	-2.31	12.08	13.98	15.61
146,297	-2.11	-1.93	2.04	9.00	10.52	11.38
167,949^	-2.04	-1.83	-1.93	7.47	8.75	9.46
175,556	-2.01	-1.82	-1.89	7.02	8.27	8.90
204,815	-1.89	-1.72	-1.76	5.61	6.70	7.17
234,075	-1.75	-1.63	-1.67	4.58	5.56	5.95

Extreme poverty line; ^ Moderate poverty line
Source: Own calculations from the Household Income and Expenditure Surveys. INEGI 1984, 1989, and 1992.

The Effects of Fiscal Adjustment On Inequality and Poverty: Public Education and PRONASOL

One of the most straightforward implications of the NEM on poverty and inequality is the redefinition of the role of the state and the efforts to stabilise the economy that lead to changes in the composition of government expenditures. Several authors have argued that, if a fiscal contraction is translated into expenditure reductions on services such as health, housing, education, water, electricity and subsidies to consumption and production, poverty and inequality will tend to rise if the poor are the main beneficiaries from them.

This section attempts to take a closer look at the fiscal contraction, and its relation to the changes in poverty and inequality observed during the 1984-1992 period. The main problem is that a comprehensive evaluation would require a detailed analysis of the impact of the main social policies at a microeconomic level, which is beyond the scope of this chapter, but we can identify broadly some of the connections between the main social-oriented expenditures and absolute and relative welfare.

Aspe (1993) has argued that, despite the generalised fiscal contraction in Mexico after 1982, particular emphasis has been paid to protect those social expenditures that affect the poor directly and, moreover, that the increase in public revenues registered since 1988 has been directed towards social policies.

Figure 3 shows the importance of the main social components of total programmable expenditures. It can be seen that public education, public health, rural development and PRONASOL, which before 1988 included the budget for regional development, accounted for around 40% of the total in 1983, and more than 52% in 1992. Therefore, in aggregate terms it seems that the main social policies have in fact been protected throughout the transformation process.

Nevertheless, expenditures on rural development have decreased consistently throughout the 1982-1992 period, as at the beginning of the crisis they represented around 10% of total programmable expenditures, but by 1992 their share had been reduced to only five per cent. Rural development expenditures include subsidies to agricultural production, rural credit and rural infrastructure, and it can be safely said that the economic crisis starting in 1982 and the initial stages of the implementation of the NEM in Mexico have had negative consequences for those policies.

The four social programmes mentioned above can be thought of in aggregate terms as having poverty and inequality reducing effects. We might expect that the improvement in the relative position of public education, public health and PRONASOL programmes would be favourable for relatively disadvantaged individuals and, in particular, that they would have avoided larger welfare losses up to 1982. In what follows, we examine in particular the public education and PRONASOL programmes.

Figure 3: Composition of Public Programmable Expenditures in Mexico 1975-1992

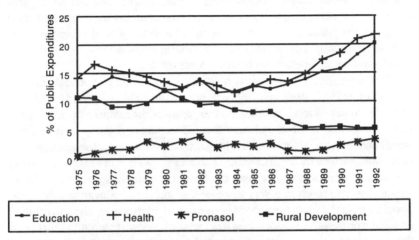

Source: Own Calculations from the 5th Presidential Report, 1993.

The effects of a change in the amount of resources allocated to public education are difficult to evaluate. There is controversy around the impact of education on incomes, and some have questioned whether education raises productivity or is simply a means of acquiring credentials that indicate other characteristics. Throughout the literature[13] there have been attempts to isolate the effects of education from other personal characteristics such as ability, family background, etc., that influence the degree to which individuals can benefit from the service. Also, the benefits from education are usually observed long after the individual acquires it, which makes it difficult to determine to what extent a change in public expenditures in education has a direct impact on the incomes received. Despite these problems, some of the effects can be analysed under the realistic assumption that higher levels of education are identified with greater incomes.

For our purposes, it is particularly important to identify the benefits individuals receive from different types of education because, as explained by Schultz (1988), different educational levels generate different private and social returns. In particular, the social component is higher at lower levels, but as the number of years of schooling rises private returns become more important, to the extent that only a small component of social benefit can be observed at post-graduate levels.

Moreover, as explained by Polachek and Siebert (1993), one of the main distinctive characteristics of the educational process is that, in order to acquire the highest private benefits, it is necessary to 'climb' through the system, which implies direct monetary and non-monetary costs for receiving formal education. Usually, poor individuals have low levels of education because they have scarce means for financing the private costs involved (especially the opportunity cost of not earning incomes while receiving education). For this reason, poor individuals usually only benefit from the initial educational levels (if at all), and are rarely able to benefit from higher education.

This argument seems to apply to Mexico, as according to our calculations from INEGI (1984, 1989, and 1992) the poorest households spend around 74% of their incomes on food, clothing, housing and health (compared to 53% for the richest households), which indicates that the amount of resources left for other goods and services is low and that longer term investments, such as in formal education, are usually not affordable. Table 11 shows that in Mexico, the lower the income level of the individual, the fewer the years of schooling received, which seems to result in a very unequal distribution of education among the population: the heads of the poorest households do not even receive full primary education on average. Besides, as at low income levels private returns are lower, the positive correlation between income and education is not only given by the difference in the number of years of schooling, but by the fact that the education received by the poor is less fruitful in terms of income than that received by the rich.

Table 11: Years of Schooling by Decile

Decile	Average Number of Years of Education of Household Head
Average	5.09
1	2.09
2	2.83
3	3.48
4	3.61
5	4.50
6	4.70
7	5.68
8	6.22
9	7.66
10	10.13

Source: Own calculations from the Household Income and Expenditure Surveys. INEGI 1984, 1989, and 1992.

Figure 4 shows that since 1982 pre-primary education (which covers more than 2.5 million students) has improved its relative position in the educational budget, while the primary education system reduced its importance from around 30% in 1982, to 22% in 1990, rising to 26% in 1993. In contrast, higher education levels, which benefit only around one per cent of the total population, improved their relative position throughout the period (reaching around 20% of the public education budget). The secondary education system also accounted for a larger share of expenditure, while high school education remained unchanged.

Figure 4: Composition of Government Expenditures in Education by Level

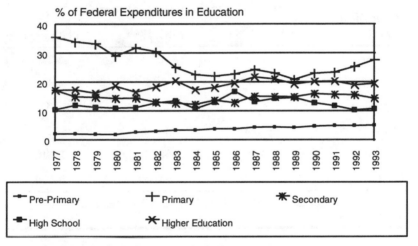

Source: Own Calculations from the 5th Presidential Report, 1993.

One way of determining the implications of changes in the expenditure shares for the demand for education is by dividing the budget assigned to each level by the number of students enrolled as a proxy for the subsidy acquired when having access to the system. Table 12 shows the results. It can be seen that between 1977 and 1984 those individuals who only acquired pre-primary and primary education had access to 8.3% of the subsidies for the whole system, while those who went to university benefited from 34.6%. It can also be seen that the 1985-1989 fiscal contraction had negative consequences for basic education, as the subsidy to the system concentrated even more at the highest level: those individuals who could only enrol in the first few years received only seven per cent of the benefits. The effects on the income of the population in the following years is likely to have been regressive.

The 1990-1992 period constitutes an improvement for those individuals that only enrolled in primary and pre-primary levels, as by doing so they had access to 10% of the subsidy. Those who reached secondary school benefited from an additional ten per cent, in contrast with the adjustment period (1985-9) in which this level only accounted for eight per cent. Nevertheless, the benefits from public education continued to be highly concentrated at university level, which continued to account for 37.2% of the subsidy as compared to 34.6% up to 1984.

Table 12: Subsidies to Education

Education Level	Proportion of Subsidy Received by Enrolling in the System (averages)		
	1977-1984	**1985-1989**	**1990-1992**
Pre-Primary	4.65	4.02	5.23
Primary	3.67	3.68	4.85
Secondary	9.31	7.97	10.43
High School	47.76	46.12	42.29
University	34.60	38.12	37.20
Total	**100.00**	**100.00**	**100.00**

Source: Own calculations from the Fifth Presidential Report. Salinas de Gortari, 1993

Although the data do not allow us to identify completely the causality between public expenditures and individual welfare, some conclusions can be obtained: if a lower proportion of the subsidy *per capita* to certain education levels means a deterioration in their quality relative to others, and if in fact poor and lower-middle class individuals benefited more from pre-primary to high school public education while the upper middle class and the rich benefit relatively more from public universities, it can be said that between 1984 and 1992 the change in the composition of public expenditures in education in Mexico has been regressive. Therefore, the progress implied by the protection in the overall education budget seems to have been counterbalanced by the regression in the distribution by education level.

One of the main distinctive characteristics of the implementation of the NEM in Mexico has been PRONASOL, which redefined significantly the strategy to combat poverty. The programme has several distinctive characteristics compared to prior policies. The first one is that it includes a wide span of mechanisms that were previously isolated, which sometimes duplicated functions and which were difficult to evaluate due to the variety of objectives they pursued besides poverty alleviation.[14] This in itself constitutes an improvement in policy design for planning purposes, as it allows us to monitor the effects of government programmes on poverty in an easier way. Secondly, PRONASOL distributes its resources among state governments and municipalities who are then placed in charge of transferring the benefit to the population, substituting the central allocation of resources observed previously. Thirdly, it incorporates the beneficiaries of the programme into its financing and operation procedures, which constitutes a major shift away from state-provided benefits. This is intended to improve targeting by incorporating the beneficiaries in the resource allocation process and it also enhances efficiency by encouraging the recipients' participation through monetary and non-monetary contributions (payments in kind, labour, etc.), increasing the amount of resources available and improving monitoring.

The creation of PRONASOL has also marked a clear shift away from traditional poverty alleviation mechanisms such as subsidies to credit, guaranteed prices for beans and maize production, and subsidies to consumption. These programmes have been substituted by the creation of credit funds, by cash handouts to increase the incomes of maize and beans producers directly (a scheme named PROCAMPO) and by the provision of consumption good bundles and food vouchers to the target population.

PRONASOL has three main strategies to combat poverty: *welfare benefits* (including the distribution of food bundles, vouchers, subsidies to consumption, health and education infrastructure improvements, and the provision of electricity, drainage, urbanisation, housing and water); *production benefits* (mainly rural credit, and loans for the acquisition of productive infrastructure and irrigation projects), and *regional development* programmes (which include the construction and repair of roads and highways, as well as municipal funds).

Due to the nature of the benefits involved, it is extremely difficult to evaluate their impact on poverty and inequality in the short-run, and moreover to compare them with the impact of prior policies. Most of the critics of PRONASOL argue that the shift to cash handouts, voucher provisions and regional targeting have been used to guarantee electoral success, rather than to enhance the operation and efficiency of poverty alleviation. In particular, it has been argued that the allocation of funds to municipalities responds directly to political interests: either to ' punish' those who have not elected the candidates from the ruling party or to 'reward' those who have.

Regarding the evaluation of the programme in economic terms, there are two main studies, one by El Colegio de México (1993), and another by Levy

(1994). Both argue that the resources distributed by PRONASOL have not been allocated to the poorest regions nor to alleviate the most urgent needs of the poorest among the poor, although it cannot be said that the objectives of the programme have not been accomplished at all.

Figure 5 shows the share of each region in total poverty obtained by multiplying the value of the FGT index by the average population share in 1984, 1989 and 1992. It can be seen that the programme allocate 32% of its resources to the two regions that account for almost 50% of the poverty of the country (the Centre and South East), and that it also gave considerable importance to the Centre West region, in which 18.5% of poverty is concentrated. At the other extreme, it did not allocate resources to the Federal District (whose share in poverty is only 1.2%), and it also assigned relatively low proportions to the North West and North East regions, which account for only 5.9% of total poverty. The two cases in which the poverty shares do not correspond to the distribution of PRONASOL expenditures are the South, which receives a relatively low proportion for its poverty level, and the South West, which receives a disproportionate share as it only accounts for 2.8% of total poverty. Therefore at the aggregate level it seems that the programme is allocating the largest and lowest proportions of expenditures to those regions that need them relatively more and less respectively, which seems to be appropriate.

Figure 5: Regional Distribution of Expenditures by PRONASOL and Share of Each Region in Total Poverty

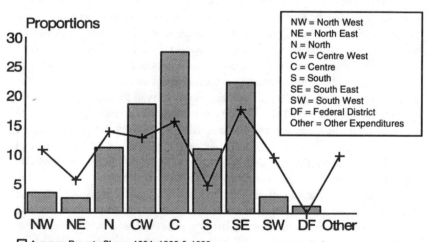

□ Average Poverty Share: 1984, 1989 & 1992
+ Total Expenditures 1988-1992

Sources: Salinas de Gortari (1993) and INEGI 1984, 1989 and 1992

In order to take a second step towards evaluating the effectiveness of the expenditures by PRONASOL, we can analyse the changes in poverty by region between 1989 and 1992[15] (see Figure 6). The first strong conclusion is that, although PRONASOL has favoured the South East (which includes the states of Oaxaca, Guerrero and Chiapas – among the poorest states in the country), this is in fact the region in which the most dramatic rise in poverty has been observed. Although the counterfactual explanation would perhaps state that without PRONASOL poverty would have increased much more, it seems more reasonable to interpret the result as evidence of the limitations of the programme in the short-run for poverty alleviation. This is supported by the fact that, despite attracting very low shares of the PRONASOL budget, poverty reductions were registered in the North East, South, and the Federal District between 1989 and 1992 while, despite being the second most important destination of resources, the Central region registered a rise in poverty. PRONASOL expenditures only seem to coincide with the changes in poverty in the case of the North and Centre West regions.

Figure 6: Poverty Level by Region in Mexico in 1984, 1989 and 1992, Measured by the FGT Index

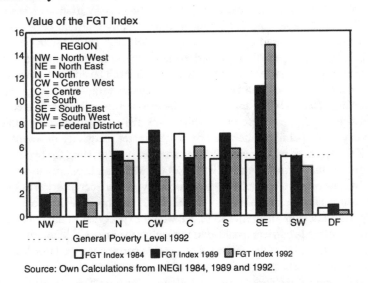

Value of the FGT Index

REGION
NW = North West
NE = North East
N = North
CW = Centre West
C = Centre
S = South
SE = South East
SW = South West
DF = Federal District

- - - - - - - General Poverty Level 1992
□ FGT Index 1984 ■ FGT Index 1989 ▩ FGT Index 1992
Source: Own Calculations from INEGI 1984, 1989 and 1992.

The results are also interesting in line with the overall changes in poverty registered during the 1984-1992 period analysed in the previous section. First, poverty as measured by the FGT index for the moderate poverty line (which is used for the regional calculations) increased between 1984 and 1989 by 8.43%

(see Table 8). However, it can be seen (see Figure 6) that this change occurred despite considerable reductions in poverty in the North West, North East, North and Centre regions. This means that poverty increased because of the deterioration in the standard of living of the poor in the Centre West, South, the Federal District and, especially, in the South East. Between 1989 and 1992 the disparities were also significant. The value of the FGT poverty index for moderate poverty between these two years (see Table 8) decreased by 6.69%, although poverty increased sharply in the Centre region, and in the South East, where the value of the FGT index rose by 35% (see Figure 6).

Payments to Factors of Production

In order to analyse the distributive consequences of payment to factors of production, we can decompose inequality by income source. For this purpose we will use the Coefficient of Variation (CV), as it can be proved that it is the only index that can be decomposed in a simple way and that at the same time fulfills the conditions suggested by Shorrocks (1982) through which unique results about the contribution of each income source to total inequality can be obtained.[16] Table 13 shows the result of this procedure and the identification of the contribution to the changes registered.[17]

Inequality in Mexico measured by the Coefficient of Variation increased by 16.5% between 1984 and 1989, remained practically constant between 1989 and 1992 and increased by 17.8% between 1984 and 1992. It can be seen in Table 13 that during the first sub-period the sharp rise in inequality was mainly due to entrepreneurial rents (especially from industrial businesses, commercial businesses and services) and imputed non-monetary rents, while wages had an equalising effect. During the second sub-period, although overall inequality hardly changed, there were major shifts, with the strong equalising effect of property rents being counteracted by much greater inequality in wages.

The effects of wage inequality are particularly interesting for two reasons. The first is that during the stabilisation of the Mexican economy wages were tightly controlled to control inflation; secondly, trade liberalisation has major implications for the prices paid for certain kinds of labour. As indicated by the Stolper-Samuelson Theorem (SST), we would expect that in the long-run the reduction of trade barriers would tend to equalise the prices of labour in Mexico with those in the USA, the country's main trade partner. As the USA has much higher salary levels, this would presumably drive Mexican wages up.

If a country is characterised by following an intra-firm or intra-industry trade pattern, the demand for skilled labour and capital will rise when tariffs decline, as the price of imported inputs needed for their production decreases. According to Woodward (1992), the consequences of a rise in the demand for capital and high skills, in a country which is neither capital nor high skill

Table 13: Variance of Income by Source

Income Source	Value of the Coefficient of Variation			Contribution to the Change in Inequality (a) (%)	
	1984	1989	1992	1984-89	1989-92
Total Income	.87	1.01	1.03	100	100
Wages	.85	.82	.93	-19.0	461.6
Entrepreneurial Rents	.94	1.37	1.46	59.6	-17.0
Industrial Business	.77	2.13	1.83	32.8	-112.0
Commercial Business	1.01	1.55	1.41	38.6	-282.1
Services	.87	1.51	1.65	38.6	221.1
Raw Material Processing	1.28	1.15	.77	0.0	-16.0
Agricultural Business	.74	.36	.73	-21.7	28.8
Livestock Business	1.32	.90	1.41	-28.7	143.2
Property Rents	1.66	2.25	1.25	10.2	-410.9
Production Cooperatives	1.15	1.08	.87	0.1	-13.6
Transfers	.74	.87	.77	3.3	-94.3
Other Monetary Income	2.27	2.24	2.21	3.5	110.2
Non-Monetary Autoconsumption	.33	.15	.31	-2.9	26.9
Non-Monetary In Kind	.91	1.20	1.12	5.6	31.0
Non-Monetary Gifts	.67	1.01	.69	3.5	-37.7
Non-Monetary Imputed Rent	.9669	1.10	1.00	36.1	43.8

(a) The figures are the sum of the inequality effect, the income share effect and the joint effect (see footnote 16). Disaggregated figures available from the authors on request.

Source: Own calculations from the Household Income and Expenditure Surveys. INEGI, 1984, 1989 and 1992, using household incomes aggregated by deciles, rather than the disaggregated data.

abundant, is that there will be a redistribution of income from plentiful labour and land to scarce physical and human capital. If the demand for unskilled labour declines, wages will fall and the lower is productivity the greater the adverse effect. On the other hand, trade liberalisation also generates demand for the highest and relatively scarce skills that are not directly used in the production process, as certain services (e.g. financial) become indispensable for exporting and importing goods. Therefore, redistribution of income towards these skills is likely.

Figure 7 shows that between 1982 and 1984 the average remuneration per worker in the economy decreased by 15% in real terms and the gap with respect to the minimum wage widened. The deterioration continued up to 1987, but since then the average remuneration has recovered some of its real value, while the minimum wage has continued to deteriorate. This has resulted in a considerable widening of the gap between the lowest and the average remunerations in the economy. Simultaneously with these changes, open unemployment in Mexico declined from 5.7% in 1984, to 2.9% in 1989 and to 2.8% in 1992, while underemployment decreased from 23.3% in 1987 to 21.6% in 1992[18] (but both measures increased again between 1992 and 1993, when the economy stagnated). This would lead us to conclude that unemployment and underemployment did not increase dramatically in Mexico during the 1984-1992 period precisely because the Pact for Economic Solidarity allowed for (downwards) wage flexibility, which could therefore be interpreted as one of the causes of the rise in extreme poverty illustrated before.

Figure 7: Annual Remuneration per Worker, Minimum Wage and Average Income by Education Level in Real Terms ('000 1992 NP)

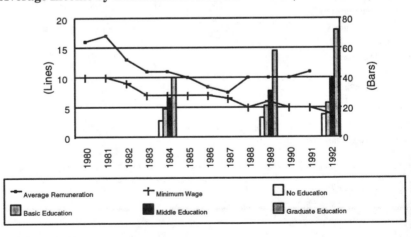

Source: Own Calculations from the 5th Presidential Report, 1993 and INEGI 1984, 1989 and 1992

The impact of wage deterioration tends to be greater at lower income levels, as it makes it relatively more costly to shift from wage-earning activities into others. The fact that between 1984 and 1989 wages had an equalising effect, while during the 1989-1992 period they had a very strong inequality effect (see Table 13), was caused mainly by the changes within wage inequality and not by households shifting away or towards this income source.

The differences in the possibilities of escaping wage deterioration can be thought of as being directly related with the skill level of an individual. For instance, during the 1984-1989 period of economic contraction, the downwards wage flexibility and small change in unemployment indicate either that individuals were willing to perform the same jobs at lower salaries or that individuals with relatively higher skills would accept jobs that did not remunerate such skills. Both effects tend to have adverse consequences for the lower-skilled workers. This argument explains some of the results in Figure 7, where it can be seen that the gap between the wages of non-educated workers and those with basic and middle education decreased between the two years, but that the gap with individuals with graduate level education increased considerably.

This would lead to the conclusion that the Pact was an effective mechanism of wage control that contributed to reduce inflation, but that the effects were very unequally distributed among the population due to the low mobility of labour during these years. The equalising effect of wages during the stabilisation period was caused due to the compression of middle and low wages, while the gap with the highest ones increased.

During the first stages of economic recovery after 1988, the gap between the average remuneration and the minimum wage continued to widen. Figure 7 also shows that the gap between the average wage of workers with no education and with basic level education narrowed, while the gap with the wages earned by those with middle graduate level education increased substantially. It therefore seems that the higher the skills of the individual, the higher the possibilities of adapting to a new economic environment and benefiting from the opportunities generated in a growing economy. The fact that Mexico has increased its trade flows with the USA in goods that require medium-skilled labour intensively indicates that the lowest incomes have not responded to the factor price equalisation effect expected.

Another source of income, where changes can be directly related to the effects of trade liberalisation, is entrepreneurial rents. During the 1984-1989 period, the sharp rise in overall inequality was due mainly to the change in entrepreneurial incomes, which accounted for almost 60% of the shift (see Table 13). Although between 1989 and 1992 the contribution to the change in inequality was negative, there were larger positive and negative effects at the sectoral level (see Table 13): incomes from industrial and commercial business had a very strong equalising effect, which was almost totally counterbalanced by the strong contribution to inequality from the provision of services, livestock business and agricultural business.

One of the explanations for the rise in inequality in entrepreneurial rents between 1984 and 1989 is given by the connection between wages and entrepreneurial incomes: wage contractions lead to higher profits, which will be greater the larger the number of workers employed. Therefore, the fact that minimum wages deteriorated consistently up to 1989 would tend to expand the gap between small-scale entrepreneurs (who are normally poorer) and larger ones (who are presumably the richest). Small businesses also have fewer possibilities of avoiding an adverse economic environment. In particular, access to credit is crucial, as it allows larger firms to compensate for demand contractions by shifting into lower quality production (small firms normally do not have access to formal credit).

With regard to the different types of entrepreneurial activity, the case of agriculture in Mexico is one of the most interesting, as most of the poverty in the country is found there. Between 1984 and 1989, the real guaranteed prices for maize and beans production declined by 20% and 50% respectively, and the yield per hectare of maize production also fell 25%. As the poorest of the rural are precisely maize and beans producers, this contributed to the gap between the incomes of the households in the first and tenth deciles and pushed the incomes of poor rural producers downwards.

The fact that entrepreneurial income from agriculture contributed to inequality between 1989 and 1992 (see Table 13) can be attributed to some extent to the sharp rise in exports registered in fruits (around 250%) and vegetables (almost 150%), as these kinds of products require larger investments than those normally undertaken by small rural producers. In contrast, the real guaranteed price of maize dropped by around 10%, and the price of beans declined by 30%, which leads us to conclude that the benefits of trade liberalisation have not yet reached the poorest rural producers.

Another interesting case is that of entrepreneurial income from commercial business, which benefits from the reduction in barriers to imports. This source had a strong impact on inequality between 1984 and 1989 (see Table 13), which was caused by a large increase in the earnings of the richest households from these incomes. Households from the second to the sixth deciles also relied more on these type of incomes during the crisis years, but part of the increase in inequality can be attributed to the fact that most low income individuals engaging in these activities are located in the informal sector. Between 1989 and 1992, the shift away from commercial business income (registered in the second to the ninth deciles) was responsible for the decline in inequality in this income source, which in fact generated a considerable equalising effect on overall income distribution. This could be explained by the saturation of these kind of activities, which lowered their profitability.

In the case of industrial business, the sharp rise in inequality during the 1984-1989 period (see Table 13) can be attributed to a large extent to the shift of the richest households towards this income source. This is at first surprising since trade liberalisation is supposed to have its greatest impact on the protected industrial sector, but the result may reflect the fact that during periods of economic contraction new markets for lower priced (and lower quality) goods emerge. The shift of households away from these kinds of incomes since 1989 may in fact be the response to this effect.

Another important entrepreneurial income source has been from services. Throughout the 1984-1992 period the distribution of these kind of incomes have registered high regressive effects on inequality (see Table 13). Between 1984 and 1989, the changes were mainly caused by the increase in inequality *within* this kind of income, but in the second sub-period the impact of the shift of households from the seventh to the tenth decile towards this source of income (the income share effect) was the major cause of the dispersion. Since services are in general a non-tradeable, and were therefore not directly affected by trade liberalisation, they have constituted an escape valve for some individuals.

Although between 1984 and 1989 property ownership rents made a relatively small contribution to the change in inequality compared to other sources of income, between 1989 and 1992 this source recorded the largest equalising contribution (see Table 13). As the main component within property ownership rents is interest payments from financial investments, there is a strong relationship with financial liberalisation.

As explained by Reyes Heroles (1988), financial liberalisation usually has an important impact on interest rate incomes. If new investment instruments are created and if the initial capital stock among households in the economy is unequal, there will be a spread of yields according to the amount of capital, and this tends to shift income towards the richest savers. Additionally, Gersovitz (1989) argues that as at higher incomes there are higher propensities to save, differential interest rates will benefit the rich more, not only because they have access to better instruments, but also because a larger part of their income is derived from higher interest rates (see also Chapter 5).

In order to test the above argument, we can calculate the potential yield of one Mexican peso invested in different financial instruments with different accessibility since 1981. Figure 8 shows that if this amount had been invested in 1981 in bank deposits (available to the whole public with a very low minimum capital requirement) or the money market (available for larger capitals only), it would have lost around 38% and 30% of its real value respectively up to 1984. Additionally, if the same peso had been deposited in the USA (only available to those who can finance the large transaction costs involved) before the 1982 devaluation, it would have gained 58%. This reflects the fact that devaluations generate capital gains for those who are able to protect themselves against them.

Figure 8: Real Value of One Peso Invested in 1981 in Different Portfolios

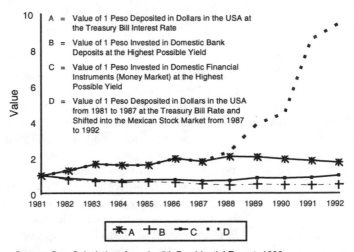

Source: Own Calculations from the 5th Presidential Report, 1993.

Although the gap between the yield of each financial instrument was already wide, it expanded further during the 1984-1989 period: those who were able to maintain their deposits in foreign currency (line A in Figure 8) avoided the 1987 devaluation and registered a 28% gain, those who only had access to bank deposits (line B) recorded a 17% loss, those who were able to invest in the money market gained 23% (line C), while those who maintained their deposits in foreign currency between 1984 and 1987 but then shifted into the stock market up to 1989 (line D), obtained a 145% yield. These differentials provide a good explanation for the rise in inequality observed in property ownership rents during the stagnation period (see Table 13).

During the 1989-1992 period, the gap between the yield generated by each financial instrument widened further, especially due to the high yields offered by the stock market. It can be seen in Figure 8 that those who kept their capital in US bank deposits lost 9.8% between 1989 and 1992 due to the appreciation of the Mexican peso, while those who invested in the money market gained three per cent and those who only had access to bank deposits lost 8.4%. On the other hand, those who had access to stock market investments during this period registered a 121.4% capital gain.

By analysing these results, we would expect further deterioration in the distribution of property ownership rents between 1989 and 1992, given by the large differentials between the yields of those financial instruments to which only the smallest and largest capital stocks respectively have access. It is therefore surprising to observe in Table 13 that there was a sharp decline in inequality in the distribution of these type of incomes which almost cancelled out the wage inequality effect. Furthermore, most of the decrease can be attributed to a shift of the richest households (income share effect) away from this source.

The most plausible explanation is that during the 1984-1989 period, the public internal debt represented on average around 23% of GDP, while between 1989 and 1992 it decreased significantly to around 8.4%. Investments from financial instruments, of which government bonds represent a considerable proportion, account for the largest part of property ownership rents. Following this argument, one plausible explanation for the simultaneous expansion of the gap in the yield on financial instruments and the sharp decrease in inequality from property ownership rents between 1989 and 1992 is that the richest households shifted from financial assets to other kind of non-financial domestic investments at some stage between those two years.[19] In this respect, it is interesting to note that the only identifiable policy change that has to do with the shift from financial assets to other investments is privatisation. Therefore, it could be argued that at least part of the shift was a response to the new opportunities offered by privatisation (it should be remembered that privatisation was intensified precisely between 1989 and 1992), as some of the richest households could have used their financial investments to participate in the acquisition of state-owned firms.

Conclusions

This chapter has explained the impact of the NEM on poverty and inequality in Mexico. First, it should be said that most of the policies identified with the NEM have in fact been implemented in Mexico since 1983, but the analysis has only been able to consider some of the short-run visible effects, leaving the longer run implications for future consideration.

In macroeconomic terms, it can be said that the adverse international environment plus the implementation of fiscal restraint, privatisation, trade and financial liberalisation, tax reform, deregulation and the redefinition of the strategy to combat poverty, had both positive and negative effects. However, it seems that the negative effects were stronger in microeconomic terms as the result has been a sharp deterioration in income distribution during the 1984-

1992 period that generated a rise in extreme poverty in a context of real average income increases of more than 35%. This resulted in an increase of 1.2 million in the number of individuals who did not have access to a minimum food bundle.

Even though economic liberalisation is expected to generate welfare gains for the whole population in the long-run, it seems that in the case of Mexico the reforms have contributed to the deterioration in income distribution by providing greater opportunities for those individuals who had a better relative initial position, given by their ownership of greater human, physical and financial assets. Moreover, it seems that some measures, such as privatisation and financial liberalisation, have contributed to the concentration of resources in fewer hands, which has implications for the distribution of income in the long-run.

Regarding the changes in poverty, the rural poor and the lowest paid industrial workers have been excluded from the benefits of growth. One of the reasons is that the main policy mechanism, which explicitly addressed the problem of reducing extreme poverty (PRONASOL), has had only a modest impact on the incomes of the poorest of the poor.

Perhaps the main conclusion is that there has been a structural shift in the economy which has long-term negative consequences. Our results indicate that the possibilities of alleviating poverty through 'trickle down' effects were already limited in 1984 as compared to the power of income redistribution. However, the gap between the two expanded after 1984 as a result of structural change. This means that it is now more difficult to alleviate poverty exclusively through growth, while at the same time the number of redistributive mechanisms has been reduced in line with the redefinition of the role of the state in the economy. Therefore, the possibility of making export-led growth compatible with poverty alleviation seems to be rather limited at the moment.

In the case of Mexico, economic liberalisation may in fact result in a further deterioration in income distribution and in greater poverty unless some kind of active redistributive policies are implemented. It seems obvious that if, for instance, trade liberalisation continues to have a dispersive effect on wages, this will tend to increase income inequality even more as it seems unlikely that there will be further progressive effects from property ownership rents.[20]

Even if high growth rates are achieved, poverty may rise if the benefits to the poor are undermined through a further concentration of income among the richest sectors of the population. This possibility has become even more relevant as a result of the 1994 financial crisis, as this event has limited the possibilities of expanding social policy. Moreover, it seems likely that the efforts to re-stabilise the economy will have adverse effects on absolute and relative welfare similar to those observed during the 1984-1989 period, as some of the measures implemented by the Mexican government are in fact analogous to those introduced in 1982.

If the economy stagnates, as expected, poverty is likely to rise. Furthermore, the burden of the adjustment costs may again be concentrated among the poorest of the poor, as the new 'emergency plan' implies large cuts in subsidies to production and consumption, real wage falls and greater unemployment (see Table A.8 and A.9). On the other hand, given the distribution of physical and human assets among the Mexican population, it seems inevitable that trade liberalisation, combined with strict controls on the minimum wage, the use of high real interest rates to contain capital flight, and the availability of a wider range of financial instruments which yield differential interest rates depending on the capital stock invested, will lead to a further deterioration in the distribution of income – at least in the short-run.

Notes

*   The authors wish to thank the valuable comments by Claudia Aburto, Adalberto García Rocha and Rodolfo de la Torre.

1.   For example, Demery and Addison (1987), Pastor (1987), Corden (1987), Heller *et al* (1988), Woodward (1992), Stewart (1995), and Berry and Stewart (1994).

2.   Greenaway and Milner (1987) explains this in more detail.

3.   It had appreciated by almost 40% in real terms since 1987.

4.   The works by Aspe (1993), Kalter (1992), and Lustig (1992) are good examples of this.

5.   The fact that the most recent household income and expenditure surveys in Mexico were held in 1984 (with 5,272 observations) 1989 (13,550 observations) and 1992 (11,920 observations) constitutes a great advantage, as it allows us to separate the 1984-1989 stagnation period from the one of economic recovery (1989-1994). The surveys were carried out by the Instituto Nacional de Estadística, Geografía e Informática (INEGI). The three data sets are strictly comparable, they were held the same days of each year, they use identical sampling techniques and utilise identical instruments for obtaining the information.

The results presented in this chapter were obtained by processing the raw dissaggregated data (every household micro-observation) of the three surveys provided directly by INEGI, but two transformations were required. The first one consisted in inflating the incomes registered in 1984 and 1989 to convert them into 1992 prices, by using an average of the Consumer Price Index (CPI) (see Salinas, 1993) for the six months prior to the survey, as this was the reference period for incomes. No differential indices were used for urban and rural areas because, as indicated by Coplamar (1983), price differentials in Mexico have been found to be insignificant between these two sectors. The second transformation is concerned with the selection of an equivalence scale. Due to the lack of recent data for Mexico, and due to the fact that the family structures remained practically constant between 1984 and 1992, we will assume that each member obtains the same proportion of total income as the others.

6.   Van Ginneken (1985) presents estimates of the Gini index applied to household data since 1950.

7.   Although we remind the reader that there is a discrepancy between the national accounts and the income and expenditure surveys.

8.   The differences in inequality between 1989 and 1992 are less clear.

9.   The Gini coefficient gives more weight to any change made at the centre of the distribution, as Atkinson (1970) shows.

10.   For the decomposition we have used the Theil index which is the General Entropy measure with α equal to +1. For the decomposition we are following the work of Cowell (1984). Strictly speaking, this decomposition should be applied to the dissaggregated data. Information about rural and urban location is only available by deciles, so the results underestimate the total amount of inequality due to the underestimation of the inequalities within deciles.

11.   The definition of the poverty line in Mexico, as elsewhere, is crucial. One of the only reliable data sources concerning basic needs requirements and prices is Coplamar (1983), which provides the market cost of several items which may be classified as 'basic needs'. For the purposes of this study, two poverty lines are used: an extreme poverty line, which only includes the necessary income to have access to a minimal food bundle, equal to 92,986 monthly 1992 pesos (equivalent to $30) and a moderate poverty line that, besides food, includes the minimum necessary income to acquire housing, health, and education, equal to 167,949 1992 pesos per month (equivalent to $54.28). In order to translate the value of these poverty lines from 1984, to 1989, and to 1992 pesos, the average price index by item of consumption, for the prior six months, was used. We then calculated the share of entrepreneurial rents in total income as an indicator of membership of the middle class or rich groups, which implies setting the 'rich-dividing' line at 5.5 times the value of the moderate poverty line, as by doing so those households with relatively high entrepreneurial incomes (more than 24%) are separated from the rest of the population in 1984.

12.   Until this moment, only INEGI-CEPAL (1993) has calculated the extent of poverty for the same three years using the same data bases and our

results do not coincide with theirs. The origin of the discrepancies is that INEGI-CEPAL applies a 'correction' factor to the incomes in the surveys, arguing that this makes them compatible with the national accounts; they also use different poverty lines.

13.   Behrman (1990) provides a summary of studies.

14.   One example of this is that PRONASOL acquired most of the tasks of the rural credit bank BANRURAL, of the subsidies to input prices for agricultural production, of the subsidies to consumption traditionally managed by CONASUPO and LICONSA, and of the provision of electricity, water and drainage to poor areas.

15.   According to INEGI (1992), although the three surveys are strictly comparable, their representativity at the regional level may differ because the size of the sample in each region has varied from year to year. This implies that the variance of the observations (and therefore their reliability) may also differ from one region to the other. However, the comparison made in this chapter is valid, as we are more interested in the trend that poverty has followed rather than its exact magnitude.

16.   Székely (1995b), has demonstrated that the (CV) index can be written in the following way:

$$CV = \sum_{j=1}^{k} \theta_j \beta_j CV_j$$

where θ_j is the correlation coefficient between income source j and total income, β_j represents the income share of income source j, and CV_j is the value of the CV index for income source j.

If we define $I_j = \theta_j CV_j$, inequality measured by this index could be said to change due to two reasons: either through changes in I_j, or by changes in β_j. As it is desirable to be able to identify both effects separately, we can apply the decomposition method suggested by Székely (1995b), which involves computing:

$$\Delta CV = \sum_{j=1}^{k} I_j^* \Delta \beta_j + \sum_{j=1}^{k} \beta_j^* \Delta I_j$$

where k is the number of income sources, and *delta* (Δ) denotes a change in time while I_j^* and β_j^* are defined as

$$I_j^* = \left(I_{j,t} + I_{j,t+1} \right) / 2$$

$$\beta_j^* = \left(\beta_{j,t} + \beta_{j,t+1} \right) / 2$$

The first term represents the contribution of the change in the income share of each source to the change in *CV*, while the second term is the contribution of the change in inequality within each source to the overall shift.

17. These results presented here can be compared with those in Székely (1995), in which the contributions to the change in inequality were obtained simply through the natural decomposition of the Coefficient of Variation.

18. See Salinas de Gortari, 1993.

19. We can rule out the possibility of capital flight as a destination for the financial assets of the richest households, as significant capital repatriations were registered in Mexico after 1989.

20. The reason is that the progressive character of property ownership rents during the 1989-1992 period can in fact be explained through the once-and-for-all asset reallocation process generated by privatisation.

CHAPTER 9

HONDURAS, THE NEW ECONOMIC MODEL AND POVERTY

Andy Thorpe*

One principal problem in interpreting the impact of the New Economic Model (NEM) policies upon poverty in Honduras, a problem shared by the accompanying case studies in this volume, is that of identifying the point at which the NEM became operational (or even whether the economic policies adopted could be construed as conforming to a 'typical' NEM). Some (Noé Pino, 1990; Noé Pino and Hernández, 1990, p. 56) talk in terms of policy after 1985 being formulated within NEM terms of reference. Others, such as the World Bank (1994a, p. 7), identify the changeover point as 3 March 1990, the date when the Honduran Congress approved the *Ley de Ordenamiento Estructural* (Decreto No.18-90), a law more popularly referred to as '*el paquetazo*'. While 1990 clearly marks an important change in economic policy (and will be used as the starting point for the NEM), there were some important changes in policy during the 1980s and these will need to be analysed.

This chapter commences by briefly *outlining* the economic crisis that hit the country at the start of the 1980s. Then, in the light of the dispute over dates, we split the period 1985-94 into two sub-periods, identifying and analysing economic policy while noting those institutional and exogenous factors which have prevented or perverted the implementation of a 'full-blown' NEM or which have tainted the results. In the third section we evaluate the impact of policy change on Honduran poverty levels within the two sub-periods.

The Period of Acute Economic Crisis, 1980-1984

Honduras returned to democratic rule in 1982 with the inauguration of the Liberal Roberto Suazo Córdova as President. Nevertheless, the weakness of the democratic system[2] provided the basis for the continued high public profile of the military establishment, principally through the Reagan-inspired 'National Security' doctrine in the mid-eighties. As a consequence, the process of political democratisation that occurred during the decade provided a fragile basis for economic policy formation, with the threat of a military return to power omnipresent.

The economic plan of the new civilian government had definite neo-liberal underpinnings and was directly influenced by what has become known as the Negroponte document.[3] The document outlined the terms of the recently approved Caribbean Basin Initiative (CBI), but made the release of aid conditional upon a number of economic policy reforms. These included (i) a rapprochement with private international banks, (ii) the elimination of export barriers, (iii) that assistance granted would be apportioned with a bias towards the private sector – and in particular to that geared towards export production, (iv) that state intervention in the economic sphere would be reduced and improvements sought in its effectiveness, (v) that moves be made towards extending the private property basis of the rural land market and (vi) that social programme expansion would be curtailed until the economic situation improved.

The document echoed the words of a private sector document published just fourteen days before the Suazo Córdova government took office by a group of entrepreneurs led by Miguel Facussé. The major points of departure between the two documents lay in a divergence of opinion over the need to maintain a protected domestic market. Whilst the Negroponte version favoured the liberalisation of both external trade and the exchange rate, the Facussé view, which was against such liberalisation, prevailed. As a result of rejecting devaluation[4] as a policy option, the maintenance of some form of import control became imperative. The desire for retaining these controls, as Hernández details (1987, p. 123), is best understood by reference to the economic constellation of industrialists behind the Facussé plan. These industrialists, orientated as they were to the domestic market, were intensely protectionist in outlook and chose to use their economic power to ensure that the captive internal market remained just that. This strategy of indirectly taxing exports (through exchange-rate overvaluation) while controlling imports seriously weakened the profitability of the agro-export sector (SRN, 1990, p. 8, USAID, 1989, p. 1), and coincided with a sharp fall in the international price of coffee, one of the country's principal export commodities.

While import controls had some success in controlling the escalation of the trade deficit (imports declined 3.6% between 1980-4), it was at the cost of excluding productive inputs and equipment seen as critical for the expansion of domestic industry and agriculture (Noé Pino and Perdomo,1992, p.8). These controls were nevertheless insufficient to protect the lempira's international value and had to be buttressed by (i) $240 million of the country's reserves over the period 1980-3 and (ii) increased external borrowing to the tune of $1,004 million.[5] External indebtedness reached $2,392 million at the end of 1984. Payment on this debt rose from around $33 million at the end of the seventies to $133 million in the early eighties, thereby accentuating the pressures on the exchange rate.

The 17.4% deterioration in the terms of trade in this 'crisis' period was reflected in a sharp deterioration in economic growth, which fell from 8.8% per year at the end of the 1970s to just 0.7% in the early eighties. *Per capita* income declined 8.2% between 1980 and 1984. Paralleling this, unemployment increased to 10.7% (from 8.8%) with underemployment rising to 24.5% (from 15.2%). While the government attempted to limit the fiscal deficit, most notably by (i) freezing minimum salary levels (1981), (ii) raising public utility prices and (iii) introducing tax changes aimed at increasing import and direct taxation shares (April 1981 and July 1982)[6], increased public investment, which rose 69% in real terms in the first half of the decade, caused the deficit to explode.[7]

Growth, Adjustment and Hybrid Models

One of the central elements of the NEM is exchange-rate policy and the necessity of a real devaluation to restore competitiveness (see Chapter 2). Despite Central Bank scepticism about the likely 'J-curve effect' (see Footnote 4) it would have been impossible to hold the line on the lempira's international value, given the sharp run-down in reserves, if it had not been for particular geopolitical developments at the time.

The emergence of the Sandinistas in Nicaragua in 1979 and the growing strength of the *Frente Farabundo Martí para la Liberación Nacional* (FMLN) in El Salvador had led to US covert intervention in the region increasing sharply in the 1980s. Honduras was to play a key role in this scenario – providing the Palmerola air-base as a Northern Command centre for US troops, allowing the Nicaraguan contras to operate from Honduran territory and preventing the Salvadorean FMLN doing the same, while keeping up the propaganda war against supposed communist subversion in the region. This support did not come cheap. Meza (1988) notes how both the quantity and structure of US lending to Honduras changed with the annual sums advanced increasing from $57 million to $283 million between 1980 and 1985, while the military's share of this rose from 7% to 76%.

This 'export of military services' offset the pressures on the lempira, allowing the government to maintain an over-valued exchange rate in the short-term. It also permitted expenditure-switching as external support for the military budget released funds that could be re-deployed elsewhere. Thus, whereas the government deficit had remained anchored around 6% of GDP in the latter half of the seventies, it now doubled to reach 12.2% by the end of the decade. In the longer term, however, the maintenance of both government deficits and exchange-rate stability were dependent upon continued capital inflows, hence Noé Pino's characterisation of the period as an 'unstable' one.

Recognition of this prompted the adoption of a new trade regime (NTR), with the international institutions accepting the Honduran case for exchange-rate stability providing the country accelerated the introduction of export promotion measures. While this had already begun in December 1983 with the *Ley de Fomento de Exportaciones*, which laid the basis for a non-traditional export drive *via* the use of favourable credit and fiscal policies, it gathered pace from late 1984 onwards.

The *Régimen de Importación Temporal* (the RIT, Decreto No.37-84) of December 1984 granted industrial firms, whose product markets were outside the Central American region, exemption from all forms of taxation and customs duties on the import of resources or capital equipment. In 1985 the *Ley de Exoneración en la Importación de Maquinaria y Equipo* extended the exemption to those industrial producers whose activities (i) involved the use of more than 50% of material inputs of a national origin and (ii) augmented value-added by 40% or more. A further relaxing of trade policy saw *El Reglamento de Compensación y Trueque* (Decreto No. 220-5/86) which permitted a company to use its export earnings to settle directly its import bills, without having to seek permission from the Central Bank first.

In May 1987 the *Ley de Fomento de Exportaciones* was superseded by a new variant which offered special credit facilities to those companies engaged in activities that added more than 20% in value-added terms, in addition to a special subsidy scheme (*Certificado de Fomento de las Exportaciones* – CEFEX) based on the product's export value. The same year the *Ley de Zonas Industriales de Procesamiento* saw the establishment of industrial parks that both allowed the free import/export of goods and offered exemption from profits tax[8] on the proviso that each park generated a minimum of 5,000 jobs within five years. It was not until 23 December 1987, however, when the CETRAS (*Certificados Transferibles con Opción a Divisas*) scheme was introduced, [9] that agricultural producers benefited to any degree from the NTR.

Despite these measures, Honduras still remained dependent upon a narrow export portfolio (mainly bananas and coffee). This ensured that the country's fate and development prospects remained shackled to the prices of these crops in world markets. Although coffee prices rose 56% to $243.3 per sack in 1986 (due to Brazilian harvest failures), by the end of the decade they had fallen back to below their 1984 level, with export receipts only slightly up despite output having risen 25.6%. Banana results were rather more positive. Both prices and volumes increased as expectancy of increased sales due to the Single European Market drew closer. Revenues rose $119.7 million in total, confirming bananas as the country's principal tradeable good. The 54% increase in international zinc prices between 1984 and 1989 caused marketed output to rise 24%, generating an additional $30 million of exports. However, none of these improved export receipts can be directly linked to the country's export promotion initiatives as these commodities only benefitted relatively late in the day from such legislation.

This improved export performance, and the record harvests of grain at the close of the decade, saw GDP grow 22% in real terms between 1984 and 1989. GDP *per capita* rose 4.6% to stand at $822 in 1990. Although the economic decline experienced at the beginning of the decade had been reversed during the second quinquennium, income *per capita* was still down 0.8% compared to 1980. Furthermore, the explosion in government indebtedness had seen public sector debt servicing requirements almost triple to 30.7% of total government expenditures, making the country ever more dependent upon external borrowing. Borrowing, however, had been conditional upon reducing the public sector deficit and the failure to conform led to IMF and World Bank blacklisting in 1989. The instability of the past growth path was now evident for all to see.

The new incoming Nationalist government of Rafael Leonardo Callejas (1990-94) would find itself faced with three major challenges. First, to reduce the public sector deficit and restore the country's creditworthiness in front of the international financial institutions. Second, to reduce the country's continued reliance upon a narrow basket of export commodities. Third, to guide the country in the new *post* Cold War environment, an environment which would undoubtably see US interest in the region wane. To accomplish this, a more serious and far-reaching economic reform programme would be necessary.[10]

The new economic policy was heralded in the Nationalist's Government Plan 1990-4: 'Honduras must mobilise enormous forces, not only to resolve the crisis that has emerged since 1980, but also to eliminate or reduce substantively the economic and social backwardness that have been generated by a development style that has been seen to be both inefficient and uncoordinated' (SRN, 1990, p. 1). The centrepiece of this programme was the *Ley de Ordenamiento Estructural* (Decreto No.18-90) and its hand-maiden, the *Ley de Fortalecimiento de la Administración Tributaria* of March 1990. This time, the reduction in the anti-export bias of Honduran economic policy was eliminated in a much more conventional manner, as the Callejas government bowed to international pressures and devalued the lempira. The lempira's value, and more importantly *El Factor de Valoración Aduanera* (FVA),[11] immediately fell 50% to four lempiras to the dollar. A number of controlled devaluations further reduced its value to 5.40 by the end of 1991. In 1992 the currency was allowed to float freely, reaching 8.60 lempiras to the dollar in June 1994. This prompted renewed control attempts, principally through the introduction of daily currency auctions by the Central Bank in June 1994. While this succeeded in reducing currency volatility, by the year-end the lempira was being quoted at 9.40 to the dollar.

Devaluation obviated the necessity for compensatory legislation and so both the *CETRAS* legislation and the *Reglamento de Compensación y Trueque* were repealed, but export promotion continued. *The Ley de Incentivos a la Producción Bananera* in May 1991 offered a series of export tax-breaks to the banana companies while the crisis in the world coffee market was ameliorated by (i) extending temporary production subsidies and (ii) replacing the fixed levy of $4.50 per sack with a variable tariff underpinned by a 'floor' price ($70 per sack).

Import liberalisation followed as *per* NEM theory, with plans to establish a common external tariff of between 5 and 20% (January 1992) compared to the rates of 5-50% that were levied earlier. In fact, import duties actually rose by 20 million lempiras between 1989 and 1990 as (i) the removal of the complex web of import exemptions generated an extra 110 million lempiras for the Treasury's purse (Cálix and Vindel de Cálix, 1992, p. 307), (ii) the government continued to levy a 10% surcharge on around 25% of all imports and a 5% surcharge on about 90% of imports until the end of 1994 (World Bank, 1994, p. 27; IMF, 1995, p. 31).

Partial fiscal adjustment along the lines proposed by the NEM occurred over the period 1990-2. Fiscal revenues were improved as the sales tax was increased from 5% to 7% (10% for cigarettes and alcohol). Personal direct taxation was also reformed. The exempted income limit was raised from 5,000 to 10,000 lempiras (in 1991 the limit was further raised to 18,000) with a progressively tapered system peaking at a rate of 40% for those declaring annual incomes of over 1 million lempiras.[12]

A key problem in Honduras is the effectiveness of the tax system, Edwards (1994, p.10) commenting that tax administration remains weak.[13] Thus, the reform's central objectives were not targeted at reducing the tax burden, but at facilitating the collectability of the tax (hence the historic preference for trade-based taxes). Therefore, despite the new personal income thresholds, the new tax measures were expected to increase revenues collected, generating an additional 74 million lempiras in the 1990 calendar year. Equally, with the corporation tax system streamlined (15% for incomes below 100,000 lempiras, 35% on incomes above), the expectancy was that corporate tax revenues would also rise. Fiscal income received a boost in 1990 as Decreto 18-90 established a temporary windfall tax on exports *(Impuesto Temporal a la Ganancia Extraordinaria de Exportación)*, diverting part of the profits derived from devaluation into government coffers.[14] Similarly, the belated recognition of the revenue potential offered by the 'dollarisation' of export taxes contributed to fiscal receipt growth in 1991.

Following World Bank insistence, the Callejas government agreed to revise utility prices. Decreto 99-90 established six new electricity tariff bands, heralding price rises of between 114-158% in January 1993 and then an additional 42% in August 1994. Administrative improvements were also on the agenda as an estimated 28% of electricity produced remained unbilled (GRH, 1994, p.9). The national water authority, SANAA, raised prices by 10% in 1990, its first increase since 1983. The telecommunications company, HONDUTEL, was also permitted to amend its tariff structure, in particular 'dollarising' charges for international calls, and is slated to be the first of the utility privatisations.[15]

On the public expenditure front we see the clearest evidence of a hybrid model. Increased efficiency in the public sector was expected to reduce ministerial operating costs by an average of 10% in 1990 (Cálix and Vindel de Cálix, 1991, p. 318), with sharper contractions programmed for subsequent years. The brunt of this was to be achieved by reducing the number of state employees by 15,000 in 1990 and by a further 10,000 in 1991 (Hernández, 1992, p. 86). The same 10% reduction in public sector expenditures is also echoed in the *paquetazo rojo* of the Reina government (1994–), although here exceptions are made in the case of both the health and education sectors. Yet while this commitment has been reflected in a 3.5% reduction in real current expenditures over the period 1989-93, in particular with respect to education, health, defence and natural resource budgets, aggregate expenditures have exploded. The culprits have been debt servicing requirements (up 46.7% over the period 1989-93) and, more significantly, increased public sector fixed investment (up 76% just between 1991 and 1992), the major part of which was ploughed into construction and, in particular, infrastructural improvements.

Interestingly enough, the reasons for this explosion lie largely in those very hands that prescribe the adoption of NEM-type policies. In the light of an impending energy crisis, Honduras received $74.1 million in 1992, principally from the World Bank and Inter-American Development Bank (IDB), for investment in its electricity generating infrastructure.[16] Of no less importance was the $45.5 million received from the Central American Bank for Economic Injection (CABEI) to develop a ringroad around the capital and the $37 million from the Italian government for the construction of the Concepción II dam (European Union, 1995, p. 34ff). Given the conditionality of these funds, and the requirement that they are matched to some degree by counterpart funds, then it is little wonder that the Callejas government found itself trapped between the Scylla of being obliged to reduce the fiscal deficit and the Charybidis of providing the required counterpart funds for these infrastructural projects. Hence the hybrid fiscal stance.

Historically, the financial system in Honduras has been highly regulated. The government set interest rates and utilised an *encaje*[17] plus rediscount lines to determine the destination of much private sector credit. NEM-inspired capital market developments have seen interest rate ceilings freed in April 1992, although the *encaje* was retained. Under this 'hybrid' capital market policy, the market rate rose from 17% to 28% in the space of a year while savings rates remained wedged at around 9%. The central component of monetary reform is the *Ley Financiera* (1995), the first comprehensive banking law since the 1950s, which intends to modernise the whole financial structure in the coming years. Public auctions of government debt received the official go-ahead on 28 June 1990, becoming weekly events in 1994. Regional capital markets became more complete with the creation of a Central American Stock Exchange in 1993 (BCH, 1994, p. 30), although its economic impact to date has been minimal.

Access to international capital markets was re-opened by a willingness to both renegotiate debt and clear arrears. Bilateral debts of $430 million (principally with the USA) were condoned in 1990, followed by smaller amounts in the following years. Present negotiations with bilateral creditors through the Club of Paris are expected to reschedule debt further, although the relatively high amount of multilateral debt (55% of the total) outstanding restricts future scope for condonation.

NEM policies to liberalise the labour market remain conspicuously absent from the agenda in Honduras. The only moves have been to *raise* minimum wage levels, which had remained unchanged since July 1981. The (now) annual review of minimum wage legislation between the private sector, government and union representatives has seen wages increase significantly in nominal terms (see Table 1). These increases are greater than the rates of inflation so that real minimum wages have risen.

In March 1992 the *Ley para la Modernización y el Desarrollo del Sector Agrícola* was passed. Intent on modernising rural Honduras, it extended the NEM to the agricultural sector. The inviolable nature of land distributed under previous agrarian reforms was challenged by permitting such land to be bought, sold or rented out. A price band system was introduced to regulate the prices of staple crops, with the operations of the state marketing agency IHMA (*Instituto Hondureño de Mercadeo Agrícola*) scaled down accordingly. Agricultural credit provision was restructured, debts condoned or re-scheduled under an accompanying law, and a land bank formally set up (Noé Pino *et al*, 1993; Thorpe, 1995).

To counteract the immediate effects of the *'paquetazo'* on the most vulnerable groups, a number of compensatory schemes were introduced. The rise in fuel energy prices was offset by the provision of transport subsidies enabling urban passenger transport rates to be frozen. A further 8,000,000 lempiras was destined to subsidise basic goods provision through the BANASUPRO stores. Rural poverty was addressed by the announcement that a land bank would be established that would offer subsidised credits to landless peasants seeking to enter the land market. More specifically, however, three new initiatives that emphasised the importance of targeting were launched to diminish the prospect of increased poverty.

TABLE 1:
Minimum Daily Wages by Activity in Honduras (Lempiras)

	1989	1990	1991	1992	1993	% Change (1989-93)
Agriculture	5.0	8.08	10.82	12.3	13.7	174
Extraction: Metals	7.1	12.53	16.13	18.37	22.6	218
Extraction: Non-Metals	7.1	10.37	13.37	15.13	16.85	137
Manufacturing	6.6	8.87	11.4	12.92	14.38	117
Construction	5.3	8.69	9.9	11.6	13.24	150
Commerce / Services	6.6	9.26	11.91	13.54	15.07	128
Transport / Storage	N/A	10.10	12.99	14.64	16.30	60 (a)
Banking / Financial Services	N/A	10.0	12.84	14.51	17.86	79 (a)
Banana / Railroad / Stevedores and Petrolworkers	7.1	11.89	16.7	19.0	20.65	191
Average Minimum Wage	**6.3**	**10.44**	**13.87**	**15.78**	**17.68**	**181**

Note:Comparisons at a disaggregated level with earlier minimum wages are not fully possible given changes in employment classification.

(a) 1990-3

Source: Calculated from BCH data and relevant minimum wage decrees

FOSOVI (*Fondo Social para la Vivienda*), which commenced operations in mid-1992, helps finance, build and improve low-cost housing. The FHIS (*Fondo Hondureño de Inversión Social*) opened its doors in May 1990, providing permanent and temporary employment opportunities through the implementation of projects in the health, education, basic foods and informal sectors. By July 1994 55,403 'person-years' of work had been generated, and FHIS projects alone accounted for 1.3% of GDP (FHIS, 1994). Two PRAF (*Programa de Asignación Familia*) programmes target females with both dependents and limited resources. An income transfer mechanism (20 lempiras monthly) saw US $16 million reaching an estimated 274,000 recipients over the period 1990-2.[18]

A number of unforeseen factors were to impinge on the effectiveness of the National Party's economic strategy. A series of strikes affected production, the most significant being the 47-day stoppage by the Tela Railroad Company's banana workers in 1991. The expectancy that the GATT talks would undermine European Union (EU) trade barriers, permitting an expansion of banana exports, also proved to be misplaced. Coffee exports suffered in 1993 as the government pledged itself to withhold 20% of production in an effort to restore the International Coffee Organisation's bargaining power. Crayfish exports too were hit by a combination of overfishing and a US ban (imposed as a consequence of the country's failure to use environmentally appropriate fishing gear).

The biggest disaster by far, however, was the energy crisis. Severe water shortages at El Cajón in 1994 (the dam generates around two-thirds of the country's energy requirements) saw its output drop sharply. By mid-1994 electricity rationing had reached 12 hours a day. Government estimates suggest this crisis could account for a loss of around 1.1% of GDP (UDAPE, 1994), with the clothing and footwear sectors particularly hard-hit as opposed to the agricultural sector where technological backwardness (with the exception of banana and refrigerated meat production) for once has proved to be a blessing. Power shortages in the banana sector were compounded by natural calamity in the shape of Hurricane Gert, which caused the loss of 10 million boxes (1993). Sigatoka disease also re-emerged, helping to send banana exports plummeting in 1994 when the banana export quantum was just 42.3% of its 1990 value. The rest of the country suffered one of its worst droughts for years (1993), and bean production fell 40% with smaller losses registered in the other basic grains.

While in the first year of the Callejas administration exchange-rate instability and interest-rate uncertainty combined to depress production, GDP falling 0.4% in real terms, recovery followed on the back of increased public sector fixed investment. By 1993 growth rates for the 1990s were averaging 4.2%, with income *per capita* at $825, 1.1% higher than in 1990.

However, the 'twin evils' of internal and external imbalance had not been reduced. The fiscal deficit had exploded to reach 10.7% of GDP, as opposed to the IMF agreed 2%[19], with a 21.7% rise in external indebtedness (to $3,761.5 million -114% of GDP) before Callejas left office (BCH, 1994). On the trade front, the export potential of coffee and bananas was curtailed by international market factors beyond the scope of domestic policy-making. A similar fate befell mineral exports (with the exception of silver). However, improved prospects for mariculture and non-traditional agro-exports, such as melon and pineapples, saw 25%+ growth rates in these sub-sectors. Even more successful was the *maquiladora* industry – increasing its exports to the USA by more than 30% to around $90 million in 1993. On the other hand, import growth has been more in evidence. Led by a construction boom, the import surge ensured that the trade deficit widened to $234 million, thereby increasing the downward pressure on the lempira.

One side-effect of the decline of the lempira has been an acceleration in the inflation rate. While inflation had been modest in the eighties, falling from 18.1% in 1980 to 2.5% in 1987 before climbing back up to 11.4% in 1989, it escalated in the 1990s. From the *paquetazo* introduction in March 1990 until the close of 1993, when the Callejas government introduced an electorally-induced emergency price freeze, the consumer price index rose 89% (BCH, 1993, p. 10), a factor which many cite as responsible for Reina's election victory. Reina himself has been unable to control inflation, and nominal prices of basic food products in mid-1994 were anywhere between 93.4% and 309.8% higher than in the pre-*paquetazo* period. In a country where it has been estimated that close to 59% of urban and 63% of rural income is solely spent on food (SECPLAN, 1994a, p. 15), inflationary rises in basic food prices must impact strongly on the incidence and magnitude of poverty and it is to this theme that we devote the rest of this chapter.

Poverty and Inequality in Honduras

Few figures are available to identify long-term trends in income inequality and poverty within Honduras. Although both the National Census (1974 and 1988) and the Agricultural Census (1952, 1964, 1974 and 1993) allow point-to-point poverty calculations to be made, their infrequency makes it difficult to judge changes in the 1980s and 1990s. The most coherent and systematic attempt to evaluate the incidence of poverty and income disparities on a regular basis is the SECPLAN bi-annual Household Surveys (EPHPM-SECPLAN), but these only date from 1986. Furthermore, temporal comparisons are impaired by the fundamental methodological changes introduced in 1989 and 1993. Our work is further hampered by the very geo-politics that tainted Honduran economic policy-making in the eighties. The National Security doctrine stifled academic freedom and led to the abandonment of micro-level economic or social analyses (particularly in the countryside), resulting in a dearth of information on the periods we have characterised as those of 'acute economic crisis' and 'unstable growth' (Thorpe, 1993, pp.74ff).

Historically, the earliest estimation of household poverty levels in Honduras dates from 1970 (Altimir, 1982), but is highly susceptible to the value imputed as representing the poverty line. As a consequence, poverty calculations based on this source can appear 'critical' – at 75% of all households (when a $125 income *per capita* figure is used) – or 'manageable'– at 40% of households ($83 income *per capita*). Similar problems exist with regard to poverty at an individual level. Tabatabai and Fouad (1994, p. 49) show how World Bank data relating to 1978 personal poverty levels can be manipulated virtually to erase poverty (14% if an income *per capita* of $255 is used) or to accentuate the nature of poverty (37% if separate rural and urban poverty lines are calculated).

The only consistent figures available for the period are those cited by FLACSO (see Table 2). In the period of acute crisis (1980-4), the decline in *per capita* income of around eight per cent had little impact upon the number of Hondurans classified as indigent. Instead, the brunt of the crisis was borne by those whose incomes had been marginally above the poverty line in 1980, but who had slipped below in the interim. The decline was much more pronounced in urban areas (where poverty increased 120%) than in rural areas (up 62%).

Table 2:
Poverty and Indigence Levels in Honduras in the 1980s (%)

YEAR	REGION	INDIGENT	POOR	NOT POOR
1980	National	56.7	11.5	31.8
	Urban	30.6	13.3	56.1
	Rural	69.7	10.5	19.8
1985	National	56.9	21.9	21.2
	Urban	32.0	29.3	38.7
	Rural	73.3	17.1	9.6
1990	National	63.0	13.0	24.0
	Urban	50.0	23.0	27.0
	Rural	72.0	7.0	21.0

Source: FLACSO, 1992.

In the urban areas the principal losers were: (i) government manual workers – whose salaries were linked to the minimum wage, a wage that remained entrenched at its July 1981 value despite annual inflation rates of 5-10%, (ii) those who became unemployed or underemployed and were unable to secure alternative full-time employment and (iii) formal sector female workers since, with 1982 wage rates ranging from 41.6% to 97.7% of the male-equivalent (SECPLAN, 1994b), the probability for female workers of becoming 'newly poor' was correspondingly greater. In the rural areas the 'new poor' were drawn from the middle-peasantry, those who produced a surplus for the market but who now found themselves with insufficient income to meet their needs (as defined by SECPLAN). In crop terms, these 'new poor' were an amalgam of small coffee producers[20] and, to a lesser extent, grain producers[21] – particularly maize, rice and sorghum.

The period of unstable growth was not only unstable in terms of the security of its economic base. Socially too, as Table 2 demonstrates, Honduran society became more polarised as a result of growing pauperisation. The cost of SECPLAN's basic food basket rose 56% in urban and 53% in rural areas over the years 1986-90, an increase way beyond the accumulated inflation over the same period. While in rural areas the real price rises for basic grains boosted incomes (Thorpe, 1993, p. 105), the main beneficiaries were coffee producers as new production began to come on line. The comparison with urban areas was stark; indigence here increased 56% as wages failed to keep pace with food price rises and outbreaks of bus-burning occurred when the government tried to remove urban transport subsidies (1989).

While the Callejas period (1990-4) coincides with the availability of more regular data, there are nevertheless serious methodological problems which affect comparison with earlier years. Equally problematic, in March 1993 further modifications in the survey data incorporated (a) other non-labour household income – principally remittances, pensions, rental income etc., (b) self-consumption and (c) revised household expenditure data. While this presents a more complete picture of income disparities than was previously available,[22] it can distort conclusions on the effects of the NEM as we intend to make clear. The position is further complicated as (i) a shortage of funds prevented a rural survey (EPHPM) being undertaken in September 1993 and (ii) the changeover in government in early 1994 resulted in a failure to undertake any EPHPM in March 1994. While a September 1994 EPHPM was carried out, results are not presently available. These subsequent comments will therefore relate to the May 1990 to September 1993 period.

The major beneficiaries of the NEM since 1990 are located in the rural sector[23] (SECPLAN, 1994, p. 23). While the dollar prices of the country's two major exports fell in the early 1990s the NTR, by permitting the lempira to slide in value, cancelled (in domestic currency terms) the negative production signals generated by the international commodity markets. In the case of bananas, strike action in 1990 and 1991 and Hurricane Gert in 1993 dented transnational profits, but these events were partly offset by the companies transferring production to new areas so as to benefit from the tax exemptions available under the banana promotion law (IDB, 1994, p.108). In the case of coffee, which remains in the hands of smallholders, the greater political leverage that participation in the export sector offers allowed producers to win one-off production subsidies and price support from the government, thereby offsetting the scissors of increased input costs and reduced final prices in 1992/3.

Devaluation in 1990 increased the price of imported wheat on the domestic market and this, linked to the reduction in general food subsidies granted under the Callejas regime, provoked rises in staple food prices (Thorpe, 1993, p.144). This was accentuated as market liberalisation led to intra-regional and domestic shortages. However, a lapse in the application of the price-band system in the case of rice, and to a lesser extent maize (imports being allowed to enter at reduced tariffs), compounded by the flooding in the north and the drought in the rest of the country, had disastrous effects upon 1993 output.

As grain prices have become more volatile, the impact on producer income has been mixed (Thorpe, 1992). For 'surplus' producers of basic grains, the first year of NEM policies saw increased profits as sale prices outstripped the rise in production costs (Cáceres, 1991). The following year the position was reversed. Stagnant (or declining) prices coincided with a devaluation-induced increase in input costs that reversed the gains of 1990/1 (Thorpe, 1993, pp.144,172). Part of these increased costs were labour costs. Rural salaries rose sharply over the period 1990-2, mirroring changes in minimum wage legislation rather than agricultural productivity or profitability (POSCAE/OXFAM, 1992, p.101). The lack of any rural EPHPM data since March 1993 (or any serious independent study) unfortunately prevents comment upon subsequent changes in rural poverty levels. We therefore turn our attention to the urban areas of Honduras.

While national household formation increased 12.3% (1990-3), the rate of increase has been disproportionately greater in Tegucigalpa, San Pedro Sula and other urban areas, reflecting internal migration rates.[24] Within the sector, the daily cost of the basic food basket rose 54.8% between May 1990 and September 1993, providing a line of indigence of 170 lempiras (May 1990 = 109.8 lempiras) and a poverty line of 340 lempiras (May 1990 = 219.6 lempiras) *per capita* per month. Despite this sharp rise, however, we have not witnessed more pronounced levels of indigence or poverty in the official figures (SECPLAN, 1994a, p.23). On the contrary, urban poverty has fallen since 1990.

To examine this in more detail, we first focus our analysis on the population employed (area of activity, occupational status) in order to identify structural

Table 3:
The Incidence of Urban Poverty Among the Employed Population
According to Type of Economic Activity, 1990 and 1993

YEAR	SECTOR	TOTAL NUMBER EMPLOYED	ABSTEN-TIONS (%)	INDIGENT (%)	POOR (%)	NOT POOR (%)
1990	Agriculture & Fishing	64,933	17.0	17.0	30.7	52.3
1993		65,853	10.7	8.1	20.4	71.5
1990	Mining	1,911	8.6	11.4	26.7	61.9
1993		896	0	18.9	19.2	61.9
1990	Manufacturing	133,355	12.0	17.8	25.9	56.3
1993		164,200	8.7	8.8	15.3	75.9
1990	Electricity , Gas & Water	7,644	11.5	0.7	7.5	91.8
1993		7,195	0	0.0	6.9	93.1
1990	Construction	50,923	6.4	7.6	25.8	66.6
1993		65,222	3.4	2.4	13.7	83.9
1990	Commerce, Hotels & Restaurants	150,839	17.8	17.1	25.4	57.5
1993		175,142	10.2	9.0	15.6	75.4
1990	Transport, Storage & Communications	28,410	6.7	4.1	10.3	85.6
1993		34,130	7.2	1.1	6.3	92.6
1990	Finance & Insurance	18,470	10.3	1.4	7.0	91.6
1993		26,003	3.6	0.0	2.9	97.1
1990	Commerce & Personnel	189,590	5.2	24.7	18.4	56.9
1993		212,634	3.5	15.0	16.1	68.9
1990	Unspecified Activities	1,844	11.2	18.6	36.1	54.7
1993		612	0	0.0	0.0	100
1990	**TOTAL**	**647,919**	**11.1**	**17.6**	**22.4**	**60.0**
1993	**TOTAL**	**751,887**	**6.9**	**9.3**	**14.9**	**75.8**

The indigent, poor and non-poor are calculated in percentage terms, after
excluding abstentions. Rows refer to both year and type of economic
activity.

Source: EPHPM (various years).

change within the labour market. Having identified these changes, we then shift our attention to the household level, examining how factors such as gender and education of the head of household account for differences in urban poverty levels in Honduras – and how these differences have been affected by the NEM.

It is apparent that over the period under consideration there have been significant shifts in the pattern of urban employment (see Table 3).[25] While total urban employment has risen 16%, there is a disproportionate increase (40.8%) in those employed within finance and insurance with big increases also in construction (28.1%) and industrial manufacturing (23.1%). This manufacturing figure is partly vindicated by IHSS *(Instituto Hondureño de Seguridad Social)* data showing a 7.2% increase in the number of companies registering for social security purposes between 1991 and 1993 (Barahona and Claros, 1995, p. 4). On the other hand, the numbers employed in mining activities have fallen 53.2%, due to a combination of poor market prices, strike activity and seam depletion.

Of these changes, only the increase in manufacturing employment could be attributed to the NEM, although some insist its origins can be traced back to the period of unstable growth (GRH, 1994). It is beyond dispute, nevertheless, that *maquiladora* production has been favoured by the lempira's devaluation along with an estimated $40 million of infrastructural spending in the industrial zones (ESA/Price Waterhouse, 1992). Employment figures for the sub-sector are hazy, however, estimates varying from 23,000 to 40,000 jobs, with a suggested employment growth rate of 43% in 1992 alone (World Bank, 1994, p.6).

The surge in the finance and insurance sector is more properly attributable to: (i) the establishment of a number of new banks by domestic entrepreneurs, (ii) an explosion of small-scale *financieras* not affected by *encaje* requirements and, although there is no hard evidence, (iii) the laundering of drug money. The growth in construction jobs is explained by the sharp increase in public expenditures (particularly on road construction).

Growth in employment has led to urban unemployment rates falling from 8.7% to 5.6%, with the most pronounced drop being in female unemployment (down 43% to 15,112 workers). The rate of underemployment, split in the EPHPM between visible (employment of less than 36 hours weekly where the worker wishes to work longer) and invisible (earnings below the established minimum wage for the sector), fell from 30.5% to 25.6%, although invisible under-employment actually rose 9.3% to 180,289 workers.

This changing urban employment structure has implications for poverty. The finance and insurance sector is a relatively high-wage sector with none of the labour force classified as indigent in 1993 (see Table 3). Employment growth in construction has contributed to a sharp reduction in indigence and poverty levels (see Table 3). Poverty remains concentrated in commerce together with communal and personal services, where the major part of invisible underemployment is also located (commerce [24.9%], communal and personal service [32.8%] in 1993) – small-scale, low productivity sectors which have been able to exploit the pool of unskilled labour that historically has existed in the country.

Table 4:
The Incidence of Poverty Among the Urban Employed Population According to Occupational Status, 1990 and 1993

YEAR	OCCUPATION	NUMBER TOTAL EMPLOYED	ABSTEN-TIONS (%)	INDIGENT (%)	POOR (%)	NOT POOR (%)
1990	Salaried workers in	93,075	4.9	1.8	5.1	93.1
1993	the public sector	100,421	2.5	0.4	2.7	96.9
1990	Salaried workers in	277,623	4.9	10.4	25.3	64.3
1993	the private sector	358,895	2.4	5.0	13.4	81.6
1990	Domestic workers	43,305	2	58.2	38.1	3.7
1993		43,489	0.5	47.1	44.4	8.5
1990	Cooperative, collective or group	3,326	9.4	13.2	4.7	82.1
1993	workers	849	12.4	62.2	3.3	34.5
1990	Unremunerated workers in family	40,654	100	N/A	N/A	N/A
1993	enterprise	35,960	100	N/A	N/A	N/A
1990	Employers who contract one or more employees on a	9,223	10.8	0.1	1.4	98.5
1993	permanent basis	10,799	4.9	0.9	6.6	92.5
1990	Own account workers (who may periodically	180,713	6.2	27.6	24.8	47.6
1993	sub-contract others)	201,474	2.1	13.1	18.7	68.2
1990	**TOTAL**	**647,919**	**11.1**	**17.6**	**22.4**	**60.0**
1993	**TOTAL**	**751,887**	**6.9**	**9.3**	**14.9**	**75.8**

The indigent, poor and non-poor are calculated in percentage terms, after excluding abstentions. Rows refer to both year and occupational status.

Source: EPHPM (various years).

On balance, urban employment growth over the NEM period since 1990 has reduced the pool of openly unemployed Hondurans. Employment growth, however, cannot be attributed to the trade element of the NEM as one of the major growth sectors, construction, produces non-tradeables, while the growth of the finance and insurance sector could be attributed to the *failure* to adopt a more conventional NEM monetary policy – piecemeal liberalisation has stimulated excessive *financiera* growth so as to circumvent current *encaje* restrictions.

In occupational terms (see Table 4), the majority of urban employed Hondurans are either employed as salaried workers in the private sector (47.7%) or located within the informal sector (31.6% of the workforce in 1993). The major dynamism in occupational terms has been in the number of private sector salaried workers employed (up 29.3%). The numbers employed by the state have grown below trend to reach 100,421, but this growth is in opposition to the public sector employment cuts that NEM rhetoric has demanded. State employees are also in a relatively more favoured position in income terms – in 1993 only 3.1% fell below the poverty line, a figure that compares favourably with all other occupational types (see Table 4).

The numbers employed as unremunerated employees in a family enterprise have declined 11.5% (see Table 4). Two explanations suggest themselves. From a labour demand perspective, improved employment opportunities may have persuaded workers to leave the family firm for better rewards elsewhere. Alternatively, the increase in basic food costs may have forced family employees to seek outside employment.

Table 5:
The Incidence of Urban Household Poverty According to Gender of Head of Household, 1990 and 1993

YEAR	GENDER	NUMBER OF HOUSEHOLDS	ABSTEN -TIONS (%)	INDIGENT (%)	POOR (%)	NOT POOR (%)
1990	F	98,251	18.6	60.5	22.6	16.9
1993	F	115,612	20.3	46.4	30.4	23.2
1990	M	266,828	7.3	47.9	24.7	27.4
1993	M	321,645	4.8	33.9	18.1	48.0
1990	TOTAL	365,079	10.3	51.0	24.2	24.8
1993	TOTAL	437,257	8.9	36.8	20.9	42.3

The indigent, poor and non-poor are calculated in percentage terms, after excluding abstentions. Rows refer to both year and gender of household head.
F = Female, M = Male.

Source: EPHPM - SECPLAN (various years)

In terms of evaluating poverty levels a more appropriate unit of analysis is the household rather than the individual, and we also need to differentiate households on the basis of the gender of the household head (see Table 5). In urban Honduras 115,612 (26.4%) of households are female-headed, an increase of 17.6% over 1990 when they represented 98,251 of households (but a similar share [26.9%] of the total). These female heads are employed principally in communal and personal services, commerce and manufacturing, with the favoured modes of employment being as a salaried worker in either the private or public sector or on own account (where household chores can be more easily arranged around working activities).

In 1993, 70,410 (76.8%) of female-headed urban households fell below the poverty line, compared to 83.1% in 1990 (see Table 5). 46.4% (42,754) were classified as destitute (60.5% in 1990). In the case of male-headed urban households the percentages falling below both the poverty and indigence lines declined over the same period (poverty down from 72.6% to 52%, indigence from 47.9% to 33.9%, see Table 5), although the sharp increase in male-headed households over the period increased the absolute number of male-headed households in poverty from 162,261 to 193,522.

Since 1990 the gender 'gap', measured as the difference between female and male households in poverty, has more than doubled (from 10.5% to 24.8%). Indeed, although indigence among female-headed urban households fell between 1990 and 1993, the proportion classified as poor increased quite sharply (see Table 5). Plausible explanations for this widening poverty gender gap can be found in (i) increased female employment within the manufacturing sector (up 8,928 to 65,853) at a time when invisible under-employment was also rising and (ii) a decline in female employment within the commerce sector (down 2,509 to 81,359) due to a massive influx of males (up 40% to 93,785). This entry has not only dampened wages in the sector, but there is evidence that where wage increases have occurred these have gone to males.[26] While female participation has increased in the public sector from 42.8% to 48.2% of the workforce (up 8,531 to 48,428 posts), it is unlikely that this is responsible for the increased differential as gender differences in salaries are only significant at the highest income levels (over 1,601 lempiras per month).

Formal education for urban household heads has historically ceased at an early stage. In 1990, 17% of heads had no formal education while a further 51.2% had not passed beyond primary grade (Table 6). Attempts to remedy educational deficiencies can be traced to the 1950s as state reform and increased fiscal revenue led the government to tackle the problem of illiteracy through the expansion of the school system (Del Cid and Posas, 1983, p. 135ff). More important, however, were the 1970 reforms that introduced free compulsory schooling for all students between the ages of seven and fifteen (equivalent to the third grade of secondary schooling). High educational expenditures in the 1980s (see Table 1) helped to extend educational provision still further (Cameron and Thorpe, 1994). As these underlying structural changes have begun to bear fruit, their impact is reflected in EPHPM data. The 30-44 age group, which has seen sharply increased household formation rates over the period 1990-3, is also the group who concluded their primary

Table 6:

The Incidence of Household Poverty According to Educational level of Head of Household, 1990 and 1993

YEAR	LEVEL OF EDUCATION	NUMBER OF HOUSEHOLDS	ABSTEN -IONS (%)	INDIGENT (%)	POOR (%)	NOT POOR (%)
1990	None	62,122	12.9	80.0	14.0	6.0
1993		65,527	13.1	60.0	29.0	11.0
1990	Primary (Up to Fourth Grade)	92,546	9.6	66.8	22.0	11.2
1993		92,376	9.3	49.3	29.5	21.2
1990	Primary (Up to Final [Sixth] Grade)	94,328	8.5	50.7	29.9	19.4
1993		131,004	8.2	37.2	33.9	28.9
1990	Secondary (Up to Level 3)	30,028	9.8	38.3	36.6	25.1
1993		32,331	7.1	32.3	33.7	34.0
1990	Secondary (To Completion)	52,415	11.4	20.9	30.7	48.4
1993		74,424	9.5	10.1	39.4	50.5
1990	Higher Education	32,767	11.8	9.2	20.4	70.4
1993		41,524	4.3	7.2	14.9	77.9
1990	Informal Education	873	0	75.3	23.2	1.5
1993		71	0	0.0	62.5	37.5
1990	TOTAL	365,079	10.3	51.0	24.2	24.8
1993	TOTAL	437,257	8.9	36.8	20.9	42.3

The indigent, poor and non-poor are calculated in percentage terms, after excluding abstentions. Rows refer to both year and the educational level completed of the head of household.

Source: EPHPM - SECPLAN (various years).

schooling at the time when primary and secondary education was expanding rapidly (EPHPM, 1990/3: Table 31). By the early 1980s, when the last cohorts of this age group were completing their secondary schooling, the university sector was increasing its student intake (Bueso, 1986). Hence, the percentage of household heads in the EPHPM survey with no formal education had shrunk to 15% by 1993, while the percentage of heads with higher level qualifications increased sharply (see Table 6).

An analysis of income data verifies the hypothesis that earnings are linked to educational levels. In 1990, 94% of households in which the head had no formal education fell into the indigent or poor bracket (see Table 6). This compared to just 71.1% of those whose head completed the primary grade, 49.5% of those passing through secondary level and just 22.1% of those with higher education.

Conclusions

In the course of this chapter it has been apparent that GDP in Honduras, and thereore income *per capita*, has remained hostage to the fickleness of international demand for its two major exports – coffee and bananas. Attempts to diversify, through increased cotton, cattle and sugar exports in the 1960s and 1970s were unsuccessful, and it remains to be seen whether the growth in non-traditional exports since the 1980s will suffer a similar fate.[27] Honduran economic policy has also been affected by the geo-political context. Its role as a US ally in the Central American crisis of the 1980s brought financial rewards that allowed the country to reject devaluation as a policy option until 1990. Since then, while the Callejas administration (1990-94) moved much further down the path towards the conventional NEM stipulated by the international lending institutions, the package remained distinctly Honduran. Interest rate ceilings were scrapped, but a reserve requirement remained. Tariffs were reduced and the structure rationalised, but revenues increased. Plans were made to cut public sector employment and yet both it and the level of government expenditures expanded. Hence, the Honduran version of the NEM was far from pure.

Our research is hampered by the frequent changes in household survey methodology which makes it extremely difficult to (i) identify whether poverty and inequality has changed over time and (ii) attribute such changes to specific policies. That said, in the period of 'unstable growth' (1985-90) the cyclical nature of coffee production appears to provide the key to understanding *rural* poverty changes. In the *urban* sector the concept of basic food baskets, as introduced by SECPLAN in 1986 (and the sharp increase in their value in the period 1986-90), explains why society became more polarised, despite income *per capita* rising 4.5% between 1984 and 1989.

In the 1990s household survey data indicate a number of important trends for urban areas.[28] The finance, construction and manufacturing sectors have grown at above average rates, while the level of both open unemployment (see Table A.9) and visible underemployment has declined. The growth in the level of manufacturing employment in particular has converted more of the economically active population into salaried workers at the expense of own account work. Public sector employment has risen, but below trend, while employment opportunities in domestic service have stagnated.

While less urban households now find themselves indigent, thanks in part to a statistical sleight of hand, there are now greater absolute numbers of urban households trapped below the poverty line (263,932 in 1993 compared to 222,963 in 1990). One partial explanation for this is the growth in invisible underemployment, as increasing numbers of workers find themselves receiving below the minimum wage. Significantly, this coincides with a 16% increase in the number of female heads of household falling below the poverty line, a group more likely than most to encounter low wages. That said, while the NEM recommends labour market flexibility, especially in a downwards direction, the Honduran model has been active in boosting minimum wages (see Table 1). While this may have placated social opposition to government economic policy, its disadvantage has been the rise in invisible underemployment as actual wages paid have failed to keep pace with the rise in minimum wages. Thus, the Honduran NEM appears to have coincided with a fall in the headcount index of poverty (at least in urban areas), but it is not clear that the fall in poverty can be attributed to those economic policies most closely associated with the NEM.

Notes

*   I wish to thank Hugo Noé Pino, Martin Barahona and Claudia Salgado for comments on ealier versions of this chapter.

1.   Noé Pino and Hernández (1989) were the first to characterise the period 1980-4 as the period of 'acute economic crisis', dubbing the subsequent years (1985-9) as the years of 'unstable growth'.

2.   A constitutional crisis occurred in 1985 when Suazo Córdova, attempting to bypass the 1977 Electoral Law, nominated Carlos Flores Facussé as the Liberal Party Candidate for the 1986 Presidential elections. The crisis was resolved, with a significant intermediating role played by the

military, through an understanding signed by all recognised political parties on 20/5/1985.

3. John Dimitri Negroponte was the USA Ambassador in Honduras at the time and the December 1981 document that bore his name represented the response of the USA to Honduran petitions for international aid.

4. The argument against a devaluation was based upon preoccupations over both the likelihood and strength of the 'J-curve effect'. The position of the Central Bank on the issue and the forces pushing it towards relaxing its position during the 1980s are well-detailed by Hernández (1992, pp. 115-24).

5. Capital flight, estimated at $275 million over the years 1979-84 (Clower, 1986, p.8), also contributed to exchange-rate pressures.

6   These were replaced in the May 1984 tax package in importance by indirect consumption-based taxes.

7. This effort peaked with the construction of the El Cajón dam in the mid-eighties. Walker (1989, p.13) is of the view that public investment activity in the eighties verged from the deceptive *(El Cajón)* to the disastrous (forestry policy).

8   Exemption for 20 years for the owner of the industrial park, indefinitely for those companies operating within its confines (Noé Pino and Perdomo, 1992, p 10).

9. This allowed all non-traditional exporters to retain 30% of the product's free-on-board (fob) export value, the expectancy being that these dollars would be deposited within the domestic banking network. After a number of changes the scheme was standardised in May 1989, permitting the retention of 50% of fob export value by any exporter.

10. In February 1994 the outgoing Nationalist government of Rafael Callejas was replaced by the Liberal government of Roberto Reina. The Reina government introduced its own adjustment measures (Decreto Ley 135-94) in October 1994 - the so-called red *paquetazo*, (as opposed to the blue *paquetazo* of the Nationalists). Given our time-frame, a full impact of this and other Reinista policies falls largely outside the chapter's remit.

11. The FVA is the 'relevant' exchange rate upon which import and export duties are calculated. It is revised periodically by the government, but generally trails the quoted exchange rate. Congress approved the full liberalisation of the FVA in October 1994 under Decreto Ley 135-94.

12. In reality the nature of the new personal taxation system was not quite so 'progressive' as it first appeared. Fiscal drag induced by inflation meant that many Hondurans became eligible for tax purposes despite the new limits. Furthermore the new tax regime initially failed to permit deductions from gross taxable income for either medical expenses or

family subsistence that had been a feature of previous legislation.

13. Decreto 137 illustrates clearly the ineffectiveness of the current tax administration and collection procedures. Passed in November 1994, it established an annual assets tax of 1% per year (applicable to companies with assets of over 750,000 lempiras). While expected to raise an additional 110 million lempiras, only around 200,000 lempiras were collected by the deadline of November 1994.

14. The rate was set at 12% for traditional exports (coffee excepted) and 9% for non-traditional exports, this rate reducing by 1% per month until it disappeared at the year-end.

15. It will not be the first state enterprise privatised. Since Decree 161-85 was passed by President Azcona (1986-90), 44 enterprises have passed into the private sector, reducing the public sector debt by approximately $40 million (GRH, 1994, p 45).

16. By way of a comparison, in 1988, just $133,000 (0.1% of external assistance) had been received for energy projects. In 1992 energy projects accounted for 21.6% of external funds received..

17. In the absence of a significant internal market for public debt, the government has resorted to using the *encaje* (a form of reserve requirement) as an instrument to manage the money supply. This has been criticised strongly by NEM proponents who claim that it (i) leads to both high real and nominal interest rates, (ii) encourages a large intermediation margin (currently 10-11%) and (iii) causes disintermediation. The *Ley Financiera* (1995) will curb disintermediation while the Reina government (1994 -) has begun to pay interest on any reserve funds above the 35% threshold it inherited from the Callejas government.

18. Common criticisms of PRAF programmes include that; (i) it assists, but does not promote development, (ii) it fails actually to reach the targeted population and (iii) it has had limited success in promoting female participation in productive projects. In the case of FHIS the beneficiaries have been (i) the urban areas at the expense of the rural, (ii) the departments classified as 'standard' as opposed to those considered 'poor' in basic needs terms and (iii) have benefitted the organised at the expense of the disorganised (OPS/INCAP, 1993; POSCAE/OXFAM 1992; SECPLAN, 1994b).

19. There is immense conflict over the true relationship between the fiscal deficit and national output. The outgoing Callejas government insisted that it had managed to reduce it from 12.2% to under 7%. The incoming Liberal government insists the real figure it inherited was 11%.

20. The role of coffee expansion in Honduras during the eighties, despite the sterling efforts of Lara (1993), has not been adequately analysed to date.

It is our thesis that the sharp switches in rural poverty levels during the decade are due, in large part, to the cyclical nature of this crop. High coffee prices in 1979/80 led to an expansion in coffee area, reflected in higher output 4-6 years later (hence increased rural poverty in 1984/5 as these bushes had grown to a size to exclude intercropping, but were still not producing significant yields of coffee). From 1986 onwards national production was high (and a further increase in the cultivated area was encouraged by the 1986 price) and, although coffee prices decline from 1987 onwards, average returns from one hectare of coffee were still sufficient to place an average-sized household above the poverty line (POSCAE-OXFAM, 1992). Over this period coffee producers gradually 'escaped' from poverty, leaving the basic grain producer as the major contributor to the rural indigent.

21. It is important to note that, until the March 1993 adjustments to the poverty statistics, self-consumption statistics were not collected/imputed, resulting in the majority of basic-grain producing households being classified as indigent.

22. The extent to which the EPHPM understated income levels (and thus over-represented poverty levels) can be gleaned from the fact that the EPHPM-calculated *per capita* income in March 1992 was 2,061 Lempiras, compared to a Central Bank-calculated GDP *per capita* of 3,693 lempiras (79.2% higher).

23. Part of this is again attributable to the incorporation of self-consumption into the March 1993 EPHPM, though just how much is impossible to say.

24. SECPLAN (1993) estimates that, while the population will increase 15.1% between 1990 and 1995, above average rates will be recorded in Francisco Morazán, Cortés (where Tegucigalpa and San Pedro Sula are located), Atlántida (where, with Cortés, the majority of the maquila industry is located) and Colón, Gracias a Dios and Olancho (the agricultural frontier). Conversely, below average rates of increase are predicted for Lempira, Valle, Choluteca, Lempira, Ocotepeque and Intibucá (regions where land is of poor quality and land pressures are intense). If those migrating do so in order to improve their economic standing, then they are first likely to locate in the marginal *barrios* of the major cities (Hall and Berumen, 1994).

25. These, and all subsequent calculations in the chapter (i) exclude abstentions and (b) assume incomes *per capita* are evenly distributed within the income bands identified in the EPHPMs.

26. This statement is based on the fact that while the dominant income groups for both sectors were 101-200 and 201-300 lempiras in 1990, in 1993 they had become 301-400 and 401-600 for males whilst female

modal income remained as before.

27.   The fragility of *maquiladora*-led growth was all too evident to see when the failure to obtain the same textile guarantees that Mexico enjoys under the NAFTA treaty in 1994 led three *maquiladoras* promptly to close their Honduran operations. The recent sexual abuse claims made by a Honduran ex-*maquiladora* worker to the US press, and the collapse of the Mexican peso, cannot have improved prospects (European Union, 1995, p.61).

28.   The impact of current changes on the rural sector is much more indeterminate given the volatility that has characterised commodity prices (in particular of basic grains) and the lack of recent data on the sector. Hence our conclusion is based solely upon urban data.

CHAPTER 10

INEQUALITY AND POVERTY IN THE LOST DECADE: BRAZILIAN INCOME DISTRIBUTION IN THE 1980s

Francisco Ferreira and Julie Litchfield[*]

None of the characteristics of the New Economic Model (NEM) outlined in Chapter 1 were present in Brazil during the 1980s. The constitutional reforms proposed in 1995 by President Cardoso represent an important step in the introduction of such a model, and some features – such as openness of the current account - were introduced earlier. Yet even these came only after 1990. Because the latest household survey data for Brazil available to us are from 1990,[1] it is impossible at this time to analyse the impact of any constituent element of the NEM on income distribution in the country.

Nevertheless, we believe that there are very good reasons for studying the evolution of the distribution of income in Brazil during the 1980s. Of the 65 countries for which the World Bank (1994) lists percentage shares of income accruing to different groups, Brazil has the largest share going to the richest 10% (51.3%), and the (joint) second lowest share going to the poorest 20% of its population (2.1%). This comparison confirms the widely held notion that it is one of the countries with the most unequal distribution of income in the world. But unlike others who approximate it in terms of inequality – e.g. Guatemala, Honduras, Kenya, Panama – Brazil is a major world economy, with the world's tenth largest GDP after the G7, China and Spain.[2]

In addition to this unique combination of size and inequality, Brazil has experienced an interesting recent economic history. In the 1960s and 1970s, when import-substituting industrialisation (ISI) and an interventionist state held sway across the developing world, Brazil was one of the largest borrowers and fastest growing economies. In the 1980s, when the debt crisis put an end to that growth cycle, and led to a decade of stagnation for a large number of developing countries, Brazil was one of the worst hit. The average annual real GDP growth rate fell from 9.0% in 1965-80 to 2.7% in 1980-90 (World Bank, 1992).

In that decade, Brazil and many other developing countries were the focus of a great deal of talk about structural adjustment and the transition from ISI to a new, export-led and market-based growth strategy. Fiscal restraint and devaluations were to be followed by deeper structural reforms. Trade was to be liberalised, state-owned enterprises (SOEs) were to be privatised, tax systems reformed and financial markets deregulated. However, unlike in many other countries, these reforms did not really go beyond talk in Brazil in the 1980s. The country saw at least four failed stabilisation plans and annual inflation in 1990 was 2,938% (IDB, 1994), the highest in the period (see Table 1). Tariff reductions and privatisations did not begin in earnest until 1990/1. Discussions on tax and social security reforms were only beginning to take place in Congress

Table 1:
Macroeconomic Indicators for Brazil, 1981-90

	1981	1982	1983	1984	1985	1986	1987	1988	1989	1990
GDP *per capita* (1988 US$) (a)	2,252	2,237	2,145	2,118	2,235	2,362	2,394	2,346	2,377	2,233
Annual Growth in GDP (%) (b)	-4.4	0.6	-3.4	5.3	7.9	7.5	3.6	-0.1	3.3	-4.6
Open Unemployment (%) (c)	7.9	6.3	6.7	7.1	5.3	3.6	3.7	3.8	3.3	4.3
Govt Spending (% of GDP) (a)	27.3	28.7	31.7	29.9	37.6	35.9	32.4	40.9	46.5	47.2
Fiscal Surplus (% of GDP) (a)	-2.2	-3.1	-4.6	-5.0	-11.1	-13.3	-11.2	-21.4	-24.9	-14.4
Annual Inflation Rate (%) (a)	106	98	142	197	227	145	230	682	1,287	2,938
Trade Surplus (US$ billions) (d)	1.19	0.78	6.47	13.09	12.47	8.30	11.16	19.17	16.11	10.75
Current Account Surplus (US$ billions) (d)	-11.75	-16.31	-6.84	0.04	-0.27	-5.30	-1.45	4.16	1.03	-3.28

(a) Source for 1981-1983: IDB (1991). Source for 1984-90: IDB (1994). Due to data revison, there are discrepancies between the time-series reported in the two volumes above, but these are not too great; (b) source: IDB (1991);(c) source: ECLAC (1994a).Open unemployment is an annual average of monthly data for the metropolitan areas of São Paulo, Rio de Janeiro, Belo Horizonte, Porto Alegre, Salvador and Recife. (d) Source: IDB (1991, 1992).

in mid-1995. In short, Brazil in the 1980s was a country *not* adjusting to the debt crisis. Government spending rose sharply as a proportion of GDP as the budget deficit reached 24.9% of GDP in 1989 (see Table 1).

This fact, combined with its economic importance and pronounced inequality, make it virtually unique as a case study for the behaviour of income distribution in the 1980s. Since the mid-1980s, an extensive literature has arisen to discuss the impact of structural adjustment on welfare, poverty and income distribution (see Bourguignon *et al* (1991), Cornia, Jolly and Stewart (1987), Demery and Addison (1987), Heller *et al* (1988), Kanbur (1990) and the World Bank (1990)). Many authors mourn the absence of a counterfactual. They variously analyse the effects of reform policies – through Computable General Equilibrium (CGE) modelling, econometric estimation, or other means – on the distribution of income or other welfare indicators, but cannot reach forceful conclusions as to the desirability or otherwise of those policies for lack of knowledge of what would have happened in their absence. Clearly, each country is a specific case, and no country can be used as an exact counterfactual for another. Nevertheless, the basic initial macroeconomic conditions facing Brazil and a number of other Latin American countries in the early 1980s – such as Chile and Mexico – were not dissimilar. But whereas those countries underwent at least some adjustment policies in the course of the decade – or even earlier, in the case of Chile – Brazil did not.[3]

Furthermore, while inequality has long been a lively issue in Brazil, both in and out of academic circles, relatively little work has been done in terms of analysing changes in the distribution of income in this decade. Araquem da Silva (1988) has used input-output analysis to look at income distribution, using 1975 data; Bonelli and Cunha (1983) look at growth and income distribution in a dynamic model; Denslow and Tyler (1984) carried out an empirical study of changes in income distribution for the 1970s; Fields (1991) has discussed adjustment and poverty for 1980-85 and Hoffman (1989) has taken it until 1986. Other works include Sedlacek and Paes de Barros (1989), and Tolosa (1991), but to our knowledge no empirical studies have been made of changes in the distribution of household incomes up to 1990, using a data set as comprehensive as the one we use, and relating them to the macroeconomic background.

This chapter analyses the evolution of the distribution of income and of poverty in Brazil in the 1980s, using a very large and comprehensive data set from the Brazilian Statistical Office's annual National Household Survey. The next section analyses the changes in the distribution of gross household income *per capita*, and hence in inequality, using standard tools as well as summary inequality measures. This is followed by a discussion of poverty where we derive our chosen poverty lines, and present three poverty indices for different years across the decade. We then look at possible explanations for Brazilian inequality and suggest some causal mechanisms through which the policies of the 1980s may have affected the changes described. The final section contains our conclusions.

Inequality in Brazil, 1981-1990

This section describes the evolution of the distribution of income in Brazil over the decade, with data for every year except for 1982,[4] based on the data sets of the *Pesquisa Nacional por Amostra de Domicílios* (PNAD) for 1981-1990, produced by the *Instituto Brasileiro de Geografia e Estatística* (IBGE). Appendix A contains a brief description of these data sets, of the sampling procedure on which they are based and of the definitions of variables we adopt. We compare the distributions for each of the years in terms of summary statistics and scalar inequality measures, income means and shares per decile.

Summary statistics of the income distribution over the decade are shown below in Table 2. The table illustrates two key features of the distribution in each year, and its evolution over the decade. The first feature of the data is the difference between mean and median income. In each year median income was only approximately half the mean. This indicates that the distribution of income was extremely skewed to the right, with 50% of the population receiving incomes less than about half of the arithmetic mean.

Table 2 also suggests a 14.7% growth in mean monthly incomes between 1981 and 1990. This is clearly at odds with the picture of stagnation that emerges from the GDP *per capita* figures in Table 1, where 1990 growth over 1981 is -0.8%. This is an example of the general problem of comparability between national accounts-based and household survey-based statistics common to many countries (see, for example, Chapter 8 for a discussion of Mexico). In the case of Brazil, it has been argued that the discrepancies (which are large) arise primarily out of under-reporting of capital and other non-labour incomes. It has also been suggested that the importance of these income sources increases monotonically with income, thus causing PNAD-based studies to underestimate income inequality (see Lluch, 1982).

The usual practice in these cases seems to be to rely more heavily on the national accounts data for the behaviour of income aggregates, while using the survey data to obtain a lower bound estimate of inequality. In this specific instance, a plausible hypothesis to explain the growth disparity is that there might have been a shift in the composition of income towards formal labour earnings – which are more accurately reported – and away from other sources more commonly understated. Tentative backing for this conjecture comes from the fall in open unemployment over the decade (see Table 1). While we will

Table 2:
Brazil 1981-1990: Summary Statistics of Inequality

	1981	1983	1984	1985	1986	1987	1988	1989	1990
Mean Monthly Income (1990 US$)	143	126	125	150	213	166	166	196	164
Median Monthly Income (1990 US$)	75	64	64	74	110	84	79	88	79
Theil Index (a)	0.647	0.676	0.653	0.697	0.694	0.710	0.750	0.796	0.745
Gini Coefficient (a)	0.574	0.584	0.577	0.589	0.581	0.592	0.609	0.618	0.606
Coefficent of Variation (a)	1.653	1.743	1.635	1.804	2.084	1.891	1.869	2.154	2.009

(a) For an explanation of these measures, see Chapter 1.

return to this disparity in the conclusions, it would be inappropriate to ignore any feature of the survey data in the analysis below. Our welfare analysis will therefore incorporate the growth in mean reported incomes apparent in Table 2. There is no reason why it should affect any results pertaining to dispersion in the distribution, but the reader should bear in mind that any net welfare improvement results are upper bound estimates.

The second key feature of Table 2 is the growth in inequality over the decade, as demonstrated by the three summary measures, the Theil index, the Gini coefficient and the Coefficient of Variation (CV). Between 1981 and 1990 the Theil index rose by fifteen percent, the Gini coefficient increased by more than five per cent and the CV increased by nearly 23 per cent. However, this rise in inequality was not monotonic over the period. Both the Theil index and the Gini rose every year from the previous one, except in 1984, 1986 and 1990. Exclude these years and both measures record strictly monotonic increases. The CV also fell in 1984 and 1990, but it rose in 1986, falling the next year, and then rising almost to its 1986 level by 1990. The differing behaviour of the measures in 1986 arises from their sensitivity to incomes in different ranges of the distribution. The Theil index is more sensitive to low incomes, the Gini to incomes in the middle of the distribution, and the CV is more sensitive to incomes at the top.[5]

Despite this observation, the three measures present a remarkably coherent picture. First, there was an unambiguous tendency for inequality in incomes to increase in Brazil in the course of the decade. All three measures rose substantially during the recession of 1981-83 (see Table 1) and, although they fall with the resumption of growth in 1984, they soon resume their upward trend, which is unchecked until all three measures peak in 1989 (except for the aforementioned falls in 1986-87).

Secondly, 1986 was an atypical year in that both the Theil index and the Gini fell, indicating falling inequality with respect to the bottom of the distribution (the sharp rise in the CV suggests a greater dispersion amongst higher incomes). These changes go against the general trend and are almost surely due to the effects of the Cruzado Plan, which was introduced in February 1986.[6] This plan lowered inflation very substantially, impacting positively upon those least able to protect their incomes against the inflation tax.[7] Although end-of-year inflation was 145.3% (still much lower than either 1985 or 1987), it would have been much less by September, the PNAD reference month for incomes. In addition to lower inflation, the lower inequality amongst the poor in 1986 may also reflect the accumulated effect of three years of growth. The fall in all three inequality measures in 1990, albeit to levels still much higher than the decade average, is also connected with a severe, if short-lived, reduction in inflation in the second and third quarters.[8]

The behaviour of mean incomes per decile sheds further light on the remarkably consistent time paths of the inequality measures (see Table 3).[9] The data show that, although overall income rose between 1981 and 1990, the average incomes of the poorest 30% fell. The top decile gained the most, with average income rising by roughly 20 per cent, whilst the middle groups stood still and the poorest decile lost by almost ten per cent.

The recession caused mean incomes for all deciles (except the third) to fall between 1981 and 1983. From 1983 to 1984 there was equalising growth, with mean incomes for the bottom six deciles (again except the third) rising and those

Table 3:
Brazil 1981-1990: Mean Incomes per Decile

Decile	1981	1983	1984	1985	1986	1987	1988	1989	1990
1	13.92	12.45	12.88	13.85	20.46	13.99	12.35	14.29	12.65
2	26.32	22.52	23.45	26.02	38.36	27.31	25.26	29.09	24.96
3	37.47	37.75	32.61	37.16	55.40	40.13	37.39	42.14	37.12
4	50.29	42.55	43.29	50.17	73.73	54.94	51.22	57.76	50.91
5	65.33	55.46	55.89	65.27	96.10	73.09	68.61	77.57	68.81
6	84.67	72.21	72.76	85.80	125.29	96.40	91.20	104.48	90.82
7	111.67	96.60	96.41	114.46	164.71	128.37	122.31	142.42	122.52
8	153.672	135.23	133.16	159.17	225.87	177.48	171.07	204.42	173.10
9	237.07	213.58	207.17	248.60	349.03	275.05	273.07	321.99	274.27
10	644.46	581.29	570.87	702.14	981.90	778.20	804.44	968.85	787.16
Top 1%	1692.5	1578.7	1487.3	1949.8	2839.3	2242.9	2285.6	2936.6	2236.1

Note: all incomes are in 1990 US $

of the top four falling. This is perfectly in line with the fall of all three inequality measures in Table 2. As growth accelerates, all decile means are higher in 1985 than in 1984. Between 1985 and 1986, incomes for all groups again increased significantly, although not uniformly. This reflects not only the large GDP growth rates of 1985 and 1986, but also the aforementioned redistributive effect of falling inflation. The mean incomes of the poor and middle groups grew proportionately more than the mean of the rich,[10] which confirms the picture obtained from falls in the Theil and Gini Coefficients. Between 1986 and 1987 all ten decile mean incomes fell, but the mean income of the poor and middle group fell by proportionately more than that of the rich.[11]

Further insight into the distribution of income may be gained by examining the shares of income of different deciles of the distribution. This abstracts from changes in the mean to look exclusively at inequality. Table 4 below shows shares of total income by decile. Between 1981 and 1990 the shares in total income of all but the richest 20% fell, and these gained chiefly at the expense of the poorest groups. The poorest decile lost 20% of its original share of total income, the fifth decile lost nine per cent of its original share and the rich gained by almost six per cent.

Again, we see that the recession early in the decade was inequality-augmenting, as deciles 2 to 8 lost income share to deciles 9 and 10.[12] Between 1983 and 1984, shares of deciles 1 to 7 rose at the expense of the top three deciles. This was partly reversed in 1985, but between 1985 and 1986 the lowest eight deciles recovered some (but not all) of their original share in total income. After 1986, there is continuing deterioration of the distribution of income for three years, with 1989 recording the highest share for decile 10, and the lowest for deciles 2 to 7. There is some recovery in 1990, but inequality is still much worse than earlier in the decade. In 1990, all except the richest 20% were worse off than in 1981 in relative terms.

This implies that gains by deciles 4 to 8 between 1981 and 1990, in terms of mean incomes as reported in Table 3, were due to economic growth – little though there was of it – rather than to redistribution. In relative terms, the top 20% of the distribution gained at the expense of the poorest 80%. In fact, despite growth in the overall mean, these inequality – augmenting redistributions caused the poorest 30% to lose out even in absolute terms.

Poverty in the 1980s

In view of the limited growth in average incomes and the increase in dispersion described in the previous section, the net effect of which was an absolute fall in mean incomes for the bottom three deciles, it is not surprising that poverty as a whole increased over the 1980s. Given the wealth of information in our

Table 4:
Brazil 1981-1990: Income Shares by Decile

Decile	1981	1983	1984	1985	1986	1987	1988	1989	1990
1	0.97	0.99	1.03	0.92	0.96	0.84	0.70	0.73	0.77
2	1.85	1.78	1.88	1.73	1.80	1.64	1.52	1.48	1.52
3	2.63	2.51	2.61	2.48	2.60	2.41	2.26	2.15	2.26
4	3.53	3.37	3.47	3.33	3.46	3.30	3.09	2.94	3.10
5	4.59	4.39	4.48	4.35	4.51	4.39	4.14	3.95	4.19
6	5.94	5.71	5.83	5.71	5.88	5.79	5.50	5.32	5.53
7	7.84	7.64	7.72	7.62	7.73	7.71	7.38	7.25	7.46
8	10.78	10.70	10.67	10.59	10.60	10.66	10.35	10.41	10.54
9	16.64	16.90	16.59	16.54	16.38	16.52	16.48	16.40	16.70
10	45.23	46.00	45.72	46.73	46.08	46.74	48.54	49.35	47.93

sample, however, we are able to be more specific than that. Following Sen (1981), we structure the section according to the two component aspects of poverty analysis: the identification problem and the aggregation problem. We first discuss our choice of poverty line, which identifies the poor within the population. We then present aggregated information on changes in the extent of poverty in Brazil, according to three different aggregation procedures – one for each of the poverty measures we compute for each year during the decade: the headcount index (H), the poverty gap (PG) and the Foster-Greer-Thorbecke (FGT) index with the poverty aversion parameter $\alpha = 2$ (see Chapter 1 for an explanation of these measures).

Although the debate on the measurement of poverty has included views that poverty should be seen as simply an aspect of inequality – referring, for example, to 'the nature and size of the differences between the bottom 20 or 10 per cent and the rest of society' (Miller and Roby, 1970, p.143) – most researchers see poverty as a concept inherently distinct from inequality.

It follows immediately that the choice of a poverty line – which separates the poor from the non-poor – is crucial; any poverty measure can only be understood with reference to a particular poverty line. This section describes the procedures used in the derivation of the poverty line we adopt. The first choice facing any empirical researcher in this area is whether to embrace an absolute or relative concept of poverty. We follow Sen (1983), who argues for an 'irreducible absolutist core in the idea of poverty' (p.332), and adopt a poverty line based on an estimate of the income needed to meet basic needs rather than simply a fraction of median income.

In particular, we use a set of regionally specific poverty lines painstakingly calculated by Rocha (1993) and intended precisely for use with PNAD 1990 data. Rocha starts her procedure by following standard practice and computing the minimum cost of food baskets required to attain the Food and Agricultural Organization (FAO) recommended calorie requirements. Because of substantial differences across the country's regions – and within these regions, from metropolitan to other urban areas and then to rural areas – in both consumption patterns and prices, a food basket was calculated for each area specifically.[13] The food costs for each area therefore respect not only price differences, but also differences in tastes and local food availability across the different areas.

Once these food baskets had been costed, Rocha decided to deviate from the standard procedure of multiplying this number by the inverse of an Engel coefficient to obtain the poverty line. She argues convincingly that substantial relative price changes in Brazil during the decade mean that the Engel coefficient was not stable, and that – given the availability of detailed expenditure data from the *Pesquisa de Orçamentos Familiares* (POF) – it was preferable to calculate non-food expenditure amongst the poor directly.[14] This she does for each separate metropolitan area again, and adding the non-food expenditure amongst the poor to the food basket cost gives her regional poverty lines. These were updated for 1990 from the 1987 current prices by use of the consumer price index (INPC). This makes it particularly compatible with our data set, where conversion to real values also used the INPC to derive constant 1990 cruzeiros (and then dollars). The value of the regionally specific poverty lines, in 1990 cruzeiros, for the relevant PNAD regions are reported in Table 5 below.[15]

Three poverty measures were chosen to describe poverty in each year and changes in poverty over the decade.[16] They are shown in Table 6. Unsurprisingly, the poverty picture reflects the behaviour of the mean incomes for the bottom deciles, reported in Table 3. Between 1981 and 1990, we observe a rise in poverty according to all measures. The rise in the headcount index indicates that there were more poor people by the end of the decade than there had been in the beginning. In addition, the fact that the poverty gap (PG) index grew by proportionately more than the headcount (H) index (six per cent against one per cent) is evidence that the poor were, on average, further away from the poverty line.[17] Finally, the ten per cent rise in the Foster-Greer-Thorbecke (FGT) Index suggests that incomes among the poor were also distributed more unequally.

Nevertheless, as in the case of the inequality measures, this increase was not monotonic. All three measures indicate a sharp increase in poverty from 1981 to 1983, due to the recession. Indeed, all of the measures have 1983 as their peak year for the decade. All measures then decline monotonically until 1986, although until 1985 each was still above its 1981 level. The really sharp reduction in poverty came in 1986, as was to be expected from the previous

Table 5:
Poverty Lines for the PNAD Regions

PNAD's Regions		Value (US$ 1990)
Region 1	Metropolis of Rio de Janeiro	110.26
	Urban	68.36
	Rural	49.62
Region 2	Metropolis of São Paulo	117.49
	Urban	74.02
	Rural	47.00
Region 3	Metropolis of Curitiba	94.44
	Metropolis of Porto Alegre	65.56
	Urban	60.00
	Rural	40.00
Region 4	Metropolis of Belo Horizonte	90.61
	Urban	60.71
	Rural	35.34
Region 5	Metropolis of Fortaleza	68.89
	Metropolis of Recife	91.71
	Metropolis of Salvador	105.29
	Urban	62.04
	Rural	37.23
Region 6	Brasília	112.72
Region 7(a)	Metropolis of Belém	63.88
	Urban	56.85
Region 8(b)	Goiânia	107.12
	Urban	81.41
	Rural	41.84

(a) No data were collected for the rural population of the North; (b) The rural poverty line in region 8 is the unweighted average of all other rural poverty lines.
Source: Rocha, 1993

welfare dominance results for that year. The underlying story seems to reflect the positive impact of growth in 1984-86 on poverty reduction, but the magnitude of the shift in 1986 is compatible with the hypothesis that the abrupt lowering in inflation brought about by the Cruzado Plan had an additional impact.

Table 6:
Poverty Measures, 1981-1990

	1981	1983	1984	1985	1986	1987	1988	1989	1990
Headcount (H)	0.445	0.553	0.520	0.457	0.296	0.417	0.439	0.403	0.450
Poverty Gap (PG)	0.187	0.235	0.232	0.195	0.109	0.178	0.194	0.177	0.199
Foster-Greer-Thorbecke (FGT)	0.104	0.135	0.135	0.109	0.056	0.099	0.112	0.101	0.114

All three measures were at their minimum in 1986 and then rise until 1990, except for a downward blip in 1989. Overall, the sharp increases in poverty during the early recession years, reinforced by the increases in the post-1986 inflationary period, more than offset the gains made in 1984-86. Poverty is shown to have increased according to all three measures from 1981 to 1990, which is fully compatible with the losses in mean decile income for the first three deciles reported above.

This evidence is somewhat ironic, in the light of the hesitation displayed by Brazilian governments – particularly by the Sarney administration (1985-1990) – to undertake serious macroeconomic adjustment, for fear of curtailing growth and hurting the poor. In the event there was little growth, and it benefited the middle classes and the rich exclusively. The bottom of the distribution became worse off and poverty increased according to three widely used measures. It increased in incidence, it increased in intensity and it became more unequal.

Some Possible Explanations

The last two sections provided a detailed description of what was happening to the distribution of income and to poverty in the 1980s in Brazil. In this section we consider in greater detail whether the macroeconomic turmoil of the 1980s had any impact on the observed changes in equity. To do so, we start with some more conventional distributional analysis based on inequality decompositions.

A standard approach to examining the nature of inequality is to analyse the role played by certain individual characteristics such as age, gender, education and geographic location.[18] There is empirical support for such partitions from studies using regression analysis, inequality decomposition or analysis of variance techniques, although income inequality can never be fully explained by such characteristics. A survey of inequality decompositions in LDCs does show that personal attributes have large effects on the distribution of income (Fields, 1980). Empirical tests of the human capital model also commonly find that fixed effects explain approximately one-third of overall variation in (log-) earnings (see Lillard and Willis, 1978; Mincer, 1974).

In this chapter we concentrate on five attributes of the household (its regional location; its urban/rural status; age of household head; gender of household head; and his or her educational attainment)[19] and on three years: 1981, 1985 and 1990. Two types of decomposition are performed: first a static decomposition analysing the importance of the above household attributes in explaining overall inequality in any one year. Finer partitions are created by incorporating more than one attribute to give a measure of total inequality explained by all such household characteristics. Secondly, a dynamic decomposition is presented to analyse the impact of changes over time of population shares, relative incomes and inequality within each group.[20]

The point of the static decompositions is to separate total inequality in the distribution into a component of inequality *between* the chosen groups (I_B) – the explained component – and the remaining *within* group inequality (I_W) – the unexplained component. Unfortunately, many widely used inequality measures are not decomposable, in the sense that overall inequality cannot be related consistently to the constituent parts of the distribution. In particular, we are interested in measures where $I_B + I_W = I$. This is not generally true, for instance, of the Gini coefficient, but it is true of a parametric class of measures known as the Generalised Entropy class (see Chapter 1). A general formula for the class is included in Appendix B to this chapter, and Table 7 below presents the ratio of explained to total inequality $(R_B = I_B / I)$ for three members of that class – the mean log deviation [G(0)], the Theil index [G(1)]' and a transformation of the Coefficient of Variation [G(2)].

There are four main results of these decompositions: first, the explanatory power of age[21] and gender of the household head is negligible in both cases; second, inequality between rural and urban areas across the country explains somewhere between 3%-17% of total inequality, while inter-regional[22] differences account for 3-12%; third, education levels[23] of household heads are by far the most important explanatory variable, accounting for up to 42% of total inequality in Brazil on its own; and fourth, when these five variables are taken together, so that the distribution is finely partitioned, they jointly account for about half of total observed inequality. Subject to the proviso (see footnote 18) that for variable factors these results cannot be used to infer the direction of causation – particularly relevant in the case of years of schooling – this is a rather informative exercise.

Table 7:
The Amount of Inequality Explained: Static Results

	1981 R$_B$			1985 R$_B$			1990 R$_B$		
	G(0)	G(1)	G(2)	G(0)	G(1)	G(2)	G(0)	G(1)	G(2)
Age	0.01	0.01	0.00	0.00	0.00	0.00	0.00	0.00	0.00
Education	0.37	0.42	0.30	0.39	0.42	0.26	0.37	0.40	0.21
Region	0.12	0.10	0.04	0.10	0.08	0.03	0.10	0.08	0.03
Urban/Rural	0.17	0.13	0.05	0.14	0.11	0.04	0.10	0.11	0.03
Gender	0.00	0.00	0.00	0.00	0.00	0.00	0.00	0.00	0.00
All	0.51	0.52	0.36	0.51	0.50	0.30	0.50	0.49	0.25

Note: G(0) - mean log deviation; G(1) - Theil index; G(2) - ½CV² [CV = coefficient of variation]

While we may now feel that we know some of the factors behind the high *levels* of inequality in Brazil, such as educational attainment, geographical location and rural / urban status, they do not tell us anything about the reasons behind the *changes* during the 1980s, with which we were concerned above. To investigate whether changes in these variables can explain those changes, we briefly report results from a dynamic decomposition of G(0), due to Mookherjee and Shorrocks (1982), which allows the change in overall inequality to be decomposed into four terms as follows.[24]

$$(1) \quad \Delta G(0) = \left[\begin{array}{l} \sum_{j=1}^{k} \bar{f}_j \Delta G(0)_j \\ + \sum_{j=1}^{k} \bar{G}(0)_j \Delta f_j + \sum_{j=1}^{k} \left[\bar{\lambda}_j - \log(\bar{\lambda}_j) \right] \Delta f_j \\ + \sum_{j=1}^{k} (\bar{v}_j - \bar{f}_j) \Delta \log(\bar{y}_j) \end{array} \right]$$

where Δ is the difference operator, f_j is the population share of group j, λ_j is the mean income of group $_j$ relative to the overall mean, i.e. $\bar{y}_j / \bar{y}$, and the overbar indicates a simple average. The first term in equation (1) captures the pure inequality effect (a) , the second and third terms capture the allocation effect [(b and c)], and the final term the income effect (d) . By dividing both sides through by $G(0)_t$ proportional changes in inequality can be compared to proportional changes in the individual effects (Jenkins, 1995). It is then straightforward to draw conclusions about the importance of each effect in explaining changes in overall inequality. Changes in terms b, c or d would indicate that changes in mean incomes for the different groups, or in their composition, are explaining the observed changes in total G(0). Changes in the first component – the pure inequality effect – are the unexplained changes, due to greater inequality within the groups. Results for changes between 1981 and 1990 are reported in Table 8.

Although some 4% of the total rise in inequality can be accounted for by combined increases in mean income differences between urban and rural areas and offsetting migration, and a more significant 32% by reallocation effects across education groups, the striking feature of the table is the dominance of component 'a' over all others. This reveals that most of the growth in inequality observed in the 1980s *cannot* be explained by changes in inequality between the groups partitioned according to the attributes in the above Table.

Since ten years is a relatively short time in terms of a structural transformation of earnings behaviour, this is perhaps not surprising. But the question remains as to what lies behind the significant changes in inequality that were registered in terms of all measures we have reported, which we now know to consist mostly of unexplained within-group effects. The tool box available to

Table 8:
The Amount of Inequality Explained: Dynamic Results

% change in G(0) 1981-1990		14.8		
% accounted for by:	a	b	c	d
Age	14.9	0.1	0	-0.2
Education	10.0	-0.5	4.5	0.9
Region	15.2	-0.1	-0.2	-0.1
Urban/Rural	14.2	0.5	-1.5	1.7
Gender	15.0	-0.3	0	0.1

Note: a shows the pure within-group inequality effect; b and c show the allocation effect; d shows the income effect

students of income distribution is not very rich on means to investigate this question further, particularly with such a short time-series. Nevertheless, Table 9 presents some evidence strongly suggestive of which elements of the prevalent macroeconomic instability might have contributed to the growth in income dispersion. This table reports Rank-Spearman Correlation coefficients between the Theil index and four macro-variables, and between the FGT poverty measure and the same variables.

While we emphasise the merely suggestive nature of the correlations in Table 9, two observations can nevertheless be made. It would appear that, although both poverty and inequality grew over the decade, the changes in poverty and inequality were driven by different forces. It is striking, for instance, that the signs on the correlation coefficients between the Theil index and both unemployment and real wages have the 'wrong' sign. Higher unemployment was associated, in Brazil in the 1980s, with lower inequality. The same is true, albeit less markedly, of lower real wages. And correlation between growth and inequality was very close to zero. The real macroeconomic force behind growth in inequality would appear to be inflation. The reasons for this have been discussed above and centre on the fact that ability to hedge against inflation – i.e to protect the value of one's earnings and assets – is widely thought to be positively related to income. In other words, the inflation tax is a highly regressive means of financing a public deficit.

Since this dispersionary effect of high inflation is also felt within all partition groupings in Table 8, it may provide an explanation for the large unexplained component in changes in inequality. It is interesting to note in passing that these results are starkly at odds with the traditional view that unemployment has an inequality augmenting effect, while inflation has an

Table 9:
Inequality and Poverty Correlation Coefficients

	Theil Index	FGT
Log inflation	0.8455	0.1038
Unemployment	-0.7986	0.5432
Real wage in manufacturing	0.1592	-0.7484
GDP growth	0.0123	-0.4349

Note: The Theil Index is a measure of income distribution; the FGT Index is a measure of poverty.

(insignificant) equalising effect, as reported for the cases of the USA by Blinder and Esaki (1978) and of the UK by Nolan (1987). It is possible to conjecture that, whereas in low inflation economies, an increase in inflation merely proxies for an increase in aggregate demand, in high inflation economies, such as Brazil, the regressive inflation tax effect dominates.

The relation between poverty and the macroeconomic aggregates is rather different (see Table 9). The effect of inflation is still positive, but not large, while unemployment and real wages now have the expected signs. Falls in unemployment, rises in real wages and rises in GDP growth are all correlated with reductions in poverty. This is less surprising than the inflation results, and perfectly in line with the stylised inverted-U shape of poverty, wages and growth in the 1980s.

Conclusions

During the 1980s, Brazil did not display any of the defining features of the NEM. There was no macroeconomic stability; trade and capital flows were not liberalised to a significant extent; the state's presence in economic life was not receding, and no substantial changes to anti-poverty policy were attempted. Nevertheless, a number of failed stabilisation plans were pursued, most of them involving price and wage freezes. Growth performance was erratic; despite substantial rises from 1984 to 1986, contractions both at the beginning and at the end of the decade meant that income *per capita* in 1990 was virtually unchanged from 1981.[25] We suggested at the outset that to study the behaviour of inequality and poverty under these circumstances is to study a counterfactual to the impact of a successful implementation of the NEM.

The evidence suggests that both poverty and inequality rose in the 1980s. Measures of inequality, such as the Theil index, have a clear upward trend. It would appear that 1988 and 1989 were the worst years for inequality, rather than 1990. However, there was substantial change around 1986, revealing the distributional non-neutrality of the Cruzado Plan. The impact of lower inflation and higher growth was to reduce inequality for almost the entire distribution. Conversely, the rise in inflation following the failure of the plan, associated with a deceleration in investment and growth, caused inequality to increase for the whole distribution in 1987.

Poverty, measured by any of three standard measures and with respect to a constant, poverty line, also rose from 1981 to 1990. In addition, growth from 1984 to 1986 and the Cruzado Plan also caused this rise to be non-monotonic. Poverty rose sharply from 1981 to 1983, then fell gradually until 1985, and sharply in 1986. It then rose again to 1990, with a blip in 1989. Even if one believes that the post – 1985 civilian government chose not to cut the fiscal deficit and reduce inflation because of its concern for poverty, it is apparent that it was not successful in preventing its rise.

These increases in poverty and inequality appear to have been influenced by the macroeconomic instability which characterised Brazil in the period. Growth in inequality cannot be explained only as the result of an increase in the dispersion of returns to age or education, or indeed by greater differences across regions or sectors. Within-group increases were by far the largest component of changes in overall inequality. On the other hand, rises in annual inflation were highly correlated with increases in the Theil index, suggesting that the suspected regressivity of the inflation tax may be an important part of the Brazilian inequality story in the 1980s. Growth, unemployment and real wages, on the other hand, do not appear to be central to that story. It would be foolish to conclude that the signs on the correlation coefficients of unemployment and wages mean that greater unemployment (or lower wages) will lead to lower inequality, at least in the absence of a longer time series and a multivariate regression analysis. Nevertheless, it does seem safe to say that the aggregate labour market variables were not responsible for the increase in inequality in Brazil in the 1980s, and that higher inflation is a much likelier candidate.

It is a different picture for poverty, where the evidence suggests a positive correlation with unemployment and negative with growth and real wages, but a much lower correlation with inflation. Just as growth and real wages were highest in the middle of the decade, and lower in the beginning and the end, the inverse was true of poverty. It would be wrong to argue, however, that this should be interpreted to mean that fighting inflation is unimportant for poverty reduction. The levels of inflation observed in the late 1980s were clearly incompatible with net investment and sustainable growth. Real wages, employment and GDP are all likelier to grow for long periods in a stable environment, leading to greater and more sustained poverty reduction. What we now know is that, in addition, price stability prevents a further worsening in the relative situation of the poor, brought about by greater inequality.

In terms of general welfare, conclusions are more mixed. Mean *per capita* income in 1990 as reported by our sample is almost 15% higher than in 1981, in sharp contrast to the stagnation revealed by the national accounts based GDP *per capita* figures. The reasons for this have been discussed above, and we have chosen to interpret our results using the PNAD sample as a lower bound on inequality and welfare analysis. Comparing the beginning and end points, we see that the top two thirds of the distribution appear to have a higher level of welfare in 1990 than ten years earlier, but the reverse is true for the bottom quarter.

If we allow for the fact that the increase in mean reported income in the sample probably overestimates real growth, the welfare conclusions will be revised downwards. Poverty and inequality rose unambiguously in Brazil in the lost decade, even if growth is higher than indicated by GDP statistics. If the PNAD mean income growth is an overestimate, the share of the population suffering welfare losses in the 1980s could grow considerably. Clearly, things can become worse for the poor even in the absence of structural adjustment. The case of Brazil seems to lend support to those who, earlier in the decade, argued that doing nothing was not an option and that delaying was not helpful.

Appendix A

The data sets are the *Pesquisa Nacional por Amostra de Domicílios* (PNAD) for 1981-1990, produced by the *Instituto Brasileiro de Geografia e Estatística* (IBGE). Data are collected each year from a representative national sample of households, selected according to a three-level multi-stage sampling procedure, and covers every state in the Federation. For more detail on the sampling procedure, see IBGE (1991).

The survey is available annually on a range of variables which form the basic data set, common to every year, with only minor exceptions. Questions are asked on subjects pertaining to the household and to individuals within the household. Information is recorded on the geographic location of the household, characteristics of the dwelling, household size, relationships between individuals in the household, activities of individuals, income from labour, transfers, other income generating activities, occupation and other labour characteristics, age, gender, education, colour and literacy. Population weights, based on the 1980 Census, are also included. In addition to this core set of indicators, a further supplementary survey was conducted in some years. The sample size varies in each year, from a minimum of 290,000 (in 1986) to a maximum of 525,000 individuals (in 1985).[26]

This data set allows us to derive the following standard definitions for statistical analysis. Income is gross monthly household income *per capita* (from all sources)[27] and the income receiver is the individual. One implication of this is that the mean of the real income imputed to each individual by our procedure will equal the sample mean of pre-tax income, which in turn will be an unbiased estimate of mean pre-tax income in the Brazilian population. Nominal Brazilian currencies[28] were converted to constant 1990 US dollars according to the following procedure. First, local currencies were converted into 1990 Brazilian Cruzeiros using the CPI deflator, the *INPC* (IBGE, 1993); second, the Cruzeiro series was converted to 1990 US dollars using the exchange rate for the interview month in 1990.[29] The small proportion of observations with missing income data[30] were excluded from the sample.

Appendix B

The Generalised Entropy class of inequality is a parametric class, composed of all measures that can be expressed as:

(1)
$$G(\alpha) = \frac{1}{\alpha^2 - \alpha} \left[\frac{1}{n} \sum_{i=1}^{n} \left(\frac{y_i}{\overline{y}} \right)^{\alpha} - 1 \right], \alpha \in R$$

When total inequality, I, is decomposed by population subgroups, the Generalised Entropy class of measures can be expressed as the sum of within-group inequality, I_w, and between group inequality, I_B. Within-group inequality I_w is calculated and weighted as follows:

(2)
$$I_w = \sum_{j=1}^{k} w_j G(\alpha)_j$$

$$w_j = v_j^{\alpha} f_j^{1-\alpha}$$

where f_j, is the population share and v_j the income share of each partition j, $j=1,2,...k$. Between-group inequality, I_B, is measured by assigning the mean income of partition j, y_j, to each member of the partition and calculating:

(3)
$$I_B = \frac{1}{\alpha^2 - \alpha} \left[\sum_{j=1}^{k} f_j \left(\frac{\overline{y_j}}{\overline{y}} \right)^{\alpha} - 1 \right]$$

Cowell and Jenkins (1995) show how these within-group components can be expressed in terms of overall inequality to give the summary measure, R_B, of the amount of inequality explained by a particular characteristic or set of characteristics:

(4)
$$R_B = \frac{I_B}{I}$$

We presented decomposition using three members of this class of measures: $G(0)$, $G(1)$ and $G(2)$. If $\alpha=1$, then using l'Hôpital's rule, $G(\alpha)$ can be written as:

(5)
$$G(0) = \frac{1}{n} \sum_{i=1}^{n} \log \left[\frac{\overline{y}}{y_i} \right]$$

Similarly, if $\alpha=1$, $G(\alpha)$ is just the Theil index presented above. If $\alpha=2$, equation (6) can be expressed in terms of the coefficient of variation (CV) as 1/2 CV².

Notes

* We are grateful to the Leverhulme Foundation, the CNPq in Brasilia and STICERD for financial support; to Frank Cowell for invaluable guidance and to Kaspar Richter for impeccable assistance.

1. The data from the household survey for 1992 became available as this book went to press.

2. Or eleventh; there is an unresolved debate as to whether the Russian Federation or Brazil has the larger GDP. This is not as straightforward as may at first appear, given the recent changes in Russia's national accounting system.

3. See Aspe (1993) on adjustment in Mexico and Edwards and Cox-Edwards (1991) on Chile.

4. 1982 is excluded on advice from IBGE, because in that year the survey was carried out over a 12-week reference period. This methodological divergence from other years was reflected in the collected data, hampering intertemporal comparability. See IBGE (1993, p.10).

5. The Theil and CV are both members of the Generalised Entropy class of inequality measures, which is defined over a set of 'inequality aversion' parameters – see Chapter 1.

6. The Cruzado Plan brought a sharp reduction in monthly inflation in its first nine months. See Winograd (1995).

7. This effect is at least partially captured by the real income data, to the extent that nominal returns on financial assets and/or capital gains are reported as nominal income by those to whom they accrue.

8. This was a consequence of the Collor Plan Mark I, introduced by President Collor de Melo in March.

9. Decile groupings were used for reporting income shares and means, whilst all graphs were generated using percentiles.

10. Between 1985 and 1986 average income of decile 1 rose by 48%, that of decile 5 by 47%, and that of decile 10 by 40%.

11. Between 1986 and 1987 average income of decile 1 fell by 31%, that of decile 5 fell by 24%, and that of decile 10 fell by 21%.

12. Although there was a 2% increase in the share of the poorest decile.

13. In fact, this was done for the nine metropolitan areas (Belém, Fortaleza, Recife, Salvador, Belo Horizonte, Rio de Janeiro, São Paulo, Curitiba and Porto Alegre), as well as Brasilia and Goiânia, for which a recent (1987) expenditure survey data set was available. This was the Pesquisa de Orçamentos Familiares (POF). For the other urban and rural areas, conversion factors were borrowed from an earlier work by Fava (1984), which were based on the most recent available data for these areas, the

1975 Estudo Nacional da Despesa Familiar (ENDEF).

14. 'The poor' amongst whom she computes non-food expenditures are those who, according to information recorded by POF, were unable to meet *minimum* calorie requirements as specified by FAO. It is interesting to note that if the criterion had been *recommended* caloric requirements, which were used to derive the food basket component of the poverty lines, some areas would have over half of the population counted as 'poor' for the purpose of studying non-food expenditure.

15. For greater detail on the construction of these lines, such as the specific food baskets in each metropolitan area, the exact non-food expenditures by category, or the conversion factors from metropolitan lines to other urban and rural areas, see Rocha (1993).

16. The headcount index (H), Poverty Gap (PG) and the Foster-Greer-Thorbecke take into account the three Is of poverty – incidence, intensity and inequality respectively amongst the poor.

17. Using the poverty measure definitions it is immediately clear that the average normalised distance between individual incomes of the poor and the poverty line equals the ratio PG / H.

18. Whilst it is possible to draw some inferences about the direction of causality between *fixed* attributes, such as gender or race and incomes, it is difficult to do so between *variable* attributes, such as education and incomes.

19. Ethnicity may also be an important source of inequality. Unfortunately very little data is available. In 1981 the question did not appear on the questionnaire and in 1985 less than 5% of the sample responded to the question. Only for the last two or three years of the decade was there a significant response rate to the question.

20. For a more detailed discussion of the decomposition methodologies and results, see Litchfield (1995).

21. Households were grouped into six categories by age of head: 1) under 25, 2) 25-34, 3) 35-44, 4) 45-54, 5) 55-64 and 6) 65+ years, using an extension of the categorisation in Bonelli and Ramos (1993).

22. States were grouped into the five official, standard geographical regions of Brazil: North, Northeast, Southeast, South and Centre-West.

23. Education is disaggregated into five groups, again using the Bonelli and Ramos (1993) procedure, of 1) illiterates – less than one year of schooling, 2) elementary school – 1 to 4 years of schooling, 3) intermediate school – 5 to 8 years of schooling, 4) high school – 9 to 11 years of schooling and 5) college education – 12 or more years of schooling.

24. This is actually an approximation to the true decomposition, but both Mookherjee and Shorrocks (1982) and Jenkins (1995) argue that for

computational purposes this approximation is sufficient.

25. In assessing overall growth performance, the GDP *per capita* statistics reported in Table 1, calculated from the national accounts, are thought to be more reliable than the sample means reported in Table 2. This is due to many factors, including misreporting of income from capital. See discussion in Section 2, and Lluch (1982).

26. The sampling method embodies a natural growth in the sample size of the survey, reflecting the underlying population growth rate. There was a sharp break in 1986, when the sample size was reduced for cost-related reasons, with special care paid to maintaining precision. See IBGE (1991).

27. In choosing this unit, we are adopting an extreme assumption on equivalence scales, by essentially ignoring any economies of scale within the household.

28. There were three changes within the decade: the Cruzeiro lasted until 1986, the Cruzado from 1986 to 1988, the Novo Cruzado until March 1990, and then back to the Cruzeiro.

29. For more detailed information on the data set, our treatment of it and comparability of our results with other published results, see Cowell, Ferreira and Litchfield (1995).

30. These constituted approximately 1% of the sample in each year; e.g. 0.80% in 1981, 0.99% in 1985 and 1.34% in 1990.

CHAPTER 11

THE MANUFACTURING SECTOR IN LATIN AMERICA AND THE NEW ECONOMIC MODEL

John Weeks

During the years from the end of the Second World War until the late 1970s, broad agreement emerged among Latin American governments with respect to the general orientation of economic policy and especially industrial policy. This broad agreement derived from two widely accepted propositions: 1) that domestic markets in Latin American countries operated inefficiently, both with regard to the allocation of resources among alternative uses and the distribution of the gains from economic growth; and 2) that the international trading system incorporated a bias against the major products exported by Latin American countries. These two propositions implied that state action was required to correct the failures of domestic markets and that governments needed to implement a broadly interventionist trade policy to transform the structure of exports and, by logical extension, domestic production. This combination of interventions in domestic markets and trade was encapsulated in the term 'import substitution'.

On the basis of this development strategy, during the 1950s and 1960s Latin American countries experienced moderate to strong growth performances. To an extent, this growth could be attributed to a relatively favourable world economic environment. While the terms of trade for many Latin American countries declined during the twenty-five years after the Second World War, flows of private and official capital tended to be offsetting. Overall, Latin American countries benefited from a relatively stable world trading system of fixed exchange rates (overseen by the International Monetary Fund), preferential trading agreements, and an increasing number of commodity agreements between producing and consuming countries.

So sustained was the growth performance of the Latin American countries that towards the end of the 1960s the distribution of the gains from growth received increasing emphasis, even to the point of making equity considerations integral to the definition of 'economic development'. While earlier development theory had tended to stress the likelihood of a *positive* relationship between income inequality and growth,[1] by the early 1970s quite the opposite perspective gained respectability. Inspired by innovative theoretical and empirical work, especially from the World Bank, a 'basic needs' approach emerged which placed alleviation of poverty at the centre of economic policy in developing countries.

During the period in which a consensus emerged about the centrality of distribution to the development process, several shocks to the international system occurred that dramatically altered the world economic environment. At the outset of the 1970s the international trading system was shaken by the decision of the US government to suspend the fix-price convertibility of the dollar for gold, which ushered in a new set of international rules for trade and finance based upon managed, but variable, exchange rates in the Organisation for Economic Cooperation Development (OECD) countries. This new exchange rate regime proved problematical for the Latin American countries, due to the vulnerability of their economies to world market fluctuations and their lack of skilled people for the increased burden of economic management. The petroleum price increases of 1973-74 followed quickly on the collapse of the post-war system of international regulation, generating large trade deficits for developing countries dependent upon imports of oil. These deficits led to large-scale borrowing by Latin American governments from the world's major commercial banks.

The overwhelming consensus within the financial establishment in the 1970s was that growing indebtedness represented no long-term danger; on the contrary, in the absence of indebtedness the hard currency surpluses of the oil-exporting countries would not have been 'recycled' into the international expenditure stream. Further, world inflation during the 1970s resulted in buoyant primary product prices, which generated optimism regarding the ability of Latin American countries to service their debts. However, the early 1980s brought new and unexpected shocks for developing countries. The most dramatic was the severe recession in the OECD countries, which resulted in a rapid decline in the rate of world inflation. Somewhat differently from previous post-war recessions, the downturn reflected in part the conscious policy of some developed country governments, especially the US government, to make control of inflation the first policy priority even at the cost of high unemployment. For the Latin American countries the recession generated high real international interest rates and falling primary product prices. At this point many Latin American countries, especially the heavily indebted, found themselves unable to service their debts and forced to turn to crisis borrowing on terms starkly unfavourable compared to the previous decade.

In 1982 Mexico announced it could no longer service its debt,[2] which converted into an international financial crisis the difficulties created by the gathering pressure of Latin American country indebtedness, low primary product prices and increased reluctance by commercial banks to make further loans. The alarm generated by the fear of the collapse of major commercial banks resulted in a change in the priorities of the international lending agencies from the previous emphasis upon poverty reduction and equity to debt service. This required immediate current account surpluses, which needed to be achieved through import reduction and export expansion.

It was in this context that there occurred a radical shift in economic policy by Latin American governments. By the end of the 1980s, almost all Latin American countries had adopted a New Economic Model (NEM). The altered agenda derived its theoretical justification from the mirror-image of the previously accepted import substitution strategy: 1) that domestic markets were paragons of efficient operation, and 2) that the international trading system would provide producers throughout Latin America with the most appropriate 'signals' upon which to base their economic decisions. With this change of policy direction went a new language of discourse, derived from the value-laden term 'free' markets. This chapter investigates the impact of that new strategy on the manufacturing sector in Latin America.

Change in the Ideology of Policy

The standard explanation for the policy shift towards neoliberalism in Latin America was that the strategy of import substitution had 'failed'. In response to this failure governments had to embrace a new policy framework, not just to rescue their countries from crisis, but to correct the damage done to their economies by the misguided policies of the past. The failure of the strategy allegedly arose from two causes, the so-called exhaustion of the 'simple stage' of import substitution (González-Vega and Céspedes (1993), pp. 97ff), and the 'distortions' generated by the state interventions to bring about a shift in production structures from primary products to industrial development (Rottenberg (1993)). The first cause derives from the theoretically and empirically unsubstantiated proposition that replacing consumer goods imports with domestic production might somehow be less problematical than doing the same for intermediate and capital goods. One can find no serious defence of this oft-asserted opinion in the literature on industrialisation.

More theoretically based is the concept of 'distortions', a term which refers to any market outcome which differs from that which would be produced under conditions in which all state interventions were absent. For example, a tariff on textiles is said to produce a distortion by making the domestic production of this commodity more profitable than it would be in the absence of that tariff. As a result, more resources are drawn into the sector than would be the case without the tariff. To this point the argument is uncontroversial for, indeed, the precise purpose of the tariff is to achieve this outcome. Orthodox ('neoclassical') economic theory judged such an outcome as inefficient and undesirable, on the grounds that markets without interventions (i.e., the tariff) produce a superior outcome in which a country's resources are optimally employed.[3]

The free market advocates instilled the impression that markets by their nature produced efficient results, but the conclusion is theoretical – not empirically based on actual results of markets. Central to the force of the free market argument are three propositions that must be established theoretically and, once established, ensure the optimal efficiency conclusion as an abstract deduction from logic. First, it must be shown that all markets are perfectly competitive; second, that competitive markets through their interaction result in full employment of resources; and third, that all economic variables assume values in the full employment outcome which are unique (that there is one and only one full employment outcome produced by unregulated markets). If unregulated markets are tainted by seller or buyer market power, then the result is *private sector regulation* which in its effect upon the orthodox concept of efficiency is equivalent to state regulation. If one suspends belief and accepts that all markets are perfectly competitive, efficiency in each market requires full employment in all markets. If all labour and other resources are not in use, then by definition the outcome is not efficient, for it is undesirable compared to full resource use.[4] The competitive and full employment outcome must be unique, because if there were multiple outcomes, a social policy decision is required to select among them, which would require interventions and regulations (Weeks, 1993).[5]

Within orthodox economic theory it is well established that 1) perfectly competitive markets result in full employment of resources only under extremely restrictive conditions, and 2) that even under these restrictive conditions there are in general multiple outcomes. So powerful was the ideology of the free market that it came to prevail in the 1980s, notwithstanding its theoretical limitations and absence of conclusive empirical support. This ideological ascendancy resulted from the successful sale of a simplified and popularised version of the 'high theory', in which powerful policy prescriptions were marketed in the absence of their underlying analytical justification.

By its nature the neoclassical argument that unregulated markets increase efficiency is difficult to test empirically. An initial problem arises as a result of the famous principle of the Second Best, which implies that the result of partial liberalisation and deregulation cannot be predicted with regard to whether it moves an economy closer to Pareto Optimality. Since in practice all liberalisation reform is partial, the investigator, even if (s)he accepts that perfect competition generates optimality, must begin with the agnostic position that reforms might or might not increase efficiency of resource allocation. If one makes a leap of faith and embraces the view that some deregulation always increases efficiency, the problem arises how to predict theoretically the *form* that improvement will take. By definition, the effect of deregulation is to create greater scope for private economic agents to pursue their goals, whatever those goals might be. It follows that any outcome is preferred to the previous – regulated - regime, since the new outcome reflects, by definition, greater scope for individual choice. To take but one example, if the effect of deregulation is to reduce the national savings rates, a strict reading of neoclassical logic would entertain no criticism of this outcome, interpreting it as revealing the true time-preferences of agents.

This *a priori* agnosticism makes assessment of the impact of the NEM on the manufacturing sector particularly difficult. Were we to find that trade liberalisation in a country was associated with a decline in manufacturing output of growth, this could be embraced by a neoclassical theorist as a positive development. It could be seen as indicating that the country in question did not have a comparative advantage in manufacturing and, therefore, was well-served by deregulation reducing resource use in the sector.

An analytical framework which predicts all outcomes in theory predicts none in practice. There is little choice but to move from stylised abstractions to more concrete considerations. As noted above, the neoclassical critique of import substitution focused upon its distorting effects with respect to the structure of domestic production, choice of technique and export orientation. If one accepts this critique, then it follows that one would expect statistically measurable and significant changes as a result of the dismantling of import substitution regimes. If the economic characteristics of manufacturing sectors in Latin America did not change in the 1980s and early 1990s, then either the NEM proved ineffective in correcting the previous distortions, or the neoclassical critique of import substitution should be judged of limited practical relevance.

On the basis of the critique of import substitution, one can identify several expected outcomes of liberalisation and deregulation. First, in as far as manufactures are tradeable, manufactured exports should increase as a result of reducing or eliminating policies of protectionism (in the discussion, considerable space will be given to the analysis of manufacturing export orientation). Second, one would expect a change in the structure of manufacturing production, though the nature of the change may vary across countries. The pattern for each country would be determined, within neoclassical analysis, by comparative advantage. One would *not* expect the structure of production across broad sectors - consumer non-durables, durables, intermediates, and capital goods – to remain the same. Third, in as far as Latin American countries are characterised by surplus labour, one would anticipate a shift in distribution from capital to labour. Both of the latter changes would be predicted by the neoclassical critique of import substitution that it stimulated choice of inappropriately capital-intensive techniques in protected industries.

Assessing outcomes is made difficult by the variation in pace and intensity of NEM reform among countries, which is documented in the country chapters in this volume. Seeking a definitive ordering of countries by degree of market reform is a quest doomed to failure; only the broadest judgements can be made (Weeks, 1995). The analysis will proceed on the presumption that a major change in economy policy occurred in Latin America in the 1980s, and that sufficient time has transpired to expect measurable changes. It is further assumed that in most cases the initiation of reform can be roughly dated, and that some comparative judgements can be made as to the degree of liberalisation at the macroeconomic level.

Structural Change in Latin American Manufacturing?

Prior to presenting our empirical results, it is useful to review the conclusions of others. In an important contribution to the evaluation of the impact of the NEM on Latin American manufacturing, Buitelaar and Mertens (1993) suggest several major structural changes during the 1980s. The importance of their analysis lies not only in the empirical trends they identify (which are open to question), but in their nuanced assessment of the impact of various policies. While it is generally alleged by neoclassical writers that the policies of the Washington Consensus (Williamson 1990) uniformly foster competitiveness (Balassa *et al,* 1986), Buitelaar and Mertens (1993) argue that such was not the case. They point out that privatisation, because it has been concentrated in transport, communications and utilities, 'led to the reallocation of private investment resources from tradeable to non-tradeable activities' (Buitelaar and Mertens, 1993, p. 50). In addition to generating a shift of investment away from export-oriented activity, in some countries privatisation of such industries increased costs of production for manufacturing.

They argue that observed increases in manufacturing production in Latin America in the 1980s derived from productive capacity installed during the period of import substitution, citing data on low rates of investment in the sector during the decade. On the basis of this rather 'gloomy picture',[6] they suggest an analytical periodisation of the evolution of the manufacturing sector in Latin America during the crisis-ridden 1980s. The first phase, approximately the period 1981-1985, they characterise as one of private entrepreneurs seeking 'to minimize the loss of profits by *rationalising* the factors of production' (emphasis in original) through 'reducing [factor use] in absolute terms'; i.e., reduction of the labour force and abandoning capital equipment 'without making any substantial technological or organisational innovations' (Buitelaar and Mertens, 1993, p. 53). This period of rationalisation was then followed, they argue, by a phase of intensification of factor use, which again involved little new investment or innovation in management techniques or the work process.[7] They then conclude that to achieve international competitiveness Latin American manufacturing must enter a phase 'involving the transformation of [productive] factors through integral innovation in the technical, organisational and human resource bases of the enterprises' (Buitelaar and Mertens, 1993, p. 54).

The conclusions of these authors provide a useful counter-analysis to the optimistic predictions of the advocates of the NEM. While the former see at best nascent indications of emerging competitiveness, the latter consider Latin American manufacturing well on its way to recovery and international competitiveness. In the context of their analysis, Buitelaar and Mertens identify one major change in the structure of Latin American industry, a relative shift towards intermediate goods, both in the structure of production and the composition of exports. If, indeed, this represents the major measurable shift, it is not without its negative aspects. On the one hand, intermediate goods throughout the region are the least employment generating of the four broad sub-sectors of manufacturing (consumer non-durable, consumer durable, intermediate and capital goods) and, on the other hand, their expansion might reflect Latin American's traditional dependence on natural resource-based exports. This hypothesis is treated below in the empirical analysis.

Perhaps the most important elements of the NEM for manufacturing are the exchange rate regime and trade liberalisation (see Chapter 2). The former affects the relative profitability between tradeables and non-tradeables, and the latter the relative return for importables and exportables. While the degree to which governments reformed each of these policies varied across countries, by the early 1990s every country in Latin America operated under a more liberalised trade regime and more flexible exchange rate mechanism than in the early 1980s.[8] Since these policies affect trade in general, of which manufactures are but a part, our analysis begins with a brief consideration of export performance as a whole.

Table A.5 shows total exports as a proportion of GDP for the main Latin American countries. One would expect that NEM policies would increase the export orientation of the countries, and this occurred in some cases. For all countries taken together, weighted by GDP (see Table A.3), the export share rose in the 1980s (it fell in the 1970s). However, if one treats countries as the unit of analysis, the increase is less impressive and begins prior to general introduction of the NEM, with the largest five-year increase occurring during

1975-1980. One can conclude that there is no strong evidence that NEM-type policies increased the openness of Latin America on a disaggregated basis, for what increase occurred can easily be associated with a trend begun in the 1970s.

Table 1 provides a measure of change in export performance for a larger group of countries, presenting UNCTAD indexes of trade diversification and concentration, for 1980 and 1991. For both indices unity indicates maximum concentration (a single export commodity). It is not clear what theoretical prediction neoclassical analysis would have for the impact of trade liberalisation on export structure. On the one hand, liberalisation of the trade regime and the exchange rate should reveal comparative advantage in commodities that was previously blocked by anti-export bias. On the other hand, the move from protectionism towards freer trade results, by definition, in specialisation. The predicted outcome is made more indeterminate because 'specialisation' refers to input use rather than to commodities as such.[9]

One can escape from this indeterminacy by recalling a neoclassical critique of import substitution regimes. Structuralist trade policy was not aimed at import substitution as such, but at fostering manufactured exports, whose superiority over primary products was seen as being derived from the Singer-Prebisch hypothesis.[10] Protection of manufacturing, it was argued, allowed for the capturing of economies of scale, leading to lower unit costs and international competitiveness. In addition to their rejection of the analytics of Singer-Prebisch, neoclassicals criticised the outcome of import substitution for not generating the export diversification sought by the structuralist strategy, i.e., the continued reliance of Latin American countries on a small number of export commodities was treated as evidence of the failure of the strategy. Thus, it would seem fair to test whether the NEM achieved what import substitution did not.

Table 1 suggests that no substantial change in export diversification occurred in most Latin American countries during the 1980s. If one averages across countries, the difference in the diversification and concentration indexes for the two years is not statistically significant. Indeed, the differences in the diversification index in both years is overwhelmingly explained by the familiar variable, size of country.[11] Only five of the countries show a non-trivial decline in both indexes: Brazil and Colombia, neither of which can be judged as bold NEM reformers during the 1980s; Guatemala and Uruguay which might be viewed as moderate reformers; and Chile, certainly a bold reformer (though the decline in the diversification index is less than for the other four). As with the share of exports in GDP, little change occurred in diversification and concentration of exports in the 1980s.

The absence of change in macroeconomic openness and diversification does not imply anything about manufacturing as such. In current value terms

Table 1:
Export Diversification and Concentration Indices for Latin America, 1980 & 1991

	Diversification		Concentration	
	1980	1991	1980	1991
Argentina	.71	.65	.15	.15
Bolivia	.88	.88	.39	.32
Brazil	.56	.52	.14	.10
Chile	.82	.79	.41	.32
Colombia	.78	.67	.58	.23
Costa Rica	.76	.72	.32	.31
Ecuador	.69	.84	.54	.45
El Salvador	.75	.74	.38	.34
Guatemala	.78	.73	.31	.24
Honduras	.85	.85	.37	.42
Mexico	.52	.50	.48	.50
Nicaragua	.83	.86	.37	.28
Panama	.73	.81	.26	.29
Paraguay	.88	.91	.28	.46
Peru	.61	.81	.26	.26
Uruguay	.78	.74	.24	.20
Venezuela	.71	.80	.67	.56
Simple Average	.74	.75	.36	.32
Standard Deviation	.10	.12	.14	.12

Notes: The 'diversification' index is measured as the absolute deviation of the country commodity shares from the world structure of exports. The concentration index is the Hirschman index normalised to make the values range from zero to unity. For both indices, unity indicates maximum concentration of export structure. To quote from the source: 'The concentration index discriminates more finely between countries which are relatively more diversified.'
Source: UNCTAD (1993), pp. 241-44

manufacturing exports increased substantially, as Table 2 shows. In 1970 total manufacturing exports were about US$ 1500 million, increasing ten-fold to $15,000 million in 1980s and to $45,000 million in 1992. Much of the increase was concentrated in Brazil and Mexico (whose total rose by a factor of 45), but the expansion for the other countries was also large. Still, the increase was unbalanced: four countries – Argentina, Brazil, Colombia, and Mexico - accounted for 76 percent of the GDP of the 17 countries in Table 2, and 88 per cent of the manufactured exports.

Table 2:
Manufactured Exports, Current Prices (US$ millions)

	1970	1975	1980	1985	1990	1992
Argentina	246	722	1852	1746	3594	3218
Bolivia	7	19	30	3	43	95
Brazil	367	2,194	7,469	11,185	46,215	20,459
Chile	59	165	518	246	929	1273
Colombia	66	306	777	600	1698	2199
Costa Rica	43	118	308	221	382	477
Ecuador	3	21	74	22	62	121
El Salvador	65	139	255	175	146	225
Guatemala	81	154	363	214	293	387
Honduras	14	31	104	32	84	95
Mexico	401	931	1,868	4,255	11,567	14,208
Nicaragua	31	63	75	22	28	20
Panama	4	13	31	39	55	84
Paraguay	6	18	37	17	95	100
Peru	19	38	559	348	603	603
Uruguay	41	114	405	393	658	661
Venezuela	32	90	289	1602	1877	1540
Total	**1,487**	**5,136**	**15,015**	**21,119**	**38,330**	**45,765**
Excluding Brazil	1,120	2,943	7,546	9,934	22,115	25,306
Excluding Brazil and Mexico	718	2,012	5,677	5,679	10,548	11,098

Source: UNCTAD (1993)

To what extent was the increase in manufactured exports associated with the NEM ? Table 3 provides a partial answer to this question, in which the rate of growth of manufactured exports is given for various time periods in current and constant prices. To approximate the latter, current exports were deflated by the US wholesale price index for manufactures. Inspection of part B of the table shows that the growth of price-deflated exports during the 1970s was considerably above the rate for the 1980s and also faster than for the first years of the 1990s. At the very least, these percentages suggest that the 1970s should not be dismissed as a period of unqualified anti-export bias. Brazil, with its aggressive industrial policy (Marcovitch, 1990), enjoyed an impressive annual growth of almost 15% per cent (price-deflated) in the 1970s. On the other hand, Mexico's rate of growth of manufactured exports was below the rate of growth of GDP during the interventionist 1970s, though this might be explained by the infamous 'Dutch disease' effects more than trade policy as such.

Table 3:
Annual Rate of Change of Manufactured Exports (%)

COUNTRY	A. Current Prices					B. Constant Prices		
	1970-75	1975-80	1980-85	1985-90	1990-92	1970-80	1980-90	1990-92
Argentina	19.7	17.6	-1.2	13.8	-5.5	8.5	4.2	-5.9
Bolivia	17.6	9.5	-33.4	35.3	37.5	3.2	1.3	37.1
Brazil	28.5	21.8	8.0	7.3	11.6	14.8	5.2	11.2
Chile	18.9	20.7	-14.3	23.3	15.6	9.7	3.4	15.3
Colombia	25.9	17.4	-5.1	19.1	12.9	11.9	5.3	12.5
Costa Rica	18.6	17.8	-6.6	10.7	11.0	8.1	-0.2	10.6
Ecuador	29.0	22.1	-21.7	19.1	32.1	15.1	-4.1	31.8
El Salvador	14.3	11.8	-7.5	-3.5	21.3	2.5	-7.6	20.9
Guatemala	12.3	16.2	-10.3	6.3	13.8	3.8	-4.4	13.4
Honduras	15.4	21.5	-21.3	18.0	6.1	8.5	-4.4	5.7
Mexico	15.9	13.4	15.6	18.5	10.2	4.2	13.2	9.9
Nicaragua	13.5	3.5	-21.9	4.8	-16.9	-2.3	-10.9	-17.2
Panama	22.2	16.0	4.1	6.9	21.0	9.2	3.1	20.7
Paraguay	20.7	13.5	-14.9	28.0	2.5	7.1	6.9	2.1
Peru	13.6	34.9	-9.3	10.7	0.0	16.3	-1.6	-0.4
Uruguay	18.9	22.4	-0.6	10.1	0.2	10.6	2.5	-0.2
Venezuela	19.0	21.0	27.8	3.2	-9.9	10.0	13.5	-10.3
Total	**22.0**	**19.6**	**6.8**	**11.6**	**8.8**	**10.8**	**6.7**	**8.5**
Excluding Brazil	18.0	17.6	5.5	15.2	6.7	7.6	7.9	6.3
Excluding Brazil and Mexico	19.0	19.1	0.0	12.	2.5	8.9	3.8	2.1

Source: Derived from Table 2 deflated by US manufacturing price index

The overall effect of the relatively rapid growth of manufactured exports from 1970 onwards was to increase their share in total trade (Table 4). Again, however, the impact of the NEM remains ambiguous, for the share increases for the periods 1980-85, 1985-1990 and 1990-1992 can be interpreted as the continuation of trends of the 1970s. Further, for ten of the seventeen countries, manufactures were not a significantly larger proportion (indeed, smaller in some cases) of total exports in the 1990s than they had been in either 1975 or 1980.[12]

The Central American countries present a special case, for in the 1960s and 1970s their exports of manufactures increased dramatically behind a regional tariff structure and non-tariff barriers to trade. However, it is the neoclassicals who argue that trade liberalisation is a more effective way to foster exports of any type than protectionist policies. In the absence of concrete evidence that the manufacturing enterprises of the Central American Common Market (CACM)

Table 4:
Exports of Manufactures as a Percentage of Total Exports

	1970	1975	1980	1985	1990	1992
Argentina	13.9	24.4	23.1	20.8	29.1	26.3
Bolivia	3.2	3.5	2.9	0.4	4.7	12.5
Brazil	13.4	25.3	37.1	43.7	51.9	56.9
Chile	4.8	10.0	11.3	6.7	10.9	13.2
Colombia	9.0	20.9	19.7	16.9	25.1	31.8
Costa Rica	18.7	23.9	29.8	22.3	27.4	24.5
Ecuador	1.8	2.2	3.0	0.8	2.3	4.0
El Salvador	28.7	27.0	35.4	25.7	35.5	40.6
Guatemala	28.1	24.7	24.4	20.2	24.5	29.9
Honduras	8.2	10.7	12.8	4.0	9.5	12.9
Mexico	33.3	31.1	12.1	20.6	43.3	52.3
Nicaragua	17.8	16.9	18.1	8.9	8.2	9.1
Panama	3.5	4.7	8.9	12.8	17.0	16.7
Paraguay	9.0	10.4	11.8	5.5	9.9	15.2
Peru	1.8	2.9	16.9	11.8	18.4	17.3
Uruguay	17.6	30.0	38.2	46.1	38.8	40.8
Venezuela	1.0	1.0	1.5	10.0	10.9	11.0
Total	**11.5**	**16.0**	**17.9**	**23.6**	**33.1**	**36.7**
Simple Average	12.6	15.9	18.1	16.3	21.6	24.4
Standard Deviation	10.2	10.7	11.8	13.2	14.5	15.6

Source: ECLAC (1994)

had no prospects for developing international competitiveness, their relatively high shares of manufactures in total exports can be interpreted as support for infant industry protectionism.

From the apparently limited change in export performance associated with the NEM period, we turn to an analysis of manufacturing growth as such. Here, again, one expects an indication of structural change associated with liberalisation. In testing for the possibility of structural change, it is necessary to make explicit what was implicit in the treatment of exports. Analytically, one can distinguish among three influencing factors in the NEM period: sectoral, cyclical and conjunctural tendencies. The first refers to long-term trends, the second to the influence of what used to be called the 'business cycle', and the third to changes that might be associated with policy reform.

In Table 5 an attempt is made to decompose the rate of growth of manufacturing as a whole and for each broad sub-sector into the secular and conjunctural elements over the period 1970-1992.[13] Secular tendencies are approximated by a time trend variable and possible policy effects by a dummy variable. For the latter, all possible time periods were taken and the most statistically significant reported.[14] A common time period is used to make cross-country comparisons more obvious. The column of the table entitled 'evidence of structural change', reports which, if any, time periods produced a statistically significant coefficient for the dummy variable. For manufacturing as a whole (Part A), the dummy variable is significant for what might be defined as the NEM period for only two countries, Mexico (1983-1992) and Chile (1975-1992). In these cases, the coefficients are negative, indicating a *slower* rate of growth of manufacturing as a whole than for the long-term trend.[15] For the other countries, except Argentina (where there was no evidence of structural change), the significant periods fall in the late 1970s and early 1980s, all with positive coefficients. Thus, it would appear that the NEM period was associated with a lower rate of manufacturing growth than previously. Parts B and C of the table apply the same test to the two more technologically-sophisticated sub-sectors of manufacturing, consumer durables (Part B) and capital goods (Part C). For durables, the results are virtually the same as for manufacturing as a whole, while for capital goods four of the seven countries show no evidence of structural change in the growth rate.

The results in Table 5 suggest either a negative or non-significant change in manufacturing growth in the NEM period, but they suffer from not distinguishing between secular and cyclical influences. An attempt is made to correct this omission in Table 6, where the *share* of manufacturing output for intermediates, consumer non-durables and capital goods is decomposed. Because of limitations of data, there are results for only five countries, but these are five of the six largest economies of the region (Venezuela being the fourth largest and

Table 5:
Rate of Growth of Manufacturing and Measures of Structural Change (1970-1992)

	Regression Rate of Growth	Evidence of Structural Change	R^2	Durbin-Watson (DW) Statistic
A. Index of Manufacturing Output				
1. Argentina	0.9**	none	0.342	1.813
2. Bolivia	1.8**	1976-85 positive**	.753	.532
3. Brazil	5.0**	1977-83 positive**	.924	2.835
4. Chile	2.6**	1975-92 negative**	.711	1.114
5. Colombia	4.3**	1976-80 positive**	.957	.595
6. Ecuador	5.9**	1977-83 positive**	.973	.695
7. Mexico	2.7**	1983-92 negative**	.731	.652
B. Index of Consumer Durable Output				
1. Argentina	-2.2**	none	.627	.978
2. Bolivia	2.4**	1973-83 positive**	.437	1.164
3. Brazil	6.2**	1976-83 positive**	.917	.552
4. Chile	3.2**	1978-87 negative**	.554	.786
5. Colombia	3.4**	1975-85 positive**	.903	.655
6. Ecuador	10.4**	1976-81 positive**	.935	1.097
7. Mexico	2.3**	1983-92 negative**	.735	.723
C. Index of Capital Goods Output				
1. Argentina	-2.1**	none	.398	1.034
2. Bolivia	4.3**	1975-86 positive**	.618	.466
3. Brazil	6.7**	1976-82 positive**	.804	.271
4. Chile	-0.6**	1975-77 &1983-88 negative**	.649	1.383
5. Colombia	5.3**	none	.899	1.278
6. Ecuador	15.9**	none	.971	.5
7. Mexico	14.3**	none	.416	.613

* significant at 5% level, ** significant at 1% level

Table 6:
Manufacturing Shares and Measures of Structural Change

A. Share of Intermediates

	Elasticity with respect to total output	Elasticity with respect to time	Evidence of Structural change	R^2	Durbin-Watson (DW) statistic
1. Argentina 1970-1992	-.316 **	.009 **	none	.919	1.283
2. Brazil 1963-1992	.19 *	-.002	1985-92 positive	.860	1.385
3. Chile 1963-1992	-.36	.021**	none	.631	1.204
4. Colombia 1963-1992	.258 **	-.007	1985-92 positive**	.840	2.096
5. Mexico 1970-1992	-.119	-.010	1983-92 positive**	.808	1.377

B. Share of Consumer Durables

	Elasticity with respect to total output	Elasticity with respect to time	Evidence of Structural change	R^2	Durbin-Watson (DW) statistic
1. Argentina 1970-1992	.669 *	-.019 **	none	.779	1.395
2. Brazil 1963-1992	.174	-.012	none	-.05	1.481
3. Chile 1963-1992	.460	0	1981-92 negative**	.762	1.253
4. Colombia 1963-1992	-.432 *	-.021 **	none	.181	1.381
5. Mexico 1970-1992	-.747 **	-.022 **	none	.707	1.708

C. Share of Capital Goods

	Elasticity with respect to total output	Elasticity with respect to time	Evidence of Structural change	R^2	Durbin-Watson (DW) statistic
1. Argentina 1970-1992	1.321**	-.034**	none	.690	1.043
2. Brazil 1963-1992	.463 **	-.022 *	none	.516	2.174
3. Chile 1963-1992	1.454**	-.020*	1983-92 negative**	.694	.766
4. Colombia 1963-1992	2.036 **	-.057 **	1969-72 positive**	.904	1.457
5. Mexico 1970-1992	.713 **	-.004	1983-92 negative**	.804	1.322

*significant at 5% level, ** significant at 1% level*

not included). The first statistical column gives the elasticity of the output share with respect to changes in the level of real output, with a positive coefficient indicating a cyclical relationship and a negative coefficient anti-cyclical movement. The second column reports the time trend, and the third, as before, evidence of structural change.

As discussed in the previous section, Buitelaar and Mertens argue that the NEM period was associated with a relative shift in manufacturing output towards intermediate goods. This hypothesis is confirmed for Brazil, Colombia, and Mexico, but not for Argentina and Chile. Since Brazil was one of the least reformed economies and Colombia a relatively late reformer, one hesitates to assign causality to NEM policies. For consumer durables, there are no structural breaks in the time series except for Chile, with the years 1981-1992 bringing a significant decline in the share. For capital goods, the two strong reformers in the table, Chile and Mexico, both show statistically significant declines in the share during 1983-1992. Colombia shows a significant positive shift during 1969-1972, well before any shift towards NEM-type policies.

Tables 5 and 6 yield negative conclusions. The policy reform periods, however, dated by country, are not in most cases associated with statistically significant shifts in the growth or structure of manufacturing. Where significant shifts occur during years of policy reform, they are generally negative: slower growth of output, and lower shares for the technologically more sophisticated and labour-intensive durable consumer and capital goods industries. The intermediate goods sector, capital-intensive and natural resources based, increased its share in three of five countries, but not in the most liberalised country (Chile).

The indeterminate outcomes measured so far might be explained by the indeterminacy of neoclassical predictions with regard to trade liberalisation and deregulation. One area where predictions *are* clear is for the distribution of income between wages and profits. Since import substitution regimes allegedly induced inefficient capital intensity, liberalisation should shift techniques to greater labour intensity and, *ceteris paribus*, a larger wage share in value added. For the economy as a whole, this shift in technique should increase the demand for labour relative to the demand for capital, raising the real wage and lowering the rate of return on capital. While this relative price shift might be off-set by real devaluation and recession at the macroeconomic level, it is hard to generate a neoclassical scenario that results in a decline in the wage share when capital-biased distortions are removed.

Table 7 investigates the distributional hypothesis using the same technique of decomposition employed in Table 6, with manufacturing disaggregated by broad sub-sectors. For each country and each sector, the wage share in value added is a function of output in the sector (cyclical effect), a time trend (secular effect) and the dummy variable (conjunctural effect).[16] The output (cyclical) variable is significant in nine cases out of 28, with the wage share moving anti-cyclically in six regressions and pro-cyclically in three. For the time trend, Bolivia shows a positive tendency for all sectors, while Argentina and Mexico have negative trends in all cases. For the measure of structural change, the result is more clear. Among the seven countries only one, Argentina, shows statistically significant positive shifts in the wage share , but reform only began at the end of the period (1985-92). For Bolivia, all sectors show a significant downward shift in the wage share after 1985 and in the case of Colombia the shift is for three sectors out of four for the same time period. For Brazil, Chile, Colombia, and Mexico, a downward shift occurs for one sector (capital goods in each case), with no significant change for Ecuador.

These results can be interpreted as indicating a significant cross-country tendency for the reform period to be associated with a decline in the wage share. This result, that liberalisation and deregulation seem most strongly associated with a redistribution from wages to profits, has been found in other research.[17] Only with some ingenuity might this result be interpreted as consistent with neoclassical analysis. The obvious explanation, that the wage share fell because wages fell in response to high levels of unemployment, is hardly neoclassical. If markets are flexible, liberalisation and deregulation should result in a shift – not the unemployment – of labour, and a shift towards techniques of greater labour absorption.

Directly verifying the fall in real wages implied by Table 7 proves extraordinarily difficult if not impossible.[18] As long as one deals with output and income shares and growth of real output in manufacturing, the data are reasonably reliable. However, money wage levels, both in the aggregate and on a sectoral level, prove virtually impossible to render consistent over time due to the hyper- and near hyper-inflation in many of the countries of Latin America at the time. For measurement purposes the problem is made all the greater by the frequent currency reforms.[19] By combining IDB statistics on real value added in manufacturing and UNIDO statistics on the share of wages and levels of employment, Table 8 seeks to estimate changes in real wages. Part A of the table provides an index of the real wage bill in ten countries and shows that for six of the ten, the wage bill fell in the 1980s and early 1990s. The other part of value added, called the operating surplus, rose or remained constant in eight countries (Part B).[20] Only for Chile, Colombia, and Ecuador, quite a mixed group in terms of pace and timing of NEM reforms, did both rise and in no country did the wage bill rise and the surplus fall. Parts A and B of the table, which can be treated as reasonably reliable calculations,[21] indicate a shift in distribution from wages to profits in all countries. Part C of the table presents calculations in which the index of the wage bill is divided by a index of total

Table 7:
Statistical Test of Structural Change: the Wage Share in Manufacturing Value Added

	Output	Time Trend	Evidence of Structural change	R^2
ARGENTINA 1970-1992				
Non-Durable Consumer Goods	pro-cyclical ***	negative ***		.484
Durables		negative ***	1985-1992 positive *	.685
Intermediates	pro-cyclical ***	negative ***	1985-1992 positive *	.553
Capital Goods		negative ***		.336
BOLIVIA 1970-1992				
Non-Durable Consumer Goods		positive ***	1985-1992 negative ***	.658
Durables		positive ***	1985-1992 negative ***	.646
Intermediates		positive ***	1985-1992 negative ***	.805
Capital Goods	anti-cyclical ***	positive ***	1985-1992 negative ***	.676
BRAZIL 1970-1991				
Non-Durable Consumer Goods				.170
Durables	anti-cyclical **			.337
Intermediates				.131
Capital Goods	anti-cyclical *	positive ***	1985-1991 negative **	.327

* significant at 10% level, ** significant at 5% level, *** significant at 1% level
No entry means that the coefficient was not significant

Table 7: continued

	Output	Time Trend	Evidence of Structural change	R^2
CHILE 1963-1992				
Non-Durable Consumer Goods	pro-cyclical *			.359
Durables				.071
Intermediates				.078
Capital Goods	anti-cyclical *	positive ***	1975-1992 negative **	.347
COLOMBIA 1963-1992				
Non-Durable Consumer Goods		negative **	1985-1992 negative ***	.946
Durables			1985-1992 negative ***	.856
Intermediates		negative *		.807
Capital Goods	anti-cyclical ***		1985-1992 negative *	.859
ECUADOR 1963-1992				
Non-Durable Consumer Goods	anti-cyclical *	positive **		.558
Durables				.095
Intermediates				.146
Capital Goods				.076
MEXICO 1963-1992				
Non-Durable Consumer Goods		negative ***		.924
Durables		negative ***		.954
Intermediates		negative ***		.904
Capital Goods		negative ***	1985-1992 negative **	.939

* significant at 10% level, ** significant at 5% level, *** significant at 1% level
No entry means that the coefficient was not significant.

Table 8: Wage and Profit Shares in Manufacturing (1980=100)

Index of Real Wage Bill

Year	Argentina	Bolivia	Brazil	Chile	Colombia	Ecuador	Guatemala	Mexico	Uruguay	Venezuela
1970	115	80	39	90	75	27	65	65	n/a	65
1975	142	107	58	48	86	44	73	80	68	74
1980	100	100	100	100	100	100	100	100	100	100
1985	72	52	78	69	102	105	90	68	54	95
1990	83	64	93	115	106	101	86	73	77	66
1992	100	71	87	126	108	106	91	78	78	90

Index of Real Operating Surplus

Year	Argentina	Bolivia	Brazil	Chile	Colombia	Ecuador	Guatemala	Mexico	Uruguay	Venezuela
1970	77	44	43	89	51	48	52	44	n/a	59
1975	89	63	79	78	75	70	68	62	85	79
1980	100	100	100	100	100	100	100	100	100	100
1985	85	63	102	98	106	105	90	123	88	111
1990	84	75	99	130	139	103	103	143	98	138
1992	10	83	94	155	148	112	109	152	99	148

Index of Real Wages

Year	Argentina	Bolivia	Brazil	Chile	Colombia	Ecuador	Guatemala	Mexico	Uruguay	Venezuela
1970	100	115	106	77	113	63	73	92	n/a	125
1975	104	103	93	42	97	67	65	96	60	100
1980	100	100	100	100	100	100	100	100	100	100
1985	86	39	79	77	117	121	71	71	55	100
1990	83	41	100	80	110	101	68	84	80	60
1992	n/a	n/a	94	80	111	98	n/a	92	81	75

Sources: Derived from IDB (1983), (1987), (1994) and UNIDO (1994).

manufacturing employment. The calculations show that real wages fell notably in seven of the ten countries in the 1980s and 1990s, with the exceptions being weak or late NEM reformers (Brazil, Colombia, and Ecuador).[22] The real wage calculations in Part C of Table 8 are therefore consistent with the more reliable estimates of the real wage bill in Part A.

The statistics in Tables 7 and 8 provide strong evidence that the NEM period was associated with a substantial redistribution from wages to profits, notwithstanding *a priori* expectations to the contrary. A detailed analysis of each country would be required to specify the causes of the redistributions. However, one can speculate that the loss of labour income was affected by the fiscal and monetary austerity associated with the NEM, the impact of real devaluations and the region-wide decline in the bargaining power of trade unions.

Conclusion

Arthur Conan Doyle wrote famously of the case in which Sherlock Holmes found himself perplexed by the dog that did not bark when a crime was committed. In the case of the manufacturing sector in Latin America one finds a similar anomaly. The canine role is assumed by NEM policies and the anticipated barking should have taken the form of a statistically significant change in the behaviour of manufactured exports and the structure of production. While changes occurred, they can be attributed in most countries to the continuation of pre-NEM trends or cyclical effects. It is possible that the latter, involving a relative or absolute contraction in manufacturing output during the 1980s, should not be separated from NEM macroeconomic policies. However, the possibility that the NEM impact on manufacturing was primarily through depression of output is a distinction that the model's advocates presumably would not care to claim. One is left to conclude that if the beast barked, it was soft and discrete with respect to exports and changes in output structure. In contrast, it would appear that the NEM may have delivered a quite robust bite to the incomes and welfare of the Latin American working class in manufacturing.

Notes

1. The Lewis model (also called 'labour surplus' model) of development was extremely influential. It stressed the importance of raising the saving rate in developing countries. On the basis of the reasonable presumption that the saving rate out of profits is greater than out of wages, one can be

led to the conclusion that greater inequality, by increasing savings, increases growth.

2. The announcement proved all the more dramatic because it coincided with the joint meeting of the IMF and the World Bank, which is in effect the annual convention of the world financial establishment (always held in Washington, D.C.).

3. This optimal employment of resources is in relation to external trade. In the orthodox analysis, each country possesses a given amount of resources of various types, in the simplest case homogeneous capital and labour, which can be used for any productive purpose; that is, the capital (machinery, buildings, etc.) is perfectly malleable to any use. In the absence of any state intervention, each country would produce a set of commodities that are best suited for its resource supplies (the metaphorical term 'endowments' is used in this context). Thus, a country with a lot of labour ('relative abundance') would under free market conditions produce labour-intensive commodities and trade these abroad for capital-intensive ones. Tariffs 'distort' this outcome, inducing in a labour-abundant country the inefficient production of capital-intensive commodities.

4. If there are unused resources, then in principle it is possible to produce at least a bit more of every commodity, in which case there is the potential for everyone in society to be better off (assuming the distribution of the additional output to be the same as for the previous level of output).

5. Consider, for example, a perfectly competitive market system which produces two possible full employment outcomes, one in which the rate of investment is ten percent of national income, and another in which it is fifteen percent. In the latter outcome, current consumption is lower (the rate of saving is higher to finance the higher investment), but the rate of growth of consumption over time is higher. A collective decision would be necessary to resolve the trade-off between higher consumption in the present or higher consumption in the future. Since, by assumption, the market produces both results, it cannot serve as a vehicle to select one rather than the other.

6. They write: 'This may seem a gloomy picture, as it would appear to indicate that Latin America has few options open to it except to take advantage of the investments made in earlier periods, exploit its natural resources in the same way, and also take advantage of its unskilled labour' (Buitelaar and Mertens 1993, p. 50). They find cause for guarded optimism in 'indications that a variety of competitive manufacturing activities are emerging, which, because of their as yet small scale, do not show up clearly in the aggregate data' (*Ibid.*).

7. This periodisation leads them to conclude, rather pessimistically, that 'it is even possible that in some cases the exports [in manufacturing] are produced on the basis of marginal costs, without any possibility of recovering the original investments' (Buitelaar and Mertens 1993, p.50)

8. The only exceptions to this judgement might be the countries whose governments adopted currency board mechanisms for exchange rate setting (e.g. Argentina). It is beyond the scope of this chapter to consider the impact of this instrument and its virtual 'dollarisation' of the currency.

9. That is, from a position of near-autarky, the movement to free trade results in a country producing more of those commodities that are intensive in the abundant factor. Whether there will be more of these than in the export pattern under protectionist distortions is an empirical question.

10. It was argued that the terms of trade tended to move systematically against primary products and in favour of manufactures, due to market structures and the role of trade unions.

11. For 1980 and 1991 cross-section regressions in logarithms (ln) were estimated, with the diversification index (diver) as the dependent variable and absolute GDP and *per capita* GDP (y/p) as independent variables. The results were:

<u>1980</u>
$$\ln(\text{diver}) = -.049 - .006 \ln(y/p) - .084* \ln(\text{GDP})$$

$$R^2 = .597 \qquad F = 10.4 \qquad DF = 14$$

<u>1991</u>
$$\ln(\text{diver}) = -.400 + .053 \ln(y/p) - .099* \ln(\text{GDP})$$

$$R^2 = .609 \qquad F = 10.9 \qquad DF = 14 \qquad *\text{significant at 1\% level}$$

The results support the standard conclusion that small economies tend to be less diversified than larger ones (see the negative coefficient on GDP). Further, the coefficients on size of economy are not significantly different for the two years and the R^2 is virtually the same. These results suggest no structural change among the countries. Regressions using the concentration index were non-significant for both variables. Data from UNCTAD (1993), pp.241-243.

12. These countries are: Argentina, Costa Rica, Chile, Ecuador, Guatemala, Honduras, Nicaragua, Paraguay, Peru, and Uruguay.

13. The seven countries in the table are those for which the UNIDO industrial data base allows for the calculations to be made.

14. The possibilities were restricted by requiring the dummy variable to cover a minimum of four years. While this number is arbitrary, it is consistent with the view that any 'structural' change should be more than momentary.

15. The dummy for Chile covers all but the first four years of the time period. For this country it is possible to take the time series back to 1963. When this is done, the period 1975-1992 remains the most statistically significant.

16. In this case, the dummy is the same across countries in order to test specifically for NEM effects.

17. Pastor found that IMF programmes in Latin America were associated with no statistically significant change in macroeconomic variables such as GDP growth, inflation, and the current account balance, but were highly correlated with a decline in the wage share in national income (Pastor, 1987a).

18. Problems of measuring manufacturing wages, and productivity, are also discussed in Buitelaar and Mertens (1993).

19. An obvious procedure to solve the problem, converting local currency to US dollars at official exchange rates to measure money wages, produces time series for several countries which are as improbable as using local currency units.

20. The operating surplus is merely the wage share subtracted from unity. It includes profits, interest, rent, and depreciation.

21. The IDB statistics on value added in principle include all producers regardless of size, while the UNIDO data on the wage share covers establishments hiring five or more. If very small establishments have a larger wage share, using the UNIDO statistics imparts a downward bias to the calculation. Since the table employs an index of the wage share, the bias presents a problem if the distribution of establishments between less than five employed and more than five employed changed over time. However, employment in very small establishments is small in most of the countries for the manufacturing sector, implying a small statistical error.

22. These results are consistent with the findings of Berry, Méndez and Tenjo (1994).

CHAPTER 12

CONCLUSIONS

Victor Bulmer-Thomas

The countries of Latin America have all started the transition away from inward-looking development towards a new paradigm based on export-led growth. The New Economic Model (NEM), based on the Washington Consensus, still has no intellectual rival and criticism of the model is either muted or coded. There is no danger for the foreseeable future of countries sliding back into the old model nor there is any coherent alternative available to be adopted.

Despite the fact that the new paradigm is still relatively young, it is abundantly apparent that the benefits claimed for the NEM are very difficult to achieve. The textbook certainties associated with the Washington Consensus have proven to be no more than possibilities, while the costs identified as unavoidable in the short-term have been all too apparent. After a decade of intense reform, hailed around the world as a model of its kind, Mexico faced in 1995 a financial and economic crisis that wiped out much of the earlier achievements. Argentina, a more recent convert to the NEM, has seen the rate of unemployment rise to levels never previously recorded in the country's history (see Table A.9).

Chile remains the great success story of the NEM in Latin America. After more than two decades of reform, the Chilean version of the model has demonstrated a vigour and robustness that puts all other western hemisphere countries to shame. The trend rate of growth of real GDP has accelerated, while population growth rates have continued to decline. Growth has been export-led with exports diversified in terms of products and markets. Domestic savings are high and provide most of the finance needed for fixed capital formation, while annual inflation has fallen into single figures. Chile was hardly affected by the shockwaves from the Mexican crisis, while neighbouring Argentina has been crippled by a liquidity squeeze and crisis of confidence.

The new paradigm will not survive in Latin America unless other countries can join Chile as examples of success. This is not impossible, although it is as well to remember the torturous road taken by Chile on the way to its present elevated status. Both Colombia and Costa Rica have established a solid base for export-led growth in the last decade, while adjustments to the NEM in Mexico in the wake of the 1994/5 financial crisis may be seen in retrospect to have played the same role as the redefinition of the NEM in Chile after 1982.

Time, however, is running out. The willingness of Latin American electorates to tolerate hardship in the short-run in pursuit of long-term gains has surprised most observers, but it should not be taken as a given. Indeed, social protest has escalated in Latin America since 1994 and has been focused above all on issues of economic deprivation. The NEM must start to deliver or it will be swept away by those whose expectations it has raised, but whose aspirations it has failed to meet.

That is why the relationship between the NEM on the one hand and income distribution and poverty on the other is so crucial. If Chile in the 1970s and Mexico in the 1980s were able to implement the model with little or no concern for its impact on equity, that is unlikely to be true for Argentina or Brazil or any other country in the 1990s. Even if the NEM has no intellectual rival as yet, the electorate can still punish those parties most closely associated with its implementation, leaving a political vacuum to be filled by opportunists of varying hues.

The Impact of Reform on Income Distribution and Poverty

The New Economic Model has been proposed as the most appropriate way of improving efficiency and accelerating growth in Latin America. Its impact on income distribution and poverty was not a central consideration in its adoption throughout the region. Yet the different elements of the NEM are non-neutral as far as income distribution and poverty are concerned. Thus, it is important to isolate the potential impact of each element of reform on these two dimensions of equity.

Many methodological problems have to be resolved before this can be done. It is necessary, for example, to distinguish between first- and second-round effects. Labour market reform can be assumed to have implications for income distribution (first-round effects); it may also contribute to a faster rate of economic growth, generating additional resources for the public sector that can be devoted to human capital investment (second-round effects). While the first-round effects are often predictable, the second-round effects will depend on whether the NEM leads to a faster rate of economic growth. That is not something that can be taken for granted and so it is necessary to isolate the first-round from the second-round effects.

Another example is provided by exchange rate policy. Real devaluation, for example, is a crucial part of trade liberalisation; it has a negative short-run effect on real wages; the medium-term effect depends on the factor intensity of tradeable and non-tradeable goods; the long-run effect, however, also depends on the change in the trend rate of growth of GDP. The short-run and medium-term effects are clearly part of the NEM and are relatively straightforward to predict; the long-run effect, however, depends on whether the NEM leads to an acceleration of the trend rate of growth. If it does, the negative impact on real wages will be reversed. As before, however, we cannot assume that the NEM will have this effect on the long-run rate of growth; that is an empirical question that can only be resolved by reference to the data.

The different elements of the NEM may be non-neutral, but they do not affect income distribution and poverty directly. Instead, their impact is felt on real wages, real interest rates etc. that in turn affect income distribution and poverty. We therefore need to proceed in three stages. In the first (see Table 1), the direct impact of each type of reform on the relevant variables is recorded using the theoretical framework established in the thematic chapters. This allows us to predict the expected impact of the NEM on the relevant variable (e.g. real wages). Each of these variables (see Chapter 1) is a factor in explaining changes in income distribution and poverty.

In the second stage the impact of the predicted change in the relevant variables on indicators of income distribution and poverty is recorded (see Table 2). This allows us to estimate the impact of the NEM on income distribution and poverty *on the assumption that the NEM is fully implemented.* This assumption is then relaxed in the next section of this chapter.

The first two stages are concerned with the direct or first-round effects of the NEM on income distribution and poverty. The third stage explores the indirect impact assuming an increase in the trend rate of growth. The next section of the chapter examines the relationship between the NEM and the trend rate of growth in practice.

Chapter 2 makes clear that trade liberalisation reduces real wages in the short-run as a result of real exchange rate depreciation. FitzGerald also argues that this will be the medium-term effect since employment losses in non-traded sectors and importables will be greater than employment gains in exportables. Thus, the impact of trade liberalisation, *ceteris paribus*, is to lower real wages and raise unemployment. The inflation-reducing impact of tariff and non-tariff barrier reductions is assumed to be less than the inflation-increasing impact of currency devaluation so that inflation increases as a result of trade liberalisation. Finally, FitzGerald argues that real interest rates will increase – in part, as a result of exchange rate risk associated with currency depreciation (see Table 1).

This impact from trade liberalisation runs counter to much conventional thinking. It is often argued that, if exportables are labour-intensive, the medium-term impact of trade liberalisation will be an increase in employment and therefore real wages. Exportables, however, are often natural-resource intensive rather than labour-intensive; furthermore, even if they are more labour-intensive than importables, they may be less labour-intensive than non-tradeables. Thus, FitzGerald's conclusions are plausible and, indeed are supported by Weeks in Chapter 11. It is the alleged *long-run* impact of trade liberalisation on economic growth that is most beneficial for real wages and unemployment; this long-run effect, however, is not included in Table 1 for the reasons given above.

Table 1: Impact of Reform on Key Economic Variables

	Trade Liberal- isation	Fiscal Reform	Labour Market Reform	Domestic Capital Reform	Foreign Capital Inflows	Overall
Real Minimum Wage		↑	↓			Neutral
Real Wages	↓	↓	↓		↑	Down
Unemploy- ment Rate	↑	↑	↑		↓	Up
Inflation Rate	↑	↓			↓	Down
Real Interest Rates	↑	↓		↑	↓	Up
Urban Informal Sector		↑	↑		↓	Up
Wealth Effects		↑		↑	↑	Up

Fiscal reform reduces budget deficits and this is reflected in a fall in the rate of inflation (see Table 1). Since the inflation tax is highly regressive (see Chapter 5), the fall in inflation is assumed to benefit the poor. Fiscal reform also lowers the public sector's need to borrow and this results in a lower real interest rate. Lower inflation may well be associated with a rise in real *minimum* wages, but the loss of public sector jobs will mean a rise in unemployment, a fall in real wages and an increase in the size of the urban informal sector. Fiscal austerity, as Whitehead makes clear in Chapter 3, may also require major changes to social security programmes, leading to a reduction in the proportion of the labour force covered by public programmes.[1] An increase in social spending - including targetting on the poor - is then only possible if economic growth accelerates.

Since other parts of the NEM imply a fall in tax receipts (e.g. export and import duties), fiscal reform is often associated with privatisation of state-owned enterprises. As Whitehead makes clear, the transfer of such assets to the private sector is not neutral in terms of income distribution since the new share ownership is highly concentrated. Assuming that the assets are sold at a big discount to their market value, there is a strong wealth effect associated with fiscal reform (from which only the top decile or quintile can be expected to benefit, see Table 1).

Labour market reform (see Chapter 4) is intended to make the labour market more flexible. As a result, real wages and real minimum wages can be expected to fall. It does not necessarily follow, however, that employment in the formal sector will rise since labour market reform is also intended to remove various restrictive practices. The ending of these practices makes it easier for firms to dismiss redundant workers. As Thomas argues, labour will then be displaced from the formal sector, leading to a rise in both unemployment and the size of the informal sector (see Table 1).

The reform of the domestic capital market is aimed at ending financial repression. This is usually associated with a rise in real interest rates (see Table 1). Fernández in Chapter 5 also argues that the real interest rate and the dispersion of the return on financial assets are heavily influenced by the rate of inflation. In particular, if macroeconomic stability brings a decline in inflation, the real rate of interest should fall; this does not mean, however, that capital market reform *ceteris paribus* will lower the real rate of interest since it is contingent on the fall in inflation. Fernández demonstrates that capital market reform can be expected to lead to a greater concentration of financial assets (including pension funds) in private hands and a strong wealth effect from stock market performance.

The impact of increased foreign capital flows on real interest rates is quite different, as shown by Stephany Griffith-Jones in Chapter 6. Higher foreign savings are associated with a *fall* in the real interest rate. The inflows of foreign capital, furthermore, have a direct (first-round) effect on economic growth so that they are associated with a fall in unemployment and a fall in the size of the urban informal sector (see Table 1). Foreign capital inflows lead to real exchange rate appreciation so that real wages are also expected to rise and inflation to fall. Finally, Griffith-Jones confirms the strong wealth effect associated with capital market reform for similar reasons to those found by Fernández.

Very few, if any, of the causal relationships developed in Table 1 can be established with certainty. Furthermore, there are almost no variables for which the direction of change is completely unambiguous. Nevertheless, the non-neutrality of the NEM is clear and the direction of change is not unduly difficult to establish. At the risk of some simplification, we may therefore conclude that the NEM will reduce the real wage, although the impact on the real *minimum* wage is indeterminate. It is likely to increase the rate of open unemployment and the size of the urban informal sector. The rate of inflation can be expected to fall, but the impact on real interest rates will depend on how much of investment is financed by domestic or foreign savings. Since current account deficits in long-run equilibrium are unlikely to exceed 2-3% of GDP while long-run investment rates are expected to be in the range 20-30%, it is safer to assume that the real interest rate will rise *ceteris paribus* in the NEM. Finally, there is a strong wealth effect associated with the NEM leading to a revaluation of both financial and physical assets.

The impact of these changes on distribution will depend on how each decile (quintile) derives its income. We know, for example, that the lower deciles are more dependent than the top decile on wage income; they are more likely to be unemployed and derive their income from the informal sector.[2] These characteristics of the poor can then be used to establish causal links to income distribution and poverty (see Table 2). Thus, for example, the fall in real wages predicted in Table 1 will lower the income share of the bottom decile (quintile) while raising the Gini coefficient and the share of the top decile; poverty, as measured by the Headcount Index, can also be expected to rise. By contrast, the rich benefit the least from a reduction in inflation, and the top decile has most to gain from a rise in real interest rates (see Table 2). This does not, however, affect the Headcount Index of poverty.

Table 2: Impact of NEM on Income Distribution and Poverty

	Bottom Decile	Bottom Quintile	Gini Coefficient	Top Decile	Poverty (Headcount Index)
Real Wage (Fall)	↓	↓	↑	↑	↑
Unemployment Rate (Up)	↓	↓	↑	↑	↑
Size of Urban Informal Sector (Up)	↓	↓	↑	↑	↑
Rate of Inflation (Down)	↑	↑	↓	↓	↓
Real Interest Rates (Up)	↓	↓	↑	↑	Neutral
Wealth Effects	↓	↓	↑	↑	Neutral

Wealth effects lead to capital gains and these are not normally included in the definition of income (they are always excluded from the definition of income used to define the poverty line). The wealth effects associated with the NEM are so strong, however, that they cannot be excluded. Table 2 suggests that they will lead to a deterioration in income equality where income is defined to include capital gains/losses, although they will not affect poverty as measured by the headcount index.

It is clear from Tables 1 and 2 that the impact of the NEM on income distribution and poverty is not unambiguous. Indeed, any other result would have been very surprising. The most positive feature of the NEM is the reduction in inflation and the gains this brings for the bottom decile (quintile), but this can easily be overwhelmed – as Table 2 shows – by forces working in the opposite direction. Indeed, what Tables 1 and 2 show is that the impact of the NEM is not necessarily positive even on the assumption of full implementation. Further-more, a strong case could easily be made that full implementation will lead to an increase in both income inequality and poverty unless the NEM is associated with rapid economic growth.

The beneficial effects of the NEM on income distribution and poverty therefore rest heavily on the assumption of an acceleration in the trend rate of growth of real GDP. If growth is export-led and if non-traditional exports are labour-intensive, there is every reason to be confident about the ability of the NEM to reduce poverty; if the inward-looking model had a positive association between growth and poverty reduction (see Chapter 1), despite the distortions in factor prices, it would seem that *a fortiori* the NEM would also lower poverty. Even if exports are intensive in natural resources rather than labour, there are no strong grounds for challenging the link between rapid growth and poverty reduction.

The impact on income distribution of an NEM-induced increase in the trend rate of growth is less clearcut. While labour and capital market reform removes factor price distortions, encouraging a shift to labour-intensive techniques, trade liberalisation lowers tariff and non-tariff barriers and promotes the adoption of high technology imports that leads to labour-shedding by firms. Factor market reform also gives a boost to the income of lenders (concentrated in the top quintile) through the rise in real interest rates, while undermining real wage rates. Under these circumstances, a faster rate of growth is only likely to be associated with an improvement in income distribution under two conditions: a tightening of the labour market leading to rising real wages and transfers to the poorest through a concentration of state subsidies on the bottom deciles.[3]

Implementation of the NEM and its Impact on Growth

Both the thematic and case study chapters leave no doubt that a New Economic Model *is* being implemented in Latin America. Even Brazil, the exception to the rule in so many cases, has since 1990 adopted many features of the NEM. Furthermore, the main structures of the NEM have proved quite robust, surviving the negative external shock applied at the beginning of 1995 as a consequence of the Mexican financial crisis. Deviations from the path of virtue (e.g. tariff increases) have been relatively minor and defended as 'temporary'.[4]

The NEM, however, has not been fully implemented anywhere. Although Chile is correctly identified as the country in which the NEM has been most consistently applied, Scott makes clear in Chapter 7 that in several important respects (e.g. capital account liberalisation) the country has fought shy of full implementation. Mexico resisted full deregulation of the labour market even before the collapse of the peso in December 1994. Argentina, although in many respects a model reformer, eschewed real exchange rate depreciation after 1990 despite its commitment in other respects to trade liberalisation. Honduras, as Andy Thorpe shows, has not even begun the process of labour market reform and the same is still true of Brazil.

What emerges from the thematic and case study chapters is, therefore, a NEM that has been only partially implemented. This partiality arises for several reasons. First, there is the question of timing: early reformers are likely to have adopted more of the NEM than late reformers. Secondly, there is the political economy of the NEM: some reforms are easier to implement than others. Thirdly, there is the question of ideological commitment: some reforms command more widespread support than others among the policy-making elite. Each of these factors will be considered in turn.

Although experiments with reform before the debt crisis are relevant in terms of the experience acquired, the first real opportunity to apply the NEM only arose after the debt crisis.[5] That is because the NEM was borne in a context demanding a rapid adjustment from a trade deficit to a trade surplus and this was not a condition for adjustment before 1982. Furthermore, the immediate response to the debt crisis (1982-5) had to be short-term balance of payments crisis management so that in practice the NEM could not be implemented until the mid-1980s. The next decade was to witness the introduction of some version of the model in each republic. Table 3 gives the starting date for a number of countries.[6]

The main consideration behind the difference in timing has been the need to overcome resistance from those pressure groups likely to be negatively affected and the need to build some sort of consensus. It is no accident that Chile is the earliest reformer in Table 3, since opposition to the Pinochet dictatorship was strictly limited and a decade of reform experiments after 1973 had already built some kind of consensus. By contrast, Argentina continued to experiment with neo-Keynesian 'pump-priming' policies for most of the 1980s as pressure groups opposed to the NEM were strong. Similarly, the collapse of the NEM in Venezuela (not shown in Table 3) was due to the absence of consensus in support of the policies adopted by Carlos Andrés Pérez in 1989.

There have been several examples of countries in which the policy-making elite favoured the NEM, but institutional barriers prevented its implementation. The electoral cycle and congressional opposition, for example, has prevented Costa Rica from implementing sustainable fiscal reform despite the fact that in many other respects the country has been a model reformer. Similarly, reform in Brazil since 1990 has had to be fought every inch of the way as a result of legal and congressional obstacles. Indeed, it was these sorts of problems that were in part responsible for the *autogolpe* of President Fujimori in Peru in 1992 when congress was temporarily suspended.[7]

The ideological commitment to the NEM is the most intriguing aspect of partial implementation. Chile, as already mentioned, has been extremely reluctant to adopt full liberalisation of the capital account – a reluctance that has been strengthened by the reaction of international capital to the Mexican financial crisis in December 1994.[8] The same has also been true of Colombia where there has also been a great deal of reservation over fiscal reform and the reduction of inflation. Many of the 'commanding heights' of the Brazilian economy are still under state control and likely to remain so for many years to come. Mexico's commitment to oil nationalisation has never wavered and Honduran fiscal discipline, as Chapter 9 shows, is wafer thin – particularly in election years.

No single explanation can account for these ideological deviations from the purest version of the NEM. They are often country-specific and sometimes rooted in the collective memory of past mistakes. Chilean resistance to capital account liberalisation, for example, is surely a natural reaction to the gross errors associated with financial liberalisation before 1982, while the symbolic importance of oil in Mexico should never be underestimated. In this respect, Latin American countries are no different from other parts of the world. German fiscal and monetary discipline is rooted in the memory of hyperinflation and French protection of the film industry is explained by the fear of a US cultural invasion.

While some deviations from the NEM are country-specific, there is no doubt that there are many similarities in terms of sequencing. As Table 3 shows, trade liberalisation is invariably the first area to be tackled. Where trade liberalisation includes exchange rate devaluation, inflation usually accelerates and this explains why fiscal reform follows after an appropriate lag. With or without devaluation, trade liberalisation tends to widen the current account deficit and this helps to explain the timing of reforms designed to attract international capital flows (including direct foreign investment).

The timing of labour and capital market reforms (see Table 3) is less clear. Recognition of the need to increase savings is a powerful argument in favour of domestic capital market reform, unless foreign savings are widely available; there is also a certain reluctance to reform capital markets while the public sector needs to fund large budget deficits since the anticipated rise in real interest rates will aggravate the problem. Labour market deregulation is needed to increase the profitability of tradeable goods. However, there are other instruments available (notably exchange rate devaluation) with lower political costs.[9]

Table 3:
Implementation of the NEM

	Trade Liberalisation	Fiscal Reform	Labour Market Reform	Domestic Capital Reform	Foreign Capital Inflows
Argentina	1989-	1991-	1993-	1991-	1990-
Brazil	1990-	1994-	n/a	n/a	1991-
Chile (a)	1984-	1986-	1986-	1986-	1986-
Colombia	1990-	1995-	n/a	1990-	1991-
Costa Rica	1986-	n/a	1990-	1994-	1990-
Honduras	1990-	1990-	n/a	1990-	1990-
Mexico	1985-	1988-	1992-	1990-	1986-

(a) The NEM began in Chile after 1973 before collapsing in the 1981-3 financial crisis. The dates in this table refer to the re-establishment of reform policies in the second phase of the NEM after 1983.

Where trade liberalisation leads to external disequilibrium, an increase in foreign capital flows to finance the deficit is a much easier option than labour market reform to increase exports. Thus, labour market reform is often postponed as long as possible.

Although trade liberalisation has been tackled first, it has not always worked as intended. In Chapter 2 FitzGerald shows how sustained real exchange rate depreciation has been rare - in large part, as a result of renewed international capital flows in the first half of the 1990s (see Chapter 6). There has been no sustained boom in the value of exports so that the first stage of export-led growth has been thwarted. Manufactured exports have grown more rapidly than primary exports, but the structure of exports is still heavily slanted towards products intensive in natural resources, leaving the region vulnerable to terms of trade shocks.

Fiscal adjustment (see Chapter 3) has often been impressive. Reforms have included a widening of the revenue base, a shift to value added tax, expenditure reductions, changes in social security provision, privatisation and administrative overhaul. Limits have been placed on central bank credits and inflation rates have fallen. Yet the fiscal system and inflation rates remain vulnerable to external shocks, as the responses to devaluation in Venezuela in 1994 and Mexico in 1995 have shown. The reallocation of social expenditure to benefit the poorest groups has not been a high priority outside of Chile. Even where targeting has taken place, it has not in general compensated the poor for the reduction in total social spending.

Domestic capital market reform, or the New Financial Regime (NFR) in Fernández's terminology, has brought substantial benefits. Negative real interest rates have been phased out and the dispersion of yields on financial instruments has fallen in line with inflation reduction. Real interest rates now encourage domestic savings, but rates are generally still too high to promote productive investment (see Table A.10). The exception is Chile where pension reform has led to a huge increase in the supply of loanable funds through compulsory savings (see Chapter 7). Other countries (notably Argentina, Mexico, and Peru) have followed the Chilean example, but have been unable to reproduce the success.

The return of foreign capital to Latin America after 1990 has proved to be a mixed blessing. As Chapter 6 shows, the benefits tended to be exaggerated and the costs ignored. Renewed international capital flows may have helped to stabilise inflation through their impact on the real exchange rate, but the profitability of the tradeables sector suffered. Foreign savings also appear to have been a substitute for domestic savings rather than a complement despite the reform of domestic capital markets. While Latin America suffered severely from too little foreign capital in the 1980s, the region appears to have been damaged by too much foreign capital in the first half of the 1990s.

The biggest disappointment from implementation of the NEM has been its impact on the trend rate of growth. While growth rates in the first half of the 1990s (when the NEM was in force) have in general been faster than in the second half of the 1980s (when short-term crisis management was still widespread), they are still below those achieved in the three decades before 1980 with the exception of Argentina and Chile (see Table 4). Projections by the IMF and

Table 4:
Growth Rates of Real GDP Per Head (%)

	1950-80	1985-90	1990-4
Argentina	1.5	-1.4	6.4
Brazil	4.2	0	0.6
Chile	1.5	4.4	5.5
Colombia	2.3	2.7	2.2
Costa Rica	3.0	0.6	2.4
Honduras	1.2	0	0.3
Mexico	3.1	-0.9	0.6

Sources: Bulmer-Thomas (1994) and Inter-American
Development Bank (1995)

other international organisations for the rest of the 1990s do not suggest that the situation will improve even under the most optimistic assumptions. When the damaging impact of the Mexican financial crisis in 1994/5 on growth rates is taken into account, it is very difficult to believe that the trend rate of growth for the 1990s will have accelerated.[10]

The NEM has therefore failed to fulfil its expectations so far. The sheer complexity of the reform package appears to have overwhelmed many governments responsible for its implementation. This does not mean it was flawed from the beginning nor does it mean that other superior alternatives were available. However, with the exception of Argentina and Chile, growth rates of GDP have been far below what could legitimately have been expected. Furthermore, growth in Argentina before 1995 was not export-led and the country is now in recession; Chile is the only case where adoption of the NEM appears to have led to an acceleration in the trend rate of growth. As a result, it is by no means certain that the NEM as applied in Latin America has had a positive impact on income distribution and poverty. It is to this controversial subject that we now turn.

The NEM, Income Distribution And Poverty

The NEM has been applied for a relatively short space of time – very short in a few cases. Income distribution and poverty, on the other hand, are influenced not only by the reforms carried out under the NEM, but also by other forces such as the demographic transition and educational levels. Some of these forces are

Table 5:
The New Economic Model, Income Distribution and Poverty

Country	Period	Poverty (a) Indigence	Poverty (a) Other	Bottom Quintile (b) Urban	Bottom Quintile (b) Rural	Bottom Quintile (b) Total	Bottom 40% (b) Urban	Bottom 40% (b) Rural	Bottom 40% (b) Total	Top Decile (b) Urban	Top Decile (b) Rural	Top Decile (b) Tota	Gini Coefficient (c) Urban	Gini Coefficient (c) Rural	Gini Coefficient (c) Total	Inform-al Sector (d)	Source
Argentina	1989-92	-10.1(g)	-13.9(g)														Lloyd-Sherlock (1995)
	1989-94			-0.1(g)			-0.6(g)			+0.7(g)							Lloyd-Sherlock (1995)
	1990-92															+2.1	PREALC (1993)
Brazil	1990-92															+2.1	PREALC (1993)
Chile	1985-92															-3.8	PREALC (1993)
	1987-90	-1.9	-1.6	+0.2(e)	-3.6(e)		+0.4	-5.2		0	+9.4				-.008		Chapter 7; CEPAL (1994)
	1990-92	-4.3	-2.6	+0.2(e)	-2.2(e)		+0.3	+3.1		+1.0	-6.1				-.007		Chapter 7; CEPAL (1994)
	1987-92	-6.2	-4.2	+0.4(e)	-1.4(e)		+0.7	-2.1		+1.0	+3.3				-.015		Chapter 7; CEPAL (1994)
Colombia	1990-92		+1.3(f)	-0.7(e)			-0.8			-0.5						+1.2	Urrutia (1993);CEPAL (1994); PREALC (1993)
	1990-93												+.044				Berry (1995)
Costa Rica	1987-93	-0.3(f)		-0.4(e)	-0.1(e)		-1.9	+0.3		-0.9	-1.1				-.01		Fields and Newton (1995)
	1988-92	+2.0	-2.0														CEPAL (1994)
Honduras	1990-93	-8.3(h)	-7.5(h)	+1.0(e)	+0.7(e)		+1.0	+1.9		-3.5	-7.5		-2.6	-5.0			Chapter 9
	1990-92																CEPAL (1994)
Mexico	1984-89	+0.4	-1.6			-0.3			-0.8			+6.4			+.057		Chapter 8
	1989-92	+0.1	-0.5			0			-0.05			-0.4			+.0001		Chapter 8
	1984-92	+0.5	-2.1			-0.3			-0.85			+5.9			+.057	+4.7	Chapter 8

(a) Absolute change in Headcount Index between beginning and end of year [Ha(t) - Ha(t-1)].
(b) Absolute change in share of decile/quintile(s) between beginning and end of year.
(c) Absolute change in Gini coefficient between beginning and end of year [G(t) - G(t-1)].
(d) Absolute change in size of informal sector as a percentage of total labour force.

(e) Quartile
(f) Indigent and other combined.
(g) Greater Buenos Aires.
(h) Urban only.

very long-term so that it cannot be assumed that changes in income distribution and poverty during the life of the NEM can be exclusively attributed to the NEM itself. The reader needs to be aware of this *caveat* while examining the changes in income distribution and poverty since the introduction of the NEM.

The data for the same countries as in Table 3 and 4 are presented in Table 5 and are derived from a variety of sources including the country study chapters. The initial year is as far as possible the same as the starting date for the NEM identified in Table 3; where this is not possible, as in the case of Chile, the most recent subsequent year has been chosen. All time-periods since the introduction of the NEM are listed where there is more than one observation.

The data in Table 5 illustrate the complex relationship between the NEM and poverty reduction. The level of indigence has fallen sharply in Argentina, Chile, and (urban) Honduras, while the level of moderate poverty has also fallen in Argentina, Chile, (urban) Honduras and Mexico. The level of indigence has, however, increased in Costa Rica and Mexico and overall poverty rose in Colombia. Furthermore, the sharp drop in poverty in Argentina is in large part due to the fact that the base year (1989) was one of hyperinflation which hit the poor very hard. Indeed, the unemployment rate (see Table A.9) rose to 20% in 1995, suggesting a big increase in poverty in the more recent period.

The NEM appears to have been less ambiguous in relation to income distribution. The share of the bottom quintile fell in (rural) Chile with the sharp decline between 1987 and 1990 not fully reversed by the improvement after 1990; it also fell in (urban) Argentina, (urban) Colombia and Mexico, although it did rise in (urban) Chile and Honduras. The top decile made spectacular gains in (rural) Chile between 1987 and 1990 and in Mexico – gains that are correlated with the change in the Gini coefficient. Although the bottom quintile lost in Costa Rica, the top decile also saw a decline in its income share as income shifted to the middle deciles. As in the 1960s, the Gini coefficient in Costa Rica fell despite the squeeze on the bottom decile. Finally, the informal sector share of the labour force rose in all countries except Chile.

The data in Table 5 show quite clearly that the NEM in Latin America is not a sufficient condition for the reduction in poverty and an improvement in income distribution. This is a considerable disappointment for those who argued that a change to a NEM would necessarily improve equity. It seems, however, that there are cases where equity is in fact made much worse. Furthermore, this is true even of the star performers under the NEM; the deterioration in income distribution in rural Chile between 1987 and 1990 was one of the most severe ever recorded, while the rise in the Gini coefficient in Mexico between 1984 and 1989 was also very sharp.

There are several reasons for these disappointing results. First, the NEM has not produced the expected acceleration in growth rates; indeed, the rate of

growth in real GDP per head since the start of the NEM is below the rate before
the debt crisis in most countries (see Table 4). Although rapid growth does not
guarantee an improvement in income distribution (cf. rural Chile), it does at least
make it much easier to reduce poverty (cf. Argentina). However, the NEM has
so far failed to produce the expected acceleration in growth despite the
favourable circumstances created by capital inflows in the first half of the 1990s.

The second problem is caused by the first. Slow growth makes it much more
difficult to increase social expenditure in areas known to improve equity such
as education and health. Indeed, it could be argued that the NEM *ceteris paribus*
makes it more difficult to achieve this because of the emphasis on fiscal
discipline. Even the privatisation of public services is unlikely to help since the
private sector will find little attraction in selling services to the poorest quintile.
It is no accident that Chile, where the growth rate *has* accelerated as a result of
the NEM, has been able to increase substantially the resources dedicated to
education and health in recent years.

The third problem is that the targeting of social expenditure appears to work
best in a context where the lowest deciles are easily accessible. Chile (see
Chapter 7) has been very successful in ensuring that the bottom quintile receives
a disproportionately large share of social spending (excluding pensions). The
same has not been true of other countries, where the poorest are either
inaccessible (e.g. Brazil and Honduras) or political considerations loom large
in disbursals (e.g. Mexico[11]). Even in Chile, however, the positive impact of
social spending since 1990, when democracy was restored, is as much to do with
additional resources made available by rapid growth as with targeting. It is naive
in the extreme to imagine that targeting can be effective in the context of slow
growth, particularly if the political context is highly charged.

The fourth explanation for the disappointing results in Table 5 is provided
by partial application of the NEM. In Chile, for example, the NEM between
1987 and 1990 emphasised trade liberalisation and labour market reform; the
result was a massive transfer of resources to the top decile in rural areas. In
Argentina trade liberalisation was distorted by the exchange rate policy after
March 1991; the result was a huge increase in the relative price of non-
tradeables, rendering the equity gains reported in Table 5 for 1989-92
vulnerable in the long-run. In Colombia, the reluctance to tackle the high rate
of inflation makes it difficult to protect the real earnings of the poor. The same
is true of Costa Rica where fiscal imbalance has led to unstable inflation rates
and a squeeze on the income of the poorest, despite an overall improvement in
equity.

Finally, and most disturbingly, there is some evidence that the first phase
of the NEM is associated with a sharp deterioration in income distribution as a
result of asset redistributions (e.g. privatisation) and the fall in real wages.

Subsequent phases of the NEM may then produce a modest recovery, but this may not be sufficient to reverse the equity losses in the first place. This is clearly the case for Mexico (see Table 5), but it also fits the Chilean case since by all accounts (see Chapter 7) income distribution deteriorated as poverty rose in the first phase of the NEM. As these two countries are the ones that implemented the NEM most thoroughly, this experience is of particular relevance.

Lessons for the Future

The New Economic Model evolved in response to the debt crisis. It was designed to overcome the balance of payments constraint that crippled economic performance in the 1980s. It was not primarily adopted to reduce poverty and improve income distribution. Greater equity is not an integral part of the NEM. Chile and Mexico were widely (and correctly) assumed to be practising the NEM in the second half of the 1980s despite the fact that many indicators of income distribution showed a deterioration; the explanation is provided by their commitment to trade liberalisation, macroeconomic stability and factor market reform. Venezuela, by contrast, was assumed to have abandoned the NEM in 1994 when the administration of President Caldera reversed trade liberalisation; the impact of heterodox policies in Venezuela on income distribution was never even considered in forming this judgement.

The theoretical impact of the NEM on income distribution and poverty cannot, therefore, be evaluated solely by reference to the model itself. While the model has quite clear implications for trade openness, financial deepening, inflation stabilisation and so on, its impact on income distribution and poverty will be determined by the changes in those endogenous variables (e.g. real wages) that have a profound bearing on equity. This is not a simple matter, but – as Tables 1 and 2 have shown – there are no strong grounds for assuming that the NEM is positive for either income equality or poverty reduction. On the contrary, the NEM in itself may well increase inequality and it will only reduce poverty if it leads to an acceleration in growth rates.

If the NEM leads to an increase in the trend rate of growth of GDP per head, it can safely be assumed that this will lead to a reduction in poverty as measured by the Headcount Index.[12] This, however, begs the question: is the NEM capable of accelerating economic growth in Latin America? So far, the evidence is flimsy. In the last ten years (1985-94), only one country (Chile) achieved a faster rate of growth than in the three decades before the debt crisis; if we take only the last five years (1990-4), only four other countries performed better despite the exceptionally favourable circumstances provided by the return of foreign capital and in all these cases (Argentina, El Salvador and Panama and Peru) the additional output consisted primarily of non-tradeable goods. Thus, the superiority of the NEM over its predecessor in terms of economic growth is far from being established.

This does not mean that Latin America is condemned to slow growth if it persists with the NEM. It does mean, however, that the model needs to be adapted and reformed in numerous ways before faster growth can be assured. The cornerstone of the NEM is increased exports and Latin American countries still have much to learn from South-East Asia in this respect. Similarly, investment rates are far too low to be consistent with rapid and sustainable economic growth. The trade-offs in the NEM are still not widely understood and economic policy needs to become clearer with regard to its main priorities. Asian export performance, for example, was not undermined by an increase in foreign capital flows in the 1990s and much of the increase flowed into investment in tradeable goods.

The impact of the NEM on poverty reduction hinges on the long-run rate of growth. In this respect the NEM is no different from its predecessor. There are no special characteristics of the NEM to suggest that it can make much impact on poverty if growth is modest and no reason to doubt that it can make a substantial impact if growth is rapid. Poverty has fallen rapidly in Chile under an orthodox version of the NEM, while the unorthodox version in Argentina after 1990 emphasising non-tradeables had the same result until the 1995 recession. Slow growth in Mexico, however, has produced an increase in indigence and only a small decline in moderate poverty. Since December 1994, it is safe to assume that both have risen since GDP has fallen.

The impact of the NEM on income distribution is more ambiguous. While a slow rate of growth is unlikely to bring an improvement (Mexico after 1984 demonstrates this clearly), there are no strong reasons for assuming that a faster rate of growth will necessarily help. The deterioration in rural Chile during a period of rapid growth (1987-90) is a warning for all those who might have thought otherwise. A failure to adopt the NEM, however, can be just as damaging; the experience of Brazil in the 1980s (see Chapter 10) shows this quite clearly.

This suggests that income distribution will continue to be determined in large part by variables exogenous to the NEM. The demographic transition is an obvious example. A slower rate of growth of population, leading eventually to a tighter labour market, is probably the single most important factor. As Scott has shown for Chile, the combination of rapid economic growth and a slow rate of growth of the labour force has been particularly important in the improvement in income distribution since 1990. If there is little that can be done to reduce the rate of growth of the labour force in the short-run, there is no doubt that the demographic variables are at least moving in the right direction long-term.[13]

The other crucial exogenous (to the NEM) variable is the level of human capital formation. All studies concur that education is a key determinant of income inequality. The NEM, however, has no special advantage in terms of the priority given to education over any other economic model. Indeed, it could easily be argued that Cuba – where income distribution is still relatively egalitarian – gives the highest priority to human capital formation in Latin America, although its economic model was until recently the antithesis of the NEM. Given the need for macroeconomic stability and balanced budgets, the NEM is unlikely to be able to devote sufficient resources to education unless the rate of economic growth accelerates. Thus, it is the rate of economic growth rather than the NEM itself that is crucial for human capital formation.

If the NEM does have an advantage over its predecessor in terms of income distribution, it ought to be found in the emphasis on targeting. The indiscriminate subsidies widely employed before the debt crisis did not benefit the poor disproportionately since the middle and upper quintiles also gained; thus, the distribution of income was only marginally affected, if at all, by increases in social spending. With the exception of Chile, however, targeting is still in its infancy in Latin America. Many governments committed to the NEM still use either indiscriminate subsidies (e.g. urban public transport) or subsidies that go mainly to the upper deciles (e.g. public expenditure on higher education and housing).[14] Where, as in Mexico, there is a commitment to targeting, political objectives have distorted the allocation of resources while slow growth has made it impossible to devote sufficient resources to poverty alleviation to have much effect.

The scale of poverty and the degree of income inequality continue to be the scourge of Latin America. The NEM does not provide a simple answer to either problem. Major improvements, particularly in income distribution, are likely to take many years to achieve and can only be secured through the adoption of policies that operate over the long-run. This presents a major dilemma since democratically elected governments naturally want to see gains in the short-run. The answer is not, as is sometimes claimed, a return to authoritarian politics; on the contrary, what is needed is a consensus among the main political parties on the substance of reforms required to improve equity over the longer-term. That consensus already exists in most Latin American countries on the main elements of the NEM; it is time to extend it to the key determinants of income distribution and poverty.

Notes

1.   A good survey of social security systems in Latin America can be found in Barreto de Oliveira (1994).

2.   For a profile of the poor using a logit model to assign probabilities, see Fiszbein and Psacharopoulos (1995).

3.   Morley (1995, Chapter 2) claims to have found evidence that both poverty and income inequality are counter-cyclical, i.e. falling with rising GDP. The empirical support for this view, however, is very weak and is contradicted by Fields (1995).

4.   A good example is the justification for tariff increases in March 1995 provided by Pedro Malan, Brazil's Finance Minister. He defended them on the grounds of balance of payments difficulties rather then industrial protection and claimed that they would be reversed if domestic firms raised their prices by the full extent of the tariff hikes.

5.   Chile, as so often, is the exception since the NEM did begin before the debt crisis (see Chapter 7).

6.   In order to increase the sample size, the four countries studied in this volume have been supplemented by three others (Argentina, Colombia and Costa Rica) whose reform programmes have been widely discussed.

7.   Although international pressure forced Fujimori to reconvene congress, the President was able to ensure that it remained a shadow of its former self. The elections of April 1995 not only gave Fujimori an overwhelming majority for the presidency, but also a working majority in congress.

8.   While most of Latin America suffered severely from the reversal of short-term capital flows in the first quarter of 1995, Chile was barely affected and the stock market index did not suffer a precipitate decline.

9.   In Argentina, where nominal exchange rate devaluation has been ruled out since March 1991, labour market deregulation has become crucial to the success – and, indeed, survival – of the model.

10. Three other countries (El Salvador, Panama and Peru) had a rate of growth of real GDP per head in 1990-4 that was faster than the trend rate of growth before 1980. In all those cases, however, the economies had collapsed in the 1980s so that post-1990 growth was in large part simply a cyclical recovery rather than attributable to the NEM.

11. Studies of PRONASOL in Mexico suggest two problems with targeting. First, resources are not always targeted on the poorest groups; secondly, the overall impact on poverty of targeting is slight. See Guevara (1995) and Chapter 8 in this volume

12. See Morley (1995) for a strong statement in support of this view. Berry (1995), however, shows that growth may take many years to achieve a significant reduction. See also Chapter 8, Table 10.

13. Latin America's annual rate of growth of population fell from 2.4% in the 1970s to 2.1% in the 1980s and to 1.9% in the first half of the 1990s. The

rural population declined in *absolute* terms after 1990. See Inter-American Bank (1995), Tables A-1 and A-2.

14.   CEPAL (1994), pp.65-6, shows the distributive impact of social expenditure in four NEM cases – Bolivia (1992), Chile (1993), Colombia (1992) and Uruguay (1989). The bottom quintile does not receive more than 20% of social expenditure on higher education (all cases), health (two cases), social security (two cases) and housing (two cases).

STATISTICAL APPENDIX

Table A.1:
Poverty in Latin America: Households Below the Poverty Line (%), c.1980 and 1992

Country	URBAN c.1980	URBAN 1992	RURAL c.1980	RURAL 1992	TOTAL c.1980	TOTAL 1992
Argentina	5(a)	10(a)	16		9	
Bolivia		46				
Brazil	30	39(b)	62	56(b)	39	43(b)
Chile	12(c)	27	25(c)	29	17(c)	28
Colombia	36	38	45		39	
Costa Rica	16	25	28	25	22	25
Guatemala	41		79	72(b)	65	
Honduras	40(c)	66	75(c)	79	65(c)	73
Mexico	28(d)	30	45(d)	46	34(d)	36
Panama	31	34(e)	45	43(e)	36	36(e)
Paraguay		36(a)				
Peru	28	45(f)	68	64(f)	46	52(f)
Uruguay	9	8	21		11	
Venezuela	18	32	35	36	22	33
Latin America	25	34(b)	54	53(b)	35	39(b)

Source: CEPAL (1994), Table 22, pp.158-9 (a) Metropolitan Area, (b) 1990 (c) 1970 (d) 1984 (e) 1991 (f) 1986

Table A.2:
Income Distribution in Latin America: Bottom Quintile (%),
Top Quintile (%) and Gini Coefficient, c.1980 and c.1990

Country	Bottom Quintile		Top Quintile		Gini Coefficient	
	c.1980	c.1990	c.1980	c.1990	c.1980	c.1990
Argentina(a)	5.3	4.2	46.6	51.9	.408	.476
Bolivia		3.5		57.5		.525
Brazil	2.6	2.1	64.0	67.5	.594	.633
Chile(b)	5.2(c)	4.4(d)	51.0(c)	54.9(d)		.573
Colombia(e)	2.5	3.4	63.0	58.3	.585	.532
Costa Rica	3.3	4.0	51.4	50.8	.475	.460
Dominican Republic		4.2		55.6		.503
El Salvador(e)		4.5		50.0		.448
Guatemala		2.1		63.0		.595
Honduras		2.7		63.5		.591
Mexico		3.2		59.3		.550
Panama	3.8	2.0	53.4	59.8	.488	.565
Paraguay(a)		5.9		46.1		.398
Peru(a)		5.6		50.4		.438
Uruguay(e)	4.9	5.4	49.3	48.3	.436	.424
Venezuela	5.0	4.8	48.3	49.5	.428	.441

Source: World Bank (1993)
(a) Metropolitan Area, (b) Figures for Quintiles refer to distribution of consumption among households in Greater Santiago. See Ffrench - Davis (1992) reported in Berry (1995), Table 4. (c) 1978; (d) 1988; (e) Urban.

Table A.3:
The External Trade of Latin America, 1980-94

	Value of Exports ($ billion)	Value of Imports ($ billion)	Exports/ GDP (%)	Share of World Exports (%)	Export Unit Values (1980= 100)	Terms of Trade (1980= 100)
1980	103.6	116.3	11.3	5.4	100	100
1981	112.2	124.4	11.9	6.0	99.3	94.2
1982	100.1	100.8	11.8	5.8	89.1	85.5
1983	98.0	75.4	13.1	5.8	82.1	86.0
1984	107.5	77.0	13.0	6.0	87.7	91.7
1985	101.0	67.9	13.2	5.5	79.5	86.6
1986	86.5	69.2	12.6	4.1	67.6	76.7
1987	99.0	78.0	13.0	3.9	71.1	76.1
1988	114.7	90.2	14.1	3.9	74.4	75.8
1989	127.2	98.2	14.9	3.9	78.8	76.9
1990	140.2	110.4	15.7	3.7	81.6	76.4
1991	140.9	129.2	15.6	3.6	78.2	71.5
1992	149.8	156.5	16.5	3.5	77.3	69.1
1993	159.7	171.6	16.9	3.6	76.3	69.0
1994	185.6	201.5	18.6	3.8	78.0	71.0

*Source: International Monetary Fund (1994); Inter-American
Development Bank (1995); ECLAC (1994a).*

Table A.4:
Exports and Imports of Major Countries, 1980-94 ($million)
(A) Exports

Year	Argentina	Brazil	Chile	Colombia	Mexico(a)	Peru	Venezuela
1980	8,021	20,132	4,671	3,945	15,570	3,898	19,221
1981	9,143	23,293	3,906	2,956	19,646	3,255	20,980
1982	7,625	20,175	3,710	3,095	21,214	3,259	16,590
1983	7,836	21,899	3,836	3,081	21,819	3,015	13,937
1984	8,107	27,005	3,657	3,462	24,407	3,147	15,997
1985	8,396	25,639	3,823	3,552	26,757	2,979	14,438
1986	6,852	22,349	4,191	5,102	21,804	2,531	8,660
1987	6,360	26,224	5,224	4,642	27,600	2,661	10,577
1988	9,135	33,789	7,052	5,037	30,692	2,701	10,244
1989	9,579	34,383	8,080	5,717	35,171	3,488	13,313
1990	12,353	31,414	8,373	6,765	40,711	3,231	17,497
1991	11,978	31,620	8,942	7,232	42,688	3,329	15,155
1992	12,235	35,793	10,007	6,917	46,196	3,484	14,185
1993	13,118	38,597	9,199	7,116	51,886	3,497	14,066
1994	15,659	43,558	11,539	8,399	60,833	4,555	15,480

Source: Inter-American Development Bank (1995)
(a) Includes maquiladoras after 1984.

Table A.4 (continued):
Exports and Imports of Major Countries, 1980-94 ($million)
(B) Imports

Year	Argentina	Brazil	Chile	Colombia	Mexico(a)	Peru	Venezuela
1980	10,541	24,961	5,797	4,663	19,460	2,499	11,827
1981	9,430	24,079	7,181	5,199	24,068	3,482	13,106
1982	5,337	21,069	3,989	5,478	15,128	3,601	12,944
1983	4,504	16,801	3,085	4,968	8,023	2,548	6,419
1984	4,585	15,210	3,574	4,498	11,788	2,212	7,774
1985	3,814	14,332	3,072	4,141	18,359	1,835	8,106
1986	4,724	15,557	3,436	3,862	16,784	2,909	8,504
1987	5,818	16,581	4,396	4,322	18,812	3,562	9,659
1988	5,322	16,055	5,292	5,002	28,082	3,348	12,726
1989	4,203	19,875	7,144	5,004	34,766	2,749	7,803
1990	4,077	22,524	7,678	5,590	41,593	3,469	7,335
1991	8,275	22,950	8,094	4,906	49,966	4,193	11,147
1992	14,872	23,068	10,129	6,516	62,169	4,861	14,066
1993	16,784	27,740	11,125	9,832	65,367	4,901	12,200
1994	21,527	35,997	11,825	11,883	79,375	6,794	8,879

Source: Inter-American Development Bank (1995)
(a) Includes maquiladoras after 1984.

Table A.5:
Exports of Goods and Services (% of GDP at current prices) for
Major Countries, 1980-94

Year	Argentina	Brazil	Chile	Colombia	Mexico	Peru	Venezuela
1980	5.1	9.1	22.8	16.2	10.7	22.2	33.6
1981	6.9	9.5	16.4	11.9	10.4	16.1	31.4
1982	9.1	7.7	19.4	10.9	15.3	16.5	25.8
1983	9.2	11.8	24.0	10.4	19.0	19.7	25.5
1984	7.6	14.2	24.3	11.9	17.4	19.3	26.8
1985	11.7	12.2	29.1	13.8	15.4	23.0	24.1
1986	8.2	8.8	30.6	18.8	17.3	13.9	19.8
1987	7.9	9.4	33.5	17.0	19.5	10.9	21.4
1988	9.5	10.9	34.6	16.3	17.6	13.5	20.6
1989	13.1	9.5	35.0	18.0	16.0	14.0	33.9
1990	10.4	7.8	34.5	20.6	15.8	12.6	39.5
1991	7.7	8.9	32.8	21.3	13.8	9.7	31.4
1992	6.6	10.4	29.8	17.7	12.6	10.3	26.3
1993	6.3	9.8	26.6	17.3	12.4	10.6	26.2
1994	7.0	9.6	28.2	18.3	14.1	11.2	30.8

Source: International Monetary Fund (several issues). Rows 90c and 99b for each country.

Table A.6:
Real Effective Exchange Rate Indices for Exports (1990=100) (a)

	1986	1987	1988	1989	1990	1991	1992	1993	1994
Argentina	100.2	122.4	129.7	143.1	100.0	83.3	77.5	74.4	76.3
Bolivia	67.9	69.8	74.1	71.9	100.0	108.3	116.1	119.9	126.3
Brazil	160.7	156.8	143.2	108.4	100.0	118.5	126.5	113.3	96.2
Chile	88.4	96.3	102.0	96.4	100.0	98.9	94.8	96.1	95.0
Colombia	77.0	85.2	86.5	88.8	100.0	101.0	89.5	83.3	76.3
Costa Rica	95.7	99.6	104.0	98.0	100.0	108.3	103.1	100.6	101.9
Dominican Republic	105.2	130.2	151.0	109.2	100.0	100.6	101.2	98.0	95.9
Ecuador	68.7	78.8	92.3	94.6	100.0	95.2	94.7	83.9	77.6
El Salvador	117.9	99.7	86.9	82.8	100.0	98.4	98.2	87.5	82.8
Guatemala	65.2	84.1	85.0	85.4	100.0	87.9	86.5	87.8	84.6
Haiti	75.0	88.2	93.1	96.4	100.0	92.8	96.2	110.2	n/a
Honduras	56.6	60.3	60.4	56.1	100.0	107.9	102.2	111.5	125.9
Mexico	130.4	135.2	110.0	103.2	100.0	91.1	83.8	78.8	80.3
Nicaragua	24.9	3.1	125.4	150.0	100.0	112.0	104.7	106.8	103.2
Paraguay	86.2	93.1	96.5	101.9	100.0	86.9	91.1	93.6	94.5
Peru	208.1	189.8	195.8	122.1	100.0	82.1	81.4	88.7	84.0
Uruguay	78.1	80.6	86.7	86.3	100.0	88.1	83.9	74.6	73.0
Venezuela	62.7	83.9	81.2	96.1	100.0	93.9	89.1	87.8	93.5

Source: ECLAC (1994a), Table A.8, p.44
(a) prepared on the basis of consumer price indices.

Table A.7:
Public Sector Deficit (-) or Surplus (+) as Percentage of GDP at Current Prices

Country	Coverage	1988	1989	1990	1991	1992	1993	1994
Argentina	NNFPS	-6.0	-3.8	-3.8	-1.6	+0.4	+1.1	+0.1
Bolivia	NFPS	-7.5	-5.0	-4.0	-4.2	-5.3	-6.5	-3.2
Brazil	NFPS	-4.8	-6.9	+1.2	-1.4	-2.1	+0.4	+0.2
Chile	NFPS	+3.5	+5.0	+3.1	+2.2	+2.9	+2.0	+2.0
Colombia	NFPS	-2.5	-2.4	-0.3	+0.1	-0.3	+0.7	+0.9
Costa Rica	CG	-2.5	-4.1	-4.4	-3.2	-1.9	-1.9	-7.0
Dominican Republic	CG	-1.6	-0.1	+0.3	+0.8	+2.6	-0.3	-0.1
Ecuador	NFPS	-5.3	-1.6	+0.6	-1.0	-1.7	-0.4	+0.1
El Salvador	CG	-3.2	-4.9	-3.2	-4.6	-4.7	-3.0	-0.7
Guatemala	CG	-2.5	-3.8	-2.3	-0.1	-0.5	-1.5	-1.4
Haiti	CG	-5.2	-6.6	-1.0	-	-2.6	-2.3	-5.4
Honduras	CF	-6.9	-7.4	-6.4	-3.3	-4.9	-9.2	-4.8
Mexico	CPS	-12.5	-5.7	-4.0	-1.5	+0.5	+0.7	-0.6
Nicaragua	CG	-26.6	-6.7	-17.2	-7.5	-7.6	-6.3	-4.8
Panama	CG	-5.4	-7.1	+6.8	-2.7	-1.4	-0.6	0
Paraguay	CG	+0.7	+1.5	+3.0	+4.4	-0.1	-0.2	+0.8
Peru	CG	-2.5	-4.2	-2.5	-1.5	-1.6	-1.4	+2.6
Uruguay	CPS	-4.5	-6.1	-2.5	-	+0.5	-1.5	-2.2
Venezuela	NFPS	-8.6	-1.3	+0.2	+0.6	-5.8	-2.8	-6.5

Sources: For 1988-93, ECLAC (1994a), Table A.7, p.43; For 1994, Inter-American Development Bank (1995), Table C-4.
CG=Central Government; NFPS=Non-Financial Public Sector; NNFPS=National Non-Financial Public Sector excluding provinces and municipalities; CPS=Consolidated Public Sector

Table A.8:
Average Real Wages (1985=100), 1988-95

Country	1988	1989	1990	1991	1992	1993	1994	1995
Argentina(1)	88.8	88.9	81.0	71.9	68.3	67.2	67.7	68.5
Bolivia	96.9	99.3	105.6	112.9	120.8	n/a	n/a	n/a
Brazil(2)	126.3	136.4	119.0	114.4	126.3	138.9	148.8	168.2
Brazil(3)	92.3	94.0	75.8	80.3	100.4	104.1	94.9	n/a
Chile	108.4	110.5	112.5	118.0	123.3	129.6	136.2	142.1
Colombia(1)	102.9	104.9	105.3	103.4	105.8	112.4	115.7	n/a
Costa Rica	103.5	107.7	110.3	107.7	108.5	118.0	120.2	n/a
Dominican Republic	108.7	96.8	92.3	97.8	112.5	118.2	126.1	n/a
El Salvador(4)	90.2	85.9	81.1	75.1	74.3	70.4	71.2	n/a
Guatemala	91.7	97.7	83.2	78.0	90.7	100.5	107.7	n/a
Mexico(1)	93.0	101.4	104.4	111.1	120.9	129.5	134.8	118.3
Panama	105.2	105.2	106.1	106.5	107.8	112.3	n/a	n/a
Paraguay	120.2	118.7	117.2	120.6	116.6	116.1	123.1	n/a
Peru	102.6	54.7	46.8	53.9	52.0	51.6	59.3	n/a
Uruguay	113.4	112.9	104.7	108.7	111.1	116.4	117.4	110.6
Venezuela(1)	74.1	62.4	57.5	52.8	54.8	51.0	n/a	n/a

(1) In manufacturing; (2) manufacturing sector in São Paulo; (3) manufacturing sector in Rio de Janeiro; (4) formal sector private employment.
Sources: For 1988-94, ECLAC (1994a) and Inter-American Development Bank (1995); for 1995, CEPAL (1995).

Table A.9:
Urban Unemployment (%), 1986-94

Country	1986	1987	1988	1989	1990	1991	1992	1993	1994	1995
Argentina	5.6	5.9	6.3	7.6	7.5	6.5	7.0	9.6	11.2	20.2
Bolivia	7.0	7.2	11.6	10.2	9.5	7.3	5.8	5.4	5.8	n/a
Brazil	3.6	3.7	3.8	3.3	4.3	4.8	5.8	5.3	5.5	4.8
Chile	13.1	11.9	10.2	7.2	6.5	7.3	4.9	4.0	6.2	5.7
Colombia	13.5	11.8	11.3	10.0	10.2	10.2	10.2	8.7	9.3	9.2
Costa Rica	6.7	5.9	6.3	3.7	5.4	6.0	4.3	4.0	n/a	n/a
Ecuador	10.7	7.2	7.4	7.9	6.1	8.5	8.9	8.9	8.1	n/a
El Salvador	n/a	n/a	9.4	8.4	10.0	7.5	7.9	8.1	7.2	n/a
Guatemala	14.0	11.4	8.8	6.2	6.4	6.7	6.1	5.5	n/a	n/a
Honduras	12.1	11.4	8.7	7.2	7.8	7.4	6.0	5.9	n/a	n/a
Mexico	4.3	3.9	3.5	2.9	2.7	2.7	2.8	3.4	3.7	6.5
Nicaragua	4.7	5.8	6.0	8.4	11.1	14.2	17.8	21.8	23.5	n/a
Panama	12.7	14.1	21.1	20.4	20.0	16.1	14.2	12.5	12.0	n/a
Paraguay	6.1	5.5	4.7	6.1	6.6	5.1	5.3	5.1	5.1	n/a
Peru	5.4	4.8	7.1	7.9	8.3	5.9	9.4	9.9	9.5	n/a
Uruguay	10.7	9.3	9.1	8.6	9.3	8.9	9.0	8.4	9.0	10.4
Venezuela	12.1	9.9	7.9	9.7	11.0	10.1	8.0	6.6	8.9	n/a

Sources: For 1986 to 1994, ECLAC (1994a), Table A.4, p.40;
For 1995, CEPAL (1995)

Table A.10:
Average Real Lending Rate (%), 1988-94

	1988	1989	1990	1991	1992	1993	1994
Argentina	NAP	NAP	NAP	-13.0	-2.6	-1.7	+4.1
Bolivia	+18.3	+20.7	+23.8	+26.6	+35.0	+44.5	+47.1
Brazil(a)	NAP	NAP	-4.8	+6.8	+30.2	+7.1	+27.7
Chile	+8.5	+14.5	+21.5	+9.9	+11.2	+12.1	+11.4
Colombia	+14.5	+16.9	+12.8	+20.3	+12.1	+13.2	+17.9
Costa Rica	+3.4	+19.2	+5.3	+13.6	+11.5	+21.0	+13.1
Ecuador	-62.7	-24.2	-12.0	-2.3	0	+16.8	+18.6
El Salvador	-1.2	-5.0	+1.9	+9.9	-3.6	+7.3	+10.1
Guatemala	+2.9	-4.2	-36.3	+23.9	+5.3	+13.1	11.3
Honduras	+8.8	+4.0	-19.3	+0.5	+15.2	+9.0	-0.9
Mexico(b)	+12.9	+24.9	+7.2	+3.7	+6.9	+10.6	+8.4
Panama	+12.2	+13.1	+11.2	+10.7	+9.0	+9.2	+9.2
Paraguay	N/A	N/A	-13.1	+23.1	+10.2	+10.4	+14.2
Peru	NAP	NAP	NAP	NAP	+117.1	+57.9	+38.2
Uruguay	+33.0	+38.4	+45.5	+71.6	+58.8	+44.4	+51.0
Venezuela	-27.0	-58.4	-8.3	-1.2	-2.0	-3.0	-24.3

N/A=not available; NAP=not applicable due to hyperinflation
Source: International Monetary Fund (several issues); line 60p (Lending Rate)
adjusted for annual inflation (December to December).
(a) Real CDI deflated by IGP-DI.
(b) Average cost of funds (line 60n in International Monetary Fund (1995)
adjusted for December to December inflation).

BIBLIOGRAPHY

Adelman, I. and S. Robinson (1989) 'Income Distribution and Development', in H. Chenery and T. N. Srinivasan (eds.) *Handbook of Development Economics*, Amsterdam: North-Holland, Vol. 2, pp. 949-1003

Agosín, M. R. and R. Ffrench-Davis (1993) 'Trade liberalization in Latin America', *Cepal Review*, Vol. 50, pp. 41-62

Ahmad, E., J. Amieva-Huerta and J. Thomas (1994) *Perú: Pobreza, Mercado de Trabajo y Políticas Sociales*, Washington, D.C.: unpublished IMF report

Ahumada, H., A. Canavese, P. Sanguinetti and W. Sosa (1992) 'Efectos Distributivos del Impuesto Inflacionario: Una estimación para el caso Argentino', *Documento de Trabajo No. FP/01, Serie: Finanzas Públicas*, Buenos Aires: Secretaría de Programación Económica

Altimir, O. (1979) 'La dimensión de la pobreza en América Latina', *Cuadernos de la CEPAL*, No. 27, Santiago: CEPAL

Altimir, O. (1982) 'La distribución del ingreso en México', in C. Bazdresch, G. Vera and J. Reyes Heroles (eds.), *Distribución del Ingreso en México: Ensayos*, México: Banco de México

Altimir, O. (1982a) *The Extent of Poverty in Latin America*, Washington, D.C.: World Bank Working Paper 522

Altimir, O. (1986) 'Estimaciones de la distribución del ingreso en la Argentina, 1953-80', *Desarrollo Económico*, Vol. 26, No. 100

Altimir, O. (1987) 'Income distribution statistics in Latin America and their reliability', *Review of Income and Wealth*, Vol. 33, No. 2

Altimir, O. (1994) 'Cambios de la desigualdad y la pobreza en la América Latina', *Trimestre Económico*, Vol. 61 (1), pp. 85-133

Altimir, O. (1994a) 'Income Distribution and Poverty through Crisis and Adjustment', *CEPAL Review*, 52, Santiago

Altimir, O. and S. Piñera (1982) 'Análisis de Descomposición de las Desigualdades de Ingreso en América Latina', *Trimestre Económico*, Vol. 49 (1)

Araquem da Silva, E. (1988) 'A Relação Salário-Lucro no Brasil: Análise de Insumo-Produto, 1970 e 1975', *Revista Brasileira de Economia*, Vol. 42, pp. 3-12

Aspe, P. (1993), *Economic Transformation the Mexican Way*, Cambridge, MA: MIT Press

Atkinson, A. B. (1989) *The Economics of Inequality*, Second Edition, Oxford: Clarendon Press

Bakker, I. (ed.) (1994) *The Strategic Silence: Gender and Economic Policy*, London: Zed Books

Balassa, B., G. Bueno, P. P. Kuczynski and M. H. Simonsen (1986) *Toward Renewed Economic Growth in Latin America*, Washington, D.C.: Institute for International Economics

Banco Central de Chile (1994), *Boletín Mensual*, No. 797, July

Barahona, M. O. and D. R. Claros (1995) *Generación y Cierre de Empleos en el Sector Moderno durante 1993*, Tegucigalpa: SECPLAN Proyecto HON/94/PO2 Política Social: Población, Género y Empleo, Documento de Trabajo

Barr, N. (1993) *The Economics of the Welfare State*, Second edition, London: Weidenfeld and Nicolson

Barreto de Oliveira, F. (ed.) (1994) *Social Security Systems in Latin America*, Washington, D.C.: Inter-American Development Bank

Barrientos, S. (1995) 'Flexible Work, Female Labour and the Global Integration of Chilean Fruit', paper presented to *Annual Conference of the Society of Latin American Studies*, University of Wales, Swansea, 24-26 March

Barrón, A. (1994) 'Mexican rural women wage earners and macro-economic policies', in Bakker (ed.), pp. 137-51

Barros, R., L. Fox and R. Mendonça (1994) *Female-Headed Households, Poverty and the Welfare of Children in Urban Brazil*, Washington D.C.: World Bank Policy Research Working Paper No. 1275

Bastias, A. (1977) *Políticas de Estabilización y Empleo: el caso de Chile, 1973-75*, Santiago: PREALC

Bautista, R. M. and A. Valdés (eds.) (1993) *The Bias Against Agriculture: Trade and Macroeconomic Policies in Developing Countries*, San Francisco: ICS Press

BCH (Banco Central de Honduras) (1991) *Honduras en Cifras*, 1989-91, Tegucigalpa

BCH (1993) *Indice de Precios al Consumidor*, Tegucigalpa

BCH (1994) *Comportamiento de la Economía Hondureña durante 1993*, Tegucigalpa

Bee, A. (1995) 'Agricultural Production and Gender Relations in the Guatulame Valley', paper presented to *Annual Conference of the Society of Latin American Studies*, University of Wales, Swansea, 24-26 March

Behrman, J. R. (1990) 'The Action of Human Resources and Poverty on One Another: What We Have Yet to Learn', Washington, D.C.: World Bank, LSMS Working Papers, No. 74

Behrman, J. (1993) 'Investing in Human Resources', Part 2 of Inter-American Development Bank, *Economic and Social Progress Report*, Washington, D.C.: IDB/Johns Hopkins University Press

Belluzzo, L. G. (1986) 'Um Esforço de Guerra' – interview to *Senhor* news magazine, 29 July

Bengoa, J. (1988) *El Poder y la Subordinación: Historia Social de la Agricultura Chilena, Tomo I*, Santiago: Ediciones Sur

Bequele, A. and J. Boyden (1988) *Combating Child Labour*, Geneva: ILO

Berry, A., M. T. Méndez and J. Tenjo (1994) 'Growth, Macroeconomic Stability and Employment Expansion in Latin America', Paper prepared under the ILO/UNDP project 'Economic Policy and Employment', Geneva: ILO

Berry, A. and F. Stewart (1994) *Market Liberalization and Income Distribution, the Experience of the 1980s*, mimeo, Queen Elizabeth House, Oxford

Berry, A. (1995) *The Social Challenge of the New Economic Era in Latin America*, Toronto: University of Toronto, Center for International Studies

Bilsborrow, R. E. (1992) *Rural Poverty, Migration, and the Environment in Developing Countries: Three Case Studies*, Washington, D.C.: World Bank Working Paper No. 1017

Binswanger, H. P., K. Deininger and G. Feder (1993) *Power, Distortions, Revolt, and Reform in Agricultural Land Relations*, Washington, D.C.: World Bank Working Paper No. 1164

Biondi-Morra, B. N. (1990) *Revolución y Política Alimentaria: Un Análisis Crítico de Nicaragua*, México: Siglo Vientiuno

Bitran, E. and R. E. Saez (1994) 'Privatization and Regulation in Chile', in Bosworth *et al* (eds.)

Blackwood, D. L. and R. G. Lynch (1994) 'The Measurement of Inequality and Poverty: A Policy Maker's Guide to the Literature', *World Development*, Vol. 22, No. 4, pp. 567-78

Blinder, A. and H. Esaki (1978) 'Macroeconomic Activity and Income Distribution in the Postwar United States', *Review of Economics and Statistics*, Vol. 60, No. 4, pp. 604-9.

Bliss, C. (1989) 'Trade and development', in H. Chenery and T. N. Srinivasan (eds.), *Handbook of Development Economics*, Amsterdam: North-Holland, Vol. 2, pp. 1187-1240

Bonelli, R. and P. V. da Cunha (1983) 'Distribuição de Renda e Padrões de Crescimento: Um Modelo Dinâmico da Economia Brasileira', *Pesquisa e Planejamento Econômico*, Vol. 13, pp. 91-154

Bonelli, R. and L. Ramos (1993) 'Income Distribution in Brazil: an evaluation of long-term trends and changes in inequality since the mid-1970s', paper presented to the 12th Latin American Meeting of the Econometric Society, Tucumán, Argentina, 17-20 August

Bosworth, B. P., R. Dornbusch and R. Laban (eds.) (1994) *The Chilean Economy: Policy Lessons and Challenges*, Washington, D.C.: The Brookings Institution

Bosworth, B. P., R. Dornbusch and R. Laban (1994a) 'Introduction', in

Bosworth *et al* (eds.)

Bourguignon, F., J. de Melo and C. Morrisson (1991) 'Poverty and Income Distribution During Adjustment: Issues and Evidence from the OECD Project', *World Development*, Vol. 19, No. 11, pp. 1485-1508

Bourguinon, F. and C. Morrison (1989) *External trade and income distribution*, Paris: OECD Development Centre

Bromley, R. and C. Gerry (eds.) (1979) *Casual Work and Poverty in the Third World*, Chichester: John Wiley

Bucheli, M. and Rossi, M. (1993) 'Poverty status in Montevideo (Uruguay) in the 1980s', Montevideo: Departamento de Economía, Universidad de la República

Bueso, J. A. (1986) *El Subdesarrollo Hondureño*, Tegucigalpa: Colección Realidad Nacional No.18, UNAH

Buitelaar, R. & L. Mertens (1993) 'The Challenge of Industrial Competitiveness', *CEPAL Review*, 51, Santiago

Buiter, W. (1983) *Measurement of the Public Sector Deficit and the Implications for Policy Evaluation and Design*, Washington, D.C.: IMF Staff papers 30(2)

Bulmer-Thomas, V. (1991) *A Long-run Model of Development for Central America*, London: Institute of Latin American Studies, Research Paper 27

Bulmer-Thomas, V. (1992) *Life after Debt: The New Economic Trajectory in Latin America*, London: Institute of Latin American Studies, Occasional Paper No.1.

Bulmer-Thomas, V. (1994) *The Economic History of Latin America since Independence*, Cambridge: Cambridge University Press

Bulmer-Thomas, V. (1995) *The State, the Market and Elections in Latin America: How Much has Really Changed?*, London: Institute of Latin American Studies, Occasional Paper, No. 10

Bulmer-Thomas, V., N. Craske and M. Serrano (eds.) (1994) *Mexico and the North American Free Trade Agreement*, London: Macmillan/ILAS

Cabrera, A., D. Hachette and R. Luders (1989) *La Privatización en Chile después de 1985: ¿Se vendieron o regalaron las empresas públicas?* Santiago: mimeo, Encuentro Anual de Economistas

Cáceres, M. (1991) *Los Efectos de las Medidas de Ajuste*, Tegucigalpa:UPSA/SRN, mimeo

Caldas, R. (1995) 'Privatisation in Brazil', Canterbury: University of Kent, mimeo

Calderón, F. (1993) 'The trade union system: its background and future prospects', *CEPAL Review*, 49, Santiago

Cálix, S. M. and Z. Vindel de Cálix (1991) *Política económica antes y después de 1989*, Tegucigalpa: Litografía López

Calvo, G., L. Leiderman and E. Reinhart (1993) 'Capital inflows and real exchange rate appreciation in Latin America: the role of external factors', *IMF Staff Papers*, Vol. 40, No. 1, March, Washington, D.C.

Cameron, S. and A. Thorpe (1994) *What Determines the Level of Human Capital Investment in Rural Agricultural Communities? Lessons from Honduras*, Bradford:University of Bradford, Working Paper

Carbonetto, D., J. Hoyle and M. Tueros (1987) *El Sector Informal Urbano en Lima Metropolitana*, Lima: CEDEP

Card, D. and A. B. Krueger (1995) *Myth and Measurement:the New Economics of the Minimum Wage*, Princeton: Princeton University Press

Cardoso, E. (1993) 'Private investment in Latin America', *Economic Development and Cultural Change*, Vol. 41, No.4

Cardoso, E. and D. Dantas (1990) 'Brazil', in John Williamson (ed.), *Latin American Adjustment. How Much has Happened?*, Washington, D.C.: Institute for International Economics

Cardoso, E., and R. Dornbusch (1989) 'Foreign Capital Flows', in H. Chenery and T. N. Srinivasan (eds.), *Handbook of Development Economics*, Amsterdam: North-Holland Vol. 2, pp. 1387-1439

Castañeda, T. (1992) *Combating Poverty:Innovative Social Reforms in Chile during the 1980s*, San Francisco: ICS Press

CEPAL (1989) *Antecedentes estadísticos de la distribución del ingreso, Perú, 1961-82*, Santiago: Serie Distribución del Ingreso, 8

CEPAL (1993) *Panorama Social de América Latina*, Santiago

CEPAL (1993a) *Productividad, crecimiento y orientación de las exportaciones en Brasil: Tendencias de largo plazo y hechos recientes*, Santiago

CEPAL (1994) *Panorama Social de América Latina*, Santiago

CEPAL (1995) *Panorama Económico de América Latina*, Santiago

Chant, S. (1985) 'Single-parent families: choice or constraint? The formation of female-headed households in Mexican shanty towns', *Development and Change*, Vol. 16 (October), pp. 635-56

Chant, S. (1991) *Women and Survival in Mexican Cities: Perspectives on Gender, Labour Markets and Low-income Households*, Manchester: University of Manchester Press

CIEPLAN-Ministerio del Interior (1994) *Evolución del Producto por Regiones*, Santiago

Clower, C. (1986) *La Fuga de Capitales en Centroamérica*, Tegugigalpa:BCIE

Codron, J-M. (1990) 'La Fruticulture Chilienne:Bilan et Perspectives', paper presented to *Coloquio Internacional sobre Agriculturas y Campesinados en América Latina:Mutaciones y Recomposiciones*, University of Toulouse, France,13-14 December

Cole, W. E. and R. D. Sanders (1985) 'Internal migration and urban employment in the Third World', *American Economic Review*, Vol. 75 (June), pp. 481-94

Collier, P. (1993) 'Higgledy-piggledy liberalization', *World Economy*, July

Collier, P., A. C. Edwards, J. Roberts and K. Bardham (1994) 'Gender aspects of labor allocation during structural adjustment', in Horton, Kanbur and Mazumdar (eds.), Vol. 1, pp. 276-345

Collier, P. and J. W. Gunning (1993) 'Trade and development: protection, shocks and liberalization', in D. Greenaway and A. Winters (eds.), *Surveys in international trade*, Oxford: Blackwell

Cominetti, R. (1994) 'Fiscal Adjustment and Social Spending', CEPAL Review, 54, Santiago

Coorey, S. (1992) 'Financial Liberalization and Reform in Mexico', in C. Loser and E. Kalter (eds.) *Mexico: The Strategy to Achieve Sustained Economic Growth*, Washington, D.C.: International Monetary Fund

Coplamar, I. (1983) *Las Necesidades Esenciales en México: Situación Actual y Perspectivas al año 2000 Vol. I, Alimentación*, Mexico: Siglo XXI

Corbo, V. and S. Fischer (1994) 'Lessons from the Chilean Stabilization and Recovery', in Bosworth *et al* (eds.)

Corden, W. M. (1987) 'Protection and Liberalization: A Review of Analytical Issues', Washington, D.C.: IMF Occasional Paper, No. 54.

Corden, W. M. (1990) 'Macro-Economic Policy and Growth: Some Lessons of Experience', *Proceedings of the World Bank Annual Conference on Development Economics*, Washington, D.C.: World Bank

Corden, W. M. (1993) 'Protection and liberalization: a review of the analytical issues', Washington, D.C. IMF Occasional Paper 54

Cornia, G. A. (1994) *Macroeconomic Policy, Poverty Alleviation and Long-Term Development: Latin America in the 1990's*, Florence: UNICEF Innocenti Occasional Papers, Economic Policy Series. No. 40

Cornia, G. A., R. Jolly and F. Stewart (1987) *Adjustment with a Human Face*, Oxford: Clarendon Press

Cornia, A. and F. Stewart, F. (1990) 'The Fiscal System, Adjustment and the Poor', *Innocenti Occasional Paper*, Florence: UNICEF

Cornia, G. A. and F. Stewart (1994) '*The Fiscal System, Adjustment and the Poor*', Queen Elizabeth House, Oxford: Development Studies Working Paper No. 29

Corry, D. and A. Glynn (1986) 'The Adjustment Process and the Timing of Trade Liberalization', in A. Choksi and D. Papageorgiou (eds.), *Economic Liberalization in Developing Countries*, Oxford: Basil Blackwell

Cortazar, R. and J. Marshall. (1980) 'Indices de Precios al consumidor en Chile, 1970-78', *Colección Estudios CIEPLAN*, Santiago, No. 4, November

Cortez Baldassano, H. (1988) 'Chile: Programas de Empleo en Chile', in *Empleos de Emergencia*, Santiago: PREALC

Cowell, F. A. (1984) 'The structure of American Income Inequality', *Review of Income and Wealth*, Vol. 30

Cowell, F. A. (1995) *Measuring Inequality*, 2nd edition, Hemel Hempstead: Harvester Wheatsheaf

Cowell, F. A., F. H. G. Ferreira and J. A. Litchfield (1995) 'The Evolution of Income Distribution in Brazil during the 1980s: Documentation and Procedures', LSE mimeo

Cowell, F. A. and Jenkins, S. P. (1995) 'How much inequality can we explain? A methodology and an application to the USA', *Economic Journal*, Vol. 105 pp. 421-30

Cruz, M. E. and R. Rivera (1983) *La Realidad Forestal Chilena*, Santiago: GIA

Damill, M. and J. M. Fanelli (1994) 'La Macroeconomía de América Latina: De la Crisis de la Deuda a las Reformas Estructurales', *Documento CEDES/100*, Buenos Aires: CEDES

Das, S. P. (1993) *New Perspectives on Business Cycles: An Analysis of Inequality and Heterogeneity*, Aldershot: Edward Elgar

De Janvry, A., D. Fajardo, M. Errázuriz and F. Balcázar (1991) *Campesinos y Desarrollo en América Latina*, Bogotá: Tercer Mundo Editores

De Janvry, A., A. Fargeix and E. Sadoulet (1992) 'The Political Feasibility of Rural Poverty Reduction', *Journal of Development Economics*, Vol. 37, pp. 351-68

De Melo, J., and S. Urata (1984) *Market Structure and Performance: the Role of International Factors in a Trade Liberalization*, Washington, D.C.: World Bank, Discussion Paper No. 71

De Soto, H. (1987) *El Otro Sendero: La Revolución Informal*, Buenos Aires: Editorial Sudamericana

Decreto Ley No. 18-90 Tegucigalpa: *La Gaceta*, March 1990

Decreto Ley 135-94 Tegucigalpa: *La Gaceta*, October 1994

Del Cid, R. and M. Posas (1983) *La Construcción del Sector Público y del Estado Nacional en Honduras 1876-1979*, San José: EDUCA

Demery, L. and T. Addison (1987) 'The Alleviation of Poverty Under Structural Adjustment', Washington, D.C.: World Bank Working Paper

Demery, L. and T. Addison, 'Stabilization Policy and Income Distribution in Developing Countries', *World Development*, Vol. 15, pp. 1483-98

Denslow, D. and W. G. Tyler (1984) 'Perspectives on Poverty and Income Inequality in Brazil', *World Development*, Vol. 12, pp. 1019-28

Devlin, R. (1993) 'Las Privatizaciones y el bienestar social en América Latina', in O. Muñoz (ed.), *Después de las Privatizaciones: Hacia el Estado Regulador*, Santiago: CIEPLAN

Diamond, P. and S. Valdes-Prieto (1994) 'Social Security Reforms', in Bosworth *et al* (eds.)

Dias Carneiro, D., R. Werneck, M. Pinto García and M. Bonomo (1994), 'El Fortalecimiento del Sector Financiero en la Economía Brasileña', in R. Frenkel (ed.), *El Fortalecimiento del Sector Financiero en el Proceso de Ajuste: Liberalización y Regulación*, Buenos Aires: CEDES/IDB

Díaz, A. (1993) *Restructuring and the New Working Classes in Chile: Trends in Waged Employment, Informality and Poverty*, 1973-1990, Geneva: UN Research Institute for Social Development Discussion Paper No. 47

Díaz-Alejandro, C. F. (1985) 'Good-bye Financial Repression, Hello Financial Crash', *Journal of Development Economics*, Vol. 19, pp. 1121-24.

Dickens, R., S. Machin and A. Manning (1994) *The Effects of Minimum Wages on Employment:Theory and Evidence from the UK*, Cambridge, Mass.: NBER, Working Paper No. 4742

Dirven, M. (1993) 'Rural society: its integration and disintegration', *CEPAL Review*, 51, pp. 69-87

Dixon, H. W. (1994) 'Imperfect competition and open economy macroeconomics', in F. van der Ploeg (ed.), *The handbook of international macroeconomics*, Oxford: Blackwell

Dornbusch, R. (1980) *Open economy macroeconomics*, New York: Basic Books

Dornbusch, R. and S. Edwards (eds.) (1991) *The Macroeconomics of Populism in Latin America*, Chicago: Chicago University Press

Dornbusch, R. and S. Edwards (1994) 'Exchange Rate Policy and Trade Strategy' in Bosworth *et al* (eds.)

Dornbusch, R. and S. Fischer (1987) 'International Capital Flows and the World Debt Problem', in A. Razin and E. Sadka (eds.), *Economic Policy in Theory and Practice*, Basingstoke: Macmillan

Dornbusch, R. and F. Helmers (1988) *The Open Economy: tools for policymakers in developing countries*, Washington, D.C.: World Bank

ECLAC (1990) *Changing Production Patterns and Social Equity*, Santiago

ECLAC (1992) *Economic Survey of Latin America and the Caribbean 1990*, Santiago

ECLAC (1992a) *Social equity and changing production patterns*, Santiago

ECLAC (1993) *Statistical Yearbook for Latin America and the Caribbean*, Santiago

ECLAC (1994) *Statistical Yearbook for Latin America and the Caribbean*, Santiago

ECLAC (1994a) *Preliminary Overview of the Latin American and Caribbean Economies*, Santiago

ECLAC (1994b) *Economic Survey of Latin America and the Caribbean 1992*, Santiago

ECLAC (1994c) *Policies to improve linkages with the global economy*, Santiago

Economist Intelligence Unit (EIU) (1991) *Chile,Country Profile 1991-92*, London: EIU

Economist Intelligence Unit (EIU) (1994) *Chile,Country Profile 1994-95*, London: EIU

Economist Intelligence Unit (EIU) (1995) *Chile,Country Report 1st Quarter 1995*, London: EIU

Economist Intelligence Unit (EIU) (1995a) *Chile,Country Report 2nd Quarter 1995*, London: EIU

Edwards, S. (1993) 'Openness, trade liberalization and growth in developing countries', *Journal of Economic Literature*, September, pp. 1358-93

Edwards, S. (1994) *Macro-economic Stabilisation in Latin America: Recent Experience and Sequencing Issues*, Washington, D.C.: NBER WP.4697

Edwards, S. and A. Cox-Edwards (1990) *Labor Market Distortions and Structural Adjustment in Developing Countries*, New York: NBER Working Paper No. 3346

Edwards, S. and A. Cox-Edwards (1991) *Monetarism and Liberalization: The Chilean Experiment*, Chicago: University of Chicago Press

Edwards, S. and A. Cox-Edwards (1994) 'Labour market distortions and structural adjustment in developing countries', in Horton, Kanbur and Mazumdar (eds.)

El Colegio de México (1993) *Solidaridad en Zacatecas: Impacto y Problemas de una Política Pública*, Mexico: Centro de Estudios Económicos, El Colegio de México

Elson, D. (ed.) (1991) *Male Bias in the Development Process*, Manchester: University of Manchester Press

EPHPM - SECPLAN, *Encuesta Permanente de Hogares de Propósitos Múltiples*, Tegucigalpa: DGEC Volumes I-V, Various Years

Erzan, R. *et al.* (1989) 'The Profile of Protection in Developing Countries', *UNCTAD Review* 1, Vol. 1, No. 1

ESA/Price Waterhouse (1993) *Estudio de Base de las Poblaciones Afectadas por los ZIP's*, Tegucigalpa

Escobar, B. and A. Repetto (1993) 'Efectos de la estrategia de desarrollo chilena en las regiones: una estimación de la rentabilidad del sector transable regional', *Colección Estudios CIEPLAN*, No 37, June

Estrella Díaz, A. (1991) *Investigación Participativa de las Trabajadoras Temporeras de la Fruta (Estudios de Casos)*, San Bernardo, Chile: Centro el Canelo de Nos Programa Mujer

European Union (1995) *Honduran Country Strategy Paper*, Brussels: mimeo

Eyzaguirre, N. (1993) 'Financial Crisis, Reform and Stabilization: The Chilean Experience', in S. Faruqi and G. Capria (eds.), *Financial Sector Reforms in Asian and Latin American Countries: lessons of comparative experience*, Washington, D.C.: World Bank

Fanelli, J. M. (1991) 'Tópicos de Teoría y Política Monetaria', CIEPLAN, *Serie Docente*, No.5, Santiago

Fanelli, J. M., R. Frenkel and G. Rozenwurcel (1992) 'Growth and Structural Reform in Latin America. Where We Stand', in A. Zini (ed.), *The Market and The State in Economic Development in the 1990s*, Amsterdam: North Holland

Fanelli, J. M. and J. L. Machinea (1994) 'Capital Movements in Argentina', *Documento CEDES/99*, Buenos Aires

FAO (1988) *Potentials for Agricultural and Rural Development in Latin America and the Caribbean: Main Report*, Rome: Food and Agricultural Organization

Fava, V. L. (1984) *Urbanização, Custo de Vida e Pobreza no Brasil*, São Paulo: IPE / USP

Ferguson, J. (1992) *Dominican Republic: Beyond the Lighthouse*, London: Latin America Bureau

Ferreira, F. H. G. (1992) 'The World Bank and the Study of Stabilization and Structural Adjustment in LDCs', London School of Economics, STICERD Development Discussion Paper No. 41

Ffrench-Davis, R. and S. Griffith-Jones (1995) *Coping with Capital Surges: Latin American macro-economics and investment*, Boulder and London: Lynne Rienner

FHIS (Fondo Hondureño de Inversíon Social) (1994) *El FHIS II en Cifras*, Tegucigalpa

Fields, G. (1975) 'Rural-urban migration, urban unemployment and underemployment, and job-search activity in LDCs', *Journal of Development Economics*, Vol. 2 (June), pp. 165-87.

Fields, G. (1980) *Poverty, Inequality and Development*, Cambridge: Cambridge University Press

Fields, G. (1990) 'Labour market modelling and the urban informal sector: theory and evidence', in Turnham, Salomé and Schwarz (eds.), pp. 49-69

Fields, G. (1991) 'Who Paid the Bill: Adjustment and Poverty in Brazil 1980-85', Washington, D.C.: World Bank Staff Working Paper No. 648

Fields, G. (1992) 'Changing Poverty and Inequality in Latin America', *Public Finances*, Vol. 47, pp. 59-76

Fields, G. and A. Newton (1995) 'Changing Labor Market Conditions and Income Distribution in Brazil, Costa Rica and Venezuela', paper presented to Latin American Studies Association, Washington, D.C., September

Fishlow, A. (1972) 'Brazilian Size Distribution of Income', *The American Economic Review*, Vol. 62, No. 2

Fiszbein, A. and G. Psacharopoulos (1995) 'Poverty alleviation, income distribution and growth during adjustment', in Lustig (ed.)

Fiszbein, A. (1992) *Do Workers in the Informal Sector Benefit from Cuts in the Minimum Wage?*, Washington, D.C.: World Bank Human Resources Operations, WPS 826

FitzGerald, E. V. K. (1994) 'ECLA and the formation of Latin American economic doctrine', in D. Rock (ed.), *Latin America in the 1940s: war and postwar transition*, Los Angeles, CA: California University Press

FitzGerald, E. V. K. (1995) 'Structural adjustment in the 1980s: stimulus or setback for private investment in the industrialization process?', in P. van Dijck and R. Buitelaar (eds.), *The Transformation of Industrialization Policies in Small Latin American Countries*, Basingstoke: Macmillan

FitzGerald, E. V. K., K. Jansen and R. Vos (1994) 'External constraints on private investment decisions in developing countries', in J. Gunning (ed.), *Trade, Growth and Development: essays in honour of Hans Linnemann*, Basingstoke: Macmillan

FitzGerald, E. V. K. and G. Perosino (forthcoming) 'Trade liberalization, employment and wages: a critical approach', *QEH/D'Agliano Working Papers*, Oxford & Turin

FLACSO (1992) *Perfil Estadístico Centroamericano*, San José

Foster, J. E. and A. F. Shorrocks (1988) 'Poverty Orderings and Welfare Dominance', in W. Gaertner and P. K. Pattanaik (eds.), *Distributive Justice and Inequality*, New York: Springer Verlag

Foster, J. E. and A. F. Shorrocks (1991) 'Subgroup Consistent Poverty Indices', *Econometrica*, Vol. 59, No. 3, pp. 687-709

Foster, J., J. Greer and E. Thorbecke (1984) 'A Class of Decomposable Poverty Measures', *Econometrica*, Vol. 52, pp. 761-6

Frenkel, R. (ed.) (1994) *Strengthening the Financial Sector in the Adjustment Process*, Washington, D.C.: Inter-American Development Bank

Galal, A. and M. Shirley (eds.) (1994) *Does Privatization Deliver? Highlights from a World Bank Conference*, Washington, D.C.: Economic Development Institute of the World Bank

Galde, W. (1989) 'Privatization in Rent-Seeking Societies', *World Development*, Vol. 17, No. 5, pp. 673-82

García, N. E. (1993) *Ajuste, Reformas y Mercado Laboral: Costa Rica (1980-1990), Chile (1973-1992), y México (1981-1991)*, Santiago: PREALC

García Rocha, A. (1990) 'Note on Mexican Economic Development and Income Distribution', Mexico: El Colegio de México, Centro de Estudios Económicos, *Documento de Trabajo* No. VII-90

García Rocha, A. (1990a) 'Distributive Effects of Financial Policies in Mexico', Mexico: El Colegio de México, Centro de Estudios Económicos, *Documento de Trabajo* No. VIII-90

Gersovitz, M. (1989) 'Savings and Development', in H. Chenery and T. N. Srinivasan (eds.) *Handbook of Development Economics*, Amsterdam: North Holland, Vol. 1, pp. 381-424

Gómez, S. (1994) 'Forestación y campesinado: análisis de los efectos de la expansion forestal sobre los campesinos de la X region, 1990-1993', Estudios Sociales, Vol. 81, No. 3, Santiago: Corporación de Promoción Universitaria

Gómez, S. and J. Echenique (1988) *La Agricultura Chilena: las dos caras de la modernización*, Santiago: FLACSO/AGRARIA

Gómez, S. and E. Klein (eds.) (1993) *Los Pobres del Campo: El Trabajador Eventual*, Santiago: PREALC

González-Vega, C. and V. H. Céspedes (1993) 'Costa Rica', in S. Rottenberg (ed.), *The Political Economy of Poverty, Equity, and Growth: Costa Rica and Uruguay*, New York: Oxford University Press

Graham, C. (1991) *From Emergency Employment to Social Investment: Alleviating Poverty in Chile*, Washington, D.C.: Brookings Institution

Graham, C. (1994) *Safety Nets, Politics and the Poor: Transitions to Market Economies*, Washington, D.C.: Brookings Institution

Greenaway, D. (1993) 'Liberalizing trade through rose-tinted glasses', *Economic Journal*, Vol. 103, pp. 208-23

Greenaway, D. and C. Milner (1987) 'Trade Theory and the Less Developed Countries', in N. Gemmell (ed.) *Surveys in Development Economics,* Oxford: Blackwell

Greenwood, J. and B. Jovanovic (1990) 'Financial Development, Growth and the Distribution of Income', *Journal of Political Economy*, Vol. 98, No. 5, pp. 1076-1107

GRH (Gobierno de la República de Honduras) (1994) *Las Medidas Económicas y su Relación con la Política de Desarrollo Sostenible y Equitativo del Gobierno de Honduras*, Tegucigalpa

Griffith-Jones, S. (1995) 'European Private Flows to Latin America: The Facts and Issues', in Ffrench-Davis and Griffith-Jones

Griffith-Jones, S. and B. Stallings (1995) 'Global Financial Trends: Implications for Third World Development', in B. Stallings (ed.), *Global Changes and the Regional Response*, Cambridge: Cambridge University Press

Grosh, M. E. (1993) *Administering Targeted Social Programs in Latin America: from platitudes to practice*, Washington, D.C.: World Bank

Grosh, M. E. (1993) *From Platitudes to Practice: Administering Targeted Social Programmes in Latin America*, Washington, D.C.: World Bank

Regional and Sectoral Studies Monograph series

Grosh, M. E. (1995) 'Five criteria for choosing among poverty programs', in Lustig (ed.)

Grossman, G. and E. Helpman (1991) *Innovation and growth in the global Economy*, Cambridge MA: MIT Press

Guevara, A. (1995) 'Poverty alleviation in Mexico: the Socio-economic aspects of PRONASOL', in M. Serrano and V. Bulmer-Thomas (eds.), *Rebuilding the State: Mexico after Salinas*, London: Institute of Latin American Studies

Haan, H. (1989) *Urban Informal Sector Information: Needs and Methods*, Geneva: ILO

Hachette, D. and R. Luders (1992) *Privatización en Chile*, Santiago: Centro Internacional para el Desarrollo Económico (CINDE)

Haindl R. E. (1989) 'Análisis de Gasto Social', in E. Haindl, E. Budinich and I. Irarrazaval, *Gasto Social Efectivo:un instrumento para la superación definitiva de la pobreza crítica*, Santiago: ODEPLAN/University of Chile

Haindl, E. and C. Weber (1986) *Impacto Redistributivo del Gasto Social*, Santiago: ODEPLAN/University of Chile

Hanson, G. H. and A. Harrison (1995) 'Trade, technology and wage inequality', mimeo, University of Texas at Austin

Harris, J. R. and M. P. Todaro (1970) 'Migration, unemployment and development: a two-sector analysis', *American Economic Review*, Vol. 60 (March), pp. 126-42

Hasenbalg, C. and N. do Valle Silva (1992) *Relações Raciais no Brasil*, Rio do Janeiro

Hausmann, R. and R. Rigobón (eds.) (1993) *Government Spending and Income Distribution in Latin America*, Washington, D.C.: Inter-American Development Bank

Heller, P., A. Bovenberg, T. Catsambas, K. Chu and P. Shome (1988) 'The Implications of Fund-Supported Adjustment Programs for Poverty: Experiences in Selected Countries', Washington, D.C.: IMF Occasional Paper No. 58

Helpman, E. and P. Krugman (1985) *Market structure and foreign trade*, Cambridge MA: MIT Press

Hernández, A. (1987) *El Neo-Liberalismo en Honduras*, Tegucigalpa: Guayamuras

Hernández, A. (1992) *Del Reformismo al Ajuste Estructural*, Tegucigalpa: Guayamuras

Hirata, H. and J. Humphrey (1991) 'Workers' response to job loss: female and male industrial workers in Brazil', *World Development*, Vol. 19 (June), pp. 671-82

Hirschman, A. (1991) *The Rhetoric of Reaction: Perversity, Futility, Jeopardy*, Cambridge, Mass: Belknap Press

Hoffman, R. (1989) 'Evolução da Distribuição da Renda no Brasil, entre Pessoas e entre Famílias, 1979-1986', in Sedlacek and Paes de Barros (eds.)

Hojman, D. E. (1993) *Chile: The Political Economy of Development and Democracy in the 1990s*, Basingstoke: Macmillan

Horton, S., R. Kanbur and D. Mazumdar (eds.) (1994) *Labor Markets in an Era of Adjustment, Volume 1: Issue Papers; Volume 2: Case Studies*, Washington, D.C.: World Bank

IICA (1990) *Modernización de la Agricultura en América Latina y el Caribe*, San José, Costa Rica: Instituto Interamericano de Cooperación para la Agricultura

IILS (1993) *Reestructuración y Regulación Institucional del Mercado de Trabajo en América Latina*, Geneva: International Institute for Labour Studies

ILO (various years), *Yearbook of Labour Statistics*, Geneva

ILO (1972) *Employment, Incomes and Equality: A Strategy for Increasing Productive Employment in Kenya*, Geneva: ILO

ILO (1988) *Assessing the Impact of Statutory Minimum Wages in Developing Countries: Four Case Studies*, Geneva: ILO Labour-Management Series No. 67

ILO (1990) *Surveys of Economically Active Population, Employment, Unemployment and Underemployment*, Geneva: ILO

ILO (1995) *World Employment 1995*, Geneva: ILO

INEGI (1984) *Encuesta Nacional de Ingresos y Gastos de los Hogares*, Mexico

INEGI (1989) *Encuesta Nacional de Ingresos y Gastos de los Hogares*, Mexico

INEGI (1992) *Encuesta Nacional de Ingresos y Gastos de los Hogares*, Mexico

INEGI-CEPAL (1993) *Informe Sobre la Magnitud y Evolución de la Pobreza en México 1984-1992*, Mexico: ONU-CEPAL and INEGI

Infante, R. (ed.) (1993) *Social Debt: The Challenge of Equity*, Santiago: PREALC

Infante, R. and C. Revoredo (1993) 'Social Expenditure and Income Levels of Poor Families', in Infante (ed.).

Instituto Brasileiro de Geografia e Estatística (IBGE) (1991) *Para Compreender a PNAD*, Rio de Janeiro: IBGE

Instituto Brasileiro de Geografia e Estatística (IBGE) (1993) *Pesquisa Nacional por Amostra de Domicílios: Síntese de Indicadores da Pesquisa Básica - 1990*, Rio de Janeiro: IBGE

Inter-American Development Bank (IDB) (1986) *Economic and Social Progress Report*, Washington, D.C.

Inter-American Development Bank (1991) *Economic and Social Progress Report*, Washington, D.C.

Inter-American Development Bank (1993) *Economic and Social Progress Report*, Washington, D.C.

Inter-American Development Bank (1994) *Economic and Social Progress Report*, Washington, D.C.

Inter-American Development Bank (1995) *Economic and Social Progress Report,* Washington, D.C.

International Finance Corporation (IFC) (1994) *Emerging Stocks Markets Factbook*, Washington, D.C.

International Monetary Fund (IMF), *International Financial Statistics*, several issues, Washington, D.C.

International Monetary Fund (1993) *World Economic Outlook*, Washington, D.C.

International Monetary Fund (1994) *World Economic and Financial Surveys*, Washington, D.C.

International Monetary Fund (1995) Honduras – *Recent Economic Developments*, Washington, D.C.: IMF Staff Country Report No. 95/19

Jarvis, L. (1985) *Chilean Agriculture under Military Rule: from Reform to Reaction, 1973-80*, Berkeley: University of California, Institute of International Studies, Research Series No. 59

Jarvis, L., C. Montero and M. Hidalgo (1993) 'El Empresario Fruticultor: fortalezas y debilidades de un sector heterogeneo', *Notas Técnicas CIEPLAN No. 154*, November

Jazairy, I., M. Alamgir and T. Panuccio (1992) *The State of World Rural Poverty: An Inquiry into Its Causes and Consequences*, London: Intermediate Technology, for IFAD

Jenkins, R. (1995). *Trade Liberalisation and Manufacturing in Bolivia,* London: Institute of Latin American Studies, Research Paper No. 39

Jenkins, S. P. (1995) 'Accounting for Inequality Trends: Decomposition Analyses for the UK, 1971-86', *Economica*, Vol. 62, pp. 29-63

Johnson, H. G. (1969) 'Minimum Wage Laws: a General Equilibrium Analysis', *The Canadian Journal of Economics*, Vol. II, No. 4, November

Johnson, H. G. (1971) *The Two-Sector Model of General Equilibrium*, London: Allen and Unwin

Kakwani, N. C. (1980) *Income Inequality and Poverty: Methods of Estimation and Policy Applications*, Washington, D.C.: World Bank/Oxford University Press

Kakwani, N. (1991) 'Poverty and Economic Growth with Application to Côte d'Ivoire', *Review of Income and Wealth*, Series 39, No. 2, pp. 121-39

Kalter, E. (1992) 'The Mexican Strategy to Achieve Sustained Economic

Growth', in C. Loser and E. Kalter (eds.), *Mexico: The Strategy to Achieve Sustained Economic Growth*, Washington, D.C.: International Monetary Fund,

Kanbur, R. (1990), 'Poverty and the Social Dimensions of Structural Adjustment in Côte d'Ivoire', Washington, D. C.: World Bank, SDA Working Paper No. 2, March

Knight, J. (1976) 'Devaluation and Income Distribution in Less Developed Economies', *Oxford Economic Papers*, pp. 208-27

Kritz, E. and J. Ramos (1976) 'The measurement of urban underemployment: a report of three experimental surveys', *International Labour Review*, Vol. 113 (January-February), pp. 115-27

Krueger, A. O. (1982) *Trade and employment in developing countries: synthesis and conclusions*, Chicago: University of Chicago Press

Lal, D. (1987) 'The Political Economy of Economic Liberalization', *The World Bank Economic Review*, Vol. 1, No. 2, pp. 273-99

Lambert, P. J. (1993) *The Distribution and Redistribution of Income. A Mathematical analysis*, 2nd edition, Manchester: Manchester University Press

Langoni, C. G. (1975) 'Review of Income Distribution Data: Brazil', in C. R. Frank and R. C. Webb (eds.), *Income Distribution and Growth in Less Developed Countries*, Washington, D.C.: The Brookings Institution

Lara, T. (1993) *La Producción Cafetelera en Honduras*, Masters Thesis, POSCAE-UNAH, Tegucigalpa

Lara Resende, A., D. Funaro, J. Sayad, L. G. Belluzzo and P. Arida (1987) *Por Que Não Deu Certo*, Porto Alegre: L&PM Editores

Larrañaga, O. (1989) *El Déficit del Sector Público y la Política Fiscal en Chile, 1978-1987*, Santiago: ECLAC

Larrañaga, O. (1993) *Poverty, Growth and Inequality: Chile after Adjustment*, Santiago: ILADES/Georgetown University, Postgraduate Research Programme in Economics Working Paper I-66

Larrañaga, O. (1994) *Gasto Social en Chile: Incidencia Distributiva e Incentivos Laborales*, Santiago: ILADES/Georgetown University, Postgraduate Research Programme in Economics Working Paper I-76

Larrañaga, O. and G. Sanhueza (1994) *Descomposición de la Pobreza en Chile con Base en la Función Lognormal Desplazada*, Santiago: ILADES/ Georgetown University, Postgraduate Research Programme in Economics Working Paper I-79

Leiva, F. I. and R. Agacino (1994) *Mercado de Trabajo Flexible, Pobreza y Desintegración Social en Chile, 1990-1994*, Santiago: Universidad de Artes y Ciencias Sociales, mimeo

Levy, S. (1994) 'La Pobreza en México', in F. Vélez (ed.), *La Pobreza en*

México: Causas y Políticas para Combatirla, México: Fondo de Cultura Económica-ITAM

Lillard, L. A. and R. J. Willis (1978) 'Dynamic Aspects of Earnings Mobility', *Econometrica*, Vol 46, pp. 985-1012

Litchfield, J. A. (1995) 'The Brazilian Income Distribution: Explaining income inequality during the 1980s', London: LSE mimeo

Lloyd-Sherlock, P. (1995) 'The New Economic Model, Poverty and Income Distribution in Argentina', London: London School of Economics, mimeo

Lluch, C. (1982) 'Sobre Medições de Renda a partir dos Censos e das Contas Nacionais no Brasil', *Pesquisa e Planejamento Econômico*, Vol. 12, No. 1, pp.133-48

Londoño, J. L. (1990) 'Income distribution during the structural transformation. Colombia 1938-88', unpublished Ph.D. thesis, University of Harvard

López, C., M. Pollack and M. Villarreal (eds.) (1992) *Género y Mercado de Trabajo en América Latina*, Santiago: PREALC

Lora, E., L. Zuleta and S. Zuluaga (1994) 'El Fortalecimiento del Sector Financiero en el Proceso de Ajuste: Liberalización y Regulación. El Caso Colombiano', in R. Frenkel (ed.), *El Fortalecimiento del Sector Financiero en el Proceso de Ajuste: Liberalización y Regulación*, Buenos Aires: CEDES/IDB

Lubell, H. (1991) *The Informal Sector in the 1980s and 1990s*, Paris: OECD Development Centre

Lustig, N. (1992) *Mexico: The Remaking of an Economy*, Washington, D.C.: The Brookings Institution

Lustig, N. (ed.) (1995) *Coping with Austerity: Poverty and Inequality in Latin America*, Washington, D.C.: The Brookings Institution

MacEwan Scott, A. (1979) 'Who are the self-employed?', in Bromley and Gerry (eds.), pp. 105-29

MacEwan Scott, A. (1991) 'Informal sector or female sector?: gender bias in urban labour market models', in Elson (ed.), pp. 105-32

Maddison, A. (ed.) (1992) *The Political Economy of Poverty, Equity, and Growth: Brazil and Mexico*, Oxford: Oxford University Press and World Bank

Maloney, W. F. (1994) 'Comment on Bitran and Saez', in Bosworth *et al* (eds.)

Mamalakis, M. (1978) 'Historical Statistics of Chile', Vol. 1, Westport, Conn.: Greenwood Press

Marcel, M. (1989) 'La privatización de empresas públicas en Chile, 1985-88', *Notas Técnicas CIEPLAN No. 125*, January

Marcel, M. and A. Solimano (1994) 'The Distribution of Income and Economic Adjustment', in Bosworth *et al* (eds.)

Marcel, M. (1989) 'Privatización y finanzas públicas: el caso de Chile,1985-88', *Colección Estudios CIEPLAN 26*, June

Marcovitch, J. (1990) 'Política industrial e tecnológica no Brasil: uma avaliação preliminar', *Pensamiento Iberoamericano*, Vol. 17

Marfan, M. and B. P. Bosworth (1994) 'Saving, Investment and Economic Growth', in Bosworth *et al* (eds.)

Márquez, G. and J. Mukherjee (1991) *Distribución del ingreso y pobreza en Venezuela*, Caracas: IESA

Martínez, M. M. (1993) 'Financial and Industrial Policies: Colombia's Challenges and Dilemmas', in S. Faruqi and G. Capria (eds.), *Financial Sector Reforms in Asian and Latin American Countries: lessons of comparative experience*, Washington, D.C.: World Bank

Martínez Pizarro, J. (1993) 'Intraregional migration of skilled manpower', *CEPAL Review*, 50, pp. 127-46

Marx, K. (1970) *Capital*, New York: Progress Publishers

Matear, A. (1995) 'Changing Relations in the Public and Private Sector: the Impact on Employment Opportunities for the Temporeras', paper presented to *Annual Conference of the Society of Latin American Studies*, University of Wales, Swansea, 24-26 March

Mazumdar, D. (1975) *The Theory of Urban Unemployment in Less Developed Countries*, Washington, D.C.: World Bank Staff Working Paper No. 198

Mazumdar, D. (1976) 'The urban informal sector', *World Development*, Vol. 4 (August), pp. 655-79

Mazumdar, D. (1976a) 'The rural-urban wage gap, migration and the shadow wage', *Oxford Economic Papers*, Vol. 28 (June), pp. 406-25

McGreevey, W. (1990) *Social Security in Latin America: Issues and Options for the World Bank*, Washington, D.C.: World Bank Discussion Paper 110

McKinnon, R. I. (1973), *Money and Capital in Economic Development*, Washington, D.C.: The Brookings Institution

McKinnon, R. I. (1988) 'Financial Liberalization in Retrospect: Interest Rate Policies, in LDCs', in G. Ranis and T. Schultz (eds.), *The State of Development Economics*, Cambridge, Mass.: Basil Blackwell

McKinnon, R. I. (1989) 'Financial Liberalization and Economic Development: A Reassesment of Interest-Rate Policies in Asia and Latin America', *Oxford Review of Economic Policy*, Vol. 6, No. 4

McKinnon, R. I. (1991), 'The Order of Economic Liberalization', *Financial Control in the Transition to a Market Economy*, Baltimore and London: Johns Hopkins University Press

McKinnon, R. and D. Mathieson (1981) *How to Manage a Repressed Economy*, Princeton: Princeton University, Essays in International Finance 145

Meller, P. (1992) *Adjustment and Equity in Chile*, Paris: OECD

Meza, V. (1988) 'The military: willing to deal', *NACLA: Report on the Americas*, Vol. 22, No. 1, pp. 14-21

Mezzera, J. (1981) 'Segmented labour markets without policy-induced labour market distortions', *World Development*, Vol. 9 (November/December), pp. 1109-14

Mezzera, J. (1989), 'Excess labor supply and the urban informal sector: an analytical framework', in M. Berger and M. Buvinic (eds.), *Women's Ventures: Assistance to the Informal Sector in Latin America*, West Hartford: Kumarian Press

MIDEPLAN (1991) *Evolución de las Políticas Sociales en Chile,1920-1991*, Santiago

MIDEPLAN (1992) *Impacto distributivo de la política económica y social en 1990-91*, Santiago

MIDEPLAN (1994) *Integración al Desarrollo-Balance de la Política Social, 1990-93*, Santiago

MIDEPLAN (1994a) *Situación de la Pobreza en Chile,1987-1992*, Santiago

Miller, S. M. and P. Roby (1970) 'Poverty: Changing Social Stratification', in P. Townsend (ed.), *The Concept of Poverty*, London: Heinemann

Mincer, J. (1958) 'Investment in human capital and personal income distribution', *Journal of Political Economy*, Vol. 66

Mizala, A. and P. Romaguera (1993) 'Remuneraciones según tamaño de firmas e índices de salarios: Chile, 1982-90', *Notas Técnicas CIEPLAN No. 149*, April

Mizala, A. and P. Romaguera (1993a) 'La importancia de la firma en la determinación de los salarios: evidencia para Chile y Brasil', *Notas Técnicas CIEPLAN No. 155*, December

Moll, T. (1992) 'Mickey Mouse Numbers and Inequality Research in Developing Countries', *Journal of Development Studies*, Vol. 28, No. 4

Montero, C., L. Jarvis and S. Gómez (1992) 'El Sector Frutícola en la Encrucijada: opciones para una expansión sostenida', *Apuntes CIEPLAN No. 112*, September

Mookherjee, D. and A. Shorrocks (1982) 'A Decomposition Analysis of the Trend in UK Income Inequality', *Economic Journal*, Vol. 92, pp. 886-902

Morley, S. A. and C. Alvarez (1992) *Poverty and Adjustment in Costa Rica*, Washington, D.C.: Inter-American Development Bank

Morley, S. A. (1994) *Poverty and Inequality in Latin America: Past Evidence, Future Prospects*, Washington, D.C.: Overseas Development Council Policy Essay No. 13

Morley, S. (1995) *Poverty and Inequality in Latin America*, Baltimore: Johns Hopkins University Press

Morris, F., M. Dorfman, J. Ortiz and M. Franco (1990) 'Latin America's

Banking System in the 1980s: A Cross-Country Comparison', *World Bank Discussion Papers*, No. 81, Washington, D.C.: World Bank

Moser, C. (1978) 'Informal sector or petty commodity production: dualism or dependence in urban development', *World Development*, Vol. 6 (September/October), pp. 1041-64

Moser, C. (1984) 'The informal sector reworked: viability and vulnerability in urban development', *Regional Development Dialogue*, Vol. 5 (June), pp. 135-78

Muchnik, E. and I. Vial (1988) *Evaluación del Programa de Alimentación Complementaria en Santiago: Participación, Cobertura y Aceptabilidad de la Leche Cereal*, Santiago: mimeo

Muñoz, O. (1993) *Después de las Privatizaciones: Hacia el Estado Regulador*, Santiago: CIEPLAN

Musgrove, P. (1986) 'Desigualdad en la distribución del ingreso en díez ciudades sudamericanas: descomposición e interpretación del coeficiente de Gini',*Cuadernos de Economía*, Año 23, No. 69, August, Santiago

Mussa, M. (1974) 'Tariffs and the Distribution of Income: The Importance of Factor Specificity, Substitutability, and Intensity in the Short and Long Run', *Journal of Political Economy*, Vol. 82, No. 6, pp. 1191-1203

Navarro, J. (1993) 'Poverty and Adjustment: The Case of Honduras', *CEPAL Review*, 49, pp. 91-101

Noé Pino, H. (1990) *El Ajuste Estructural en Honduras*, Tegucigalpa: CEDOH Special Bulletin No.45

Noé Pino, H. and A. Hernández (1990) 'La Economía Hondureña en los Años Ochenta y Perspectivas para los Noventas', *Honduras: Crisis Económica y Proceso de Democratización Política*, Tegucigalpa: CEDOH

Noé Pino, H. and R. Perdomo (1992) *Impacto de las Exportaciones No Tradicionales sobre Pequeños y Medianos Productores: Casos de Melón y Camarón*, Tegucigalpa: POSCAE Working Paper No. 4, UNAH

Noé Pino, H., A. T. Thorpe and R. Sandoval Corea (eds.) (1993) *El Sector Agrícola y la Modernización en Honduras*, Tegucigalpa: CEDOH-POSCAE

Nolan, B. (1987) *Income Distribution and the Macroeconomy*, Cambridge: Cambridge University Press

OECD (1993/4) *Financial Market Trends*, Various Issues, Paris

OPS/INCAP (1993) *Evaluación del Bono Mujer Jefe de la Familia* [PRAF], Tegucigalpa: mimeo

O'Connor, J. (1973) *The Fiscal Crisis of the State*, New York: St Martins Press

Ortiz, G. (1993), 'The Modernization of the Mexican Financial System', in S. Faruqi and G. Capria (eds.), *Financial Sector Reforms in Asian and Latin American Countries: lessons of comparative experience*, Washington,

D.C.: World Bank

Palma A. C. (1995) 'The agricultural sector in Chile', in J. Weeks, *Structural Adjustment and The Agricultural Sector in Latin America and the Caribbean*, Basingstoke: Macmillan/ILAS

Panorama Económico de la Agricultura, No. 95, July-August 1994, Santiago: Departamento de Economía Agraria, Pontificia Universidad Catolíca de Chile

Papageorgiou, D., M. Michaely, M. and A. Choksi (eds.) (1991) *Liberalizing foreign trade*, Oxford: Blackwell, Vol. 1 Argentina, Chile and Uruguay, D. Cavallo and associates, Vol. 4 Brazil, Colombia and Peru, D. Coes and associates

Pastor, M. (1987) 'The Effects of IMF Programs in the Third World: Debate and Evidence for Latin America', *World Development*, Vol. 15, No. 2, pp. 249-62

Pastor, M. (1987a) *The International Monetary Fund and Latin America: Economic stabilisation and class conflict*, Boulder: Westview

Pérez, E. (ed.) (1991) *El Campesinado en Colombia Hoy: Diagnóstico y Perspectivas*, Bogotá: Ecoe Ediciones

Perry, G. and A. M. Herrera (1994) *Public Finances, Stabilization and Structural Reform in Latin America*, Washington, D.C.: Inter-American Development Bank

PET (Programa de Economía del Trabajo) (1992) *Series de Indicadores Económicos Sociales: Series Anuales,1960-1991*, Santiago: PET

PET (1992a) *Las Trabajadoras Temporeras del Sector Agrario, Serie Mujer y Trabajo, Cartilla No. 1*, Santiago

PET (1994) *Economía y Trabajo en Chile,1993-94*, Santiago

Petras, J. F. and F. I. Leiva with H. Veltmeyer (1994) *Democracy and Poverty in Chile*, Boulder, Col.: Westview Press

Plant, R. (1994) *Labour Standards and Structural Adjustment*, Geneva: ILO

Polachek, S. W., and W. S. Siebert (1993) *The Economics of Earnings*, Cambridge: Cambridge University Press

Pollack, M. (1992) *Los Instrumentos Compensatorios del Ajuste: El FSE de Bolivia*, La Paz: Fondo Social de Emergencia

POSCAE/OXFAM (1992) *Los Campesinos Hondureños ante los Retos de los Noventas*, Tegucigalpa: mimeo

PREALC (1982) *Mercado de Trabajo en Cifras: 1950-1980*, Santiago: PREALC

PREALC (1984) *Employment Planning*, Santiago

PREALC (1990) *Employment and Equity: The Challenge of the 1990s*, Santiago: PREALC WEP Working Paper No 354

PREALC (1992) *Newsletter Number 30*, Santiago

PREALC (1993) *Newsletter Number 32*, Santiago

Psacharopoulos, G. and Z. Tzannatos (1992) *Case Studies on Women's Employment and Pay in Latin America*, Washington, D.C.: World Bank

Psacharopoulos, G. and Z. Tzannatos (1992a) *Women's Employment and Pay in Latin America: Overview and Methodology*, Washington, D.C.: World Bank

Raczynski, D. (1994) 'Políticas Sociales y Programas de Combate a la Pobreza en Chile: Balance y Desafíos', *Colección Estudios CIEPLAN, No. 39*, June

Ramírez, P. (1968) *Cambio en las Formas de Pago a la Mano de Obra Agrícola*, Santiago: ICIRA

Ramos, J. (1986) *Neoconservative Economics in the Southern Cone of Latin America, 1973-83*, Baltimore: Johns Hopkins University Press

Ravallion, M. (1992) *Poverty Comparisons: A guide to concepts and methods*, Washington, D.C.: World Bank, Living Standards Measurement Study Working Paper No. 88

Reyes Heroles, J. (1988) 'Las Políticas Financieras y la Distribución del Ingreso en México', *El Trimestre Económico*, No. 55, pp. 649-702

Rivera, R. (1988) *Los Campesinos Chilenos*, Santiago: GIA

Rivera, R. and M. E. Cruz (1984) *Pobladores Rurales*, Santiago: GIA

Rocha, S. (1993) 'Poverty Lines for Brazil: New Estimates from Recent Empirical Evidence', Rio de Janeiro: IPEA, mimeo, January

Rodríguez, C. A. (1994) *Interest Rates in Latin America*, Washington, D.C.: World Bank Internal Discussion Paper, Office of the Chief Economist for LAC Region, April

Rodrik, D. (1989) 'Credibility of trade reform – a policy maker's guide', *World Economy*, Vol. 12, pp. 1-16

Rojas-Suárez, L. and S. Weisbrod (1994) 'Financial Market Fragilities in Latin America: From Banking Crisis Resolution to Current Policy Challenges', *IMF Working Paper* No. 117, Washington, D. C.: International Monetary Fund

Romaguera, P. (1990) 'Dispersión Salarial: Modelos y Evidencias para el Caso Chileno', *Colección Estudios CIEPLAN No. 29*, September

Rossini, R. and J. J. Thomas (1990) 'The size of the informal sector in Peru: a critical comment on Hernando de Soto's *El Otro Sendero*', *World Development*, Vol. 18 (January), pp. 125-35

Rottenberg, S. (1993), 'Introduction', in S. Rottenberg (ed.), *The Political Economy of Poverty, Equity, and Growth: Costa Rica and Uruguay*, New York: Oxford University Press

Rozenwurcel, G. and R. Fernández (1994), 'El Fortalecimiento del Sector Financiero en el Proceso de Ajuste: El Caso Argentino', *Serie de Documento de Trabajo 141*, Washington, D.C.: Inter-American Development Bank

Rozenwurcel, G. and R. Fernández (1994a), 'La Desconcentración del Acceso a los Servicios Financieros', *Documento CEDES/97*, Buenos Aires

Saez, R. E. (1993) 'Las Privatizaciones de Empresas en Chile', in O. Muñoz (ed.), *Después de las Privatizaciones: Hacia el Estado Regulador*, Santiago: CIEPLAN

Sainz, P. and A. Calcagno (1992) 'En Busca de otra Modalidad de Desarrollo', *CEPAL Review*, 48, pp. 65-77

SALA (1993) *Statistical Abstract for Latin America*, Vol. 30, Part 2

SALA (1995) *Statistical Abstract for Latin America*, Vol. 31, Part 1 and Part 2

Salinas de Gortari, C. (1993) *Quinto Informe De Gobierno: Anexo Estadístico*, México: Presidencia de la República

Sánchez, M. and R. Corona (eds.) (1993) *Privatization in Latin America*, Washington, D.C.: Inter-American Development Bank

Schkolnik, M. (1992) 'Encuesta de Caracterización Socioeconómica Nacional: Características de la CASEN 1990', in S. Gómez (ed.) *La Realidad en Cifras:Estadísticas Sociales*, Santiago: FLACSO/INE/UNRISD

Schkolnik, M. and P. Aguero (1993) 'Efecto del gasto social en la distribución de ingresos', in *Programas Sociales: Su Impacto en los Hogares Chilenos,CASEN 1990*, Santiago: MIDEPLAN

Schultz, T. P. (1989) 'Education Investments and Returns', in H. Chenery and T. N. Srinivasan (eds.), *Handbook of Development Economics*, Amsterdam: North Holland, Vol. 1, pp. 543-630

Scott, C. D. (1986) *Peasantry and Property under Pinochet: an analysis of land ownership among small farmers in contemporary Chile*, mimeo, London School of Economics and Political Science

Scott, C. D. (1990) 'Land Reform and Property Rights among Small Farmers in Chile, 1968-86', in D. E. Hojman (ed.), *Neo liberal Agriculture in Rural Chile*, London: Macmillan

Scott, C. D. (1990a) 'Plus Ça Change, Plus C'Est La Même Chose: la evolución de la estructura agraria en zonas del minifundio tradicional en Chile,1968-1986', paper presented to *Coloquio Internacional sobre Agriculturas y Campesinados en América Latina: Mutaciones Recomposiciones*, University of Toulouse, France,13-14 December

Scott, C. D. (1993) 'Rural Credit, Agricultural Extension and Poverty Alleviation: past experience and future perspectives', in D. E. Hojman (ed.), *Change in the Chilean Countryside:from Pinochet to Aylwin and beyond*, Basingstoke: Macmillan

Scott, C. D. (1994) 'Progreso y pauperización en la pequeña agricultura: un análisis de la pobreza rural en ocho comunidades de minifundios tradicionales en Chile,1968-1986', paper presented to the *Fourth Latinamerican Congress of Rural Sociology*, University of Concepción,

Chile, 7-8 December

SECPLAN (1993) *Honduras: Población y Municipio, 1990-*, Tegucigalpa: SECPLAN/OIT/FNUAP–HON/90/PO3: Políticas de Población, Pobreza y Empleo

SECPLAN (1994) *Honduras, Libro Q*, Tegucigalpa:SECPLAN/OIT/FNUAP – HON/90/PO3: Políticas de Población, Pobreza y Empleo

SECPLAN (1994a) *Desarrollo Humano, Infancia y Juventud: Primer Informe de Seguimiento y Evaluación del Plan de Acción Nacional*, Tegucigalpa: UNIS-DGEC-SECPLAN/UNICEF/PNUD

SECPLAN (1994b) *Brecha sin Tregua: Género y Condiciones de Vida de la Mujer Hondureña*, Tegucigalpa: SECPLAN/OIT/FNUAP - HON/90/ PO3, Políticas de Población, Pobreza y Empleo

Sedlacek, G. L. and R. Paes de Barros (eds.) (1989) *Mercado de Trabalho e Distribuição de Renda: Uma Coletânea*, Rio de Janeiro: IPEA/INPES

Sen, A. K. (1981) *Poverty and Famines: An Essay on Entitlement and Deprivation*, Oxford: Clarendon Press

Sen, A.K. (1983), 'Poor, Relatively Speaking', *Oxford Economic Papers*, Vol. 35, pp.153-69

Sen, A. K. (1992) *Inequality Reexamined*, New York: Russell Sage Foundation; Cambridge Mass: Harvard University Press

Sethuraman, S. V. (1976) 'The urban informal sector: concept, measurement and policy', *International Labour Review*, Vol. 114 (July-August), pp. 69-81

Sethuraman, S. V. (ed.) (1981) 'The Urban Informal Sector in Developing Countries: Employment, Poverty and Environment', Geneva: ILO

Shorrocks, A. F. (1982) 'Inequality Decomposition by Factor Components', *Econometrica*, Vol. 50, No. 1, January, pp. 193-211

Shorrocks, A. F. (1983) 'Ranking Income Distributions', *Economica*, Vol. 50, pp. 3-17

Shorrocks, A. F. (1988) 'Aggregation Issues in Inequality Measurement', in W. Eichhorn (ed.), *Measurement in Economics*, Heidelberg: Physica Verlag

SRN (Secretario de Recursos Naturales) (1990) *Resumen de la Política de la Administración de Callejas, 1990-4*, Tegucigalpa: draft, February

Stalker, P. (1994) *The Work of Strangers: A Survey of International Labour Migration*, Geneva: ILO

Standing, G. and V. Tokman (eds.) (1991) *Towards Social Adjustment: Labour Market Issues in Structural Adjustment*, Geneva: ILO

Stark, O. (1991) *The Migration of Labor*, Oxford: Basil Blackwell

Stewart, F. (1995) 'The Impact of Adjustment Policies on the Incomes of the Poor: a Review of Alternative Approaches', in F. Stewart (ed.), *Adjustment and Poverty: Options and Choices, the Story of the 1980s*,

London: Routledge

Stiglitz, J. E. (1993) 'The Role of the State in Financial Markets', *Annual Bank Conference on Development Economics*, Washington, D.C.: World Bank

Stiglitz, J. E. and A. Weiss (1981) 'Credit Rationing in Markets with Imperfect Information', *American Economic Review*, Vol. 71, No. 3, June, pp. 393-410

Stiglitz, J. E. and A. Weiss (1987) 'Macroeconomic Equilibrium and Credit Rationing', *NBER Working Paper*, No. 2164

Stolper, W. and P. Samuelson (1941) 'Protection and real wages', *Review of Economic Studies*, pp. 58-73

Streeten, P. (1994) *Strategies for Human Development*, Copenhagen

Sugden, R. (1993) 'Welfare, Resources and Capabilities: a Review of Inequality Reexamined by Amaryta Sen', *Journal of Economic Literature*, Vol. XXXI, No. 4

Szapiro, S., M. Damill and J.M. Fanelli (1989) 'El Impuesto Inflacionario: Metodología de Cálculo y Estimaciones para la Economía Argentina', *Documento CEDES/18*, Buenos Aires

Székely, M. (1994) 'Estabilización y Ajuste con Desigualdad y Pobreza: El Caso de México', *El Trimestre Económico*, Vol. 61, No. 241, pp. 135-75

Székely, M. (1995) 'Economic Liberalization, Poverty and Income Distribution in Mexico', *Documento de Trabajo*, Num. III-95, México: Centro de Estudios Económicos, El Colegio de México, February

Székely, M. (1995a) 'Poverty in Mexico During Adjustment', *The Review of Income and Wealth*, Series 41, No. 3, September

Székely, M (1995b), 'Decomposing Changes in Inequality by Factor Components', Oxford: mimeo, St. Antony's College

Szymczak, P. (1992) 'International Trade and Investment Liberalization: Mexico's Experience and Prospects', in C. Loser and E. Kalter (eds.), *Mexico: The Strategy to Achieve Sustained Economic Growth*, Washington, D.C.: International Monetary Fund

Tabatabai, H. and M. Fouad (1994) *The Incidence of Poverty in Developing Countries*, Geneva: ILO

Taylor, L. (1991), *Income Distribution, Inflation and Growth: Lectures on Structuralist Macroeconomic Theory*, Cambridge, MA: MIT Press

Teitelboim, B. (1991) *Metodología del Cálculo del IPC de los Pobres*, Santiago: PET, Documento de Trabajo No. 80

Teitelboim, B. (1992) 'Dimensión y Características de la Pobreza', in *Población, Educación, Vivienda, Salud, Empleo y Pobreza: CASEN 1990*, Santiago: MIDEPLAN

Teitelboim, B. and B. Chacon (1993) 'Características de los hogares según quintiles de ingreso autónomo per capita', in *Programas Sociales: Su*

354   *The New Economic Model in Latin America*

Impacto en los Hogares Chilenos,CASEN 1990, Santiago: MIDEPLAN

Thomas, J. J. (1992) *Informal Economic Activity*, Hemel Hempstead: Harvester Wheatsheaf

Thomas, J. J. (1995) *Surviving in the City: The Urban Informal Sector in Latin America*, London: Pluto Press

Thorpe, A. T. (1993) 'Caminos Políticos y Económicos hacia la Reactivación y Modernización del Sector Agrícola', in Noé Pino, Thorpe and Sandoval Corea (eds.)

Thorpe, A. T. (1995) 'Adjusting to Reality: The Impact of Structural Adjustment on Honduran Agriculture', in J. Weeks (ed.), *Structural Adjustment and the Agricultural Sector in Latin America and the Caribbean*, Basingstoke: Macmillan

Tobin, J. (1982), 'Money and finance in the macroeconomic process', *Journal of Money, Credit and Banking*, Vol. 68, No. 2

Tobin, J. (1969) 'A general equilibrium approach to monetary theory', *Journal of Money, Credit and Banking*, Vol. 55, No. 1

Todaro, M. P. (1969) 'A model of labor migration and urban unemployment in less developed countries', *American Economic Review*, Vol. 59 (March), pp. 138-48

Todaro, M. P. (1986) 'Internal migration and urban employment: Comment', *American Economic Review*, Vol. 76 (June), pp. 566-9

Tolosa, H.C. (1991) 'Pobreza no Brasil: Uma Avaliação dos Anos 80', in J.P. dos Reis Veloso (ed.), *A Questão Social no Brasil*, São Paulo: Nobel

Trejos, R. A. (ed.) (1992) *Ajuste Macroeconómico y Pobreza Rural en América Latina*, San José, Costa Rica: Instituto Interamericano de Cooperación para la Agricultura

Turnham, D., B. Salomé and A. Schwarz (eds.) (1990) *The Informal Sector Revisited*, Paris: OECD Development Centre

Twomey, M. J. and A. Helwege (eds.) (1991) *Modernization and Stagnation: Latin American Agriculture in the 1990s*, New York: Greenwood Press

UDAPE (1994) *Impacto de la Crisis de Energía Eléctrica en la Economía*, Tegucigalpa: mimeo

UNCTAD (1992) *Handbook of International Trade and Development Statistics*, Geneva

UNCTAD (1993) *Handbook of International Trade and Development Statistics*, Geneva

UNCTAD (1993/4) *Industry and Development Global Report*, Geneva

United Nations Development Programme (UNDP) (1994) *Human Development Report 1994*, Washington, D.C.

United Nations Development Programme (UNDP) (1995) *Human Development Report 1995*, Washington, D.C.

United Nations Industrial Development Organisation (UNIDO) (1994) *Industrial Statistics Data Base*, Vienna

Urrutia, M. (1993) 'Distribución del Ingreso y la Pobreza en Colombia: Evolución Reciente', *Revista del Banco de la República*, Bogotá, August

USAID (1989) *A Strategy Paper for the Agricultural Sector in Honduras*, Tegucigalpa: mimeo

UTASA (Unidad Técnica de Apoyo al Sector Agrícola) (1994) *Caracterización y Perspectivas del Sector Agrícola Hondureño para el Año 2000*, Tegucigalpa: mimeo

Valenzuela, J. (1991) *Bandidaje Rural en Chile Central: Curico, 1850-1900*, Santiago: Editorial Universitaria

Van de Walle, N. (1989) 'Privatization in Developing Countries: A Review of the Issues', *World Development*, Vol. 17, No. 5, pp. 601-15

Van der Gaag, J., M. Stelcner and W. Vijverberg (1989) *Public-Private Sector Wage Comparisons and Moonlighting in Developing Countries: Evidence from Côte d'Ivoire and Peru*, Washington, D.C.: World Bank Living Standards Measurement Study Working Paper No. 52

Van Ginneken, W. (1985) *Los Grupos Socioeconómicos y la Distribución del Ingreso en México*, Mexico: Fondo de Cultura Económica

Vargas-Lundius, R. (1991) *Peasants in Distress: Poverty and Unemployment in the Dominican Republic*, San Francisco

Velasco, A. (1994) 'The State and Economic Policy: Chile, 1952-1992', in Bosworth *et al* (eds.)

Venegas, S. (1992) *Una Gota al Día... Un Chorro al Año..: el impacto social de la expansión frutícola*, Santiago: GEA

Verdera, F. (1994) *El Mercado de Trabajo de Lima Metropolitana: Estructura y Evolución, 1979-1990*, Lima: Instituto de Estudios Peruanos Working Paper No. 59

Vickers, J. and G. Yarrow (1988) *Privatization: An Economic Analysis*, Cambridge, Mass.: MIT Press

Vogel, I. (1995) 'Work and the Family: Rural Women's Perceptions', paper presented to *Annual Conference of the Society of Latin American Studies*, University of Wales, Swansea, 24-26 March

Wainerman, C.H. (1992) *Improving the Accounting of Women Workers in Population Censuses: Lessons from Latin America*, Geneva: ILO Population and Labour Policies Programme Working Paper No. 178

Walker, D. I. (1989) *Deuda y Ajuste Estructural: El Caso de Honduras, 1980-88*, Tegucigalpa: mimeo

Weeks, J. (1975) 'Policies for expanding employment in the informal urban sector of developing economies', *International Labour Review*, Vol. 111 (January), pp. 1-13

Weeks, J. (1981) *Capital and Exploitation*, Princeton: Princeton University Press

Weeks, J. (1989) *A Critique of Neoclassical Macroeconomics*, Basingstoke: Macmillan

Weeks, J. (1991) 'The myth of labour market clearing', in Standing and Tokman (eds.), pp. 53-77

Weeks, J. (1993) *Fallacies of Competition*, London: School of Oriental & Africa Studies

Weeks, J. (1995) 'Macroeconomic Adjustment and Latin American Agriculture since 1980', in J. Weeks (ed.), *Structural Adjustment and the Agricultural Sector in Latin America and the Caribbean*, Basingstoke: Macmillan/ ILAS

Welch, J. (1992) *Capital Markets in Brazil*, Basingstoke: Macmillan and New York: St. Martin's Press

Williamson, J. (1990) *Latin American Adjustment: How Much has Happened?*, Washington, D.C.: Institute for International Economics

Williamson, J. (1993) 'Issues posed by portfolio investment in developing countries', World Bank Symposium, Washington, D.C., 9-10 September

Winograd, C. (1995) *Learning from Failed Stabilisation: The Cruzado Plan in Brazil*, London: Institute of Latin American Studies, Research Paper No. 38

Wood, A. (1994) *North-South Trade, Employment and Inequality: Changing Fortunes in a Skill-oriented World*, Oxford: Oxford University Press

Woodward, D. (1992) *The Impact of Debt and Adjustment at the Household Level in Developing Countries*, Vol. II., London: Printer Publishers

World Bank (various years) *World Tables*, Washington, D.C.

World Bank (1980) *Chile: An Economy in Transition*, Washington DC

World Bank (1990) *World Development Report 1990*, Washington DC

World Bank (1992) *World Development Report 1992*, New York: Oxford University Press

World Bank (1993) *Poverty and Income Distribution in Latin America: the Story of the 1980s*, Washington, D.C. Regional Studies Program, Report No. 27

World Bank (1993a) *Latin America and the Caribbean: A Decade after the Debt Crisis*, Washington, D.C.

World Bank (1993b) *Argentina From Insolvency to Growth*, Washington, D.C.: World Bank Country Study

World Bank (1994), *World Development Report, 1994*, New York: Oxford University Press

World Bank (1994a) *Honduras: Country Economic Memorandum/Poverty Assessment*, Tegucigalpa

World Bank (1995) *World Development Report 1995*, Washington, D.C.

Wurgaff, J. (1993) *Fondos de Inversión Social en América Latina*, Santiago: PREALC

Zellner, A. (1962) 'An Efficient Method of Estimating Seemingly Unrelated Regressions and Test for Aggregation Bias', *Journal of the American Statistical Association*, Vol. 57

Zemelman, H. (1967) *El Migrante Rural*, Santiago: ICIRA, mimeo

INDEX